City and Country
in America

City and Country
in America

Edited by

David R. Weimer
Rutgers University

 New York
APPLETON-CENTURY-CROFTS
Division of Meredith Publishing Company

For

My Mother and Father

Preface _____

Once there were no American cities and now they abound. In the leap from the America of Crèvecoeur to the America of Victor Gruen much more has passed than 180 years; much more has changed than a topography of wood and earth for one of concrete and steel. A culture has disappeared, if not quite a civilization. Americans will never recapture that pristine sentiment that came spontaneously to men and women as they first glimpsed the deep green forests of Appalachia or the rich vast compost spread of the Mississippi Valley. To catch one's breath at the Prudential skyscraper in Chicago is to know a very different kind of wonder.

And yet for most of us a feeling for the earth and trees and sky remains. It is a feeling for the real thing, for the untouched or at most only slightly cultivated thing. In a civilization as fabricated and packed as that now riveting London to Melbourne and Detroit to Berlin, the natural world still promises us what it promised so varied a cluster of men as Crèvecoeur, Jefferson, and Thoreau: proximity to the real thing, to the stratum beneath all strata. And curiously enough, as from differing perspectives both the nineteenth-century Romantics and biologists perceived, through analogy and idea and imagination the world of untamed brooks and beasts always promises knowledge of man's own nature.

Just as cities have risen from the land, so our attachment to a less synthetic environment has persisted. Of course, our devotion to nature has lasted partly *because* cities appeared. The passages in this book from Emerson, Ruskin, and Howard make that clear. But what sometimes appears to be merely an escapist love of "the country," as we call it, is usually much more com-

plicated than a simple emotional negativism. Life outside the
city is not solely the absence of urban conditions; it has its own
realities and meaning. That is one reason men have long found
it possible to believe that a rural life, particularly one rooted in
agriculture, is also the most humanly valuable.

Today this belief goes by the name *agrarianism*. Considering
the general decline in numbers of the rural population in the
United States and similarly urbanized nations, some readers may
be astonished to learn the strength and variety of twentieth-
century agrarian arguments. A body of opinion represented by
Frank Lloyd Wright, Baker Brownell, and a dozen leading
Southern intellectuals is, to say the least, formidable.

Defenders of the American city have been less vocal and generally less articulate than the agrarians. Triumphant as the city
has waxed in American life for a hundred years, the urbanists
have not needed to say much. Until recently, they have occupied
themselves with the practicalities of design and administration.
The writers we think of as being urban spokesmen before the
First World War were decidedly planners, and so silent were
most of them during this period that we commonly recall the
names of only two: L'Enfant and Burnham. Beginning in the
1920's, a note of apology sounded in their ranks, and a growing
conviction that the city needed friends is evidenced by the increasing number of persons who took to print in its behalf.
While the sanguine tone of Robert Moses, Tunnard, and other
contemporary urbanists echoes Burnham's sturdy confidence in
the future, it is also apprehensive in ways the Chicago planner
might not have understood. Perhaps this very tension in recent
urbanist thought helped produce the most eloquent essay on
the city in the pages ahead: that by Joseph Hudnut.

It was actually in Burnham's day, at the peak of Progressive
agitations for municipal reforms, that the American city went on
the defensive. In some respects this shift away from the optimism
of a L'Enfant or a Burnham may strike us as strangely tardy.
For throughout the nineteenth century, and particularly in the
second half, the city was under attack from most of the major
thinkers in the nation. Every one of the agrarians represented in
this volume displayed a considerable hostility toward urban life,
tempered as it often was into a kind of ambivalence.

It seems to have taken the urban-centered disillusionments of the Progressive era and those following World War I to forge the social conscience essential to a mature critique of the city. It took other conditions, too, such as the filtering of planning ideas through the active middle classes in the British Commonwealth and the United States. These ideas came chiefly from socialist sources on the Continent and, to a lesser degree, from reports of the experiment in Soviet Russia after 1917. By the 1920's some American intellectuals were prepared for the messages of Ruskin, Howard, Kropotkin, and Geddes. The modern city had to be made over.

But Americans had to make it over in their own way, obedient to their own as well as to European traditions. And so the young social critics of the day, most notably Lewis Mumford, turned to American writers of an earlier century who had suggested particular urban renovations. They turned, for instance, to Frederick Law Olmsted. The single great indigenous tradition on which they could draw, however, was agrarianism, and they did in fact draw heavily upon it. Allusions to Thoreau, Henry George, and other agrarians are common in the works of Mumford, MacKaye, and their fellow critics of the postwar period.

In time these critics created a third point of view. Roughly out of a dialectic whose thrust and counter-thrust were urbanism and agrarianism there emerged various attempts at a rational synthesis. One of these attempts was regionalism, centered in the 1920's in the Regional Planning Association of America, mainly a discussion group numbering among its members Clarence Stein, Henry Wright, Mumford, and MacKaye. Other attempts to synthesize the two older traditions have been made by individuals unrelated to this group. Clarence Perry's idea of a "neighborhood" and the Goodmans' eclectic proposals are examples.

This view of a dialectical relationship among the three traditions unavoidably simplifies the truth. In some ways Daniel Burnham is a regionalist, Victor Gruen a decentralist, and Frank Lloyd Wright more of an urbanist than he appears at first. Nevertheless, a fact this book makes plain is that most American writers on the city have been highly aware of accepting or rejecting earlier writers in one or another of the three broad currents of urban ideas.

In this collection the three traditions are exemplified and in part redefined. Those familiar with the literature of agrarianism or city planning will, I hope, find new relationships of ideas suggested by this particular juxtaposition of writings.

The selections are not primarily descriptive and rarely narrative. In the main they are didactic and analytical. Taken together, they comprise the polemics of the American city. I have not included Lincoln Steffens, Jacob Riis, and similar critics because they seem to me to write out of traditions other than the ones illustrated here, and I have considered it more desirable to present a few thoroughly than to illustrate many points of view superficially. Where for one reason or another the original texts are not readily available in public or university libraries (Le Corbusier, Burnham, Borsodi, etc.), I have used longer passages than the inner logic of the anthology would otherwise dictate.

Although *City and Country in America* offers a unique selection of readings, I have inevitably followed others' historical analyses to a degree in making that selection. My conception of the course of American agrarianism was initially formed a decade ago in seminars at the University of Minnesota under Henry Nash Smith. My notion of the lineage of urbanist and regionalist ideas derives principally from writings of Lewis Mumford, Christopher Tunnard, and Paul and Percival Goodman.

Wittingly and unwittingly, still other persons have helped me complete this book. Walter E. Bezanson, Wright Britton, and James Leiby, fellow teachers in the American Civilization Program at Rutgers University, have in their lectures and conversations shed much light for me on the American city. By their invitation to Minneapolis last summer, Bernard Bowron and Brom Weber furnished a stimulating change of scene that enabled me to carry out the necessary reading in a much shorter time than I had expected. I owe something, moreover, to my friends Barry A. Marks and Hugh M. English, Jr.—Barry, for sometimes taking my ideas seriously; Hugh, for not letting me take them too seriously.

Rene C. Eldon II of Fairchild Aerial Surveys was more generous with his time and expertise than anyone could reasonably ask him to be. Mrs. Eileen Silver, George Barrows, and Willard Tangen of the Museum of Modern Art unhesitatingly laid aside their daily work to help me explore the photograph collections at the Museum. As always, the staff members of the libraries at the University of Minnesota, Rutgers University, and the Marchand collection at Princeton University were obliging and courteous in meeting my requests. W. C. Ferguson of New Brunswick cheerfully sacrificed his twin ailanthus trees to my photography. Fred Main considerately remedied my ignorance of the mystique of permission fees and other publishing matters. Mrs. Bonnie Jean Northrop kindly came to my rescue with expert secretarial assistance.

Over many years my sons, Mark and Britton, and my wife, Patricia, have demonstrated the necessity of valuing individuals ahead of all abstractions about the city, the country, or anything else.

D.R.W.

Contents

Preface   vii

I. Early Ambiguities

J. HECTOR ST. JOHN DE CREVECOEUR
Letters from an American Farmer   1

II. An Unambiguous Vision: The Plan of Washington, D.C.

PIERRE CHARLES L'ENFANT
Letter to George Washington, September 11, 1789   11
Letter to Thomas Jefferson, April 4, 1791   12
Report on Proposed Site of the Federal City, March–April
1791   13
Report on the Plan for the Intended City, June 22, 1791   16
Inscriptions on the Plan of the City (1791)   21

III. Into Nature: Imaginative Energy

THOMAS JEFFERSON
Notes on the State of Virginia   28
Letter to James Madison, December 20, 1787   30
Letter to John Adams, April 25, 1794   31
Letter to John Taylor, May 1, 1794   32
Letter to Doctor Caspar Wistar, June 21, 1807   33
Letter to Benjamin Austin, January 9, 1816   34

RALPH WALDO EMERSON
Farming   36

HENRY DAVID THOREAU
Walden   46

HENRY GEORGE
Progress and Poverty   59

FREDERICK JACKSON TURNER
The Significance of the Frontier in American History   69

IV. Into the City: Imaginative Control

EDWARD BELLAMY
Looking Backward   77

DANIEL H. BURNHAM and EDWARD H. BENNETT
Plan of Chicago (1909)   85

V. Europe to America: Ameliorative Revolutions

JOHN RUSKIN
From The Stones of Venice   104
From Modern Painters (Vol. IV)   105
From Modern Painters (Vol. V)   107
From The Study of Architecture   109
From Lectures on Art   110
From On the Old Road   112
From The Guild of St. George   115

EBENEZER HOWARD
The Garden City (1898)   117

PETR ALEKSÎEEVICH KROPOTKIN
Fields, Factories and Workshops   136

PATRICK GEDDES
Cities in Evolution   156

ANDREW JACKSON DOWNING
Our Country Villages   162
Shade-Trees in Cities   169

FREDERICK LAW OLMSTED and CALVERT VAUX
Description of a Plan for the Improvement of the Central
Park   173

FREDERICK LAW OLMSTED
Public Parks and the Enlargement of Towns   180

BENTON MACKAYE
The New Exploration   188

CLARENCE ARTHUR PERRY
Housing for the Machine Age   196

CLARENCE S. STEIN
Radburn, New Jersey (1928—1933)
Greenbelt, Maryland (1935—1937)   209

LEWIS MUMFORD
Regions—To Live In   219
What Is a City?   224

PAUL and PERCIVAL GOODMAN
Communitas   232

VI. From Europe: Bold Conservatisms

CAMILLO SITTE
The Art of Building Cities   249

LE CORBUSIER
A Contemporary City of Three Million Inhabitants (1922)
The Voisin Plan (1924)   257

VII. The New Centrifuge

RALPH BORSODI
Flight from the City   279

TWELVE SOUTHERNERS
A Statement of Principles   290

ANDREW NELSON LYTLE
The Hind Tit   292

FRANK LLOYD WRIGHT
Broadacre City: A New Community Plan (1935)   304
When Democracy Builds   313

BAKER BROWNELL
The Human Community   323

LOUIS BROMFIELD
Out of the Earth   338

VIII. The New Centripety

JOSEPH HUDNUT
The Invisible City   349

ROBERT MOSES
The Spreading City   359

CHRISTOPHER TUNNARD
The Leaf and the Stone   368

HENRY HOPE REED, JR.
The Golden City   377

VICTOR GRUEN
In Defense of the City   382

Guides to Study

Analysis of the Readings and Illustrations   393
Ideas for Essays   397
Further Inquiry   398

I
Early Ambiguities

J. Hector St. John de Crèvecoeur_____
LETTERS FROM AN AMERICAN FARMER

J. Hector St. John de Crèvecoeur, *Letters from an American Farmer* [1782] (New York, Fox, Duffield, 1904).

[*Here the author speaks, though the words are ostensibly those of a minister with whom he discusses the writing of his letters.*]

In Italy all the objects of contemplation, all the reveries of the traveller, must have a reference to ancient generations, and to very distant periods, clouded with the mist of ages.—Here, on the contrary, every thing is modern, peaceful, and benign. Here we have had no war to desolate our fields: [1] our religion does not oppress the cultivators: we are strangers to those feudal institutions which have enslaved so many. Here nature opens her broad [7] lap to receive the perpetual accession of new comers, and to supply them with food. I am sure I cannot be called a partial American when I say, that the spectacle afforded by these pleasing scenes must be more entertaining, and more

[1] The troubles, that now convulse the American colonies, had not broke out when this, and some of the following letters were written.

1

philosophical than that which arises from beholding the musty
ruins of Rome. Here every thing would inspire the reflecting
traveller with the most philanthropic ideas; his imagination,
instead of submitting to the painful and useless retrospect of
revolutions, desolations, and plagues, would, on the contrary,
wisely spring forward to the anticipated fields of future cultivation and improvement, to the future extent of those generations
which are to replenish and embellish this boundless continent.
There the half-ruined amphitheatres, and the putrid fevers of
the Campania, must fill the mind with the most melancholy
reflections, whilst he is seeking for the origin, and the intention
of those structures with which he is surrounded, and for the cause
of so great a decay. Here he might contemplate the very beginnings and out-lines of human society, which can be traced
no where now but in this part of the world. The rest of the earth,
I am told, is in some places too full, in others half depopulated.
Misguided religion, tyranny, and absurd laws, every where
depress and afflict mankind.[8] Here we have in some measure
regained the ancient dignity of our species; our laws are simple
and just, we are a race of cultivators, our cultivation is unre-
strained, and therefore every thing is prosperous and flourishing.
For my part I had rather admire the ample barn of one of our
opulent farmers, who himself felled the first tree in his plantation,
and was the first founder of his settlement, than study the
dimensions of the temple of Ceres. . . . [9]

[*Now speaking directly as the author, Crèvecoeur addresses his
"friend in England" who is to receive the letters.*]

    . . . Remember that you have laid the foundation of this
correspondence; you well know that I am neither a philosopher,
politician, divine, nor naturalist, but a simple farmer. I flatter
myself, therefore, that you'll receive my letters as conceived,
not according to scientific rules to which I am a perfect stranger,
but agreeable to the spontaneous impressions which each subject
may inspire. This is the only line I am able to follow, the line
which nature has herself traced for me; this was the covenant
which I made with you, and with which you seemed to be well
pleased. Had you wanted the stile of the learned, the reflections

The partially cultivated land Crèvecoeur knew. This oil painting, done in 1855 by Joseph O. Montalant, shows **The Site of Azilum.** In the 1790's the village of Azilum was built on the Susquehanna River near Wyalusing in northern-central Pennsylvania as a refuge for Royalist émigrés after the French Revolution. Crèvecoeur visited or owned farms not far from this site in Pennsylvania, northwestern New Jersey, and southern-central New York State.

of the patriot, the discussions of the politician,[20] the curious
observations of the naturalist, the pleasing garb of the man of
taste, surely you would have applied to some of those men of
letters with which our cities abound. But since on the contrary,
and for what reason I know not, you wish to correspond with
a cultivator of the earth, with a simple citizen, you must receive
my letters for better or worse.[21]

WHAT IS AN AMERICAN?

I wish I could be acquainted with the feelings and thoughts
which must agitate the heart and present themselves to the
mind of an enlightened Englishman, when he first lands on this
continent. He must greatly rejoice that he lived at a time to see
this fair country discovered and settled; he must necessarily
feel a share of national pride, when he views the chain of
settlements which embellishes these extended shores. When he
says to himself, this is the work of my countrymen, who, when
convulsed by factions, afflicted by a variety of miseries and
wants, restless and impatient, took refuge here. They brought
along with them their national genius, to which they principally
owe what liberty they enjoy, and what substance they possess.
Here he sees the industry of his native country displayed in a
new manner, and traces in their works the embrios of all the arts,
sciences, and ingenuity which flourish in Europe. Here he
beholds fair cities, substantial villages, extensive fields, an immense country filled with decent houses,[48] good roads, orchards,
meadows, and bridges, where an hundred years ago all was
wild, woody and uncultivated! What a train of pleasing ideas
this fair spectacle must suggest; it is a prospect which must
inspire a good citizen with the most heartfelt pleasure. The
difficulty consists in the manner of viewing so extensive a scene.
He is arrived on a new continent; a modern society offers itself
to his contemplation, different from what he had hitherto seen.
It is not composed, as in Europe, of great lords who possess
every thing, and of a herd of people who have nothing. Here
are no aristocratical families, no courts, no kings, no bishops,
no ecclesiastical dominion, no invisible power giving to a few

a very visible one; no great manufacturers employing thousands, no great refinements of luxury. The rich and the poor are not so far removed from each other as they are in Europe. Some few towns excepted, we are all tillers of the earth, from Nova Scotia to West Florida. We are a people of cultivators, scattered over an immense territory, communicating with each other by means of good roads and navigable rivers, united by the silken bands of mild government, all respecting the laws, without dreading their power, because they are equitable. We are all animated with the spirit of an industry which is [49] unfettered and un-restrained, because each person works for himself. If he travels through our rural districts he views not the hostile castle, and the haughty mansion, contrasted with the clay-built hut and miser-able cabbin, where cattle and men help to keep each other warm, and dwell in meanness, smoke, and indigence. A pleasing uni-formity of decent competence appears throughout our habita-tions. The meanest of our log-houses is a dry and comfortable habitation. Lawyer or merchant are the fairest titles our towns afford; that of a farmer is the only appellation of the rural inhabitants of our country. It must take some time ere he can reconcile himself to our dictionary, which is but short in words of dignity, and names of honour. There, on a Sunday, he sees a congregation of respectable farmers and their wives, all clad in neat homespun, well mounted, or riding in their own humble waggons. There is not among them an esquire, saving the unlet-tered magistrate. There he sees a parson as simple as his flock, a farmer who does not riot on the labour of others. We have no princes, for whom we toil, starve, and bleed: we are the most perfect society now existing in the world. Here man is free as he ought to be; nor is this pleasing equality so transitory as many others are. Many ages [50] will not see the shores of our great lakes replenished with inland nations, nor the unknown bounds of North America entirely peopled. Who can tell how far it extends? Who can tell the millions of men whom it will feed and contain? for no European foot has as yet travelled half the extent of this mighty continent! . . . [51]

What attachment can a poor European emigrant have for a country where he had nothing? The knowledge of the language, the love of a few kindred as poor as himself, were the only cords that tied him: his country is now that which gives him land, bread, protection, and consequence: *Ubi panis ibi patria,* is the motto of all emigrants. What then is the American, this new man? He is either an European, or the descendant of an European, hence that strange mixture of blood, which you will find in no other country. I could point out to you a family whose grandfather was an Englishman, whose wife was Dutch, whose son married a French woman, and whose present four sons have now four wives of different nations. *He* is an American, who leaving behind him all his ancient prejudices and manners, receives new ones from the new mode of life he has embraced, the new government he obeys, and the new rank he holds.[54] He becomes an American by being received in the broad lap of our great *Alma Mater.* Here individuals of all nations are melted into a new race of men, whose labours and posterity will one day cause great changes in the world. Americans are the western pilgrims, who are carrying along with them that great mass of arts, sciences, vigour, and industry which began long since in the east; they will finish the great circle. The Americans were once scattered all over Europe; here they are incorporated into one of the finest systems of population which has ever appeared, and which will hereafter become distinct by the power of the different climates they inhabit. The American ought therefore to love this country much better than that wherein either he or his forefathers were born. Here the rewards of his industry follow with equal steps the progress of his labour; his labour is founded on the basis of nature, *self-interest;* can it want a stronger allurement? Wives and children, who before in vain demanded of him a morsel of bread, now, fat and frolicsome, gladly help their father to clear those fields whence exuberant crops are to arise to feed and to clothe them all; without any part being claimed, either by a despotic prince, a rich abbot, or a mighty lord. Here religion demands but little of him; [55] a small voluntary salary to the minister, and gratitude to God; can he refuse these? The American is a new man, who acts upon new principles; he must therefore entertain new ideas, and form new opinions. From involuntary idleness, servile dependence, penury, and useless labour, he has passed to toils of a very different nature, rewarded by ample subsistence.—This is an American.

British America is divided into many provinces, forming a large association, scattered along a cost 1500 miles extent and about 200 wide. This society I would fain examine, at least such as it appears in the middle provinces; if it does not afford that variety of tinges and gradations which may be observed in Europe, we have colours peculiar to ourselves. For instance, it is natural to conceive that those who live near the sea, must be very different from those who live in the woods; the intermediate space will afford a separate and distinct class.

Men are like plants; the goodness and flavour of the fruit proceeds from the peculiar soil and exposition in which they grow. We are nothing but what we derive from the air we breathe, the climate we inhabit, the government we obey, the system of religion we profess, and the nature of our employment. [56] Here you will find but few crimes; these have acquired as yet no root among us. I wish I were able to trace all my ideas; if my ignorance prevents me from describing them properly, I hope I shall be able to delineate a few of the outlines, which are all I propose.

Those who live near the sea, feed more on fish than on flesh, and often encounter that boisterous element. This renders them more bold and enterprising; this leads them to neglect the confined occupations of the land. They see and converse with a variety of people; their intercourse with mankind becomes extensive. The sea inspires them with a love of traffic, a desire of transporting produce from one place to another; and leads them to a variety of resources which supply the place of labour. Those who inhabit the middle settlements, by far the most numerous, must be very different; the simple cultivation of the earth purifies them, but the indulgences of the government, the soft remonstrances of religion, the rank of independent freeholders, must necessarily inspire them with sentiments, very little known in Europe among people of the same class. What do I say? Europe has no such class of men; tne early knowledge they acquire, the early bargains they make, give them a great degree of sagacity. As freemen [57] they will be litigious; pride and obstinacy are often the cause of law suits; the nature of our laws and governments may be another. As citizens it is easy to imagine, that they will carefully read the newspapers, enter into every political disquisition, freely blame or censure governors and others. As farmers they will be careful and anxious to get as much as they can, because what they get is their own. As northern men they will love the chearful cup. As Christians, religion curbs them not in their opinions; the general indulgence leaves every one to think for themselves in spiritual matters; the laws inspect our actions, our thoughts are left to God. Industry, good living, selfishness, litigiousness, country politics, the pride of freemen, religious indifference, are their characteristics. If you recede still farther from the sea, you will come into more modern settlements; they exhibit the same strong lineaments, in a ruder appearance. Religion seems to have still less influence, and their manners are less improved.

Now we arrive near the great woods, near the last inhabited districts; there men seem to be placed still farther beyond the reach of government, which in some measure leaves them to themselves. How can it pervade every corner; as they were driven there by misfortunes,[58] necessity of beginnings, desire of acquiring large tracks of land, idleness, frequent want of œconomy, ancient debts; the re-union of such people does not afford a very pleasing spectacle. When discord, want of unity and friendship; when either drunkenness or idleness prevail in such remote districts; contention, inactivity, and wretchedness must ensue. There are not the same remedies to these evils as in a long established community. The few magistrates they have, are in general little better than the rest; they are often in a perfect state of war; that of man against man, sometimes decided by blows, sometimes by means of the law; that of man against every wild inhabitant of these venerable woods, of which they are come to dispossess them. There men appear to be no better than carnivorous animals of a superior rank, living on the flesh of wild animals when they can catch them, and when they are not able, they subsist on grain. He who would wish to see America in its proper light, and have a true idea of its feeble beginnings and barbarous rudiments, must visit our extended line of frontiers where the last settlers dwell, and where he may see the first labours of settlement, the mode of clearing the earth, in all their different appearances; where men are wholly left dependent on their native tempers,[59] and on the spur of uncertain industry, which often fails when not sanctified by the efficacy of a few moral rules. There, remote from the power of example, and check of shame, many families exhibit the most hideous parts of our society. They are a kind of forlorn hope, preceding by ten or twelve years the most respectable army of veterans which come after them. In that space, prosperity will polish some, vice and the law will drive off the rest, who uniting again with others like themselves will recede still farther; making room for more industrious people, who will finish their improvements, convert the loghouse into a convenient habitation, and rejoicing that the first heavy labours are finished, will change in a few years that hitherto barbarous country into a fine fertile, well regulated district. Such is our progress, such is the march of the Europeans toward the interior parts of this continent. In all societies there are off-casts; this impure part serves as our precursors or pioneers; my father himself was one of that class, but he came upon honest principles, and was therefore one of the few who held fast; by good conduct and temperance, he transmitted to me his fair inheritance, when not above one in fourteen of his contemporaries had the same good fortune.[60]

Forty years ago this smiling country was thus inhabited; it is now purged, a general decency of manners prevails throughout, and such has been the fate of our best countries. . . . [61]

There is no wonder that this country has so many charms, and presents to Europeans so many temptations to remain in it. A traveller [73] in Europe becomes a stranger as soon as he quits his own kingdom; but it is otherwise here. We know, properly speaking, no strangers; this is every person's country; the variety of our soils, situations, climates, governments, and produce, hath something which must please every body. No sooner does an European arrive, no matter of what condition, than his eyes are opened upon the fair prospect; he hears his language spoke, he retraces many of his own country manners, he perpetually hears the names of families and towns with which he is acquainted; he sees happiness and prosperity in all places disseminated; he meets with hospitality, kindness, and plenty every where; he beholds hardly any poor, he seldom hears of punish-

ments and executions; and he wonders at the elegance of our
towns, those miracles of industry and freedom. He cannot
admire enough our rural districts, our convenient roads, good
taverns, and our many accommodations; he involuntarily loves
a country where every thing is so lovely. . . . [74]

II

An Unambiguous Vision:
The Plan of Washington, D.C.

Pierre Charles L'Enfant————————————
LETTER TO GEORGE WASHINGTON,
SEPTEMBER 11, 1789

Elizabeth S. Kite, ed., *L'Enfant and Washington, 1791–1792* (Baltimore, Johns Hopkins Press, 1929).

Ser;

The late determination of Congress to lay the foundation of a Federal City which is to become the Capital of this vast Empire, offers so great an occasion for acquiring reputation . . . that Your Excellency will not be surprised that my ambition and the desire I have of becoming a useful citizen should lead me to wish to share in the undertaking.

No nation had ever before the opportunity offered them of deliberately deciding on the spot where their Capital City should be fixed, or of combining every necessary consideration in the choice of situation, and although the means now within the power of the Country are not such as to pursue the design to any great extent, it will be obvious that the plan should

be drawn on such a scale as to leave room for that aggrandize-
ment and embellishment which the increase of the wealth of
the nation will permit it to pursue at any period however
remote. . . .

. . . Nothing will be wanting to my happiness if the remem-
brance of my former services connected with a variety of
peculiar circumstances during fourteen years residence in this
country can plead with your Excellency in support of the favor
I sollicit. . . .

(Signed) P. C. L'Enfant.[34]

LETTER TO THOMAS JEFFERSON, APRIL 4, 1791

. . . The number and nature of the publick building with the
necessary appendix I should be glad to have a statement of as
speedily as possible—and I would be very much obliged to
you in the mean time if you could procure for me whatever
map may fall within your reach—of any of the differents
grand city now Existing such as—for example—as london—madry
[Madrid]—paris—Amsterdam—naples—venice—genoa—florence together with particular maps of any such sea-ports or dock-yards
and arsenals as you may know to be the most compleat in their
Improvement, for, notwithstanding, I would reprobate the
Idea of Imitating and that contrary of Having this Intention it is
my wish and shall be my endeavor to delinate on a new and
original way the plan the contrivance of which the President
has left to me without any restriction soever—yet the contemplation of what exists of well improved situation iven the parallel
of these with deffective ones, may serve to suggest a variety of
new Ideas and is necessary to refine and strengthen the Judgment particularly in the present instance when having to unite
the useful with the comodious and agreeable viewing these will
by offering means of comparing enable me the better to determine with a certainty the propriety of a local which offer an
Extensive field for combinations.

I have the Honor to be, with great respect,
Your most humble and most obedient servant
(Signed) P. C. L'Enfant.[42]

REPORT [1] ON PROPOSED SITE OF THE FEDERAL CITY, MARCH-APRIL 1791

After coming upon the hill from the Eastern branch ferry, the country is level and on a space of about two miles each way presents a most eligible position for the first settlement of a grand City, and one which if not the only [one] within the limits of the Federal territory, is at least the more advantageous in that part lying between the Eastern Branch and Georgetown.

The soil is dry and, notwithstanding well watered—abounding in springs; it has an wholesome air and being of an easy ascent it is however so high that it commands on most of the surrounding country and may be effectually guarded from those hills overlooking it. . . .

With respect to navigation it lies at the head of an extensive one and . . . from the bank of a harbor in every respect to be preferred to that of the Potomac toward Georgetown [because] less impeded by ice and never so swelled by fresh [water]—The channel is deeper and will admit any vessels that may pass over the shallows below at Maryland point being moored to wharfs whilst they must remain a half mile off from the banks of the Potomac owing to the main channel bearing into the Eastern branch, immediately and all the way up on the Virginia shore until it comes to strike on Mason Island, round which in turning it comes for to wash ashore . . . on rock at Hampton Pt. or Funktown, making its way to and from the wharfs at Georgetown where the grand navigation ends.

This spot made to derive every possible advantage from water surveyance would at the same time be free from the [44] great inconveniency attending the crossing of navigable river. The deep

[1] [According to the editor, Elizabeth S. Kite, Major L'Enfant "undoubtedly" handed this report personally to President Washington.—Ed.]

water in that branch not coming up further than Evans Pt. about half a mile above the ferry, there the large bed of the river immediately changes into a run over which bridges might easily be erected to secure a constant intercourse with the eastern continent, in the mean while as it would facilitate seats being fixed on each border of a grand stream whose depths abound in fish and whose aspect . . . rests the eyes from the grand sight below [of] the city.

All the total of this ground is such as will favor every improvement as may render the City agreeable, commodious, and capable of promoting all sorts of manufacturing establishments on its water side from the mouth of the Eastern branch at Carrollsburg as far up as to Evans Pt. a distance of about three miles. The frequent winding of the shore form many natural wet docks which, though not having every where a great depth of water nevertheless would become very convenient for the establishing of naval stores and for arsenals the which as well as warehouses for merchantmen might safely be raised on the edge of the water without fear of impeding the prospect from the high flat behind.

There, where the level ground [borders] on the water and all round where it descends, but most particularly on that part terminating in a ridge to Jenkin's Hill and running in a parallel with and at half a mile off from the river Potomac, separated by a low ground intersected with three grand streams—many of the most desirable positions offer for to erect the Public Edifices thereon—From these hights every grand building would rear with a majestic aspect over the Country all around and might be advantageously seen from twenty miles off . . . [from] the first settlement of the City they would stand to ages in a central point to it, facing on the grandest prospect of both . . . branches of the Potomac [45] with the town of Alexandria in front, seen in its full extent over many points of land projecting from the Maryland and Virginia shores in a manner as adds much to the perspective, at the end of which the Cape of Hunting Creek appears directly where a corner stone of the Federal District is to be placed and in the room of which a majestic column or a grand pyramid being erected would produce the happiest effect and completely finish the landscape.

Thus in every respect advantageously situated, the Federal City would soon grow of itself and spread as the branches of a tree do towards where they meet with most nourishment. . . .

Having a bridge laid over the Eastern branch somewhere about Evans Pt. there the natural limit of the eastern branch of the City may be extended while in its western extremity may be included Georgetown itself, which being situated at the head of grand navigation of the Potomac should be favored with the same advantage of better communication with the southern [country] by having also a bridge erected over the Potomac at the place of the two Sisters where nature would effectually favor the undertaking.

There between those two points, beginning with the settlement . . . on the bank of the Eastern branch and promoting the first improvements all along the high flat as far as where it ends on Jenkins Hill, would place central to the ground left open, its growth, which most undoubtedly would be rapid towards both extremities, provided that . . . attention be paid immediately . . . to open a direct and large avenue from the bridge on the Potomac to that on the Eastern branch . . . with a middle way paved for heavy carriages and a walk on each side planted with double rows of trees to the end that by making it a communication as agreeable as it will be convenient, it may induce the improvement of either place all along and prompt the citizens in [46] both to exertions to shorten the distance by buildings, insensibly effecting the wished injunction and [so] complete a street laid out on a dimension proportioned to the greatness which . . . the Capital of a powerful Empire ought to manifest.

In viewing the intended establishment in the light and considering how in process of time a city so happily situated will extend over a large surface of ground, much deliberation is necessary for to determine on a plan for the total distribution and . . . that plan [should be conceived] on [such] a system . . . as to render the place commodious and agreeable to the first settler, [while] it may be capable of . . . [being] enlarged by progressive improvement . . . [all] which should be foreseen in the first delineation in a grand plan of the whole city combined with the various grounds it will cover and with the particular circumstance of the country all around.

In endeavouring to effect this, it is not the regular assemblage of houses laid out in squares and forming streets all parallel and uniform that it is so necessary, for such a plan could only do on a level plain and where no surrounding object being interesting it becomes indifferent which way the opening of streets may be directed.

But on any other ground, a plan of this sort must be defective, and it never would answer for any of the spots proposed for the Federal City, and on that held here as the most eligible it would absolutely annihilate every [one] of the advantages enumerated and . . . alone injure the success of the undertaking.

Such regular plans indeed, however answerable they may appear upon paper or seducing as they may be on the first aspect to the eyes of some people must even when applyed upon the ground the best calculated to admit of it become at last tiresome and insipid and it never could be in its origin [47] but a mean continuance of some cool imagination wanting a sense of the real grand and truly beautiful only to be met with where nature contributes with art and diversifies the objects.[48]

REPORT ON THE PLAN FOR THE INTENDED CITY, JUNE 22, 1791

Sir; [2]

In delineating the plan for the intended city here annexed, I regretted very much being hindered by the shortness of time from making any particular drawing of the several buildings, squares, and other improvements which the smallness of the scale of the general map, together with the hurry with which it had been drawn could not admit of having lain them down, as correct as . . . is necessary to give a [52] perfect idea of the effect when executed. My whole attention was directed to a

[2] [This report is presumably addressed to President Washington.—Ed.]

combination of the general distribution of the several situations,
an object which, being of almost immediate moment, and importance, made me sacrifice every other consideration—and here
again must I solicit your indulgence, in submitting to your
judgment—my ideas, and in presenting to you a first drawing,
correct only as it respects the situation and distance of objects,
all which were determined and well ascertained having for more
accuracy had several lines run upon the ground cleared of the
wood, and measured with posts fixed at certain distances to
serve as bases from which I might arrange the whole with a
certainty of making it fit the various parts of the ground.

Having determined some principal points to which I wished
to make the others subordinate, I made the distribution regular
with every street at right angles, North and South, east and
west, and afterwards opened some in different directions, as
avenues to and from every principal place, wishing thereby
not merely to contract with the general regularity, nor to afford
a greater variety of seats with pleasant prospects, which will be
obtained from the advantageous ground over which these
avenues are chiefly directed, but principally to connect each
part of the city, if I may so express it, by making the real
distance less from place to place, by giving to them reciprocity of
sight and by making them thus seemingly connected, promote
a rapid settlement over the whole extent, rendering those even
of the most remote parts an addition to the principal, which
without the help of these, were any such settlement attempted,
it would be languid, and lost in the extent, and become detri-
mental to the establishment. Some of these avenues were also
necessary to effect the junction of several roads to a central point
in the city, by making these roads shorter, which is effected
[by directing them] to those leading to Bladensburg and the
Eastern branch—both of which are [53] made above a little
shorter, exclusive of the advantage of their leading immediately
to the wharves at Georgetown. The hilly ground which surrounds that place the growth of which it must impede, by
inviting settlements on the city side of Rock Creek, which
cannot fail soon to spread along all those avenues which will
afford a variety of pleasant rides, and become the means for
a rapid intercourse with all parts of the city, to which they

will serve as does the main artery in the animal body, which diffuses life through the smaller vessels, and inspires vigor, and activity throughout the whole frame.

These avenues I made broad, so as to admit of their being planted with trees leaving 80 feet for a carriage way, 30 feet on each side for a walk under a double row of trees, and allowing ten feet between the trees and the houses. The first of these avenues and the most direct one, begins at the Eastern branch and ends over Rock Creek at the wharves at Georgetown, along the side of which it is continued to the bridge over to the Virginia shore, and down to the lower canal to the Potomac, along the sides of which it may be of great advantage to have such a road extended to the upper canal to facilitate dragging the boats up and down.

With respect to the point upon which it is expedient first to begin the main establishment, however various the opinions thereon are, I believe the question may be easily solved, not viewing in part but embracing in one view the whole extent from the Eastern branch to Georgetown, and from the banks of the Potomac to the mountains, for in considering impartially the whole extent, viewing it as that of the intended city, it will appear that to promote a rapid settlement throughout, across the Tiber above tide water is the most eligible one, for an offset of the establishment which . . . should be begun at various points equi-distant as possible from the center; not merely because settlements of this [54] sort are likely to diffuse an equality of advantages over the whole territory allotted, and consequently to reflect benefit from an increase of the value of property, but because each of these settlements by a natural jealousy will most tend to stimulate establishments on each of the opposed extremes, to both of which it will undoubtedly become, as so many points of union, particularly considering that a canal is easily opened from the Eastern branch across those primary settlements of the city to issue at the mouth of the Tiber into the Potomac, giving entrance to the boats from the falls of that river into the Eastern branch harbor, which will undoubtedly facilitate a conveyance, which will be of the utmost convenience to all trading people, and the supplies of the city by markets, as designed in the map, which may be

built over ground capable of sheltering any number of boats
and to serve as a depository, when the city is grown to its whole
extent, from whence all the internal parts may be supplied.
At the place first mentioned above, where the tide water comes
into Tiber Creek, is the position the most capable of any within
the limits of the city, to favor those grand improvements of
public magnitude which may serve as a sample for all subsequent undertakings, an edifice erected there such as the peculiarity of the ground may admit, well combined with the various
directions of those avenues concentrating there, should stand
to future ages a monument of magnificence.

After a minute search for other eligible situations, I may assert
without an apprehension of appearing prejudiced in favor of a
first opinion, that I could not discover one in all respects so
advantageous . .   for erecting the Federal House . . . [as] the
western end of Jenkin's Heights [which] stands really as a
pedestal waiting for a superstructure, and I am confident were
all the ground cleared of wood, no other situation could bear
a competition with this. Some [55] might perhaps require less
labor to be made agreeable, but after all none could be made
so grand, and all would appear secondary to this.

The other position of a different nature offers a local equality,
answerable for a Presidential palace, better calculated for a
commodious house and which may be rendered majestic and
agreeable. This position which very justly attracted your attention
when first viewing the ground which is upon the west side and
near the mouth of the Tiber, on that height dividing Burns and
Pierces plantations—

The spot I assigned I chose somewhat more in the wood, and
off the creek than when you stood in the partition line . . . two
considerations determined me; first, to lessen the distance to
the Federal House, and secondly to obtain a more extensive
view down the Potomac, with a prospect of the whole harbor
and town of Alexandria; also to connect with more harmony the
public walks and avenue of the Congress House with the garden
park and other improvements round the palace, which, standing
upon this high ridge, with a garden in a slope towards the canal
would overlook the vast esplanade in the center of which, and
at the point of intersection of the sight from each of the Houses,

would be the most advantageous place for an equestrian statue,
which with proper appendages and walks artfully managed,
would produce a most grand effect. In the present unimproved
state of the ground it will appear that the hight upon which
the plan of this monument is marked, will intercept the view
of the water from the palace, which in part it would were it not
to be observed that to bound the entrance of the Tiber to 200
feet, which is the extreme width of the canal to prevent its being
drained at low water, will require a great quantity of ground
to fill up, at least as much as will serve to level all the high
ground in the way to the edge of the water, especially as there
will be a propriety to extend it as far as low water mark upon
the Potomac.[56]

Fixed as expressed on the map [3] the distance from the Congressional house will not be too great . . . as . . . no message
to nor from the President is to be made without a sort of
decorum which will doubtless point out the propriety of Committee waiting on him in carriage should his palace be even
contiguous to Congress.

To make however the distance less to other officers I placed
the three grand Departments of State contiguous to the principal palace; and on the way leading to the Congressional
house, the gardens of the one together with the park and
other improvements . . . are connected with the public walk
and avenue to the Congress house in a manner as must form
a whole as grand as it will be agreeable and convenient to the
whole city . . . and all along side of which may be placed
play houses, rooms of assembly, academies and all such sort
of places as may be attractive to the learned and afford diversion
to the idle.

I proposed continuing the canal much farther up, but this
not to be effected but with the aid of lock, and from a level
obtained from the hight of the spring of the Tiber, the greatest
facility being to bring those waters over the flat back of Jenkins.
I gave the more readily the preference . . . to supply that part
of the city as it will promote the execution of a plan which I
propose in this map, of letting the Tiber return to its proper

[3] "Map" and "Plan" of the city seem to have been used interchangeably
by L'Enfant and others at this time.

channel by a fall, which issuing from under the base of the
Congress building, may there form a cascade of forty feet high,
or more than one hundred wide, which would produce the most
happy effect in rolling down to fill up the canal and discharge
itself in the Potomac, of which it would then appear the main
spring when seen through that grand and majestic avenue
intersecting with [57] the prospect from the palace, at a point
which being seen from both, I have designated as the proper
for to erect a grand equestrian statue.

. . . The whole will acquire new sweetness being laid over
the green of a field well level and made brilliant by shade of a
few trees artfully planted.

I am with respectful submission,
Your most humble and obedient servant,
P. C. L'Enfant.[58]

INSCRIPTIONS [4] ON THE PLAN
OF THE CITY (1791)

PLAN OF THE CITY, INTENDED FOR THE PERMANENT
SEAT OF GOVERNMENT OF THE UNITED STATES, PRO-
JECTED AGREEABLE TO THE DIRECTION OF THE PRES-
IDENT OF THE UNITED STATES, in pursuance of an ACT
of CONGRESS passed the SIXTEENTH DAY OF JULY
MDCCXC, ESTABLISHING THE PERMANENT SEAT on
the banks of the POTOMAC. Pierre Charles L'Enfant.

OBSERVATIONS EXPLANATORY OF THE PLAN

I. The positions for the different Grand Edifices, and for the
several Grand Squares or Areas of different shapes as they are
laid down, were first determined on the most advantageous

[4] [Editor Kite transcribed these explanatory notes from the border of a
copy of the initial map engraving. Later engravings differ in details from
the initial version, which is the one reproduced on page 24.—Ed.]

ground, commanding the most extensive prospects, and the better susceptible of such improvements as the various intents of the several objects may require.

II. Lines or Avenues of direct communication have been devised, to connect the separate and most distant objects with the principal, and to preserve through the whole a reciprocity of sight at the same time. Attention has been paid to the passing of those leading avenues over the most favorable ground for prospect and convenience.

III. North and South lines, intersected by others running due East and West, make the distribution of the city into [62] streets, squares etc., and those lines have been so combined as to meet at certain given points with those divergent avenues, so as to form on the spaces "first determined," the different Squares or Areas which are all proportional in magnitude to the number of avenues leading to them.

BREADTH OF THE STREETS

Every Grand transverse Avenue, and every principal divergent one, such as the comunication from the President's House to the Congress House etc. are 160 feet in breadth and thus divided:

10 feet of pavement on each side..........	20
30 feet of gravel walk planted with trees on each side	60
80 feet in the middle for carriage way......	80
	160 Feet

The other streets are of the following dimensions viz.

Those leading to public buildings or markets.	130
Others	110

In order to execute the above plan, Mr. Ellicott drew a true Meridional line by celestial observation, which passes through the area intended for the Congress House, this line he crossed by another due East and West, which passes through the same area. These lines are accurately measured, and made the bases on which the whole plan was executed. He ran all the lines by a transit instrument and determined the acute angles by actual measurement, and left nothing to the uncertainty of the compass.[63]

REFERENCES

A. THE equestrian figure of GEORGE WASHINGTON, a Monument voted in 1783 by the late Continental Congress.

B. An historic Column—also intended for a Mile or itinerary Column, from whose station (a mile from the Federal house) all distances of places throughout the Continent to be calculated.

C. A Naval itinerary Column, proposed to be erected to celebrate the first prize of a Navy and to stand a ready Monument to consecreate its progress and achievements.

D. This Church is intended for national purposes, such as public prayer, thanksgiving, funeral orations etc. and assigned to the special use of no particular Sect or denomination, but equally open to all. It will be likewise a proper shelter for such monuments as were voted by the late Continental Congress for those heroes who fell in the cause of liberty, and for such others as may hereafter be decreed by the voice of a grateful Nation.

E. Five grand fountains intended with a constant spout of water. N. B. There are within the limits of the City, above 25 good springs of excellent water abundantly supplied in the driest season of the year.

F. Grand Cascade, formed of water from the sources of the Tiber.

G. Public walk, being a square of 1200 feet, through which carriages may ascend to the upper Square of the Federal House.

H. Grand Avenue, 400 feet in breadth, and about a mile in length, bordered with gardens, ending in a slope from the houses on each side. This Avenue leads to Monument A. and connects the Congress Garden with the [64]

I. President's park and the

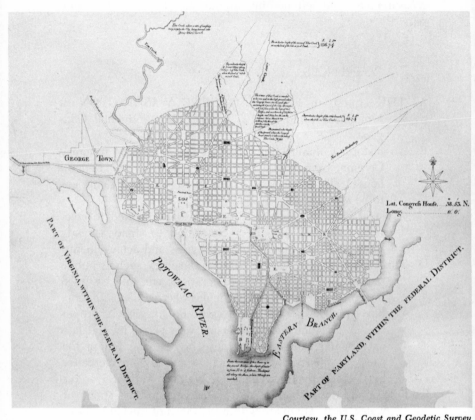

The L'Enfant Plan of the Federal City, 1791. Here, formed not solely from the imagination but from the land as well and then reimposed upon the land, forming in turn the lives of millions of individuals and the contours of government for over a century and a half, is the geometry of L'Enfant's idea.

An Air View of **Washington, D.C., 1956.** Comparisons of the plan with the actuality may be made by locating such focal points as the Capitol building ("Congress house" on the plan), near the center of both the drawing and the photograph.

K. well-improved field, being a part of the walk from the President's house of about 1800 feet in breadth, and ¾ of a mile in length. Every lot, deep-colored red with green plots, designates some of the situations which command the most agreeable prospects, and which are the best calculated for spacious houses and gardens, such as may accomodate foreign Ministers etc.

L. Around this Square and all along the

M. Avenue from the two bridges to the Federal House, the pavement on each side will pass under an Arched way under whose cover Shops will be most conveniently and agreeably situated. This street is 160 feet in breadth and a mile in length.

The Squares colored yellow, being fifteen in number, are proposed to be divided among the several States of the Union, for each of them to improve, or subscribe a sum additional to the value of the land; that purpose and the improvements around the Square to be completed in a limited time.

The center of each Square will admit of Statues, Columns, Obelisks, or any other ornament such as the different States may choose to erect: to perpetuate not only the memory of such individuals whose counsels or Military achievements were conspicuous in giving liberty and independence to this Country; but also those whose usefulness hath rendered them worthy of general imitation, to invite the youth of succeeding generations to tread in the paths of those sages, or heroes whom their country has thought proper to celebrate.

The situation of these Squares is such that they are the most advantageously and reciprocally seen from each other and as equally distributed over the whole [65] City district, and connected by spacious avenues round the grand Federal Improvements and as contiguous to them, and at the same time as equally distant from each other, as circumstances would admit. The Settlements round those Squares must soon become connected.

This mode of taking possession of and improving the

whole district at first must leave to posterity a grand idea of the patriotic interest which prompted it.

These figures colored red, are intended for the use of all religious denominations, on which they are to erect places of worship, and are proposed to be allowed to them in the manner as those colored yellow to the different States in the Union, but no burying grounds are to be admitted within the limits of the City, an appropriation being intended for that purpose without.

N. B. There are a number of squares or areas unappropriated, and in situations appropriate for Colleges and Academies and of which every Society whose object is national can be accomodated.

Every house within the City will stand square on the Streets, and every lot, even those on the divergent avenues will run square with their fronts, which on the most acute angle will not measure less than 56 feet and many will be above 140 feet.[66]

III

Into Nature:
Imaginative Energy

*Thomas Jefferson*_____
NOTES ON THE STATE OF VIRGINIA

Thomas Jefferson, *Notes on the State of Virginia* [1785], in *The Writings of Thomas Jefferson*, Vol. III, ed. by Paul Leicester Ford (New York, G. P. Putnam's Sons, 1894).

We never had an interior trade of any importance. Our exterior commerce has suffered very much from the beginning of the present contest. During this time we have manufactured within our families the most necessary articles of cloathing. Those of cotton will bear some comparison with the same kinds of manufacture in Europe; but those of wool, flax and hemp are very coarse, unsightly, and unpleasant: and such is our attachment to agriculture, and such our preference for foreign manufactures, that be it wise or unwise, our people will certainly return as soon as they can, to the raising raw materials, and exchanging them for finer manufactures than they are able to execute themselves.

The political œconomists of Europe have established it as a principle, that every State should endeavour to manufacture for itself; and this principle, like many others, we transfer to America, without calculating the difference of circumstance which should often produce a difference of result. In Europe the lands are either cultivated, or locked up against the cultivator. Manufacture must therefore be resorted to, of necessity, not of choice, to support the surplus of their people. But we have an immensity of land courting the industry of the husbandman. Is it best then that all our citizens should be employed in its improvement, or that one half should be called off from that to exercise manufactures and handicraft arts for the other? Those who labour in the earth are the chosen people of God, if ever he had a chosen people, whose breasts he has made his peculiar deposit for substantial and genuine virtue. It is the focus in which he keeps alive that sacred fire, which otherwise might escape from the face of the earth. Corruption of morals in the [268] mass of cultivators is a phænomenon of which no age nor nation has furnished an example. It is the mark set on those, who not looking up to heaven, to their own soil and industry, as does the husbandman, for their subsistence, depend for it on casualties and caprice of customers. Dependance begets subservience and venality, suffocates the germ of virtue, and prepares fit tools for the designs of ambition. This, the natural progress and consequence of the arts, has sometimes perhaps been retarded by accidental circumstances: but, generally speaking the proportion which the aggregate of the other classes of citizens bears in any state to that of its husbandmen, is the proportion of its unsound to its healthy parts, and is a good enough barometer whereby to measure its degree of corruption. While we have land to labour then, let us never wish to see our citizens occupied at a workbench, or twirling a distaff. Carpenters, masons, smiths, are wanting in husbandry: but, for the general operations of manufacture, let our work-shops remain in Europe. It is better to carry provisions and materials to workmen there, than bring them to the provisions and materials, and with them their manners and principles. The loss by the transportation of commodities across the Atlantic will be made up in happiness and permanence of government. The mobs of great cities add just so much to the support of pure government, as sores do to the strength of the human body. It is the manners and spirit of a people which

preserve a republic in vigour. A degeneracy in these is a canker
which soon eats to the heart of its laws and constitution.[269]

LETTER TO JAMES MADISON,
DECEMBER 20, 1787

Thomas Jefferson, "To James Madison," in The Writings of Thomas Jefferson,
Vol. IV, ed. by Paul Leicester Ford (New York, G. P. Putnam's Sons,
1894).

. . . I own I am not a friend to a very energetic government.
It is always oppressive. The late rebellion in Massachusetts
has given more alarm than I think it should have done. Calculate
that one rebellion in 13 states in the course of 11 years, is but one
for each state in a century & a half. No country should
be so long without one. Nor will any degree of power
in the hands of government prevent insurrections. France,
with all it's despotism, and two or three hundred thousand men
always in arms has had three insurrections in the three years
I have been here in every one of which greater numbers were
engaged than in Massachusetts & a great deal more blood was
spilt. In Turkey, which Montesquieu supposes more despotic,
insurrections are the events of every day. In England, where
the hand of power is lighter than there, but heavier than with
us they happen every half dozen years. Compare again the
ferocious depredations of their insurgents with the order, the
moderation & the almost self extinguishment of ours.—After all,
it is my principle that the will of the majority should always
prevail. If they approve the proposed Convention in all it's
parts, I shall concur in it chearfully, in hopes that they will
amend it whenever they shall find it work wrong. I think our
governments will remain virtuous for many centuries; as long
as they are chiefly agricultural; and this will be as long as
there shall be vacant lands in any part of America. When they
get piled upon [479] one another in large cities, as in Europe,

they will become corrupt as in Europe. Above all things I hope the education of the common people will be attended to; convinced that on their good sense we may rely with the most security for the preservation of a due degree of liberty. I have tired you by this time with my disquisitions & will therefore only add assurances of the sincerity of those sentiments of esteem & attachment with which I am Dear Sir your affectionate friend & servant. . . . [480]

LETTER TO JOHN ADAMS, APRIL 25, 1794

Thomas Jefferson, "To John Adams," in *The Writings of Thomas Jefferson,* Vol. VI, ed. by Paul Leicester Ford (New York, G. P. Putnam's Sons, 1895).

DEAR SIR,—I am to thank you for the book you were so good as to transmit me, as well as the letter covering it, and your felicitations on my present [504] quiet. The difference of my present & past situation is such as to leave me nothing to regret, but that my retirement has been postponed four years too long. The principles on which I calculate the value of life, are entirely in favor of my present course. I return to farming with an ardor which I scarcely knew in my youth, and which has got the better entirely of my love of study. Instead of writing 10. or 12. letters a day, which I have been in the habit of doing as a thing of course, I put off answering my letters now, farmer-like, till a rainy day, & then find it sometimes postponed by other necessary occupations. The case of the Pays de Vaud is new to me. The claims of both parties are on grounds which, I fancy, we have taught the world to set little store by. The rights of one generation will scarcely be considered hereafter as depending on the paper transactions of another. My countrymen are groaning under the insults of Gr Britain. I hope some means will turn up of reconciling our faith & honor with peace. I confess to you I have seen enough of one war never to wish to see another. With wishes of every degree of happiness to you,

both public & private, and with my best respects to mrs. Adams,
I am, your affectionate & humble servant.[505]

LETTER TO JOHN TAYLOR, MAY 1, 1794

Thomas Jefferson, "To John Taylor," in *The Writings of Thomas Jefferson*,
Vol. VI, ed. by Paul Leicester Ford (New York, G. P. Putnam's Sons, 1895).

DEAR SIR,—In my new occupation of a farmer I find a good
drilling machine indispensably necessary. I remember your
recommendation of one invented by [505] one of your neighbors;
& your recommendation suffices to satisfy me with it. I must
therefore beg of you to desire one to be made for me, & if you
will give me some idea of it's bulk, & whether it could travel
here on it's own legs, I will decide whether to send express for
it, or get it sent around by Richmond. Mention at the same time
the price of it & I will have it put in your hands.—I remember
I showed you, for your advice, a plan of a rotation of crops
which I had contemplated to introduce into my own lands.
On a more minute examination of my lands than I had before
been able to take since my return from Europe, I find their
degradation by ill-usage much beyond what I had expected, &
at the same time much more open land than I had calculated on.
One of these circumstances forces a milder course of cropping
on me, & the other enables me to adopt it. I drop therefore two
crops in my rotation, & instead of 5. crops in 8. years take 3. in
6. years, in the following order. 1. wheat. 2. corn & potatoes in
the strongest moiety, potatoes alone or peas alone in the other
moiety according to it's strength. 3. wheat or rye. 4. clover.
5. clover. 6. folding & buckwheat dressing. In such of my fields
as are too much worn for clover, I propose to try Stfoin, which
I know will grow in the poorest land, bring plentiful crops, &
is a great ameliorator. It is for this chiefly I want the drilling
machine. . . . [506]

LETTER TO DOCTOR CASPAR WISTAR, JUNE 21, 1807

Thomas Jefferson, "To Doctor Caspar Wistar," in *The Writings of Thomas Jefferson*, Vol. IX, ed. by Paul Leicester Ford (New York, G. P. Putnam's Sons, 1898).

DEAR SIR,—I have a grandson, the son of Mr. Randolph, now about 15 years of age, in whose education I take a lively interest. His time has not [78] hitherto been employed to the greatest advantage, a frequent change of tutors having prevented the steady pursuit of any one plan. Whether he possesses that lively imagination, usually called genius, I have not had opportunities of knowing. But I think he has an observing mind & sound judgment. He is assiduous, orderly, & of the most amiable temper & dispositions. As he will be at ease in point of property, his education is not directed to any particular possession, but will embrace those sciences which give to retired life usefulness, ornament or amusement. I am not a friend to placing growing men in populous cities, because they acquire there habits & partialities which do not contribute to the happiness of their after life. But there are particular branches of science, which are not so advantageously taught anywhere else in the U. S. as in Philadelphia. The garden at the Woodlands for Botany, Mr. Peale's Museum for Natural History, your Medical school for Anatomy, and the able professors in all of them, give advantages not to be found elsewhere. We propose, therefore, to send him to Philadelphia to attend the schools of Botany, Natural History, Anatomy, & perhaps Surgery; but not of Medicine. And why not of Medicine, you will ask? Being led to the subject, I will avail myself of the occasion to express my opinions on that science, and the extent of my medical creed. But, to finish first with respect to my grandson, I will state the favor I ask of you, which is the object of this letter.

Having been born & brought up in a mountainous & healthy country, we should be unwilling he should go [79] to Philadelphia until the autumnal diseases cease. It is important therefore for us to know, at what period after that, the courses of lectures in Natural history, Botany, Chemistry, Anatomy & Surgery begin and end, and what days or hours they occupy. . . . [80]

LETTER TO BENJAMIN AUSTIN, JANUARY 9, 1816

Thomas Jefferson, "To Benjamin Austin," in *The Writings of Thomas Jefferson*, Vol. X, ed. by Paul Leicester Ford (New York, G. P. Putnam's Sons, 1899).

You tell me I am quoted by those who wish to continue our dependence on England for manufactures. There was a time when I might have been so quoted with more candor, but within the thirty years which have since elapsed, how are circumstances changed! We were then in peace. Our independent place among nations was acknowledged. A commerce which offered the raw material in exchange for the same material after receiving the last touch of industry, was worthy of welcome to all nations. It was expected that those especially to whom manufacturing industry was important, would cherish the friendship of such customers by every favor, by every inducement, and particularly cultivate their peace by every act of justice and friendship. Under this prospect the question seemed legitimate, whether, with such an immensity of unimproved land, courting the hand of husbandry, the industry of agriculture, or that of manufactures, would add most to the national wealth? And the doubt was entertained on this consideration chiefly, that to the labor of the husbandman a vast addition is made by the spontaneous energies of the earth on which it is employed: for one grain of wheat committed to the earth, she renders twenty, thirty, and even fifty fold, whereas to the labor of the manufacturer nothing is added. Pounds of flax, in his hands, yield, on the contrary, but pennyweights of lace. This exchange, too, laborious as it might seem, what a field did it promise for the occupations of the ocean; what a nursery for that class of citizens who were to exercise and maintain our equal rights on that element? This was the state of things in 1785, when the "Notes on Virginia" were first printed; when, the ocean being open to all nations, and their common right in it acknowledged and exercised under regulations sanctioned by the assent and usage of all, it was thought that the doubt might claim some consideration. But who in 1785 could foresee the rapid depravity which was to render the close of that century the disgrace of the history of man? Who could have imagined that the two most distinguished in the rank of nations, for science and civilization, would have suddenly descended from that honorable eminence, and setting at defiance all those moral laws established by the Author of nature between nation and nation, as between man and man, would cover earth and sea with robberies and piracies, merely because strong enough to do it with temporal impunity; and that under this disbandment of nations from social order, we should have been despoiled of a thousand ships, and have thousands of our citizens reduced to Algerine slavery. Yet all this has taken place. One of these nations interdicted to our vessels [9] all harbors of the globe without having first proceeded to some one of hers, there paid a tribute proportioned to the cargo, and obtained her license to proceed to the port of destination. The other declared them to be lawful prize if they had touched at the port, or been visited by a ship of the enemy nation. Thus were we completely excluded from the ocean. Compare this state of things with that of '85, and say whether an opinion founded in the circumstances of that day can be fairly applied to those of the present. We have experienced what we did not then believe, that there exists both profligacy and power enough to exclude us from the field of interchange with other nations: that to be independent for the comforts of life we must fabricate them ourselves. We must now place the manufacturer by the side of the agriculturist. The former question is suppressed, or rather assumes a new form. Shall we make our own comforts, or go without them, at the will of a foreign nation? He, therefore, who is now against

domestic manufacture, must be for reducing us either to dependence on that foreign nation, or to be clothed in skins, and to
live like wild beasts in dens and caverns. I am not one of these;
experience has taught me that manufactures are now as necessary
to our independence as to our comfort; and if those who quote
me as of a different opinion, will keep pace with me in purchasing
nothing foreign where an equivalent of domestic fabric can
be obtained, without regard to difference of price, it will not
be our fault if we do not soon have a supply at home equal
to our demand, and wrest that weapon of distress from the hand
which has wielded it. If it shall be proposed to go beyond our
own supply, the question of '85 will then recur, will our *surplus*
labor be then most beneficially employed in the culture of the
earth, or in the fabrications of art? We have time yet for
consideration, before that question will press upon us; and the
maxim to be applied will depend on the circumstances which
shall then exist; for in so complicated a science as political
economy, no one axiom can be laid down as wise and expedient
for all times and circumstances, and for their contraries. . . . [10]

Ralph Waldo Emerson_____

FARMING

Ralph Waldo Emerson, "Farming," in *Society and Solitude: Twelve Chapters*
(Boston, Houghton, Mifflin, 1870).

The glory of the farmer is that, in the division of labors, it is
his part to create. All trade rests at last on his primitive activity.
He stands close to nature; he obtains from the earth the bread
and the meat. The food which was not, he causes to be. The first
farmer was the first man, and all historic nobility rests on possession and use of land. Men do not like hard work, but every
man has an exceptional respect for tillage, and a feeling that
this is the original calling of his race, that he himself is only
excused from it by some circumstance which made him delegate

it for a time to other hands. If he have not some skill which recommends him to the farmer, some product for which the farmer will give him corn, he must himself return into his due place among the planters. And the profession has in all eyes its ancient charm, as standing nearest to God, the first cause.

Then the beauty of nature, the tranquillity and innocence of the countryman, his independence, and his pleasing arts,—the care of bees, of poultry, of [133] sheep, of cows, the dairy, the care of hay, of fruits, of orchards and forests, and the reaction of these on the workman, in giving him a strength and plain dignity like the face and manners of nature,—all men acknowledge. All men keep the farm in reserve as an asylum where, in case of mischance, to hide their poverty,—or a solitude, if they do not succeed in society. And who knows how many glances of remorse are turned this way from the bankrupts of trade, from mortified pleaders in courts and senates, or from the victims of idleness and pleasure? Poisoned by town life and town vices, the sufferer resolves: 'Well, my children, whom I have injured, shall go back to the land, to be recruited and cured by that which should have been my nursery, and now shall be their hospital.'

The farmer's office is precise and important, but you must not try to paint him in rose-color; you cannot make pretty compliments to fate and gravitation, whose minister he is. He represents the necessities. It is the beauty of the great economy of the world that makes his comeliness. He bends to the order of the seasons, the weather, the soils and crops, as the sails of a ship bend to the wind. He represents continuous hard labor, year in, year out, and small gains. He is a slow person, timed to nature, and not to city watches. He takes the pace of seasons, plants, and chemistry. Nature [134] never hurries: atom by atom, little by little, she achieves her work. The lesson one learns in fishing, yachting, hunting, or planting, is the manners of Nature: patience with the delays of wind and sun, delays of the seasons, bad weather, excess or lack of water,—patience with the slowness of our feet, with the parsimony of our strength, with the largeness of sea and land we must traverse, etc. The farmer times himself to Nature, and acquires that livelong patience which belongs to her. Slow, narrow man, his rule is that the earth shall feed and clothe him; and he must wait for his crop to grow. His entertainments, his liberties and his spending must be on a farmer's scale, and not on a merchant's. It were as false for farmers to use a wholesale and massy expense, as for states to use a minute economy. But if thus pinched on one side, he has compensatory advantages. He is permanent, clings to his land as the rocks do. In the town where I live, farms remain in the same families for seven and eight generations; and most of the first settlers (in 1635), should they reappear on the farms to-day, would find their own blood and names still in possession. And the like fact holds in the surrounding towns.

This hard work will always be done by one kind of man; not by scheming speculators, nor by soldiers, nor professors, nor readers of Tennyson; but [135] by men of endurance—deep-chested, long-winded, tough, slow and sure, and timely. The farmer has a great health, and the appetite of health, and means to his end; he has broad lands for his home, wood to burn great fires, plenty of plain food; his milk at least is unwatered; and for sleep, he has cheaper and better and more of it than citizens.

He has grave trusts confided to him. In the great household of Nature, the farmer stands at the door of the bread-room, and weighs to each his loaf. It is for him to say whether men shall marry or not. Early marriages and the number of births are indissolubly connected with abundance of food; or, as Burke said, "Man breeds at the mouth." Then he is the Board of Quarantine. The farmer is a hoarded capital of health, as the farm is the capital of wealth; and it is from him that the health and power, moral and intellectual, of the cities came. The city is always recruited from the country. The men in cities who are the centres of energy, the driving-wheels of trade, politics, or practical arts, and the women of beauty and genius, are the children or grandchildren of farmers, and are spending the energies which their fathers' hardy, silent life accumulated in frosty furrows, in poverty, necessity, and darkness.

He is the continuous benefactor. He who digs a well, constructs a stone fountain, plants a grove [136] of trees by the roadside, plants an orchard, builds a durable house, reclaims a swamp, or so much as puts a stone seat by the wayside, makes the land so far lovely and desirable, makes a fortune which he cannot carry away with him, but which is useful to his country long afterwards. The man that works at home helps society at large with somewhat more of certainty than he who devotes himself to charities. If it be true that, not by votes of political parties but by the eternal laws of political economy, slaves are driven out of a slave State as fast as it is surrounded by free States, then the true abolitionist is the farmer, who, heedless of laws and constitutions, stands all day in the field, investing his labor in the land, and making a product with which no forced labor can compete.

We commonly say that the rich man can speak the truth, can afford honesty, can afford independence of opinion and action;— and that is the theory of nobility. But it is the rich man in a true sense, that is to say, not the man of large income and large expenditure, but solely the man whose outlay is less than his income and is steadily kept so.

In English factories, the boy that watches the loom, to tie the thread when the wheel stops to indicate that a thread is broken, is called a *minder*. And in this great factory of our Copernican globe, shifting its slides, rotating its constellations, times,[137] and tides, bringing now the day of planting, then of watering, then of weeding, then of reaping, then of curing and storing,—the farmer is the *minder*. His machine is of colossal proportions; the diameter of the water-wheel, the arms of the levers, the power of the battery, are out of all mechanic measure; and it takes him long to understand its parts and its working. This pump never "sucks;" these screws are never loose; this machine is never out of gear; the vat and piston, wheels and tires, never wear out, but are self-repairing.

Who are the farmer's servants? Not the Irish, nor the coolies, but Geology and Chemistry, the quarry of the air, the water of the brook, the lightning of the cloud, the castings of the worm, the plough of the frost. Long before he was born, the sun of ages decomposed the rocks, mellowed his land, soaked it with light and heat, covered it with vegetable film, then with forests, and accumulated the sphagnum whose decays made the peat of his meadow.

Science has shown the great circles in which nature works; the

manner in which marine plants balance the marine animals, as
the land plants supply the oxygen which the animals consume,
and the animals the carbon which the plants absorb. These
activities are incessant. Nature works on a method of *all for each
and each for all*. The [138] strain that is made on one point bears
on every arch and foundation of the structure. There is a perfect
solidarity. You cannot detach an atom from its holdings, or strip
off from it the electricity, gravitation, chemic affinity, or the relation to light and heat, and leave the atom bare. No, it brings
with it its universal ties.

Nature, like a cautious testator, ties up her estate so as not to
bestow it all on one generation, but has a forelooking tenderness
and equal regard to the next and the next, and the fourth and
the fortieth age. There lie the inexhaustible magazines. The eternal rocks, as we call them, have held their oxygen or lime un-
diminished, entire, as it was. No particle of oxygen can rust or
wear, but has the same energy as on the first morning. The good
rocks, those patient waiters, say to him: 'We have the sacred
power as we received it. We have not failed of our trust, and
now,—when in our immense day the hour is at last struck—take
the gas we have hoarded, mingle it with water, and let it be free
to grow in plants and animals and obey the thought of man.'

The earth works for him; the earth is a machine which yields
almost gratuitous service to every application of intellect. Every
plant is a manufacturer of soil. In the stomach of the plant development begins. The tree can draw on the whole air, [139] the
whole earth, on all the rolling main. The plant is all suction-
pipe,—imbibing from the ground by its root, from the air by its
leaves, with all its might.

The air works for him. The atmosphere, a sharp solvent, drinks
the essence and spirit of every solid on the globe,—a menstruum
which melts the mountains into it. Air is matter subdued by heat.
As the sea is the grand receptacle of all rivers, so the air is the
receptacle from which all things spring, and into which they all
return. The invisible and creeping air takes form and solid mass.
Our senses are skeptics, and believe only the impression of the
moment, and do not believe the chemical fact that these huge
mountain-chains are made up of gases and rolling wind. But
Nature is as subtle as she is strong. She turns her capital day by

day; deals never with dead, but ever with quick subjects. All things are flowing, even those that seem immovable. The adamant is always passing into smoke. The plants imbibe the materials which they want from the air and the ground. They burn, that is, exhale and decompose their own bodies into the air and earth again. The animal burns, or undergoes the like perpetual consumption. The earth burns, the mountains burn and decompose, slower, but incessantly. It is almost inevitable to push the generalization up into [140] higher parts of nature, rank over rank into sentient beings. Nations burn with internal fire of thought and affections, which wastes while it works. We shall find finer combustion and finer fuel. Intellect is a fire: rash and pitiless it melts this wonderful bone-house which is called man. Genius even, as it is the greatest good, is the greatest harm. Whilst all thus burns,—the universe in a blaze kindled from the torch of the sun,—it needs a perpetual tempering, a phlegm, a sleep, atmospheres of azote, deluges of water, to check the fury of the conflagration; a hoarding to check the spending, a centripetence equal to the centrifugence; and this is invariably supplied.

The railroad dirt-cars are good excavators, but there is no porter like Gravitation, who will bring down any weights which man cannot carry, and if he wants aid, knows where to find his fellow laborers. Water works in masses, and sets its irresistible shoulder to your mills or your ships, or transports vast boulders of rock in its iceberg a thousand miles. But its far greater power depends on its talent of becoming little, and entering the smallest holes and pores. By this agency, carrying in solution elements needful to every plant, the vegetable world exists.

But as I said, we must not paint the farmer in rose-color. Whilst these grand energies have [141] wrought for him and made his task possible, he is habitually engaged in small economies, and is taught the power that lurks in petty things. Great is the force of a few simple arrangements; for instance, the powers of a fence. On the prairie you wander a hundred miles and hardly find a stick or a stone. At rare intervals a thin oak-opening has been spared, and every such section has been long occupied. But the farmer manages to procure wood from far, puts up a rail-fence, and at once the seeds sprout and the oaks rise. It was only browsing and fire which had kept them down. Plant fruit-

trees by the roadside, and their fruit will never be allowed to
ripen. Draw a pine fence about them, and for fifty years they
mature for the owner their delicate fruit. There is a great deal
of enchantment in a chestnut rail or picketed pine boards.

Nature suggests every economical expedient somewhere on a
great scale. Set out a pine-tree, and it dies in the first year, or
lives a poor spindle. But nature drops a pine-cone in Mariposa,
and it lives fifteen centuries, grows three or four hundred feet
high, and thirty in diameter,—grows in a grove of giants, like a
colonnade of Thebes. Ask the tree how it was done. It did not
grow on a ridge, but in a basin, where it found deep soil, cold
enough and dry enough for the pine; defended itself from the
sun by growing in groves, and from [142] the wind by the walls of
the mountain. The roots that shot deepest, and the stems of happiest exposure, drew the nourishment from the rest, until the less
thrifty perished and manured the soil for the stronger, and the
mammoth Sequoias rose to their enormous proportions. The
traveller who saw them remembered his orchard at home, where
every year, in the destroying wind, his forlorn trees pined like
suffering virtue. In September, when the pears hang heaviest and
are taking from the sun their gay colors, comes usually a gusty
day which shakes the whole garden and throws down the
heaviest fruit in bruised heaps. The planter took the hint of the
Sequoias, built a high wall, or—better—surrounded the orchard
with a nursery of birches and evergreens. Thus he had the mountain basin in miniature; and his pears grew to the size of melons,
and the vines beneath them ran an eighth of a mile. But this
shelter creates a new climate. The wall that keeps off the strong
wind keeps off the cold wind. The high wall reflecting the heat
back on the soil gives that acre a quadruple share of sunshine,—

> "Enclosing in the garden square
> A dead and standing pool of air,"

and makes a little Cuba within it, whilst all without is Labrador.

The chemist comes to his aid every year by following [143] out
some new hint drawn from nature, and now affirms that this
dreary space occupied by the farmer is needless; he will concentrate his kitchen-garden into a box of one or two rods square,
will take the roots into his laboratory; the vines and stalks and

stems may go sprawling about in the fields outside, he will attend to the roots in his tub, gorge them with food that is good for them. The smaller his garden, the better he can feed it, and the larger the crop. As he nursed his Thanksgiving turkeys on bread and milk, so he will pamper his peaches and grapes on the viands they like best. If they have an appetite for potash, or salt, or iron, or ground bones, or even now and then for a dead hog, he will indulge them. They keep the secret well, and never tell on your table whence they drew their sunset complexion or their delicate flavors.

See what the farmer accomplishes by a cartload of tiles: he alters the climate by letting off water which kept the land cold through constant evaporation, and allows the warm rain to bring down into the roots the temperature of the air and of the surface-soil; and he deepens the soil, since the discharge of this standing water allows the roots of his plants to penetrate below the surface to the subsoil, and accelerates the ripening of the crop. The town of Concord is one of the oldest towns in this country, far on now in its third century. The selectmen [144] have once in every five years perambulated the boundaries, and yet, in this very year, a large quantity of land has been discovered and added to the town without a murmur of complaint from any quarter. By drainage we went down to a subsoil we did not know, and have found there is a Concord under old Concord, which we are now getting the best crops from; a Middlesex under Middlesex; and, in fine, that Massachusetts has a basement story more valuable and that promises to pay a better rent than all the superstructure. But these tiles have acquired by association a new interest. These tiles are political economists, confuters of Malthus and Ricardo; they are so many Young Americans announcing a better era,—more bread. They drain the land, make it sweet and friable; have made English Chat Moss a garden, and will now do as much for the Dismal Swamp. But beyond this benefit they are the text of better opinions and better auguries for mankind.

There has been a nightmare bred in England of indigestion and spleen among landlords and loomlords, namely, the dogma that men breed too fast for the powers of the soil; that men multiply in a geometrical ratio, whilst corn multiplies only in an arithmetical; and hence that, the more prosperous we are, the faster we approach these frightful limits: nay, the plight of every new generation [145] is worse than of the foregoing, because the first comers take up the best lands; the next, the second best; and each succeeding wave of population is driven to poorer, so that the land is ever yielding less returns to enlarging hosts of eaters. Henry Carey of Philadelphia replied: "Not so, Mr. Malthus, but just the opposite of so is the fact."

The first planter, the savage, without helpers, without tools, looking chiefly to safety from his enemy,—man or beast,—takes poor land. The better lands are loaded with timber, which he cannot clear; they need drainage, which he cannot attempt. He cannot plough, or fell trees, or drain the rich swamp. He is a poor creature; he scratches with a sharp stick, lives in a cave or a hutch, has no road but the trail of the moose or bear; he lives on their flesh when he can kill one, on roots and fruits when he cannot. He falls, and is lame; he coughs, he has a stitch in his side, he has a fever and chills; when he is hungry, he cannot always kill and eat a bear,—chances of war,—sometimes the bear eats him. 'T is long before he digs or plants at all, and then only a patch. Later he learns that his planting is better than hunting; that the earth works faster for him than he can work for himself, —works for him when he is asleep, when it rains, when heat overcomes him. The sunstroke which knocks him down brings his [146] corn up. As his family thrive, and other planters come up around him, he begins to fell trees and clear good land; and when, by and by, there is more skill, and tools and roads, the new generations are strong enough to open the lowlands, where the wash of mountains has accumulated the best soil, which yield a hundred-fold the former crops. The last lands are the best lands. It needs science and great numbers to cultivate the best lands, and in the best manner. Thus true political economy is not mean, but liberal, and on the pattern of the sun and sky. Population increases in the ratio of morality; credit exists in the ratio of morality.

Meantime we cannot enumerate the incidents and agents of the farm without reverting to their influence on the farmer. He carries out this cumulative preparation of means to their last effect. This crust of soil which ages have refined he refines again for the feeding of a civil and instructed people. The great elements with which he deals cannot leave him unaffected, or unconscious of his ministry; but their influence somewhat resembles that which the same Nature has on the child,—of subduing and silencing him. We see the farmer with pleasure and respect when we think what powers and utilities are so meekly worn. He knows every secret of labor; he changes the face of the landscape. Put him on a new planet and he would [147] know where to begin; yet there is no arrogance in his bearing, but a perfect gentleness. The farmer stands well on the world. Plain in manners as in dress, he would not shine in palaces; he is absolutely unknown and inadmissible therein; living or dying, he never shall be heard of in them; yet the drawing-room heroes put down beside him would shrivel in his presence; he solid and unexpressive, they expressed to gold-leaf. But he stands well on the world,—as Adam did, as an Indian does, as Homer's heroes, Agamemnon or Achilles, do. He is a person whom a poet of any clime—Milton, Firdusi, or Cervantes—would appreciate as being really a piece of the old Nature, comparable to sun and moon, rainbow and flood; because he is, as all natural persons are, representative of Nature as much as these.

That uncorrupted behavior which we admire in animals and in young children belongs to him, to the hunter, the sailor,—the man who lives in the presence of Nature. Cities force growth and make men talkative and entertaining, but they make them artificial. What possesses interest for us is the *naturel* of each, his constitutional excellence. This is forever a surprise, engaging and lovely; we cannot be satiated with knowing it, and about it; and it is this which the conversation with Nature cherishes and guards. [148]

Henry David Thoreau_____
WALDEN

Henry David Thoreau, *Walden* [1854] (Boston, Houghton, Mifflin, 1893).

When I wrote the following pages, or rather the bulk of them, I lived alone, in the woods, a mile from any neighbor, in a house which I had built myself, on the shore of Walden Pond, in Concord, Massachusetts, and earned my living by the labor of my hands only. I lived there two years and two months. At present I am a sojourner in civilized life again. . . . [7]

I would fain say something, not so much concerning the Chinese and Sandwich Islanders as you who read these pages, who are said to live in New England; something about your condition especially your outward condition or circumstances in this world, in this town, what it is, whether it is necessary that it be as bad as it is, whether it cannot be improved as well as not. I have travelled a good deal in Concord; and everywhere, in shops, and offices, and fields, the inhabitants have appeared to me to be doing penance in a thousand remarkable ways. . . . [9]

I see young men, my townsmen, whose misfortune it is to have inherited farms, houses, barns, cattle, and farming tools; for these are more easily acquired than got rid of. Better if they had been born in the open pasture and suckled by a wolf, that they might have seen with clearer eyes what field they were called to labor in. Who made them serfs of the soil? Why should they eat their sixty acres, when man is condemned to eat only his peck of dirt? Why should they begin digging their graves as soon as they are born? They have got to live a man's life, pushing all these things before them, and get on as well as they can. How many a poor immortal soul have I met [10] well nigh crushed and smothered under its load, creeping down the road of life, pushing before it a barn seventy-five feet by forty, its Augean stables never cleansed, and one hundred acres of land, tillage, mowing, pasture, and wood-lot! The portionless, who struggle with no such unnecessary inherited encumbrances, find it labor enough to subdue and cultivate a few cubic feet of flesh. . . . [11]

The mass of men lead lives of quiet desperation. What is called resignation is confirmed desperation. From the desperate city you go into the desperate country, and have to console yourself with the bravery of minks and muskrats. A stereotyped but unconscious despair is concealed even under what are called the games and amusements of mankind. There is no play in them, for this comes after work. But it is a characteristic of wisdom not to do desperate things.

When we consider what, to use the words of the catechism, is the chief end of man, and what are the true necessaries and means of life, it appears as if men had deliberately chosen the common mode of living because [15] they preferred it to any other. Yet they honestly think there is no choice left. But alert and healthy natures remember that the sun rose clear. It is never too late to give up our prejudices. No way of thinking or doing, however ancient, can be trusted without proof. . . . [16]

Let us consider for a moment what most of the trouble and anxiety which I have referred to is about, and how much it is necessary that we be troubled, or at least careful. It would be some advantage to live a primitive and frontier life, though in the midst of an outward civilization, if only to learn what are the gross necessaries of life and what methods have been taken to obtain them; or even to look over the old day-books of the merchants, to see what it was that men most commonly bought at the stores, what they stored, that is, what are the grossest groceries. For the improvements of ages have had but little influence on the essential laws of man's existence: as our skeletons, probably, are not to be distinguished from those of our ancestors.

By the words, *necessary of life,* I mean whatever, of all that man obtains by his own exertions, has been from the first, or from long use has become, so important to human life that few, if any, whether from savageness, or poverty, or philosophy, ever attempt to do without it. To many creatures there is in this sense but one necessary of life, Food. To the bison of the prairie it is a few inches of palatable grass, with [21] water to drink; unless he seeks the Shelter of the forest or the mountain's shadow. None of the brute creation requires more than Food and Shelter. The necessaries of life for man in this climate may, accurately enough, be distributed under the several heads of Food, Shelter, Clothing, and Fuel; for not till we have secured these are we prepared to entertain the true problems of life with freedom and a prospect of success. Man has invented, not only houses, but clothes and cooked food; and possibly from the accidental discovery of the warmth of fire, and the consequent use of it, at first a luxury, arose the present necessity to sit by it. We observe cats and dogs acquiring the same second nature. By proper Shelter and Clothing we legitimately retain our own internal heat; but with an excess of these, or of Fuel, that is, with an external heat greater than our own internal, may not cookery properly be said to begin? Darwin, the naturalist, says of the inhabitants of Tierra del Fuego, that while his own party, who were well clothed and sitting close to a fire, were far from too warm, these naked savages, who were farther off, were observed, to his great surprise, "to be streaming with [22] perspiration at undergoing such a roasting." So, we are told, the New Hollander goes naked with impunity, while the European shivers in his clothes. Is it impossible to combine the hardiness of these savages with the intellectualness of the civilized man? . . .

The grand necessity, then, for our bodies, is to keep warm, to keep the vital heat in [23] us. What pains we accordingly take, not only with our Food, and Clothing, and Shelter, but with our beds, which are our night-clothes, robbing the nests and breasts of birds to prepare this shelter within a shelter, as the mole has its bed of grass and leaves at the end of its burrow! The poor man is wont to complain that this is a cold world; and to cold, no less physical than social, we refer directly a great part of our ails. The summer, in some climates, makes possible to man a sort of Elysian life. Fuel, except to cook his Food, is then unnecessary; the sun is his fire, and many of the fruits are sufficiently cooked by its rays; while Food generally is more various, and more easily obtained, and Clothing and Shelter are wholly or half unnecessary. At the present day, and in this country, as I find by my own experience, a few implements, a knife, an axe, a spade, a wheelbarrow, etc., and for the studious, lamplight, stationery, and access to a few books, rank next to necessaries, and can all be obtained at a trifling cost. Yet some, not wise, go to the other side of the globe, to barbarous and unhealthy regions, and devote themselves to trade for ten or twenty years, in order that [24] they may live,—that is, keep comfortably warm,—and die in New England at last. The luxuriously rich are not simply kept comfortably warm, but unnaturally hot; as I implied before, they are cooked, of course à la mode.

Most of the luxuries, and many of the so-called comforts of life, are not only not indispensable, but positive hindrances to the elevation of mankind. With respect to luxuries and comforts, the wisest have ever lived a more simple and meagre life than the poor. The ancient philosophers, Chinese, Hindoo, Persian, and Greek, were a class than which none has been poorer in outward riches, none so rich in inward. We know not much about them. It is remarkable that we know so much of them as we do. The same is true of the more modern reformers and benefactors of their race. None can be an impartial or wise observer of human life but from the vantage ground of what we should call voluntary poverty. Of a life of luxury the fruit is luxury, whether in agriculture, or commerce, or literature, or art. There are nowadays professors of philosophy, but not philosophers. Yet it is admirable to profess because it was once [25] admirable to live. To be a philosopher is not merely to have subtle thoughts, nor even to found a school, but so to love wisdom as to live according to its dictates, a life of simplicity, independence, magnanimity, and trust. It is to solve some of the problems of life, not only theoretically, but practically. The success of great scholars and thinkers is commonly a courtier-like success, not kingly, not manly. They make shift to live merely by conformity, practically as their fathers did, and are in no sense the progenitors of a nobler race of men. But why do men degenerate ever? What makes families run out? What is the nature of the luxury which enervates and destroys nations? Are we sure that there is none of it in our own lives? The philosopher is in advance of his age even in the outward form of his life. He is not fed, sheltered, clothed, warmed, like his contemporaries. How can a man be a philosopher and not maintain his vital heat by better methods than other men?

When a man is warmed by the several modes which I have

described, what does he want next? Surely not more warmth of the same kind, as more and richer food, larger [26] and more splendid houses, finer and more abundant clothing, more numerous incessant and hotter fires, and the like. When he has obtained those things which are necessary to life, there is another alternative than to obtain the superfluities; and that is, to adventure on life now, his vacation from humbler toil having commenced. The soil, it appears, is suited to the seed, for it has sent its radicle downward, and it may now send its shoot upward also with confidence. Why has man rooted himself thus firmly in the earth, but that he may rise in the same proportion into the heavens above? —for the nobler plants are valued for the fruit they bear at last in the air and light, far from the ground, and are not treated like the humbler esculents, which, though they may be biennials, are cultivated only till they have perfected their root, and often cut down at top for this purpose, so that most would not know them in their flowering season.

I do not mean to prescribe rules to strong and valiant natures, who will mind their own affairs whether in heaven or hell, and perchance build more magnificently and spend more lavishly than the richest, without ever impoverishing themselves, not knowing how [27] they live,—if, indeed, there are any such, as has been dreamed; nor to those who find their encouragement and inspiration in precisely the present condition of things, and cherish it with the fondness and enthusiasm of lovers,—and, to some extent, I reckon myself in this number; I do not speak to those who are well employed, in whatever circumstances, and they know whether they are well employed or not;—but mainly to the mass of men who are discontented, and idly complaining of the hardness of their lot or of the times, when they might improve them. There are some who complain most energetically and inconsolably of any, because they are, as they say, doing their duty. I also have in my mind that seemingly wealthy, but most terribly impoverished class of all, who have accumulated dross, but know not how to use it, or get rid of it, and thus have forged their own golden or silver fetters. . . . [28]

In the savage state every family owns a shelter as good as the best, and sufficient for its coarser and simpler wants; but I think that I speak within bounds when I say that, though the birds of the air have their nests, and the foxes their holes, and the savages their wigwams, in modern civilized society not more than one half the families own a shelter. In the large towns and cities, where civilization especially prevails, the number of those who own a shelter is a very small fraction of the whole. The rest pay an annual tax for this outside garment of all, become indispensable summer and winter, which would buy a village of Indian wigwams, but now helps to keep them poor as long as they live. I do not mean to insist here on the disadvantage of hiring compared with owning, but it is evident that the savage owns his shelter because it costs so little, while the civilized man hires his commonly because he cannot afford to own it; nor can he, in the long run, any better afford to hire. But, answers one, by merely paying this tax the poor civilized man secures an abode which is a palace compared with the savage's. An annual rent of from twenty-five to a hundred dollars (these are the country [50] rates) entitles him to the benefit of the improvements of centuries, spacious apartments, clean paint and paper, Rumford fireplace, back plastering, Venetian blinds, copper pump, spring lock, a commodious cellar, and many other things. But how happens it that he who is said to enjoy these things is so commonly a *poor* civilized man, while the savage, who has them not, is rich as a savage? If it is asserted that civilization is a real advance in the condition of man,—and I think that it is, though only the wise improve their advantages,—it must be shown that it has produced better dwellings without making them more costly; and the cost of a thing is the amount of what I will call life which is required to be exchanged for it, immediately or in the long run. . . . [51]

When I think of acquiring for myself one of our luxurious dwellings, I am deterred, for, so to speak, the country is not yet adapted to *human* culture, and we are still forced to cut our *spiritual* bread far thinner than our forefathers did their wheaten. Not that all architectural ornament is to be neglected even in the rudest periods; but let our houses first be lined with beauty, where they come in contact with our lives, like the tenement of the shell-fish, and not overlaid with it. But, alas! I have been inside one or two of them, and know what they are lined with.

Though we are not so degenerate but that we might possibly live in a cave or a wigwam or wear skins to-day, it certainly is

better to accept the advantages, though so dearly bought, which
the invention and industry of mankind offer. In such a neighborhood as this, boards and shingles, lime and bricks, are cheaper
and more easily obtained than suitable caves, or whole logs,
or [65] bark in sufficient quantities, or even well-tempered clay or
flat stones. I speak understandingly on this subject, for I have
made myself acquainted with it both theoretically and practically. With a little more wit we might use these materials so. as
to become richer than the richest now are, and make our civilization a blessing. The civilized man is a more experienced and
wiser savage. . . . [66]

It would be worth the while to build still more deliberately
than I did, considering, for instance, what foundation a door, a
window, a cellar, a garret, have in the nature of man, and perchance never raising any superstructure until we found a better
reason for it than our temporal necessities even. There is some
of the same fitness in a man's building his own house that there
is in a bird's building his own nest. Who knows but if men constructed their dwellings with their own hands, and provided food
for themselves and families simply and honestly enough, the
poetic faculty would be universally developed, as birds universally sing when they are so engaged? But alas! we do like cow-
birds and cuckoos, which lay their eggs in nests which other birds
have built, and cheer no traveller with their chattering and un-
musical notes. Shall we forever resign the pleasure of construction to the carpenter? What does architecture amount to in the
experience of the mass of men? I never in all my walks came
across a man engaged in so simple and natural an occupation as
building [74] his house. We belong to the community. . . . [75]

I went to the woods because I wished to live deliberately, to
front only the essential facts of life, and see if I could not learn
what it had to teach, and not, when I came to die, discover that
I had not lived. I did not wish to live what was not life, living is
so dear; nor did I wish to practise resignation, unless it was quite
necessary. I wanted to live deep and suck out all the marrow of
life, to live so sturdily and Spartan-like as to put to rout all that
was not life, to cut a broad swath and shave close, to drive life
into a corner, and reduce it to its lowest terms, and, if it proved
to be mean, why then to get the whole and genuine meanness of

it, and publish its meanness to the world; or if it were sublime, to know it by experience, and be able to give a true account of it in my next excursion. For most men, it appears to me, are in a strange uncertainty [143] about it, whether it is of the devil or of God, and have *somewhat hastily* concluded that it is the chief end of man here to "glorify God and enjoy him forever."

Still we live meanly, like ants; though the fable tells us that we were long ago changed into men; like pygmies we fight with cranes; it is error upon error, and clout upon clout, and our best virtue has for its occasion a superfluous and evitable wretchedness. Our life is frittered away by detail. An honest man has hardly need to count more than his ten fingers, or in extreme cases he may add his ten toes, and lump the rest. Simplicity, simplicity, simplicity! I say, let your affairs be as two or three, and not a hundred or a thousand; instead of a million count half a dozen, and keep your accounts on your thumb nail. In the midst of this chopping sea of civilized life, such are the clouds and storms and quicksands and thousand-and-one items to be allowed for, that a man has to live, if he would not founder and go to the bottom and not make his port at all, by dead reckoning, and he must be a great calculator indeed who succeeds. Simplify, simplify. Instead of three meals a day, if it be necessary eat [144] but one; instead of a hundred dishes, five; and reduce other things in proportion. Our life is like a German Confederacy, made up of petty states, with its boundary forever fluctuating, so that even a German cannot tell you how it is bounded at any moment. The nation itself, with all its so-called internal improvements, which, by the way are all external and superficial, is just such an unwieldy and overgrown establishment, cluttered with furniture and tripped up by its own traps, ruined by luxury and heedless expense, by want of calculation and a worthy aim, as the million households in the land; and the only cure for it as for them is in a rigid economy, a stern and more than Spartan simplicity of life and elevation of purpose. It lives too fast. Men think that it is essential that the *Nation* have commerce, and export ice, and talk through a telegraph, and ride thirty miles an hour, without a doubt, whether *they* do or not; but whether we should live like baboons or like men, is a little uncertain. If we do not get out sleepers, and forge rails, and devote days and nights to the

work, but go to tinkering upon our *lives* to improve *them,* who
will build railroads? And if railroads are [145] not built, how shall
we get to heaven in season? But if we stay at home and mind our
business, who will want railroads? We do not ride on the railroad; it rides upon us. . . . [146]

Let us spend one day as deliberately as Nature, and not be
thrown off the track by every nutshell and mosquito's wing that
falls on the rails. Let us rise early and fast, or break fast, gently
and without perturbation; let company come and let company
go, let the bells ring and the children cry,—determined to make
a day of it. Why should we knock under and go with the stream?
Let us not be upset and overwhelmed in that terrible rapid and
whirlpool called a dinner, situated in the meridian shallows.
Weather this danger and you are safe, for the rest [153] of the
way is downhill. With unrelaxed nerves, with morning vigor, sail
by it, looking another way, tied to the mast like Ulysses. If the
engine whistles, let it whistle till it is hoarse for its pains. If the
bell rings, why should we run? We will consider what kind of
music they are like. Let us settle ourselves, and work and wedge
our feet downward through the mud and slush of opinion, and
prejudice, and tradition, and delusion, and appearance, that allu-
vion which covers the globe, through Paris and London, through
New York and Boston and Concord, through church and state,
through poetry and philosophy and religion, till we come to a
hard bottom and rocks in place, which we can call *reality,* and
say, This is, and no mistake; and then begin, having a *point
d'appui,* below freshet and frost and fire, a place where you
might found a wall or a state, or set a lamppost safely, or perhaps
a gauge, not a Nilometer, but a Realometer, that future ages
might know how deep a freshet of shams and appearances had
gathered from time to time. If you stand right fronting and face
to face to a fact, you will see the sun glimmer on both its surfaces, as if it were a cimeter, and feel [154] its sweet edge dividing
you through the heart and marrow, and so you will happily
conclude your mortal career. Be it life or death, we crave only
reality. . . . [155]

The Fitchburg Railroad touches the pond about a hundred
rods south of where I dwell. I usually go to the village along its
causeway, and am, as it were, related to society [180] by this link.

Reprinted from *Thoreau's Walden: A Photographic Register* by Henry Bugbee Kane, by permission of Alfred A. Knopf, Inc.

Near Concord, still a small town in Massachusetts, lies **Walden Pond.** The photograph here is of a portion of the north shore. Of real consequence first only to Henry David Thoreau, since 1854 this fragment of nature has become known throughout the world not for what it is but for one man's attitude toward it.

The men on the freight trains, who go over the whole length of the road, bow to me as to an old acquaintance, they pass me so often, and apparently they take me for an employee; and so I am. I too would fain be a track-repairer somewhere in the orbit of the earth.

The whistle of the locomotive penetrates my woods summer and winter, sounding like the scream of a hawk sailing over some farmer's yard, informing me that many restless city merchants are arriving within the circle of the town, or adventurous country traders from the other side. As they come under one horizon, they shout their warning to get off the track to the other, heard sometimes through the circles of two towns. Here come your groceries, country; your rations, countrymen! Nor is there any man so independent on his farm that he can say them nay. And here's your pay for them! screams the countryman's whistle; timber like long battering rams going twenty miles an hour against the city's walls, and chairs enough to seat all the weary and heavy laden that dwell within them. With such huge and lumbering civility the country hands a chair to the [181] city. All the Indian huckleberry hills are stripped, all the cranberry meadows are raked into the city. Up comes the cotton, down goes the woven cloth; up comes the silk, down goes the woollen; up come the books, but down goes the wit that writes them. . . . [182]

There can be no very black melancholy to him who lives in the midst of Nature and has his senses still. There was never yet such a storm but it was Æolian music to a healthy and innocent ear. Nothing can rightly compel a simple and brave man to a vulgar sadness. While I enjoy the friendship of the seasons I trust that nothing can make life a burden to me. The gentle rain which waters my beans and keeps me in the house to-day is not drear and melancholy, but good for me too. Though it prevents my hoeing them, it is of far more worth than my hoeing. If [205] it should continue so long as to cause the seeds to rot in the ground and destroy the potatoes in the low lands, it would still be good for the grass on the uplands, and, being good for the grass, it would be good for me. Sometimes, when I compare myself with other men, it seems as if I were more favored by the gods than they, beyond any deserts that I am conscious of; as if I had a warrant and surety at their hands which my fellows have not, and were especially guided and guarded. I do not flatter myself, but if it be possible they flatter me. I have never felt lonesome, or in the least oppressed by a sense of solitude, but once, and that was a few weeks after I came to the woods, when, for an hour, I doubted if the near neighborhood of man was not essential to a serene and healthy life. To be alone was something unpleasant. But I was at the same time conscious of a slight insanity in my mood, and seemed to foresee my recovery. In the midst of a gentle rain while these thoughts prevailed, I was suddenly sensible of such sweet and beneficent society in Nature, in the very pattering of the drops, and in every sound and sight around my house, an infinite and unaccountable friendliness [206] all at once like an atmosphere sustaining me, as made the fancied advantages of human neighborhood insignificant, and I have never thought of them since. Every little pine needle expanded and swelled with sympathy and befriended me. I was so distinctly made aware of the presence of something kindred to me, even in scenes which we are accustomed to call wild and dreary, and also that the nearest of blood to me and humanest was not a person nor a villager, that I thought no place could ever be strange to me again.—

> "Mourning untimely consumes the sad;
> Few are their days in the land of the living,
> Beautiful daughter of Toscar."

Some of my pleasantest hours were during the long rain storms in the spring or fall, which confined me to the house for the afternoon as well as the forenoon, soothed by their ceaseless roar and pelting; when an early twilight ushered in a long evening in which many thoughts had time to take root and unfold themselves. In those driving northeast rains which tried the village houses so, when the maids stood ready with mop and pail in front entries to keep the deluge out, I sat behind my door in my little [207] house, which was all entry, and thoroughly enjoyed its protection. In one heavy thunder shower the lightning struck a large pitch-pine across the pond, making a very conspicuous and perfectly regular spiral groove from top to bottom, an inch or more deep, and four or five inches wide, as you would groove a walking-stick. I passed it again the other day, and was struck with awe on looking up and beholding that mark, now more distinct than ever, where a terrific and resistless bolt came down out of the harmless sky eight years ago. Men frequently say to me, "I should think you would feel lonesome down there, and want to be nearer to folks, rainy and snowy days and nights especially." I am tempted to reply to such,—This whole earth which we inhabit is but a point in space. How far apart, think you, dwell the two most distant inhabitants of yonder star, the breadth of whose disk cannot be appreciated by our instruments? Why should I feel lonely? is not our planet in the Milky Way? This which you put seems to me not to be the most important question. What sort of space is that which separates a man from his fellows and makes him solitary? I have found that no exertion of the [208] legs can bring two minds much nearer to one another. What do we want most to dwell near to? Not to many men surely, the depot, the post-office, the bar-room, the meeting-house, the school-house, the grocery, Beacon Hill, or the Five Points, where men most congregate, but to the perennial source of our life, whence in all our experience we have found that to issue, as the willow stands near the water and sends out its roots in that direction. This will vary with different natures, but this is the place where a wise man will dig his cellar. . . . [209]

If a man does not keep pace with his companions, perhaps it is because he hears a different drummer. Let him step to the music which he hears, however measured or far away. It is not important that he should mature as soon as an apple-tree or an oak. Shall he turn his spring into summer? If the condition of things which we were made for is not yet, what were any reality which we can substitute? We will not be shipwrecked on a vain reality. Shall we with [502] pains erect a heaven of blue glass over ourselves, though when it is done we shall be sure to gaze still at the true ethereal heaven far above, as if the former were not? [503]

Henry George————————————————————

PROGRESS AND POVERTY

Henry George, *Progress and Poverty* [1879] (New York, D. Appleton, 1884).

. . . Where the conditions to which material progress every-where tends are most fully realized—that is to say, where population is densest, wealth greatest, and the machinery of production and exchange most highly developed—we find the deepest poverty, the sharpest struggle for existence, and the most enforced idleness.[6]

. . . Just as . . . a community realizes the conditions which all civilized communities are striving for, and advances in the scale of material progress—just as closer settlement and a more intimate connection with the rest of the world, and greater utilization of labor-saving machinery, make possible greater economies in production and exchange, and wealth in consequence increases, not merely in the aggregate, but in proportion to population—so does poverty take a darker aspect. Some get an infinitely better and easier living, but others find it hard to get a living at all. The "tramp" comes with the locomotive, and almshouses and prisons are as surely the marks of "material progress" as are costly dwellings, rich warehouses, and magnificent churches. Upon streets lighted with gas and patrolled by uniformed policemen, beggars wait for the passer-by, and in the shadow of college, and library, and museum, are gathering the more hideous Huns and fiercer Vandals of whom Macaulay prophesied. . . . [7]

It is true that wealth has been greatly increased, and that the average of comfort, leisure, and refinement has been raised; but these gains are not general. In them the lowest class do not share.[1] I do not mean that the condition of the lowest class has nowhere nor in anything been improved; but that there is nowhere any improvement which can be credited to increased productive power. I mean that the tendency of what we call material progress is in nowise to improve the condition of the lowest class in the essentials of healthy, happy human life. Nay, more, that it is to still further depress the condition of the lowest class. The new forces, elevating in their nature though they be, do not act upon the social fabric from underneath, as was for a long time hoped and believed, but strike it at a point intermediate between top and bottom. It is as though an immense wedge were being forced, not underneath society, but through society. Those who are above the point of separation are elevated, but those who are below are crushed down.

This depressing effect is not generally realized, for it is not apparent where there has long existed a class just able to live. Where the lowest class barely lives, as [8] has been the case for a long time in many parts of Europe, it is impossible for it to get any lower, for the next lowest step is out of existence, and no tendency to further depression can readily show itself. But in the progress of new settlements to the conditions of older communities it may clearly be seen that material progress does not merely fail to relieve poverty—it actually produces it. In the United States it is clear that squalor and misery, and the vices and crimes that spring from them, everywhere increase as the village grows to the city, and the march of development brings the advantages of the improved methods of production and exchange. It is in the older and richer sections of the Union that pauperism and distress among the working classes are becoming most painfully apparent. If there is less deep poverty in San Francisco than in New York, is it not because San Francisco is yet behind New York in all that both cities are striving for? When San Francisco reaches the point where New York now

---

[1] It is true that the poorest may now in certain ways enjoy what the richest a century ago could not have commanded, but this does not show improvement of condition so long as the ability to obtain the necessaries of life is not increased. The beggar in a great city may enjoy many things from which the backwoods farmer is debarred, but that does not prove the condition of the city beggar better than that of the independent farmer.

is, who can doubt that there will also be ragged and barefooted children on her streets?

This association of poverty with progress is the great enigma of our times. . . . [9]

Now, the industrial pyramid manifestly rests on the land. The primary and fundamental occupations, which create a demand for all others, are evidently those which extract wealth from nature, and, hence, if we trace from one exchange point to another, and from one occupation to another, this check to production, which shows itself in decreased purchasing power, we must ultimately find it in some obstacle which checks labor in expending itself on land. And that obstacle, it is clear, is the speculative advance in rent, or the value of land, which produces the same effects as (in fact, it is) a lock-out of labor and capital by land owners. This check to production, beginning at the basis of interlaced industry, propagates itself from exchange point to exchange point, cessation of supply becoming failure of demand, until, so to speak, the whole machine is thrown out of gear, and the spectacle is everywhere presented of labor going to waste while laborers suffer from want.

This strange and unnatural spectacle of large numbers of willing men who cannot find employment, is enough to suggest the true cause to whoever can think consecutively. For, though custom has dulled us to it, it *is* a strange and unnatural thing that men who wish to labor, in order to satisfy their wants, cannot find the opportunity—as, since labor is that which produces wealth, the man who seeks to exchange labor for food, clothing, or any other form of wealth, is like one who proposes to give bullion for coin, or wheat for flour. We talk about the supply of labor and the demand for labor, but, evidently, these are only relative terms. The supply of labor is everywhere the same—two hands always come into the world with one mouth, twenty-one boys to every twenty girls; and the demand for labor must always exist as long as men want things which labor alone can procure. We talk about the "want of [243] work," but, evidently it is not work that is short while want continues; evidently, the supply of labor cannot be too great, nor the demand for labor too small, when people suffer for the lack of things that labor produces. The real trouble must be that supply is somehow prevented from satisfying demand, that somewhere there is an obstacle which prevents labor from producing the things that laborers want.

Take the case of any one of these vast masses of unemployed men, to whom, though he never heard of Malthus, it to-day seems that there are too many people in the world. In his own wants, in the needs of his anxious wife, in the demands of his half-cared for, perhaps even hungry and shivering children, there is demand enough for labor, Heaven knows! In his own willing hands is the supply. Put him on a solitary island, and though cut off from all the enormous advantages which the co-operation, combination, and machinery of a civilized community give to the productive powers of man, yet his two hands can fill the mouths and keep warm the backs that depend upon them. Yet where productive power is at its highest development he cannot. Why? Is it not because in the one case he has access to the material and forces of nature, and in the other this access is denied?

Is it not the fact that labor is thus shut off from nature which can alone explain the state of things that compels men to stand idle who would willingly supply their wants by their labor? The proximate cause of enforced idleness with one set of men may be the cessation of demand on the part of other men for the particular things they produce, but trace this cause from point to point, from occupation to occupation, and you will find that enforced idleness in one trade is caused by enforced idleness in another, and that the paralysis which produces dullness in all trades cannot be said to spring from too great a supply of labor or too small a demand for labor, but must proceed from the fact that supply cannot meet demand by producing the things which satisfy want and are the object of labor.[244]

Now, what is necessary to enable labor to produce these things, is land. When we speak of labor creating wealth, we speak metaphorically. Man creates nothing. The whole human race, were they to labor forever, could not create the tiniest mote that floats in a sunbeam—could not make this rolling sphere one atom heavier or one atom lighter. In producing wealth, labor, with the aid of natural forces, but works up, into the forms desired, pre-existing matter, and, to produce wealth, must, therefore, have access to this matter and to these forces—that is to say, to land. The land is the source of all wealth. It is the mine from which must be drawn the ore that labor fashions. It is the substance to which labor gives the form. And, hence, when labor cannot satisfy its wants, may we not with certainty infer that it can be from no other cause than that labor is denied access to land?

When in all trades there is what we call scarcity of employment; when, everywhere, labor wastes, while desire is unsatisfied, must not the obstacle which prevents labor from producing the wealth it needs, lie at the foundation of the industrial structure? That foundation is land. Milliners, optical instrument makers, gilders, and polishers, are not the pioneers of new settlements. Miners did not go to California or Australia because shoemakers, tailors, machinists, and printers were there. But those trades followed the miners, just as they are now following the gold diggers into the Black Hills and the diamond diggers into South Africa. It is not the storekeeper who is the cause of the farmer, but the farmer who brings the storekeeper. It is not the growth of the city that develops the country, but the development of the country that makes the city grow. And, hence, when, through all trades, men willing to work cannot find opportunity to do so, the difficulty must arise in the employment that creates a demand for all other employments—it must be because labor is shut out from land.

In Leeds or Lowell, in Philadelphia or Manchester, in London or New York, it may require a grasp of first principles [245] to see this; but where industrial development has not become so elaborate, nor the extreme links of the chain so widely separated, one has but to look at obvious facts. Although not yet thirty years old, the city of San Francisco, both in population and in commercial importance, ranks among the great cities of the world, and, next to New York, is the most metropolitan of American cities. Though not yet thirty years old, she has had for some years an increasing number of unemployed men. Clearly, here, it is because men cannot find employment in the country that there are so many unemployed in the city; for when the harvest opens they go trooping out, and when it is over they come trooping back to the city again. If these now unemployed men were producing wealth from the land, they would not only be employing themselves, but would be employing all the mechanics of the city, giving custom to the storekeepers, trade to the merchants, audiences to the theaters, and subscribers and advertisements to the newspapers—creating effective demand that would be felt in New England and Old England, and wherever throughout the world come the articles that, when they have the means to pay for them, such a population consumes.

Now, why is it that this unemployed labor cannot employ itself upon the land? Not that the land is all in use. Though all the symptoms that in older countries are taken as showing a redundancy of population are beginning to manifest themselves in San Francisco, it is idle to talk of redundancy of population in a State that with greater natural resources than France has not yet a million of people. Within a few miles of San Francisco is unused land enough to give employment to every man who wants it. I do not mean to say that every unemployed man could turn farmer or build himself a house, if he had the land; but that enough could and would do so to give employment to the rest. What is it, then, that prevents labor from employing itself on this land? Simply, that it has been monopolized and is held at speculative prices, based not upon [246] present value, but upon the added value that will come with the future growth of population. . . . [247]

The reason why, in spite of the increase of productive power, wages constantly tend to a minimum which will give but a bare living, is that, with increase in productive power, rent tends to even greater increase, thus producing a constant tendency to the forcing down of wages.[254]

. . . It is not in the relations of capital and labor; it is not in the pressure of population against subsistence, that an explanation of the unequal development of our civilization is to be found. The great cause of inequality in the distribution of wealth is inequality in the ownership of land. The ownership of land is the great fundamental fact which ultimately determines the social, the political, and consequently the intellectual and moral condition of a people. And it must be so. For land is the habitation of man, the storehouse upon which he must draw for all his needs, the material to which his labor must be applied for the supply of all his desires; for even the products of the sea cannot be taken, the light of the sun enjoyed, or any of the forces of nature utilized, without the use of land or its products. On the land we are born, from it we live, to it we return again—children of the soil as truly as is the blade of grass or the flower of the field. Take away from man all that belongs to land, and he is but a disembodied spirit. Material progress cannot rid us of our dependence upon land; it can but add to the power of producing wealth from land; and hence, when land is monopolized, it might go on to infinity without increasing wages or improving the condition of those who have but their labor. . . . [266]

I do not propose either to purchase or to confiscate private property in land. The first would be unjust; the second, needless. Let the individuals who now hold it still retain, if they want to, possession of what they are pleased to call *their* land. Let them continue to call it *their* land. Let them buy and sell, and bequeath and devise it. We may safely leave them the shell, if we take the kernel. *It is not necessary to confiscate land; it is only necessary to confiscate rent.*

Nor to take rent for public uses is it necessary that the State should bother with the letting of lands, and assume the chances of the favoritism, collusion, and corruption that might involve. It is not necessary that any new machinery should be created. The machinery already exists. Instead of extending it, all we have to do is to simplify and reduce it. By leaving to land owners a percentage of rent which would probably be much less than the cost and loss involved in attempting to rent lands through State agency, and by making use of this existing machinery, we may, without jar or shock, assert the common right to land by taking rent for public uses.

We already take some rent in taxation. We have only to make some changes in our modes of taxation to take it all.

What I, therefore, propose, as the simple yet sovereign remedy, which will raise wages, increase the earnings of capital, extirpate pauperism, abolish poverty, give remunerative employment to whoever wishes it, afford free scope to human powers, lessen crime, elevate morals, and taste, and intelligence, purify government and carry civilization to yet nobler heights, is—*to appropriate rent by taxation.*

In this way, the State may become the universal landlord without calling herself so, and without assuming a single new function. In form, the ownership of land would remain just as now. No owner of land need be dispossessed, and no restriction need be placed upon the amount of land any one could hold. For, rent being taken by the State in taxes, land, no matter in whose name it stood, or in what [364] parcels it was held, would be really common property, and every member of the community would participate in the advantages of its ownership.

Now, insomuch as the taxation of rent, or land values, must necessarily be increased just as we abolish other taxes, we may put the proposition into practical form by proposing—

To abolish all taxation save that upon land values. . . . [365]

And so with the farmer. I speak not now of the farmers who never touch the handles of a plow, who cultivate thousands of acres and enjoy incomes like those of the rich Southern planters before the war; but of the working farmers who constitute such a large class in the United States—men who own small farms, which they cultivate with the aid of their boys, and perhaps some hired help, and who in Europe would be called peasant proprietors. Paradoxical as it may appear to these men until they understand the full bearings of the proposition, of all classes above that of the mere laborer they have most to gain by placing all taxes upon the value of land. That they do not now get as good a living as their hard work ought to give them, they generally feel, though they may not be able to trace the cause. The fact is that taxation, as now levied, falls on them with peculiar severity. They are taxed on all their improvements —houses, barns, fences, crops, stock. The personal property which they have cannot be as readily concealed or undervalued as can the more valuable kinds which are concentrated in the cities. They are not only taxed on personal property and improvements, which the owners of unused land escape, but their land is generally taxed at a higher rate than land held on speculation, simply because it is improved. But further than this, all taxes imposed on commodities, and especially the taxes which, like our protective duties, are imposed with a view of raising the prices of commodities, fall on the farmer without mitigation. For in a country like the United States, which exports agricultural produce, the farmer cannot be protected. Whoever gains, he must lose. . . . [404]

The farmer would be a great gainer by the substitution of a single tax upon the value of land for all these taxes, for the taxation of land values would fall with greatest weight, not upon the agricultural districts, where land values are comparatively small, but upon the towns and cities where land values are high; whereas taxes upon personal property and improvements fall as heavily in the country as in the city. And in sparsely settled districts there would be hardly any taxes at all for the farmer to pay. For taxes, being levied upon the value of the bare land, would fall as heavily upon unimproved as upon improved land. Acre for acre, the improved and cultivated farm, with its buildings, fences, orchard, crops, and stock could be taxed no more than unused land of equal quality. The result would be that speculative values would be kept down, and that cultivated and improved farms would have no taxes to pay until the country around them had been well settled. In fact, paradoxical as it may at first seem to them, the effect of putting all taxation upon the value of land would be to relieve the harder working farmers of all taxation.

But the great gain of the working farmer can only be seen when the effect upon the distribution of population is considered. The destruction of speculative land values would tend to diffuse population where it is too dense and to concentrate it where it is too sparse; to substitute for the tenement house, homes surrounded by gardens, and to fully settle agricultural districts before people were driven far from neighbors to look for land. The people of the cities would thus get more of the pure air and sunshine of the country, the people of the country more of the economies and social life of the city. If, as is doubtless the case, the application of machinery tends to large fields, agricultural population will assume the primitive form and cluster in villages. The life of the average farmer is now unnecessarily dreary. He is not only compelled to work early and late, but he is cut off by the [405] sparseness of population from the conveniences, the amusements, the educational facilities, and the social and intellectual opportunities that come with the closer contact of man with man. He would be far better off in all these respects, and his labor would be far more productive, if he and those around him held no more land than they wanted to use. While his children, as they grew up, would neither be so impelled to seek the excitement of a city nor would they be driven so far away to seek farms of their own. Their means of living would be in their own hands, and at home. . . . [406]

What has destroyed every previous civilization has been the tendency to the unequal distribution of wealth and power. This same tendency, operating with increasing force, is observable in our civilization to-day. . . . Wages and interest tend constantly to fall, rent to rise, the rich to become very much richer, the poor to become more helpless and hopeless, and the middle class to be swept away. . . . [475]

The type of modern growth is the great city. Here are to be found the greatest wealth and the deepest poverty. And it is here that popular government has most clearly broken down. In all the great American cities there is to-day as clearly defined a ruling class as in the most aristocratic countries of the world. Its members carry wards in their pockets, make up the slates for nominating conventions, distribute offices as they bargain together, and—though they toil not, neither do they spin—wear the best of raiment and spend money lavishly. They are men of power, whose favor the ambitious must court and whose vengeance he must avoid. Who are these men? The wise, the good, the learned—men who have earned the confidence of their fellow-citizens by the purity of their lives, the splendor of their talents, their probity in public trusts, their deep study of the problems of government? No; they are gamblers, saloon keepers, pugilists, or worse, who have made a trade of controlling votes and of buying and selling offices and official acts. They stand to the government of these cities as the Prætorian Guards did to that of declining Rome. He who would wear the purple, fill the curule chair, or have the fasces carried before him, must go or send his messengers to their camps, give them donations and make them promises. It is through these men that the rich corporations and powerful pecuniary interests can pack the Senate and the bench with their creatures. It is these men who make School Directors, Supervisors, Assessors, members of the Legislature, Congressmen. Why, there are many election districts in the United States in which a George Washington, a Benjamin Franklin, or a Thomas Jefferson could no more go to the lower house of a State Legislature than under the Ancient Regime a base-born peasant could become a Marshal of France. Their very character would be an insuperable disqualification.[480]

Frederick Jackson Turner
THE SIGNIFICANCE OF THE FRONTIER IN AMERICAN HISTORY

Frederick Jackson Turner, "The Significance of the Frontier in American History" [1893], in *The Frontier in American History*. Copyright 1920 by Henry Holt and Company; copyright renewed 1947 by Caroline Mae S. Turner.*

In a recent bulletin of the Superintendent of the Census for 1890 appear these significant words: "Up to and including 1880 the country had a frontier of settlement, but at present the unsettled area has been so broken into by isolated bodies of settlement that there can hardly be said to be a frontier line. In the discussion of its extent, its westward movement, etc., it can not, therefore, any longer have a place in the census reports." This brief official statement marks the closing of a great historic movement. Up to our own day American history has been in a large degree the history of the colonization of the Great West. The existence of an area of free land, its continuous recession, and the advance of American settlement westward, explain American development.[1]

Behind institutions, behind constitutional forms and modifications, lie the vital forces that call these organs into life and shape them to meet changing conditions. The peculiarity of American institutions is the fact that they have been compelled to adapt themselves to the changes of an expanding people—to

* Reprinted by permission of Holt, Rinehart and Winston, Inc.

the changes involved in crossing a continent, in winning a wilderness, and in developing at each area of this progress out of the primitive economic and political conditions of the frontier into the complexity of city life. Said Calhoun in 1817, "We are great, and rapidly—I was about to say fearfully—growing!" So saying, he touched the distinguishing feature of American life. All peoples show development; the germ theory of politics has been sufficiently emphasized. In the case of most nations, however, the development has occurred in a limited area; and if the nation has expanded, it has met other growing peoples whom it has conquered. But in the case of the United States we have a different phenomenon. Limiting our attention to the Atlantic coast, we have the familiar phenomenon of the evolution of institutions in a limited area, such as the rise of representative government; the differentiation of simple colonial governments into complex organs; the progress from primitive industrial society, without division of labor, up to manufacturing civilization. But we have in addition to this a recurrence of the process of evolution in each western area reached in the process of expansion. Thus American development has exhibited not merely advance along a single line, but a return to primitive conditions on a continually advancing frontier line, and a new development for that area. American social development has been continually beginning over again on the frontier. This perennial rebirth, this fluidity of American life, this expansion westward with its new opportunities, its continuous touch with [2] the simplicity of primitive society, furnish the forces dominating American character. The true point of view in the history of this nation is not the Atlantic coast, it is the Great West. Even the slavery struggle, which is made so exclusive an object of attention by writers like Professor von Holst, occupies its important place in American history because of its relation to westward expansion.

In this advance, the frontier is the outer edge of the wave—the meeting point between savagery and civilization. Much has been written about the frontier from the point of view of border warfare and the chase, but as a field for the serious study of the economist and the historian it has been neglected.

The American frontier is sharply distinguished from the

European frontier—a fortified boundary line running through dense populations. The most significant thing about the American frontier is, that it lies at the hither edge of free land. In the census reports it is treated as the margin of that settlement which has a density of two or more to the square mile. The term is an elastic one, and for our purposes does not need sharp definition. We shall consider the whole frontier belt, including the Indian country and the outer margin of the "settled area" of the census reports. . . .

In the settlement of America we have to observe how European life entered the continent, and how America modified and developed that life and reacted on Europe. Our early history is the study of European germs developing in an American environment. Too exclusive attention has been paid by institutional students to the Germanic origins, too little to the American factors. The frontier is the line of [3] most rapid and effective Americanization. The wilderness masters the colonist. It finds him a European in dress, industries, tools, modes of travel, and thought. It takes him from the railroad car and puts him in the birch canoe. It strips off the garments of civilization and arrays him in the hunting shirt and the moccasin. It puts him in the log cabin of the Cherokee and Iroquois and runs an Indian palisade around him. Before long he has gone to planting Indian corn and plowing with a sharp stick; he shouts the war cry and takes the scalp in orthodox Indian fashion. In short, at the frontier the environment is at first too strong for the man. He must accept the conditions which it furnishes, or perish, and so he fits himself into the Indian clearings and follows the Indian trails. Little by little he transforms the wilderness, but the outcome is not the old Europe, not simply the development of Germanic germs, any more than the first phenomenon was a case of reversion to the Germanic mark. The fact is, that here is a new product that is American. At first, the frontier was the Atlantic coast. It was the frontier of Europe in a very real sense. Moving westward, the frontier became more and more American. As successive terminal moraines result from successive glaciations, so each frontier leaves its traces behind it, and when it becomes a settled area the region still partakes of the frontier characteristics. Thus the advance of the frontier has meant a steady movement away from the influence of Europe, a steady growth of independence on American lines. And to study this advance, the men who grew up under these conditions, and the political, economic, and social results of it, is to study the really American part of our history. . . . [4]

In these successive frontiers we find natural boundary lines which have served to mark and to affect the characteristics of the frontiers, namely: the "fall line"; the Allegheny Mountains; the Mississippi; the Missouri where its direction approximates north and south; the line of the arid lands, approximately the ninety-ninth meridian; and the Rocky Mountains. The fall line marked the frontier of the seventeenth century; the Alleghenies that of the eighteenth; the Mississippi that of the first quarter of the nineteenth; the Missouri that of the middle of this century (omitting the California movement); and the belt of the Rocky Mountains and the arid tract, the present frontier. Each was won by a series of Indian wars. . . . [9]

And yet, in spite of this opposition of the interests of the trader and the farmer, the Indian trade pioneered the way for civilization. The buffalo trail became the Indian trail, and this became the trader's "trace"; the trails widened into roads, and the roads into turnpikes, and these in turn were transformed into railroads. The same origin can be shown for the railroads of the South, the Far West, and the Dominion of Canada. The trading posts reached by these trails were on the sites of Indian villages which had been placed in positions suggested by nature; and these trading posts, situated so as to command the water systems of the country, have grown into such cities as Albany, Pittsburgh, Detroit, Chicago, St. Louis, Council Bluffs, and Kansas City. Thus civilization in America has followed the arteries made by geology, pouring an ever richer tide through them, until at last the slender paths of aboriginal intercourse have been broadened and interwoven into the complex mazes of modern commercial lines; the wilderness [14] has been inter-penetrated by lines of civilization growing ever more numerous. It is like the steady growth of a complex nervous system for the originally simple, inert continent. If one would understand why we are to-day one nation, rather than a collection of isolated states, he must study this economic and social consolidation of the country. In this progress from savage conditions lie topics for the evolutionist.

. . . It is evident that the unifying tendencies of the Revolutionary period were facilitated by the previous cooperation in the regulation of the frontier. In this connection may be mentioned the importance of the frontier, from that day to this, as a military training school, keeping alive the power of resistance to aggression, and developing the stalwart and rugged qualities of the frontiersman. . . .[15]

Having now roughly outlined the various kinds of frontiers, and their modes of advance, chiefly from the point of view of the frontier itself, we may next inquire what were the influences on the East and on the Old World. A rapid enumeration of some of the more noteworthy effects is all that I have time for.

First, we note that the frontier promoted the formation of a composite nationality for the American people. The coast was preponderantly English, but the later tides of continental immigration flowed across to the free lands. This was the case from the early colonial days. . . .[22] In the crucible of the frontier the immigrants were Americanized, liberated, and fused into a mixed race, English in neither nationality nor characteristics. The process has gone on from the early days to our own. . . .

In another way the advance of the frontier decreased our dependence on England. The coast, particularly of the South, lacked diversified industries, and was dependent on England for the bulk of its supplies. In the South there was even a dependence on the Northern colonies for articles of food. Governor Glenn, of South Carolina, writes in the middle of the eighteenth century: "Our trade with New York and Philadelphia was of this sort, draining us of all the little money and bills we could gather from other places for their bread, flour, beer, hams, bacon, and other things of their produce, all which, except beer, our new townships begin to supply us with, which are settled with very industrious and thriving Germans. This no doubt diminishes the number of shipping and the appearance of our trade, but it is far from being a detriment to us." [23] Before long the frontier created a demand for merchants. As it retreated from the coast it became less and less possible for England to bring her supplies directly to the consumer's wharfs, and carry away staple crops, and staple crops began to give way to diversified agriculture for a time. The effect of this phase of the frontier action upon the northern section is perceived when we realize how the advance of the frontier aroused seaboard cities like Boston, New York, and Baltimore to engage in rivalry for what Washington called "the extensive and valuable trade of a rising empire."

The legislation which most developed the powers of the national government, and played the largest part in its activity, was conditioned on the frontier. . . .

. . . The pioneer needed the goods of the coast, and so the grand series of internal improvement and railroad legislation began, with potent nationalizing effects. Over internal improvements occurred great debates, in which [24] grave constitutional questions were discussed. Sectional groupings appear in the votes, profoundly significant for the historian. Loose construction increased as the nation marched westward. But the West was not content with bringing the farm to the factory. Under the lead of Clay—"Harry of the West"—protective tariffs were passed, with the cry of bringing the factory to the farm. The disposition of the public lands was a third important subject of national legislation influenced by the frontier. . . .[25]

But the most important effect of the frontier has been in the promotion of democracy here and in Europe. As has been indicated, the frontier is productive of individualism. Complex society is precipitated by the wilderness into a kind of primitive organization based on the family. The tendency is anti-social. It produces antipathy to control, and particularly to any direct control. The tax-gatherer is viewed as a representative of oppression. Prof. Osgood, in an able article, has pointed out that the frontier conditions prevalent in the colonies are important factors in the explanation of the American Revolution, where individual liberty was sometimes confused with absence of all effective government. The same conditions aid in explaining the difficulty of instituting a strong government in the period of the confederacy. The frontier individualism has from the beginning promoted democracy.

The frontier States that came into the Union in the first quarter of a century of its existence came in with democratic suffrage provisions, and had reactive effects of the highest importance upon the older States whose peoples were being attracted there. An extension of the franchise became essential. It was *western* New York that forced an extension of suffrage in the constitutional convention of that State in 1821; and it was *western* Virginia that compelled the tide-water [30] region to put a more liberal suffrage provision in the constitution framed in 1830, and to give to the frontier region a more nearly proportionate representation with the tide-water aristocracy. The rise of democracy as an effective force in the nation came in with western preponderance under Jackson and William Henry Harrison, and it meant the triumph of the frontier—with all of its good and with all of its evil elements. . . .[31]

So long as free land exists, the opportunity for a competency exists, and economic power secures political power. But the democracy born of free land, strong in selfishness and individualism, intolerant of administrative experience and education, and pressing individual liberty beyond its proper bounds, has its dangers as well as its benefits. Individualism in America has allowed a laxity in regard to governmental affairs which has rendered possible the spoils system and all the manifest evils that follow from the lack of a highly developed civic spirit. In this connection may be noted also the influence of frontier conditions in permitting lax business honor, inflated paper currency and wild-cat banking. . . . Each one of the periods of lax financial integrity coincides with periods when a new set of frontier communities had arisen, and coincides in area with these successive frontiers, for the most part. The recent Populist agitation is a case in point. Many a State that now declines any connection with the tenets of the Populists, itself adhered to such ideas in an earlier stage of the development of the State. A primitive society can hardly be expected to show the intelligent appreciation of the complexity of business interests in a developed society. . . .[32]

From the conditions of frontier life came intellectual traits of profound importance. The works of travelers along each frontier from colonial days onward describe certain common traits, and these traits have, while softening down, still persisted as survivals in the place of their origin, even when a higher social organization succeeded. The result is that to the frontier the American intellect owes its striking characteristics. That coarseness and strength combined with acuteness and inquisitiveness; that practical, inventive turn of mind, quick to find expedients; that masterful grasp of material things, lacking in the artistic but powerful to effect great ends; that restless, nervous energy; that dominant individualism, working for good and for evil, and withal that buoyancy and exuberance which comes with freedom —these are traits of the frontier, or traits called out elsewhere because of the existence of the frontier. Since the days when the fleet of Columbus sailed into the waters of the New World, America has been another name for opportunity, and the people of the United States have taken their tone from the incessant expansion which has not only been open but has even been forced upon them. He would be a rash prophet who should assert that the expansive character of American life has now entirely ceased. Movement has been its dominant fact, and, unless this training has no effect upon a people, the American energy will continually demand a wider field for its exercise. But never again will such gifts of free land offer themselves. For a moment, at the [37] frontier, the bonds of custom are broken and unrestraint is triumphant. There is not *tabula rasa*. The stubborn American environment is there with its imperious summons to accept its conditions; the inherited ways of doing things are also there; and yet, in spite of environment, and in spite of custom, each frontier did indeed furnish a new field of opportunity, a gate of escape from the bondage of the past; and freshness, and confidence, and scorn of older society, impatience of its restraints and its ideas, and indifference to its lessons, have accompanied the frontier. What the Mediterranean Sea was to the Greeks, breaking the bond of custom, offering new experiences, calling out new institutions and activities, that, and more, the ever retreating frontier has been to the United States directly, and to the nations of Europe more remotely. And now, four centuries from the discovery of America, at the end of a hundred years of life under the Constitution, the frontier has gone, and with its going has closed the first period of American history.[38]

IV
Into the City:
Imaginative Control

*Edward Bellamy*_____

LOOKING BACKWARD

Edward Bellamy, *Looking Backward, 2000–1887* [1888] (New York, Grosset and Dunlap, n.d.).

[*Julian West, thirty years old in 1887, falls asleep one night in his Boston apartment. He awakens in the house of one Dr. Leete, who informs him that a considerable period of time has elapsed since the night before.*]

"You do not, then, believe that this is the year 2000?"

"Do you really think it necessary to ask me that?" I returned.

"Very well," replied my extraordinary host. "Since I cannot convince you, you shall convince yourself. Are you strong enough to follow me upstairs?"

"I am as strong as I ever was," I replied angrily, "as I may have to prove if this jest is carried much farther."

"I beg, sir," was my companion's response, "that you will not allow yourself to be too fully persuaded that you are the victim of a trick, lest the reaction, when you are convinced of the truth of my statements, should be too great."

The tone of concern, mingled with commiseration, with which he said this, and the entire absence of any sign of resentment at my hot words, strangely daunted me, and I followed him from the room with an extraordinary mixture of emotions. He led the way up two flights of stairs and [37] then up a shorter one, which landed us upon a belvedere on the house-top. "Be pleased to look around you," he said, as we reached the platform, "and tell me if this is the Boston of the nineteenth century."

At my feet lay a great city. Miles of broad streets, shaded by trees and lined with fine buildings, for the most part not in continuous blocks but set in larger or smaller inclosures, stretched in every direction. Every quarter contained large open squares filled with trees, among which statues glistened and fountains flashed in the late afternoon sun. Public buildings of a colossal size and an architectural grandeur unparalleled in my day raised their stately piles on every side. Surely I had never seen this city nor one comparable to it before. Raising my eyes at last towards the horizon, I looked westward. That blue ribbon winding away to the sunset, was it not the sinuous Charles? I looked east; Boston harbor stetched before me within its head-lands, not one of its green islets missing.

I knew then that I had been told the truth concerning the prodigious thing which had befallen me.[38]

. . . The impressions of amazement and curiosity which my new surroundings produced occupied my mind, after the shock, to the exclusion of all other thoughts. For the time the memory of my former life was, as it were, in abeyance.

No sooner did I find myself physically rehabilitated through the kind offices of my host, than I became eager to return to the house-top; and presently we were comfortably established there in easy-chairs, with the city beneath and around us. After Dr. Leete had responded to numerous questions on my part, as to the ancient landmarks I missed and the new ones which had replaced them, he asked me what point of the contrast between the new and the old city struck me most forcibly.

"To speak of small things before great," I responded, "I really think that the complete absence of chimneys and their smoke is the detail that first impressed me."

"Ah!" ejaculated my companion with an air [41] of much interest, "I had forgotten the chimneys, it is so long since they went out of use. It is nearly a century since the crude method of combustion on which you depended for heat became obsolete."

"In general," I said, "what impresses me most about the city is the material prosperity on the part of the people which its magnificence implies."

"I would give a great deal for just one glimpse of the Boston of your day," replied Dr. Leete. "No doubt, as you imply, the cities of that period were rather shabby affairs. If you had the taste to make them splendid, which I would not be so rude as to question, the general poverty resulting from your extraordinary industrial system would not have given you the means. Moreover, the excessive individualism which then prevailed was inconsistent with much public spirit. What little wealth you had seems almost wholly to have been lavished in private luxury. Nowadays, on the contrary, there is no destination of the surplus wealth so popular as the adornment of the city, which all enjoy in equal degree." . . .[42]

[*Julian West and Edith, the daughter of Dr. Leete, go shopping in the great new city.*]

"If I am going to explain our way of shopping to you," said my companion, as we walked along the street, "you must explain your way to me. I have never been able to understand it from all I have read on the subject. For example, when you had such a vast number of shops, each with its different assortment, how could a lady ever settle upon any purchase till she had visited all the shops? for, until she had, she could not know what there was to choose from."

"It was as you suppose; that was the only way she could know," I replied.

"Father calls me an indefatigable shopper, but I should soon be a very fatigued one if I had to do as they did," was Edith's laughing comment.

"The loss of time in going from shop to shop was indeed a waste which the busy bitterly complained of," I said; "but as for the ladies of the idle class, though they complained also, I think the system was really a godsend by furnishing a device to kill time."

"But say there were a thousand shops in a city, hundreds, per-haps, of the same sort, how could even the idlest find time to make their rounds?" [100]

"They really could not visit all, of course," I replied. "Those who did a great deal of buying, learned in time where they might expect to find what they wanted. This class had made a science of the specialties of the shops, and bought at advantage, always getting the most and best for the least money. It required, however, long experience to acquire this knowledge. Those who were too busy, or bought too little to gain it, took their chances and were generally unfortunate, getting the least and worst for the most money. It was the merest chance if persons not ex-perienced in shopping received the value of their money."

"But why did you put up with such a shockingly inconvenient arrangement when you saw its faults so plainly?" Edith asked me.

"It was like all our social arrangements," I replied. "You can see their faults scarcely more plainly than we did, but we saw no remedy for them."

"Here we are at the store of our ward," said Edith, as we turned in at the great portal of one of the magnificent public buildings I had observed in my morning walk. There was nothing in the exterior aspect of the edifice to suggest a store to a representative of the nineteenth century. There was no display of goods in the great windows, or any device to advertise wares, or attract custom. Nor was there any sort of sign or legend on the front of the building to indicate the character [101] of the business carried on there; but instead, above the portal, standing out from the front of the building, a majestic life-size group of statuary, the central figure of which was a female ideal of Plenty, with her cornucopia. Judging from the composi-tion of the throng passing in and out, about the same proportion of the sexes among shoppers obtained as in the nineteenth cen-tury. As we entered, Edith said that there was one of these great distributing establishments in each ward of the city, so that no residence was more than five or ten minutes' walk from one of them. It was the first interior of a twentieth-century public building that I had ever beheld, and the spectacle naturally impressed me deeply. I was in a vast hall full of light, received not alone from the windows on all sides, but from the dome, the point of which was a hundred feet above. Beneath it, in the centre of the hall, a magnificent fountain played, cooling the atmosphere to a delicious freshness with its spray. The walls and ceiling were frescoed in mellow tints, calculated to soften without absorbing the light which flooded the interior. Around the fountain was a space occupied with chairs and sofas, on which many persons were seated conversing. Legends on the walls all about the hall indicated to what classes of commodities the counters below were devoted. Edith directed her steps towards one of these, where samples of muslin of a bewildering variety were displayed, and proceeded to inspect them. [102]

"Where is the clerk?" I asked, for there was no one behind the counter, and no one seemed coming to attend to the customer.

"I have no need of the clerk yet," said Edith; "I have not made my selection."

"It was the principal business of clerks to help people to make their selections in my day," I replied.

"What! To tell people what they wanted?"

"Yes; and oftener to induce them to buy what they didn't want."

"But did not ladies find that very impertinent?" Edith asked, wonderingly. "What concern could it possibly be to the clerks whether people bought or not?"

"It was their sole concern," I answered. "They were hired for the purpose of getting rid of the goods, and were expected to do their utmost, short of the use of force, to compass that end."

"Ah, yes! How stupid I am to forget!" said Edith. "The storekeeper and his clerks depended for their livelihood on selling the goods in your day. Of course that is all different now. The goods are the nation's. They are here for those who want them, and it is the business of the clerks to wait on people and take their orders; but it is not the interest of the clerk or the nation to dispose of a yard or a pound of anything to anybody who does not want it." She smiled as she added, "How exceedingly odd it must have seemed to [103] have clerks trying to induce one to take what one did not want, or was doubtful about!"

"But even a twentieth-century clerk might make himself useful in giving you information about the goods, though he did not tease you to buy them," I suggested.

"No," said Edith, "that is not the business of the clerk. These printed cards, for which the government authorities are responsible, give us all the information we can possibly need."

I saw then that there was fastened to each sample a card containing in succinct form a complete statement of the make and materials of the goods and all its qualities, as well as price, leaving absolutely no point to hang a question on.

"The clerk has, then, nothing to say about the goods he sells?" I said.

"Nothing at all. It is not necessary that he should know or profess to know anything about them. Courtesy and accuracy in taking orders are all that are required of him."

"What a prodigious amount of lying that simple arrangement saves!" I ejaculated.

"Do you mean that all the clerks misrepresented their goods in your day?" Edith asked.

"God forbid that I should say so!" I replied, "for there were many who did not, and they were entitled to especial credit, for when one's livelihood and that of his wife and babies depended on the amount of goods he could dispose of, the temptation [104] to deceive the customer—or let him deceive himself—was well-nigh overwhelming. But, Miss Leete, I am distracting you from your task with my talk."

"Not at all. I have made my selections." With that she touched a button, and in a moment a clerk appeared. He took down her order on a tablet with a pencil which made two copies, of which he gave one to her, and enclosing the counterpart in a small receptacle, dropped it into a transmitting tube.

"The duplicate of the order," said Edith as she turned away from the counter, after the clerk had punched the value of her purchase out of the credit card she gave him, "is given to the purchaser, so that any mistakes in filling it can be easily traced and rectified."

"You were very quick about your selections," I said. "May I

ask how you knew that you might not have found something to suit you better in some of the other stores? But probably you are required to buy in your own district."

"Oh, no," she replied. "We buy where we please, though naturally most often near home. But I should have gained nothing by visiting other stores. The assortment in all is exactly the same, representing as it does in each case samples of all the varieties produced or imported by the United States. That is why one can decide quickly, and never need visit two stores."[105]

"And is this merely a sample store? I see no clerks cutting off goods or marking bundles."

"All our stores are sample stores, except as to a few classes of articles. The goods, with these exceptions, are all at the great central warehouse of the city, to which they are shipped directly from the producers. We order from the sample and the printed statement of texture, make, and qualities. The orders are sent to the warehouse, and the goods distributed from there."

"That must be a tremendous saving of handling," I said. "By our system, the manufacturer sold to the wholesaler, the wholesaler to the retailer, and the retailer to the consumer, and the goods had to be handled each time. You avoid one handling of the goods, and eliminate the retailer altogether, with his big profit and the army of clerks it goes to support. Why, Miss Leete, this store is merely the order department of a wholesale house, with no more than a wholesaler's complement of clerks. Under our system of handling the goods, persuading the customer to buy them, cutting them off, and packing them, ten clerks would not do what one does here. The saving must be enormous."

"I suppose so," said Edith, "but of course we have never known any other way. But, Mr. West, you must not fail to ask father to take you to the central warehouse some day, where they receive the orders from the different sample houses all over the city and parcel out and send the goods [106] to their destinations. He took me there not long ago, and it was a wonderful sight. The system is certainly perfect; for example, over yonder in that sort of cage is the dispatching clerk. The orders, as they are taken by the different departments in the store, are sent by transmitters to him. His assistants sort them and enclose each class in a carrier-box by itself. The dispatching clerk has a dozen

pneumatic transmitters before him answering to the general
classes of goods, each communicating with the corresponding
department at the warehouse. He drops the box of orders into
the tube it calls for, and in a few moments later it drops on the
proper desk in the warehouse, together with all the orders of
the same sort from the other sample stores. The orders are
read off, recorded, and sent to be filled, like lightning. The
filling I thought the most interesting part. Bales of cloth are
placed on spindles and turned by machinery, and the cutter, who
also has a machine, works right through one bale after another
till exhausted, when another man takes his place; and it is the
same with those who fill the orders in any other staple. The
packages are then delivered by larger tubes to the city districts,
and thence distributed to the houses. You may understand how
quickly it is all done when I tell you that my order will probably
be at home sooner than I could have carried it from here."

"How do you manage in the thinly settled rural districts?" I
asked.[107]

"The system is the same," Edith explained; "the village sample
shops are connected by transmitters with the central county
warehouse, which may be twenty miles away. The transmission
is so swift, though, that the time lost on the way is trifling. But,
to save expense, in many counties one set of tubes connect
several villages with the warehouse, and then there is time
lost waiting for one another. Sometimes it is two or three
hours before goods ordered are received. It was so where I was
staying last summer, and I found it quite inconvenient." [1]

"There must be many other respects also, no doubt, in which
the country stores are inferior to the city stores," I suggested.

"No," Edith answered, "they are otherwise precisely as good.
The sample shop of the smallest village, just like this one, gives
you your choice of all the varieties of goods the nation has, for
the county warehouse draws on the same source as the city
warehouse." . . .[108]

[*We return now to still another conversation between Julian and
Dr. Leete.*]

---

[1] I am informed since the above is in type that this lack of perfection in
the distributing service of some of the country districts is to be remedied,
and that soon every village will have its own set of tubes.

"After what you have told me," I said, "I do not so much wonder that the nation is richer now than then, but that you are not all Crœsuses."

"Well," replied Dr. Leete, "we are pretty well off. The rate at which we live is as luxurious as we could wish. The rivalry of ostentation, which in your day led to extravagance in no way conducive to comfort, finds no place, of course, in a society of people absolutely equal in resources, and our ambition stops at the surroundings which minister to the enjoyment of life. We might, indeed, have much larger incomes, individually, if we chose so to use the surplus of our product, but we prefer to expend it upon public works and pleasures in which all share, upon public halls and buildings, art galleries, bridges, statuary, means of transit, and the conveniences of our cities, great musical and theatrical exhibitions, and in providing on a vast scale for the recreations of the people. You have not begun to see how we live yet, Mr. West. At home we have comfort, but the splendor of our life is, on its social side, that which we share with our fellows. . . .[243]

Daniel H. Burnham and
Edward H. Bennett_____

PLAN OF CHICAGO (1909)

Daniel H. Burnham and Edward H. Bennett, *Plan of Chicago*, ed. by Charles Moore (Chicago, Commercial Club, 1909).

ORIGIN OF THE PLAN OF CHICAGO

The tendency of mankind to congregate in cities is a marked characteristic of modern times. This movement is confined to no one country, but is world-wide. Each year Rome, and the cities of the Orient, as well as Berlin, New York, and Chicago, are adding to their population at an unprecedented rate. Co-

incident with this urban development there has been a wide-
spread increase in wealth, and also an enlarged participation on
the part of the people in the work of government. As a natural
result of these causes has come the desire to better the conditions
of living. Men are becoming convinced that the formless growth
of the city is neither economical nor satisfactory; and that overcrowding and congestion of traffic paralyze the vital functions
of the city. The complicated problems which the great city
develops are now seen not to be beyond the control of aroused
public sentiment; and practical men of affairs are turning their
attention to working out the means whereby the city may be
made an efficient instrument for providing all its people with
the best possible conditions of living.

Chicago, in common with other great cities, realizes that the
time has come to bring order out of the chaos incident to rapid
growth, and especially to the influx of people of many nationalities
without common traditions or habits of life. Among the various
instrumentalities designed to accomplish this result, a plan for
a well-ordered and convenient city is seen to be indispensable;
and to the task of producing such a plan the Commercial Club
has devoted its energies for the past three years.

It is not to be expected that any plan devised while as yet
few civic problems have received [1] final solution will be perfect
in all its details. It is claimed for the plan herein presented, that
it is the result of extended and careful study of the needs of
Chicago, made by disinterested men of wide experience, amid
the very conditions which it is sought to remedy; and that during
the years devoted to its preparation the plan has had the benefit
of varied and competent criticism. The real test of this plan will
be found in its application; for, such is the determination of the
people to secure more perfect conditions, it is certain that if the
plan is really good it will commend itself to the progressive
spirit of the times, and sooner or later it will be carried
out. . . . [2]

To many who have given little consideration to the subject, a
plan seems to call for large expenditures and a consequent increase in taxation. The reverse is the case. It is certain that civic
improvement will go on at an accelerated rate; and if those
improvements shall be marshaled according to a well-ordered

According to the original caption, this painting by Jules Guerin for Burnham and Bennett's **Plan of Chicago** is of the "railway station scheme west of the river between Canal and Clinton Streets, showing the relation with the Civic Center." As the painting reveals, the key word in this conception of a new Chicago is "relation."

plan great saving must result. Good order and convenience are not expensive; but haphazard and ill-considered projects invariably result in extravagance and wastefulness. A plan insures that whenever any public or semi-public work shall be undertaken, it will fall into its proper and predetermined place in the general scheme, and thus contribute to the unity and dignity of the city.

The plan frankly takes into consideration the fact that the American city, and Chicago pre-eminently, is a center of industry and traffic. Therefore attention is given to the betterment of commercial facilities; to methods of transportation for persons and for goods; to removing the obstacles which prevent or obstruct circulation; and to the increase of convenience. It is realized, also, that good workmanship requires a large degree of comfort on the part of the workers in their homes and their surroundings, and ample opportunity for that rest and recreation without which all work becomes drudgery. Then, too, the city has a dignity to be maintained; and good order is essential to material advancement. Consequently, the plan provides for impressive groupings of public buildings, and reciprocal relations among such groups. Moreover, consideration is given to the fact that in all probability Chicago, within the lifetime of persons now living, will become a greater city than any existing at the present time; and that therefore the most comprehensive plans of to-day will need to be supplemented in a not remote future. Opportunity for such expansion is provided for.

The origin of the plan of Chicago can be traced directly to the World's Columbian Exposition. The World's Fair of 1893 [1] was the beginning, in our day and in this country, of the orderly arrangement of extensive public grounds and buildings. . . .[4]

In creating the ideal arrangement, every one who lives here is better accommodated in his business and his social activities. In

---

[1] [Readers wishing to consult a compact selection of primary sources in the controversy over the 1893 Chicago Exposition should see *Architecture in America: A Battle of Styles* (New York, Appleton-Century-Crofts, 1961). This paperbound volume, edited by William A. Coles and Henry Hope Reed Jr., also includes critical writings on four other architectural controversies in the United States: the National Gallery of Art, the United Nations Building, the Lever House, and the Price Tower at Bartlesville, Oklahoma. The book is generously illustrated.—Ed.]

bringing about better freight and passenger facilities, every merchant and manufacturer is helped. In establishing a complete park and parkway system, the life of the wage-earner and of his family is made healthier and pleasanter; while the greater attractiveness thus produced keeps at home the people of means and taste, and acts as a magnet to draw those who seek to live amid pleasing surroundings. The very beauty that attracts him who has money makes pleasant the life of those among whom he lives, while anchoring him and his wealth to the city. The prosperity aimed at is for all Chicago. . . .[8]

CITY PLANNING IN ANCIENT AND MODERN TIMES

City planning, in the sense of regarding the city as an organic whole and of developing its various units with reference to their relations one to another, had its origin in Paris during the Bourbon period. Among great cities, Paris has reached the highest stage of development; and the method of this attainment affords lessons for all other cities. Paris owes its origin and its growth to the convenience of its location in view of increasing commercial conditions. Its beginnings go back to the century before the Christian era, when it was but a straggling village called Lutetia, occupying one of the islands in the Seine. On the vast level plain adjoining the town, houses could be erected indefinitely, while the numerous watercourses extending into the surrounding regions gave easy access to the trader. Fertile lands furnished an abundance of provisions; and brick-clay, lime, and sand, with timber from the neighboring forests, provided materials for building. The surroundings of Paris, so rich in all the requisites for the creation of a great city, are similar to those of London and Berlin and Chicago; and in each instance there is the same breadth in the landscape.

The architects to whom Louis XIV. entrusted his planning went far beyond the compact walled city of their day. In the open fields which the growth of Paris must sooner or later transform into streets and avenues they drew the central axis of the city. Straight, vast in width, and without limit of length, this

avenue passed entirely through open country, with scarcely a
dozen buildings [14] throughout its great extent. To the noted
city-builders of the seventeenth and eighteenth centuries,—
Louis XIV., Colbert, Le Nôtre, Blondel, and the Academy of
Architects,—Paris owes those vast reaches of avenue and boulevard which to-day are the crowning features of the most beautiful
of cities. The Paris of their day was indeed a crowded, congested
city; but the Paris which they conceived and laid out in the
deserts and waste places was the widespreading, well-adorned,
and convenient city in which to-day all the world takes delight.
The Madeleine, the Place de la Concorde, the Invalides, and
the great axial avenue from the garden of the Tuileries to the
Place de l'Etoile,—all existed on paper decades before they were
finally realized in the progress of city building. The point of
interest to us is, that as Paris increased in population, the city
grew according to a well-devised, symmetrical, highly developed
plan; and that the greater portion of the beauty and convenience
recognized to-day was attained at no money cost whatever.
Artistic sense and foresight were the only price paid. It is unnecessary to do more than point out the fact that a similar opportunity is open to Chicago.

Old Paris remained, with its dirty, crowded, ill-smelling, narrow, winding streets, the hotbeds of vice and crime. Napoleon
Bonaparte was quick to see that while the Paris of the future
might indeed grow in attractiveness and convenience, the Paris
of the present demanded his attention. Napoleon was disturbed
over the condition of his capital. He realized that the city, then
numbering some seven hundred thousand people, was destined
to become the home of two, three, or even four millions; and he
proposed to give it a splendor never before realized by any city
in the world. He began to open the Rue de Rivoli, north of the
Tuileries gardens; he created the Rue Napoleon (now the Rue
de la Paix) in the axis of the Place Vendôme; from the mediæval
bridges he [15] swept the superstructures, adding three superb
new crossings of the Seine; he built the first sidewalks in Paris,
and lighted the streets at night; and he transformed the banks of
the river by the construction of three thousand meters of new
quays. He also gave to Paris her great commemorative monuments, the Arc de Triomphe de l'Étoile, which was finished by

Louis Philippe, the Arc du Carrousel, and the Column Vendôme, all of which were foreshadowed in the designs of Louis XIV.

It remained for the third Napoleon, however, to accomplish the great work of breaking through the old city, of opening it to light and air, and of making it fit to sustain the army of merchants and manufacturers which makes Paris to-day the center of a commerce as wide as civilization itself. In 1853, Georges Eugène Haussmann became prefect of the Seine, the appointment being in the nature of a promotion due to the successful administration of the office of prefect in other French cities. Immediately Haussmann began a career which has established [17] for all time his place among the city-builders of the world. As if by intuition he grasped the entire problem. Taking counsel neither of expediency nor of compromise, he ever sought the true and proper solution. To him Paris appeared as a highly organized unit, and he strove to create ideal conditions throughout the entire city. The world gives him credit for the highest success. The people of Paris have always supported those who aimed to make their city grand and beautiful. Proud, ambitious, endowed with good taste and an artistic sense, the Parisians have ever been zealous to make their city the capital not only of the state, but also of civilization.

Haussmann never overlooked the great and broad lines laid down by his predecessors; so that to a considerable extent his work was but the continuation of the plans prepared by Louis XIV. in the later years of the seventeenth century. His peculiar task, however, was to provide adequate means of circulation within the old city, by cutting new streets and widening old ones, by sweeping away unwholesome rookeries, and by opening up great spaces in order to disengage monuments of beauty and historic interest. He placed the great railway stations of Paris in a circle about the old center of the city, and opened up fine avenues of approach to them. At times he found it less expensive, and also less disturbing, to build a new street through the blocks, rather than to widen old streets; and it was his special care to create diagonal thoroughfares in order to shorten distances, and also to give picturesqueness to the street system by the creation of those corner lots which the architects of Paris have learned so well how to improve.

The task which Haussmann accomplished for Paris corresponds with the work which must be done for Chicago, in order to overcome the intolerable conditions which invariably arise from a rapid growth of population. . . .[18]

With the Germans the cutting through of new streets was undertaken for the twofold reason of facilitating traffic and of admitting light and air into a too congested and unwholesome city quarter. In Frankfort-on-the-Main, in Hamburg, in Berlin, and in Dresden it became necessary to abolish with firm hand evil conditions that had become intolerable, no matter at what sacrifice of buildings enveloped with historical associations. But the Germans have come to modify the French theory of the unconditional superiority of the rectilinear avenue; and now they seek to maintain the essential character of the city, as in the case of Darmstadt, by admitting strong curves, and, wherever desirable, by narrowing or widening the thoroughfare, making compensations by creating open spaces. They have found, also, that a too extensive clearing away of the old buildings which cluster about a great minster or cathedral results in an enhancement of effectiveness only at a sacrifice of scale and a loss of picturesqueness. As a consequence, the Germans have sought a golden mean by creating about a monumental structure free room for the beholder to see the essential parts of the building from a sufficiently remote point of view, while leaving undisturbed single structures small in scale, in order that the main building may appear to have grown out of its surroundings.

In general, then, it may be said that while the French or classical theory results in monumental effects for a city and establishes unity, the German or individualistic treatment preserves for an old city a homelike feeling and a pleasing variety. It is worthy of note, however, that where city planning has been undertaken by masters, whether in France or Germany, the two theories have been used as circumstances warranted. It is only where designers are not able to handle their [20] subject in its entirety, but have become slaves to a system, that results have been attained at great money cost and with a loss of charm and picturesqueness that by intelligent study might have been saved. . . .[21]

We have found that those cities which retain their domination

over the imaginations of mankind achieve that result through the
harmony and beauty of their civic works; that these artistic creations were made possible largely by the gains of commerce promoted by years of peace; and that intense loyalty on the part of
the great body of the citizens was the chief impulse which led
them to strive to enhance the prestige and dignity of their city.
We have found, also, that in modern times the cities of Europe
are everywhere making those changes which a rapid increase in
trade and population requires, and which the awakened artistic
sense of the people demands. We turn now to our own country,
to note the conditions which have controlled the development of
the American city, and to recount briefly some of the more noteworthy attempts that are being made in the United States to give
form and comeliness to our great towns.

Washington was planned and founded as the capital of a nation. The architects of Louis [22] XIV. drew the lines of the new
Paris beyond the walls of the existing town, and mapped avenues converging at central points where only gardens and farms
then existed; and their plans were a wise provision for a not
distant future. Under the direction of President Washington, and
with the aid and encouragement of Secretary Jefferson, Peter
Charles L'Enfant, a young French engineer, deliberately drew
the map of an entirely new capital city designed to accommodate
a population one-third greater than was comprised in Paris at
that date. In that plan no element of civic convenience, beauty,
or adornment was lacking. The entire city was regarded as a
unit, and that unit was to be developed in a form not surpassed
by any existing city. Upon a rectilinear system of streets L'Enfant
imposed diagonal avenues of stately width, converging upon focal
points designed to be the location of important public buildings,
statues, or monuments commemorating historic events. The Capitol and the President's House were connected by a spacious
park, and axial relations between the two structures were developed; every other building necessary for national uses was provided for; and canals, cascades, and fountains were located with
reference to existing springs and watercourses. This comprehensive and magnificent plan, designed for an area which then consisted of wide swamps and wooded hills, became the laughing-
stock alike of foreign traveler and American citizen. But

fortunately the foundations were laid broad and deep by means
of the [23] donation of the lands necessary for streets, avenues,
and parks. Fortunately the plan was adopted and the streets,
avenues, public squares, and circles were fixed; and although the
development of the city during three-quarters of a century was
slow, yet the rapid increase in [24] wealth and power that followed
the ending of the Civil War found Washington ready and waiting
for the improvements which have lifted it from a straggling, ill-
kept town, into one of the beautiful and stately capitals of the
world.

Before the opening of the twentieth century, Washington had
begun to expand over the surrounding country; and there unfortunately the L'Enfant plan stopped short. Moreover, within the
city there had been perversions of the plan; and there had also
been additions to the park area awaiting development. Congress
dealt in part with the difficulties by extending the L'Enfant plan
of streets and avenues over the entire District of Columbia; and
in 1901 the task of preparing a report on the development of the
park system of the Federal territory and the placing of public
buildings was committed to an expert commission. As Haussmann aimed in large part to carry out the work that had been
planned by the architects of Louis XIV., so the Senate Park Commission sought to re-establish and reanimate the plans of L'Enfant, which had the sanction of Washington and Jefferson. In
spite of much opposition on the part of those who regard only the
present, and take no thought for future advancement, the new
plans have been carried to such a point that their general lines
are well established, and already works to cost nearly $50,000,-
000 are in progress, each one of which strengthens the hold of
the general scheme.

The plans for the improvement of Washington were prepared
by the same hands that guided the artistic development of the
World's Columbian Exposition in Chicago. The dream city on
Lake Michigan, people said, should take on enduring form in the
capital of the nation. Then as the Washington plans fired the
imagination [25] of the American people, the cities throughout the
country began to ask why they too should not achieve whatever
of beauty and convenience their situation and their civic pride
would allow. . . .[27]

Each city differs from every other city in its physical characteristics and in the nature of its opportunities, so that the development of every city must be along individual lines. This very fact allows full scope for the development of that peculiar charm which, wherever discovered and developed irresistibly draws to that city people of discrimination and taste, and at the same time begets a spirit of loyalty and satisfaction on the part of the citizens. . . .[29]

The experience of other cities both ancient and modern, both abroad and at home, teaches Chicago that the way to true greatness and continued prosperity lies in making the city convenient and healthful for the ever-increasing numbers of its citizens; that civic beauty satisfies a craving of human nature so deep and so compelling that people will travel far to find and enjoy it; that the orderly arrangement of fine buildings and monuments brings fame and wealth to the city; and that the cities which truly exercise dominion rule by reason of their appeal to the higher emotions of the human mind. The problem for Chicago, therefore, resolves itself into making the best use of a situation, the central location and resources of which have already drawn together millions of people, and are clearly destined to assemble many times that number; and planning for that civic development which promotes present content and insures permanence. . . .[30]

CHICAGO, THE METROPOLIS OF THE MIDDLE WEST

The growth of the city has been so rapid that it has been impossible to plan for the economical disposition of the great influx of people, surging like a human tide to spread itself wherever opportunity for profitable labor offered place. Thoughtful people are appalled at the results of progress; at the waste in time, strength, and money which congestion in city streets begets; at the toll of lives taken by disease when sanitary precautions are neglected; and at the frequent outbreaks against law and order which result from narrow and pleasureless lives. So that while the keynote of the nineteenth century was expansion, we of the twentieth century find that our dominant idea is conservation.

The people of Chicago have ceased to be impressed by rapid growth or the great size of the city. What they insist asking now is, How are we living? Are we in reality prosperous? Is the city a convenient place for business? Is it a good labor market in the sense that labor is sufficiently comfortable to be efficient and content? Will the coming generation be able to stand the nervous strain of city life? When a competence has been accumulated, must we go elsewhere to enjoy the fruits of independence? If the city does not become better as it becomes bigger, shall not the defect be remedied? These are questions that will not be brushed aside. They are the most pressing questions of our day, and everywhere men are anxiously seeking the answers. . . .[32]

City life has attractions that make a strong appeal to human nature. Opportunities for large success, for wealth and power and social consideration, for amusement and instruction, for the increase of knowledge and the cultivation of taste, are greater for the average person in the city than in the country. The city, therefore, is constantly drawing from the country the young men and women of ambition and self-reliance, who are lured thither by the great prizes which in a democracy are open to the competition of all.

When Chicago is adverted to as the metropolis of the Middle West, the meaning is that throughout this area Chicago newspapers circulate, and Chicago banks hold the banking reserves; [33] that in Chicago are the chief offices of the large industrial enterprises, and the market for their products. New ideas in government, in civic improvement, in the creation and maintenance of parks, and pleasure grounds are apt to appear first in the metropolis, spreading thence to the surrounding country. On high-days and holidays the great city allures the people from the neighboring parts, and sends its own people on the water or into the country for rest and refreshment, so that there is a constant interchange of comers and goers. In the art schools of Chicago more than four thousand students are gathered; the theaters draw audiences from long distances, and in music Chicago is attaining a worthy position. In Chicago great political conventions are held, party policies are determined, and from the party headquarters here national campaigns are conducted.

It is not in the spirit of boasting that these facts are stated, but rather to show the responsibility which the very pre-eminence of the city imposes, and the necessity for establishing and maintaining those standards of commercial integrity, of taste, and of knowledge which are the prerequisites of lasting success, and the only real satisfaction of the human mind. The constant struggle of civilization is to know and to attain the highest good; and the city which brings about the best conditions of life becomes the most prosperous.

While the influence of Chicago extends throughout a domain larger than any European country except Russia, there exist between this city and outlying towns within a certain radius vital and almost organic relations. The steam and the trolley railways and the automobile have opened to the city workers all varieties of life, and have made possible to a large proportion of the people a habitation amid what might be healthful and attractive surroundings. Unfortunately, however, conditions near any rapidly growing city are apt to be both squalid and ugly.

Occasionally a suburb grows up at some sightly point on the Lake shore, or gathers about some educational institution; or a group of people engaged in a common enterprise select a picturesque spot on river banks and there build homes which, by their very relations one to another, indicate neighborliness. In each of these instances a community of feeling pervades the place and finds expression in well-shaded streets, broad lawns, and homelike architecture. Too often, however, the suburb is laid out by the speculative real estate agent who exerts himself to make every dollar invested turn into as many dollars as possible. Human ingenuity contrives to crowd the maximum number of building lots into the minimum space; if native trees exist on the land they are ruthlessly sacrificed. Then the speculative builder takes matters in hand and in a few months the narrow, grassless streets are lined with rows of cheaply constructed dwellings, and with ugly apartment houses occupying the more desirable sites. In ten years or less the dwellings are dropping to pieces; and the apartment houses, having lost their newness, become rookeries.

This manner of things is as true of London or of Rome as of Chicago; it is the rule wherever population increases rapidly, because human nature is alike the world over. England, however, is remedying this evil by means of town-planning laws executed by

a central board; and is endeavoring to regulate the width and
direction of streets, and to provide for sufficient open spaces for
the health and convenience of the people. After the English manner, a commission should be appointed to lay out all that territory adacent to the city of Chicago which is likely to become incorporated in the city at least during the next decade. . . .[34]

While good highways are of great value to the terminal cities,
they are of even greater value to the outlying towns, and of
greatest value to the farming communities through which they
pass. Good roads add an element of better living to an agricultural community; they afford ready communication with the city
and reduce materially the cost of handling farm products of all
kinds; and also they promote communication between farms.
These state highways should invariably include a work-road for
heavy loads, and also a pleasure drive. The two should be separated by a grassway and there should be grass plots at the sides,
and not less than three rows of trees should be planted. The
country schools should be on these highways. . . .[39]

A satisfactory method of running highways is to parallel the
railroads. The work-road should be next to the right-of-way; then
should come the carriage driveway. Where electric railways exist,
or are projected on thoroughfares, the most agreeable treatment
is found in setting apart for the tracks a space which may be
grassed over and well shaded. Besides adding to the comfort of
the passengers, the uninterrupted use of the tracks permits high
speed and thereby saves time. The improvement of the three
roadways as a unit, with the appropriate planting, would give a
charm to suburban travel where now there is none, while at the
same time expenses of maintenance would be lessened. As a rule,
the creation of highways along railroads involves only the bare
cost of inexpensive land and the building of the road. The railroads are in themselves great diagonals; and by following them
the shortest lines between important points are secured. Then,
too, the right-of-way traversed by the tracks should be improved.
The drainage should be perfect, so that pools of stagnant water
shall not be an offense to the eye and a menace to health. The
unsightly billboard should be replaced by shrubbery or by a wall;
and the entire space should be free from the litter of papers or
the accumulations of dirt and ashes.

The suburban resident is vitally interested in the means of communication between his home and his place of business. If his morning and his evening ride are made on the steam railway, he is interested not only in passing through pleasant scenes on his way to and from Chicago, but he is concerned also in having the railway station in his suburban town conveniently located, constructed simply but artistically, and placed amid [41] surroundings which in themselves are harmonious and appropriate. A well-kept lawn, with shrubbery shutting out the necessarily unpleasant feature of a steam railway station; a sheltered platform well lighted at night, and a commodious station, architecturally in good taste—these accessories go a long way towards mitigating the nerve strain which every business man feels and from which too many suffer.

The electric railroads, with their frequent cars passing one's very door, have done a vast deal to bind the outlying towns firmly to the central city. More than this, they have promoted neighborliness among people of adjoining towns, and have broken up the isolation of farm life. These roads now strive to obtain private rights-of-way, excepting where for the convenience of passengers they pass through city streets; and the same observations as to good order along the routes and at the terminals that appertain to steam roads apply equally to trolley lines.

The rapidly increasing use of the automobile promises to carry on the good work begun by the bicycle in the days of its popularity in promoting good roads and reviving the roadside inn as a place of rest and refreshment. With the perfection of this machine, and the extension of its use, out-of-door life is promoted, and the pleasures of suburban life are brought within the reach of multitudes of people who formerly were condemned to pass their entire time in the city.[42]

THE CHICAGO PARK SYSTEM

Chicago, on becoming a city, chose for its motto *Urbs in horto*— a city set in a garden. Such indeed it then was, with the opalescent waters of the Lake at its front, and on its three sides the boundless prairie carpeted with waving grass bedecked with brilliant wild flowers. The quick advance of commerce and manufactures, the rapid building of railroads and factories, and the hastily constructed homes of operatives crowded out nature's parterres of flowers. Still the motto lingered in the minds of men, and in 1839 the struggle began to secure for the fast-growing population park spaces which should at least recall the gardens that of necessity had been sacrificed. . . .[43]

Next in the importance to the development of the Lake shore possibilities is the acquisition and improvement of forest spaces. Both the water front and the near-by woodlands should be brought within easy reach of all the people, and especially of the wage-earners. Natural scenery furnishes the contrasting element to the artificiality of the city. All of us should often run away from the works of men's hands and back into the wilds, where mind and body are restored to a normal condition, and we are enabled to take up the burden of life in our crowded streets and endless stretches of buildings with renewed vigor and hopefulness. Those who have the means and are so placed in their daily employments that they can do so constantly seek the refreshment of the country. Should not the public see to it that every one may enjoy this change of scene, this restorer of bodily and mental vigor, and will not citizenship be better thereby? He who habitually comes in close contact with nature develops saner methods of thought than can be the case when one is habitually shut up within the walls of a city. If a census of the purposes and acts of all of the people of Chicago as they affect the general good could be made for this year of grace 1909, and again in 1933, after the creation of extensive forests in the suburbs, the percentage of improvement affecting the whole community would probably be quite surprising. The existing public parks go far in this direction, but not far enough. The spaces to be acquired should be wild forests, filled with such trees, vines, flowers,[53] and shrubs as will grow in this climate, and all should be developed in a natural condition. Country roads and a few paths should run through these forests, but they should not be cut into small divisions. There should be open glades here and there, and other natural features, and the people should be allowed to use them freely. . . .[54]

TRANSPORTATION

This report does not go into details of the roadways and stations, either trunk or intramural. Routes are suggested which seem to be the natural and logical ones. The expert engineers will find the best solutions of the constructive and mechanical problems as they arise. But all citizens are interested to see that the best and most comprehensive general schemes shall be adopted, and that in carrying out of any one of them, every detail shall be designed and executed with regard to its effect on the senses as well as on the basis of mere mechanical or constructive excellence. A million Chicago people who habitually use railway facilities will possess a higher average of good citizenship when the irritation of nerves is reduced to the minimum, and within a few years most of the waking hours of a million Americans will be spent in the business center of Chicago, where unpleasant sights and sounds should be abolished. The community will get far more out of its million workers when their nerves cease to be wracked by irritating conditions.

Again, the noise of surface and elevated road cars is often excruciating. It is not denied that this evil can be largely mitigated. These conditions actually cause misery to a large majority of people who are subjected to the constant strain, and in addition they undoubtedly cause a heavy aggregate loss of money to the business community. For the sake of the state, the citizen should be at his best, and it is the business of the state to maintain conditions conducive to his bodily welfare. Noises, ugly sights, ill smells, as well as dirty streets and workshops or offices, tend to lower average efficiency. It does not pay the state to allow them to continue. Moreover,[74] citizens have pride in and loyalty to a city that is quiet, clean, and generally beautiful. It is not believed that "business" demands that our present annoying conditions be continued. In a state of good order all business must be done better and more profitably. With things as they should be, every business man in Chicago would make more money than he does now. . . .[76]

STREETS WITHIN THE CITY

. . . Paris is the international capital because in its planning the universal mind recognizes that complete articulation which satisfies the craving for good order and symmetry in every part.

If Chicago were to be relocated to-day, it would still be placed at the spot where it now is; and if the streets were again to be mapped, the same general system would be adopted, because the present rectilinear street system best comports with the line of the Lake front which nature has unalterably fixed. The rectilinear system certainly accords with the ideas of rightness inherent in the human mind; and also it involves a minimum waste of ground space. Moreover, the River, for the most part, allows the use of the right-angled system without playing havoc with the orderly arrangement of the streets. It is only when and as the city increases in population that diagonals become necessary in order to save considerable amounts of time and to prevent congestion by dividing and segregating the traffic. Thus it happens that no rectilinear city is perfect without the diagonal streets; and conversely, having the rectilinear system, the creation of diagonals produces the greatest convenience.

Now, while it happens that the planning of a new city imposes straightness as a duty, and [89] diagonals as a necessity, it is equally true that a virtue should be made of these hard-and-fast conditions. There is a true glory in mere length, in vistas longer than the eye can reach, in roads of arrow-like purpose that speed unswerving in their flight; and when and where the opportunity of level ground permits, this glory should be sought after. Older cities may indeed bend and curve their new streets to preserve what is picturesque or historic; but new cities, built on level country, should see to it that as subdivisions are platted, the streets and avenues shall be adequate to bear the traffic which will come to them from the city itself, and that such thoroughfares shall form an integral part of the entire system of circulation.

At the same time the elliptical avenue may be used to introduce variety, and especially to serve as a link to connect parks.

Chicago had no encircling fortifications to turn into boulevards such as those which beautify and distinguish the cities of Vienna, Brussels, Rouen, Milan, and especially Paris; but such avenues may well be created in order to relieve the monotony of the straight streets. . . .[90]

V

Europe to America:
Ameliorative Revolutions

John Ruskin _____

THE STONES OF VENICE

John Ruskin, *The Stones of Venice*, Vol. I [1851], in *The Works of John Ruskin*, Vol. IX, ed. by E. T. Cook and Alexander Wedderburn (London, George Allen, 1903).

. . . If, in the square of the city, you can find a delight, finite, indeed, but pure and intense, like that which you have in a valley among the hills, then its art and architecture are right; but if, after fair trial, you can find no delight in them, nor any instruction like that of Nature, I call on you fearlessly to condemn them.

We are forced, for the sake of accumulating our power and knowledge, to live in cities: but such advantage as we have in association with each other is in great part counterbalanced by our loss of fellowship with Nature. We cannot all have our gardens now, nor our pleasant fields to meditate in at eventide. Then the function of our architecture is, as far as may be, to replace these; to tell us about Nature; to possess us with memories of her quietness; to be solemn and full of tenderness, like her, and rich in portraitures of her; full of delicate imagery of the flowers we can no more gather, and of the living creatures now far away from us in their own solitude. If ever you felt or found this in a London street,—if ever it furnished you with one serious thought, or one ray of true and gentle pleasure,—if there is in your heart a true delight in its grim railings and dark casements, and wasteful finery of shops, and feeble coxcombry of club-houses,—it is well: promote the building of more like them. But if they never taught you anything, and never made you happier as you passed beneath them, do not think they have any mysterious goodness nor occult sublimity. Have done with the wretched affectation, the futile barbarism, of pretending to enjoy; for, as surely as you know that the meadow grass, meshed with fairy rings, is better than the wood pavement, cut into hexagons; and as surely as you know the fresh winds and sunshine of the upland are better than the choke-damp of the vault, or the gas-light of the ball-room, you may know, as I told you that you should, that the good architecture,[411] which has life, and truth, and joy in it, is better than the bad architecture, which has death, dishonesty, and vexation of heart in it, from the beginning to the end of time.[412]

MODERN PAINTERS (VOL. IV)

John Ruskin, *Modern Painters*, Vol. IV [1856], in *The Works of John Ruskin*, Vol. VI, ed. by E. T. Cook and Alexander Wedderburn (London, George Allen, 1904).

. . . We seem to involve the supposition that mountain influence is either unfavourable or inessential to literary power; but for this also the mountain influence is still necessary, only in a subordinate degree. It is true, indeed, that the Avon is no mountain torrent, and that the hills round the vale of Stratford are not sublime; true, moreover, that the cantons Berne and Uri have never yet, so far as I know, produced a great poet; but neither, on the other hand, has Antwerp or Amsterdam. And, I believe, the natural scenery which will be found, on the whole, productive of most literary intellect is that mingled of hill and plain, as all available light is of flame and darkness; the flame being the active element, and the darkness the tempering one.

In noting such evidence as bears upon this subject,[437] the reader must always remember that the mountains are at an unfair disadvantage, in being much *out of the way* of the masses of men employed in intellectual pursuits. The position of a city is dictated by military necessity or commercial convenience: it rises, flourishes, and absorbs into its activity whatever leading intellect is in the surrounding population. The persons who are able and desirous to give their children education naturally resort to it; the best schools, the best society, and the strongest motives assist and excite those born within its walls; and youth after youth rises to distinction out of its streets, while among the blue mountains, twenty miles away, the goatherds live and die in unregarded lowliness. And yet this is no proof that the mountains have little effect upon the mind, or that the streets have a helpful one. The men who are formed by the schools and polished by the society of the capital, may yet in many ways have their powers shortened by the absence of natural scenery; and the mountaineer, neglected, ignorant, and unambitious, may have been taught things by the clouds and streams which he could not have learned in a college, or a coterie.

And in reasoning about the effect of mountains we are therefore under a difficulty like that which would occur to us if we had to determine the good or bad effect of light on the human constitution, in some place where all corporal exercise was necessarily in partial darkness, and only idle people lived in the light. The exercise might give an advantage to the occupants of the gloom, but we should neither be justified in therefore denying the preciousness of light in general, nor the necessity to the workers of the few rays they possessed; and thus I suppose the hills around Stratford, and such glimpses as Shakespere had of sandstone and pines in Warwickshire, or of chalk cliffs in Kent, to have been essential to the development of his genius. This supposition can only be proved false by the rising of a Shakespere at Rotterdam or Bergen-op-Zoom, which I think not probable. . . .[438]

MODERN PAINTERS (VOL. V)

John Ruskin, *Modern Painters*, Vol. V [1860], in *The Works of John Ruskin,* Vol. VII, ed. by E. T. Cook and Alexander Wedderburn (London, George Allen, 1905).

. . . No one can be far wrong in either who loves the trees enough, and every one is assuredly wrong in both who does not love them, if his life has brought them in his way. It is clearly possible to do without them, for the great companionship of the sea and sky are all that sailors need; and many a noble heart has been taught the best it had to learn between [16] dark stone walls. Still if human life be cast among trees at all, the love borne to them is a sure test of its purity. And it is a sorrowful proof of the mistaken ways of the world that the "country," in the simple sense of a place of fields and trees, has hitherto been the source of reproach to its inhabitants, and that the words "countryman, rustic, clown, paysan, villager," still signify a rude and untaught person, as opposed to the words "townsman" and "citizen." We accept this usage of words, or the evil which it signifies, somewhat too quietly; as if it were quite necessary and natural that country-people should be rude, and townspeople gentle. Whereas I believe that the result of each mode of life may, in some stages of the world's progress, be the exact reverse; and that another use of words may be forced upon us by a new aspect of facts, so that we may find ourselves saying: "Such and such a person is very gentle and kind—he is quite rustic; and such and such another person is very rude and ill-taught—he is quite urbane."

At all events, cities have hitherto gained the better part of their good report through our evil ways of going on in the world generally; chiefly and eminently through our bad habit of fighting with each other. No field, in the Middle Ages, being safe from devastation, and every country lane yielding easier passage to the marauders, peacefully-minded men necessarily congregated in cities, and walled themselves in, making as few cross-country roads as possible: while the men who sowed and reaped the harvests of Europe were only the servants or slaves of the barons. The disdain of all agricultural pursuits by the nobility, and of all plain facts by the monks, kept educated Europe in a state of mind over which natural phenomena could have no power; body and intellect being lost in the practice of war without purpose, and the meditation of words without meaning. Men learned the dexterity with sword and syllogism, which they [17] mistook for education, within cloister and tilt-yard; and looked on all the broad space of the world of God mainly as a place for exercise of horses, or for growth of food.

There is a beautiful type of this neglect of the perfectness of the Earth's beauty, by reason of the passions of men, in that picture of Paul Uccello's of the battle of Sant' Egidio, in which the armies meet on a country road beside a hedge of wild roses; the tender red flowers tossing above the helmets, and glowing between the lowered lances. For in like manner the whole of Nature only shone hitherto for man between the tossing of helmet-crests; and sometimes I cannot but think of the trees of the earth as capable of a kind of sorrow, in that imperfect life of theirs, as they opened their innocent leaves in the warm springtime, in vain for men; and all along the dells of England her beeches cast their dappled shade only where the outlaw drew his bow, and the king rode his careless chase; and by the sweet French rivers their long ranks of poplar waved in the twilight, only to show the flames of burning cities on the horizon, through the tracery of their stems; amidst the fair defiles of the Apennines, the twisted olive-trunks hid the ambushes of treachery; and on their valley meadows, day by day, the lilies which were white at the dawn were washed with crimson at sunset.

And indeed I had once purposed, in this work, to show what kind of evidence existed respecting the possible influence of country life on men. . . . [18]

THE STUDY OF ARCHITECTURE

John Ruskin, *The Study of Architecture* [1865], in *The Works of John Ruskin*, Vol. XIX, ed. by E. T. Cook and Alexander Wedderburn (London, George Allen, 1905).

. . . All lovely architecture was designed for cities in cloudless air; for cities in which piazzas and gardens opened in bright populousness and peace; cities built that men might live happily in them, and take delight daily in each other's presence and powers. But our cities, built in black air which, by its accumulated foulness, first renders all ornament invisible in distance, and then chokes its interstices with soot; cities which are mere crowded masses of store, and warehouse, and counter, and are therefore to the rest of the world what the larder and cellar are to a private house; cities in which the object of men is not life, but labour; and in which all chief magnitude of edifice is to enclose machinery; cities in which the streets are not the avenues for the passing and procession of a happy people, but the drains for the discharge of a tormented mob, in which the only object in reaching any spot is to be transferred to another; in which existence becomes mere transition, and every creature is only one atom in a drift of human dust, and current of interchanging particles, circulating here by tunnels underground, and there by tubes in the air; for a city, or cities, such as this no architecture is possible—nay, no desire of it is possible to their inhabitants.[24]

LECTURES ON ART

John Ruskin, *Lectures on Art* [1870], in *The Works of John Ruskin*, Vol. XX, ed. by E. T. Cook and Alexander Wedderburn (London, George Allen, 1905).

. . . At some not very advanced period of life, men should desire to have a home, which they do not wish to quit any more, suited to their habits of life, and likely to be more and more suitable to them until their death. And men must desire to have these their dwelling-places built as strongly as possible, and furnished and decorated daintily, and set in pleasant places, in bright light, and good air, being able to choose for themselves that at least as well as swallows. And when the houses are grouped together in cities, men must have so much civic fellowship as to subject their architecture to a common law, and so much civic pride as to desire that the whole gathered group of human dwellings should be a lovely thing, not a frightful one, on the face of the earth. Not many weeks ago an English clergyman, a master of this University, a man not given to sentiment, but of middle age, and great practical sense, told me, by accident, and wholly without reference to the subject now before us, that he never could enter London from his country parsonage but with closed eyes, lest the sight of the blocks of [112] houses which the railroad intersected in the suburbs should unfit him, by the horror of it, for his day's work.

Now, it is not possible—and I repeat to you, only in more deliberate assertion, what I wrote just twenty-two years ago in the last chapter of the *Seven Lamps of Architecture*—it is not possible to have any right morality, happiness, or art, in any country where the cities are thus built, or thus, let me rather say, clotted and coagulated; spots of a dreadful mildew, spreading by patches and blotches over the country they consume. You must have lovely cities, crystallized, not coagulated, into form; limited in size, and not casting out the scum and scurf of them into an encircling eruption of shame, but girded each with its sacred pomœrium, and with garlands of gardens full of blossoming trees and softly guided streams.

That is impossible, you say! it may be so. I have nothing to do with its possibility, but only with its indispensability. More than that must be possible, however, before you can have a school of art; namely, that you find places elsewhere than in England, or at least in otherwise unserviceable parts of England, for the establishment of manufactories needing the help of fire, that is to say, of all the τέχναι βαναυσικαὶ and ἐπίρρητοι, of which it was long ago known to be the constant nature that "ἀσχολίας μάλιστα ἔχουσι καὶ φίλων καὶ πόλεως συνεπιμελεῖσθαι," and to reduce such manufactures to their lowest limit, so that nothing may ever be made of iron that can as effectually be made of wood or stone; and nothing moved by steam that can be as effectually moved by natural forces. And observe, that for all mechanical effort required in social life and in cities, water power is infinitely more than enough; for anchored mills on the large rivers, and mills moved by sluices from [113] reservoirs filled by the tide, will give you command of any quantity of constant motive power you need.

Agriculture by the hand, then, and absolute refusal or banishment of unnecessary igneous force, are the first conditions of a school of art in any country. And until you do this, be it soon or late, things will continue in that triumphant state to which, for want of finer art, your mechanism has brought them;—that, though England is deafened with spinning wheels, her people have not clothes—though she is black with digging of fuel, they die of cold—and though she has sold her soul for gain, they die of hunger. Stay in that triumph, if you choose; but be assured of this, it is not one which the fine arts will ever share with you.[114]

ON THE OLD ROAD

John Ruskin, On the Old Road [1885], in The Works of John Ruskin, Vol.
XXXIV, ed. by E. T. Cook and Alexander Wedderburn (London, George
Allen, 1908).

. . . The reactions of moral disease upon itself, and the conditions of languidly monstrous character developed in an atmosphere of low vitality, have become the most valued material of
modern fiction, and the most eagerly discussed texts of modern
philosophy.

The many concurrent reasons for this mischief may, I believe,
be massed under a few general heads.

(I.) There is first the hot fermentation and unwholesome
secrecy of the population crowded into large cities, each mote
in the misery lighter, as an individual soul, than a dead leaf, but
becoming oppressive and infectious each to his neighbour, in the
smoking mass of decay. The resulting modes of mental ruin and
distress are continually new; and in a certain sense, worth study
in their monstrosity: they have accordingly developed a corresponding science of fiction, concerned mainly with the description of such forms of disease, like the botany of leaf-lichens.

In De Balzac's story of *Father Goriot*, a grocer makes a large
fortune, of which he spends on himself as much as may keep him
alive; and on his two daughters, all that [268] can promote their
pleasures or their pride. He marries them to men of rank, supplies their secret expenses, and provides for his favourite a separate and clandestine establishment with her lover. On his death-
bed, he sends for this favourite daughter, who wishes to come,
and hesitates for a quarter of an hour between doing so, and going
to a ball at which it has been for the last month her chief ambition to be seen. She finally goes to the ball.

The story is, of course, one of which the violent contrasts and
spectral catastrophe could only take place, or be conceived, in a

large city. A village grocer cannot make a large fortune, cannot marry his daughters to titled squires, and cannot die without having his children brought to him, if in the neighbourhood, by fear of village gossip, if for no better cause.

(II.) But a much more profound feeling than this mere curiosity of science in morbid phenomena is concerned in the production of the carefullest forms of modern fiction. The disgrace and grief resulting from the mere trampling pressure and electric friction of town life, become to the sufferers peculiarly mysterious in their undeservedness, and frightful in their inevitableness. The power of all surroundings over them for evil; the incapacity of their own minds to refuse the pollution, and of their own wills to oppose the weight, of the staggering mass that chokes and crushes them into perdition, brings every law of healthy existence into question with them, and every alleged method of help and hope into doubt. Indignation, without any calming faith in justice, and self-contempt, without any curative self-reproach, dull the intelligence, and degrade the conscience, into sullen incredulity of all sunshine outside the dunghill, or breeze beyond the wafting of its impurity; and at last a philosophy develops itself, partly satiric, partly consolatory, concerned only with the regenerative vigour of manure and the necessary obscurities of fimetic Providence; [269] showing how everybody's fault is somebody else's, how infection has no law, digestion no will, and profitable dirt no dishonour.

And thus an elaborate and ingenious scholasticism, in what may be called the Divinity of Decomposition, has established itself in connection with the more recent forms of romance, giving them at once a complacent tone of clerical dignity, and an agreeable dash of heretical impudence; while the inculcated doctrine has the double advantage of needing no laborious scholarship for its foundation, and no painful self-denial for its practice.

(III.) The monotony of life in the central streets of any great modern city, but especially in those of London, where every emotion intended to be derived by men from the sight of nature, or the sense of art, is forbidden for ever, leaves the craving of the heart for a sincere, yet changeful, interest, to be fed from one source only. Under natural conditions the degree of mental excitement necessary to bodily health is provided by the course of the seasons, and the various skill and fortune of agriculture. In the country every morning of the year brings with it a new aspect of springing or fading nature; a new duty to be fulfilled upon earth, and a new promise or warning in heaven. No day is without its innocent hope, its special prudence, its kindly gift, and its sublime danger; and in every process of wise husbandry, and every effort of contending or remedial courage, the wholesome passions, pride, and bodily power of the labourer are excited and exerted in happiest unison. The companionship of domestic, the care of serviceable, animals, soften and enlarge his life with lowly charities, and discipline him in familiar wisdoms and unboastful fortitudes; while the divine laws of seed-time which cannot be recalled, harvest which cannot be hastened, and winter in which no man can work, compel the impatiences and coveting of his heart into labour too submissive to be anxious, and rest too sweet to be wanton. What thought can enough comprehend the contrast between [270] such life, and that in streets where summer and winter are only alternations of heat and cold; where snow never fell white, nor sunshine clear; where the ground is only a pavement, and the sky no more than the glass roof of an arcade; where the utmost power of a storm is to choke the gutters, and the finest magic of spring, to change mud into dust: where—chief and most fatal difference in state—there is no interest of occupation for any of the inhabitants but the routine of counter or desk within doors, and the effort to pass each other without collision outside; so that from morning to evening the only possible variation of the monotony of the hours, and lightening of the penalty of existence, must be some kind of mischief, limited, unless by more than ordinary godsend of fatality, to the fall of a horse, or the slitting of a pocket?

I said that under these laws of inanition, the craving of the human heart for some kind of excitement could be supplied from *one* source only. It might have been thought by any other than a sternly tentative philosopher, that the denial of their natural food to human feelings would have provoked a reactionary desire for it; and that the dreariness of the street would have been gilded by dreams of pastoral felicity. Experience has shown the fact to be otherwise; the thoroughly trained Londoner can enjoy no other excitement than that to which he has been accustomed, but asks for *that* in continually more ardent or more virulent concentration; and the ultimate power of fiction to entertain him is by varying to his fancy the modes, and defining for his dulness the horrors, of Death. . . .[271]

THE GUILD OF ST. GEORGE

John Ruskin, *The Guild of St. George*, in *The Works of John Ruskin*, Vol. XXX, ed. by E. T. Cook and Alexander Wedderburn (London, George Allen, 1907).

. . . I have never expressed distinctly, or completely enough, the difference between the proper relation of the field to the city, and that which has become the principal folly and danger, alike of the citizen and countryman, in the social organization of the nineteenth century. In all healthy states, the city is the central expression of the national religion, the throne of its legal authority, and the exponent and treasure-house of its artistic skill. A perfect city exhibits always these three functions in perfection, and the nobleness of its cathedral, the dignity of its king's palace (or council-house if it be a republic), and the beauty of its architecture and publicly seen painting, concentrate within its sacred walls the final energies and the loftiest pleasures of which the nation is capable. To such a city, the country people of the district look, as the brightest standard of their national faith, the guardian of justice and peace in their social life, the arbiter of their relations with foreign states, and the treasure-house of all that has been most admirable and is most active in the national genius. Such, and such in a supreme degree, were the great cities of Italy, France, Spain, and England in the faith and practice of Christian law. In the faith and practice of unchristian licence, the modern cities of all European states have alike in these days become, literally, cities of the plain, or pits of the plain into which, in precise opposition to the former going up of the tribes as to the mountain of the Lord, the

iniquity of the tribes sinks by instinctive drainage into a slime-
pit of central corruption, where sin reacting upon sin, and
iniquity festering upon iniquity, curdle and coagulate into forms
so monstrous, that the eye hath not seen, nor the ear heard
them. Where all the principal follies of the nation excite themselves into fraternal fury, and all the principal vices of the
nation knot themselves into the loathsomest alliance, and out
of which the virus of infectious sin and the glare and rumour
of infinitely echoed falsehood spread themselves in overshadow-
ing and thunderous darkness, over the length and breadth of
land soon to be left desolate, and through the innocent places
of peace, soon to be overthrown. So great is the force of this
national gravitation in this present era, that it has paralyzed the
powers of thought alike in our politicians and philanthropists,
until they accept the foulest conditions of disease as if they
were alike inevitable and irresistible. The laws of nature and
of common prudence are, however, at last beginning to vindicate
themselves on the opposite side, and by methods and with
evidence which will be soon found irresistible indeed. To take
one example only. The markets of a city which proposes to
itself the gathering together only of the wise for counsel and
of the skilful in art will never be found to exhaust the resources
of the neighbouring country, but a city to which all the fools
in the kingdom resort for pleasure, all the luxurious for channels
of extravagance, and all the vicious for varieties of temptation,
will soon be found to require for its supply the greater part of
the produce of neighbouring provinces, and the result in the
most literal sense inevitable will be, that which is at last
beginning to surprise our own metropolis, namely, that while
in a million of square miles round it, it is impossible to get fresh
fish on the seashore, or ripe fruit in the gardens, its population
have to spend some millions a year in shorage with a result of
stranding their British Navy on banks of metropolitan abomina-
tion.[156]

Ebenezer Howard_____

THE GARDEN CITY (1898)

Ebenezer Howard, *Garden Cities of Tomorrow* [orig. publ. as *Tomorrow: A Peaceful Path to Real Reform*, 1898], ed. by F. J. Osborn (London, Faber and Faber, 1946).*

AUTHOR'S INTRODUCTION

. . . It is wellnigh universally agreed by men of all parties, not only in England, but all over Europe and America and our colonies, that it is deeply to be deplored that the people should continue to stream into the already over-crowded cities, and should thus further deplete the country districts. . . .[42]

All . . . are agreed on the pressing nature of this problem, all are bent on its solution, and though it would doubtless be quite Utopian to expect a similar agreement as to the value of any remedy that may be proposed, it is at least of immense importance that, on a subject thus universally regarded as of supreme importance, we have such a consensus of opinion at the outset. This will be the more remarkable and the more hopeful sign when it is shown, as I believe will be conclusively shown in this work, that the answer to this, one of the most pressing questions of the day, makes of comparatively easy solution many other problems which have hitherto taxed the ingenuity of the greatest thinkers and reformers of our time. Yes, the key to the problem how to restore the people to the land—that beautiful land of ours, with its canopy of sky, the air that blows upon it, the sun that warms it, the rain and dew that moisten it —the very embodiment of Divine love for man—is indeed a *Master Key*, for it is the key to a portal through which, even when scarce ajar, will be seen to pour a flood of light on the

* Reprinted by permission of Faber and Faber Ltd.

problems of intemperance, of excessive toil, of restless anxiety, of grinding poverty—the true limits of Governmental interference, ay, and even the relations of man to the Supreme Power.

It may perhaps be thought that the first step to be taken towards the solution of this question—how to restore the people to the land—would involve a careful consideration of the very numerous causes which have hitherto led to their aggregation in large cities. Were this the case, a very prolonged enquiry would be necessary at the outset. Fortunately, alike for writer and for reader, such an analysis is not, however, here requisite, and for a very simple reason, which may be stated thus: Whatever may have been the causes which have operated in the past, and are operating now, to draw the people into the cities, those causes may all be summed up as 'attraction'; and it is obvious,[44] therefore, that no remedy can possibly be effective which will not present to the people, or at least to considerable portions of them, greater 'attractions' than our cities now possess, so that the force of the old 'attractions' shall be overcome by the force of new 'attractions' which are to be created. Each city may be regarded as a magnet, each person as a needle; and, so viewed, it is at once seen that nothing short of the discovery of a method for constructing magnets of yet greater power than our cities possess can be effective for redistributing the population in a spontaneous and healthy manner.

So presented, the problem may appear at first sight to be difficult, if not impossible, of solution. 'What', some may be disposed to ask, 'can possibly be done to make the country more attractive to a workaday people than the town—to make wages, or at least the standard of physical comfort, higher in the country than in the town; to secure in the country equal possibilities of social intercourse, and to make the prospects of advancement for the average man or woman equal, not to say superior, to those enjoyed in our large cities?' The issue one constantly finds presented in a form very similar to that. The subject is treated continually in the public press, and in all forms of discussion, as though men, or at least working men, had not now, and never could have, any choice or alternative, but either, on the one hand, to stifle their love for human society—at least in wider relations than can be found in a straggling village—or, on the other hand, to forgo almost entirely all the keen and pure delights of the country. The question is universally considered as though it were now, and for ever must remain, quite impossible for working people to live in the country and yet be engaged in pursuits other than agricultural; as though crowded, unhealthy cities were the last word of economic science; and as if our present form of industry, in which sharp lines divide agricultural from industrial pursuits, were necessarily an enduring one. This fallacy is the very common one of ignoring altogether the possibility of alternatives other than those presented to the mind. There are in reality not only, as is so constantly assumed, two alternatives—town life and country life—but a third alternative, in which all the advantages of the most energetic and active town life, with all the beauty and delight of the country,[45] may be secured in perfect combination; and the certainty of being able to live this life will be the magnet which will produce the effect for which we are all striving—the spontaneous movement of the people from our crowded cities to the bosom of our kindly mother earth, at once the source of life, of happiness, of wealth, and of power. The town and the country may, therefore, be regarded as two magnets, each striving to draw the people to itself—a rivalry which a new form of life, partaking of the nature of both, comes to take part in. This may be illustrated [46] by a diagram of 'The Three Magnets', in which the chief advantages of the Town and of the Country are set forth with their corresponding drawbacks, while the advantages of the Town-Country are seen to be free from the disadvantages of either.

The Town magnet, it will be seen, offers, as compared with the Country magnet, the advantages of high wages, opportunities for employment, tempting prospects of advancement, but these are largely counterbalanced by high rents and prices. Its social opportunities and its places of amusement are very alluring, but excessive hours of toil, distance from work, and the 'isolation of crowds' tend greatly to reduce the value of these good things. The well-lit streets are a great attraction, especially in winter, but the sunlight is being more and more shut out, while the air is so vitiated that the fine public buildings, like the sparrows, rapidly become covered with soot, and the very

Diagram 1. The Three Magnets.*

* [This diagram and those following appeared in this
form in the 1902 edition of Howard's book.—Ed.]

statues are in despair. Palatial edifices and fearful slums are the strange, complementary features of modern cities.

The Country magnet declares herself to be the source of all beauty and wealth; but the Town magnet mockingly reminds her that she is very dull for lack of society, and very sparing of her gifts for lack of capital. There are in the country beautiful vistas, lordly parks, violet-scented woods, fresh air, sounds of rippling water; but too often one sees those threatening words, 'Trespassers will be prosecuted'. Rents, if estimated by the acre, are certainly low, but such low rents are the natural fruit of low wages rather than a cause of substantial comfort; while long hours and lack of amusements forbid the bright sunshine and the pure air to gladden the hearts of the people. The one industry, agriculture, suffers frequently from excessive rainfalls; but this wondrous harvest of the clouds is seldom properly ingathered, so that, in times of drought, there is frequently, even for drinking purposes, a most insufficient supply.[1] Even the [47] natural healthfulness of the country is largely lost for lack of proper drainage and other sanitary conditions, while, in parts almost deserted by the people, the few who remain are yet frequently huddled together as if in rivalry with the slums of our cities.

But neither the Town magnet nor the Country magnet represents the full plan and purpose of nature. Human society and the beauty of nature are meant to be enjoyed together. The two magnets must be made one. As man and woman by their varied gifts and faculties supplement each other, so should town and country. The town is the symbol of society—of mutual help and friendly co-operation, of fatherhood, motherhood, brotherhood, sisterhood, of wide relations between man and man—of broad,

[1] Dr. Barwise, Medical Officer of Health for the County Council of Derbyshire, giving evidence before a Select Committee of the House of Commons, on 25th April 1894, on the Chesterfield Gas and Water Bill, said, in answer to Question 1873: 'At Brimington Common School I saw some basins full of soapsuds, and it was all the water that the whole of the children had to wash in. They had to wash one after another in the same water. Of course, a child with ringworm or something of that kind might spread it through the whole of the children. . . . The schoolmistress told me that the children came in from the playground hot, and she had seen them actually drink this dirty water. In fact, when they were thirsty there was no other water for them to have.'

expanding sympathies—of science, art, culture, religion. And the country! The country is the symbol of God's love and care for man. All that we are and all that we have comes from it. Our bodies are formed of it; to it they return. We are fed by it, clothed by it, and by it are we warmed and sheltered. On its bosom we rest. Its beauty is the inspiration of art, of music, of poetry. Its forces propel all the wheels of industry. It is the source of all health, all wealth, all knowledge. But its fullness of joy and wisdom has not revealed itself to man. Nor can it ever, so long as this unholy, unnatural separation of society and nature endures. Town and country *must be married,* and out of this joyous union will spring a new hope, a new life, a new civilization. It is the purpose of this work to show how a first step can be taken in this direction by the construction of a Town-country magnet; and I hope to convince the reader that this is practicable, here and now, and that on principles which are the very soundest, whether viewed from the ethical or the economic standpoint.

I will undertake, then, to show how in 'Town-country' equal, nay better, opportunities of social intercourse may be enjoyed than are enjoyed in any crowded city, while yet the beauties of [48] nature may encompass and enfold each dweller therein; how higher wages are compatible with reduced rents and rates; how abundant opportunities for employment and bright prospects of advancement may be secured for all; how capital may be attracted and wealth created; how the most admirable sanitary conditions may be ensured; how beautiful homes and gardens may be seen on every hand; how the bounds of freedom may be widened, and yet all the best results of concert and co-operation gathered in by a happy people.

The construction of such a magnet, could it be effected, followed, as it would be, by the construction of many more, would certainly afford a solution of the burning question set before us by Sir John Gorst, 'how to back the tide of migration of the people into the towns, and to get them back upon the land'.

A fuller description of such a magnet and its mode of construction will form the theme of subsequent chapters.[49]

THE TOWN-COUNTRY MAGNET

'I will not cease from mental strife,
Nor shall my sword sleep in my hand,
Till we have built Jerusalem
In England's green and pleasant land.'
—BLAKE.

'Thorough sanitary and remedial action in the houses that we have;
and then the building of more, strongly, beautifully, and in groups of
limited extent, kept in proportion to their streams and walled round,
so that there may be no festering and wretched suburb anywhere, but
clean and busy street within and the open country without, with a
belt of beautiful garden and orchard round the walls, so that from
any part of the city perfectly fresh air and grass and sight of far
horizon might be reachable in a few minutes' walk. This the final
aim.'—JOHN RUSKIN, *Sesame and Lil es.*

The reader is asked to imagine an estate embracing an area
of 6,000 acres, which is at present purely agricultural, and
has been obtained by purchase in the open market at a cost of
£40 [1] an acre, or £240,000. The purchase money is supposed to
have been raised on mortgage debentures, bearing interest at an
average rate not exceeding £4 per cent.[2] The estate is legally
vested in the names of four gentlemen of responsible position
and of undoubted probity and honour, who hold it in trust,
first, as a security for the debenture-holders, and, secondly, in [50]
trust for the people of Garden City, the Town-country magnet,
which it is intended to build thereon. One essential feature of

[1] This was the average price paid for agricultural land in 1898; and,
though this estimate may prove far more than sufficient, it is hardly likely
to be much exceeded.

[2] The financial arrangements described in this book are likely to be
departed from in form, but not in essential principle. And until a definite
scheme has been agreed upon, I think it better to repeat them precisely as
they appeared in *To-morrow,* the original title of this book—the book which
led to the formation of the Garden City Association. (Footnote to 1902
edition. *Ed.*)

the plan is that all ground rents, which are to be based upon the annual value of the land, shall be paid to the trustees, who, after providing for interest and sinking fund, will hand the balance to the Central Council of the new municipality,[3] to be employed by such Council in the creation and maintenance of all necessary public works—roads, schools, parks, etc.

The objects of this land purchase may be stated in various ways, but it is sufficient here to say that some of the chief objects are these: To find for our industrial population work at wages of *higher purchasing power,* and to secure healthier surroundings and more regular employment. To enterprising manufacturers, co-operative societies, architects, engineers, builders, and mechanicians of all kinds, as well as to many engaged in various professions, it is intended to offer a means of securing new and better employment for their capital and talents, while to the agriculturists at present on the estate as well as to those who may migrate thither, it is designed to open a new market for their produce close to their doors. Its object is, in short, to raise the standard of health and comfort of all true workers of whatever grade—the means by which these objects are to be achieved being a healthy, natural, and economic combination of town and country life, and this on land owned by the municipality.

Garden City, which is to be built near the centre of the 6,000 acres, covers an area of 1,000 acres, or a sixth part of the 6,000 acres, and might be of circular form, 1,240 yards (or nearly three-quarters of a mile) from centre to circumference. (Diagram 2 is a ground plan of the whole municipal area, showing the town in the centre; and Diagram 3, which represents one section or ward of the town, will be useful in following the description of the town itself—*a description which is, however, merely suggestive, and will probably be much departed from.*)

Six magnificent boulevards—each 120 feet wide—traverse the city from centre to circumference, dividing it into six equal parts or wards. In the centre is a circular space containing about [51] five and a half acres, laid out as a beautiful and well-watered garden; and, surrounding this garden, each standing in its own ample grounds, are the larger public buildings—town hall,

[3] This word, 'municipality', is not used in a technical sense.

principal concert and lecture hall, theatre, library, museum, picture-gallery, and hospital.

The rest of the large space encircled by the 'Crystal Palace' is a public park, containing 145 acres, which includes ample recreation grounds within very easy access of all the people.[53]

Running all round the Central Park (except where it is intersected by the boulevards) is a wide glass arcade called the 'Crystal Palace', opening on to the park. This building is in wet weather one of the favourite resorts of the people, whilst the knowledge that its bright shelter is ever close at hand tempts people into Central Park, even in the most doubtful of weathers. Here manufactured goods are exposed for sale, and here most of that class of shopping which requires the joy of deliberation and selection is done. The space enclosed by the Crystal Palace is, however, a good deal larger than is required for these purposes, and a considerable part of it is used as a Winter Garden —the whole forming a permanent exhibition of a most attractive character, whilst its circular form brings it near to every dweller in the town—the furthest removed inhabitant being within 600 yards.

Passing out of the Crystal Palace on our way to the outer ring of the town, we cross Fifth Avenue—lined, as are all the roads of the town, with trees—fronting which, and looking on to the Crystal Palace, we find a ring of very excellently built houses, each standing in its own ample grounds; and, as we continue our walk, we observe that the houses are for the most part built either in concentric rings, facing the various avenues (as the circular roads are termed), or fronting the boulevards and roads which all converge to the centre of the town. Asking the friend who accompanies us on our journey what the population of this little city may be, we are told about 30,000 in the city itself, and about 2,000 in the agricultural estate, and that there are in the town 5,500 building lots of an *average* size of 20 feet x 130 feet —the minimum space allotted for the purpose being 20 x 100. Noticing the very varied architecture and design which the houses and groups of houses display—some having common gardens and co-operative kitchens—we learn that general observance of street line or harmonious departure from it are the chief points as to house building, over which the municipal

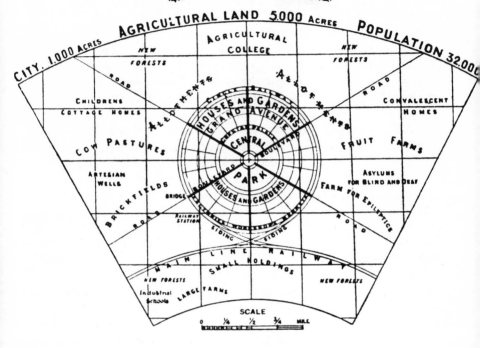

Diagram 2. **Garden City and Rural Belt.**

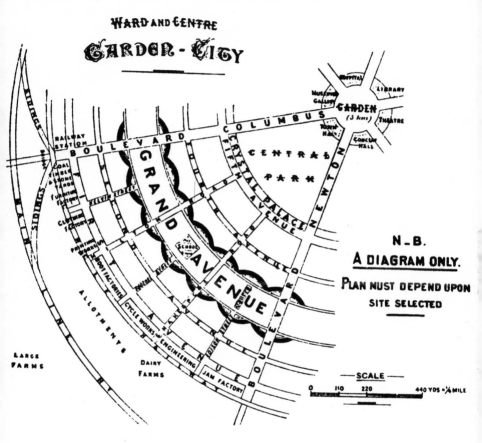

Diagram 3. **Ward and Center of Garden City.**

authorities exercise control, for, though proper sanitary arrangements are strictly enforced, the fullest measure of individual
taste and preference is encouraged.

Walking still toward the outskirts of the town, we come upon
'Grand Avenue'. This avenue is fully entitled to the name it [54]
bears, for it is 420 feet wide, and, forming a belt of green up-
wards of three miles long, divides that part of the town which
lies outside Central Park into two belts. It really constitutes an
additional park of 115 acres—a park which is within 240 yards
of the furthest removed inhabitant. In this splendid avenue six
sites, each of four acres, are occupied by public schools and
their surrounding playgrounds and gardens, while other sites
are reserved for churches, of such denominations as the religious
beliefs of the people may determine, to be erected and maintained out of the funds of the worshippers and their friends. We
observe that the houses fronting on Grand Avenue have departed (at least in one of the wards—that of which Diagram 3
is a representation)—from the general plan of concentric rings,
and, in order to ensure a longer line of frontage on Grand
Avenue, are arranged in crescents—thus also to the eye yet further enlarging the already splendid width of Grand Avenue.

On the outer ring of the town are factories, warehouses,
dairies, markets, coal yards, timber yards, etc., all fronting on
the circle railway, which encompasses the whole town, and
which has sidings connecting it with a main line of railway which
passes through the estate. This arrangement enables goods to
be loaded direct into trucks from the warehouses and workshops, and so sent by railway to distant markets, or to be taken
direct from the trucks into the warehouses or factories; thus not
only effecting a very great saving in regard to packing and
cartage, and reducing to a minimum loss from breakage, but
also, by reducing the traffic on the roads of the town, lessening
to a very marked extent the cost of their maintenance. The
smoke fiend is kept well within bounds in Garden City; for all
machinery is driven by electric energy, with the result that the
cost of electricity for lighting and other purposes is greatly
reduced.

The refuse of the town is utilized on the agricultural portions
of the estate, which are held by various individuals in large

farms, small holdings, allotments, cow pastures, etc.; the natural
competition of these various methods of agriculture, tested
by the willingness of occupiers to offer the highest rent [55]
to the municipality, tending to bring about the best system of
husbandry, or, what is more probable, the best *systems* adapted
for various purposes. Thus it is easily conceivable that it may
prove advantageous to grow wheat in very large fields, involving united action under a capitalist farmer, or by a body of
co-operators; while the cultivation of vegetables, fruits, and
flowers, which requires closer and more personal care, and more
of the artistic and inventive faculty, may possibly be best dealt
with by individuals, or by small groups of individuals having a
common belief in the efficacy and value of certain dressings,
methods of culture, or artificial and natural surroundings.

This plan, or, if the reader be pleased to so term it, this absence of plan, avoids the dangers of stagnation or dead level,
and, though encouraging individual initiative, permits of the
fullest co-operation, while the increased rents which follow from
this form of competition are common or municipal property,
and by far the larger part of them are expended in permanent
improvements.

While the town proper, with its population engaged in various
trades, callings, and professions, and with a store or depot in
each ward, offers the most natural market to the people engaged on the agricultural estate, inasmuch as to the extent to
which the townspeople demand their produce they escape altogether any railway rates and charges; yet the farmers and others
are not by any means limited to the town as their only market,
but have the fullest right to dispose of their produce to whom-
soever they please. Here, as in every feature of the experiment,
it will be seen that it is not the area of rights which is con-
tracted, but the area of choice which is enlarged.

This principle of freedom holds good with regard to manufacturers and others who have established themselves in the
town. These manage their affairs in their own way, subject, of
course, to the general law of the land, and subject to the provision of sufficient space for workmen and reasonable sanitary
conditions. Even in regard to such matters as water, lighting,
and telephonic communication—which a municipality, if effi-

cient and honest, is certainly the best and most natural body to
supply—no rigid or absolute monopoly is sought; and if any
private corporation or any body of individuals proved itself [56]
capable of supplying on more advantageous terms, either the
whole town or a section of it, with these or any commodities the
supply of which was taken up by the corporation, this would be
allowed. No really sound system of *action* is in more need of
artificial support than is any sound system of *thought*. The area
of municipal and corporate action is probably destined to become greatly enlarged; but, if it is to be so, it will be because
the people possess faith in such action, and that faith can be
best shown by a wide extension of the area of freedom.

Dotted about the estate are seen various charitable and
philanthropic institutions. These are not under the control of
the municipality, but are supported and managed by various
public-spirited people who have been invited by the municipality to establish these institutions in an open healthy district,
and on land let to them at a pepper-corn rent, it occurring to
the authorities that they can the better afford to be thus generous, as the spending power of these institutions greatly benefits
the whole community. Besides, as those persons who migrate to
the town are among its most energetic and resourceful members,
it is but just and right that their more helpless brethren should
be able to enjoy the benefits of an experiment which is designed
for humanity at large.[57]

THE REVENUE OF GARDEN CITY

We now come to deal with an element of economy which will
be simply incalculable. This is to be found in the fact that the
town is definitely planned, so that the whole question of municipal administration may be dealt with by one far-reaching
scheme. It is not by any means necessary, and it is not, humanly
speaking, possible, that the final scheme should be the work of
one mind. It will no doubt be the work of many minds—the
minds of engineers, of architects and surveyors, of landscape
gardeners and electricians. But it is essential, as we have said,
that there should be unity of design and purpose—that the town

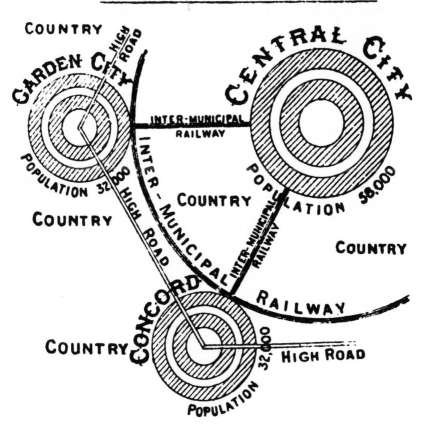

— DIAGRAM —

ILLUSTRATING CORRECT PRINCIPLE OF A CITY'S GROWTH – OPEN COUNTRY EVER NEAR AT HAND, AND RAPID COMMUNICATION BETWEEN OFF-SHOOTS.

Diagram 4. **Correct Principle of a City's Growth.**

should be planned as a whole, and not left to grow up in a chaotic manner as has been the case with all English towns, and more or less so with the towns of all countries. A town, like a flower, or a tree, or an animal, should, at each stage of its growth, possess unity, symmetry, completeness, and the effect of growth should never be to destroy that unity, but to give it greater purpose, nor to mar that symmetry, but to make it more [76] symmetrical; while the completeness of the early structure should be merged in the yet greater completeness of the later development.[4]

Garden City is not only planned, but it is planned with a view to the very latest of modern requirements,[5] and it is obviously always easier, and usually far more economical and completely satisfactory, to make out of fresh material a new instrument than to patch up and alter an old one. This element of economy will be perhaps best dealt with by a concrete illustration, and one of a very striking nature at once presents itself.

In London the question of building a new street between [77]

[4] It is commonly thought that the cities of the United States are planned. This is only true in a most inadequate sense. American towns certainly do not consist of intricate mazes of streets, the lines of which would appear to have been sketched out by cows: and a few days' residence in any American city except a few of the oldest, will ordinarily enable one to find his way about it; but there is, notwithstanding, little real design, and that of the crudest character. Certain streets are laid out, and as the city grows, these are extended and repeated in rarely broken monotony. Washington is a magnificent exception as to the laying out of its streets; but even this city is not designed with a view of securing to its people ready access to nature, while its parks are not central, nor are its schools and other buildings arranged in a scientific manner.

[5] 'London has grown up in a chaotic manner, without any unity of design, and at the chance discretion of any persons who were fortunate enough to own land as it came into demand at successive periods for building operations. Sometimes a great landlord laid out a quarter in a manner to tempt the better class of residents by squares, gardens, or retired streets, often cut off from through traffic by gates and bars; but even in these cases London as a whole has not been thought of, and no main arteries have been provided for. In other and more frequent cases of small land-owners, the only design of builders has been to crowd upon the land as many streets and houses as possible, regardless of anything around them, and without open spaces or wide approaches. A careful examination of a map of London shows how absolutely wanting in any kind of plan has been its growth, and how little the convenience and wants of the whole population or the considerations of dignity and beauty have been consulted.' Right Hon. G. J. Shaw-Lefevre, *New Review*, 1891, p. 435.

Holborn and the Strand has been for many years under consideration, and at length a scheme is being carried out, imposing
an enormous cost on the people of London. 'Every such change
in the street geography of London displaces thousands of the
poor'—I quote from the *Daily Chronicle* of 6th July 1898—'and
for many years all public or quasi-public schemes have been
charged with the liability to rehouse as many of them as possible. This is as it should be; but the difficulty begins when the
public is asked to face the music and pay the bill. In the present
case some three thousand souls of the working population have
to be turned out. After some searching of heart, it is decided
that most of them are so closely tied to the spot by their employment that it would be a hardship to send them more than
a mile away. The result, in cash, is that London must spend in
rehousing them about £100 a head—or £300,000 in all. As to
those who cannot fairly be asked to go even a mile away—
hangers-on to the market, or others tethered to the spot—the
cost will be even higher. They will require to have parcels of the
precious land cleared by the great scheme itself, and the result
of that will be to house them at the handsome figure of £260
apiece, or some £1,400 for every family of five or six. Financial
statements convey little to the ordinary mind. Let us make it a
little more intelligible. A sum of £1,400 means, in the house
market, a rental of nearly £100 a year. It would buy an excellent
in fact a sumptuous, house and garden at Hampstead, such as
the better middle-class delight in. It would purchase anywhere
in the nearer suburbs such houses as men with £1,000 a year
inhabit. If one went further afield, to the new neighbourhoods
which the City clerk can easily reach by rail, a £1,400 house
represents actual magnificence.' But on what scale of comfort
will the poor Covent Garden labourer with a wife and four
children live? The £1,400 will by no means represent a fair standard of comfort, to say nothing of magnificence. 'He will live
in three rooms sufficiently small in a block at least three storeys
high.' Contrast this with what might be done on a new area, by
carefully planning a bold scheme at the outset. Streets of greater
width than this new street would be laid out and constructed at
a mere fraction of the cost, while a sum of £1,400, instead of
providing one family with 'three rooms sufficiently small in [78]

blocks at least three storeys high', would provide seven families
in Garden City with a comfortable six-roomed cottage each,
and with a nice little garden; and, manufacturers being con-
currently induced to build on the sites set apart for them, each
breadwinner would be placed within easy walking distance of
his work.[6]

There is another modern need which all towns and cities
should be designed to meet—a need which has arisen with the
evolution of modern sanitation, and which has of recent years
been accentuated by the rapid growth of invention. Subways
for sewerage and surface drainage, for water, gas, telegraph and
telephone wires, electric lighting wires, wires for conveying motive power, pneumatic tubes for postal purposes, have come to
be regarded as economic if not essential. But if they would be a
source of economy in an old city, how much more so in new
ones; for on a clean sheet it will be easy to use the very best
appliances for their construction, and to avail ourselves to the
fullest extent of the ever-growing advantages which they possess
as the number of services which they accommodate increases.
Before the subways can be constructed, trenches somewhat wide
and deep must be excavated. In making these the most approved
excavating machinery could be employed. In old towns this
might be very objectionable, if not, indeed, quite impossible.
But here, in Garden City, the steam navvy would not make its
appearance in the parts where people were living, but where
they were coming to live after its work in preparing the way had
been completed. What a grand thing it would be if the people
of England could, by an actual illustration under their very eyes,
be convinced that machinery can be so used as to confer not
only an ultimate national benefit, but a direct and immediate advantage, and that not only upon those who actually own it or use
it, but on others who are given work by its magic aid. What [79]
a happy day it would be for the people of this country, and of
all countries, if they could learn, from practical experience, that

[6] The great Kingsway street improvement scheme (1900–10) cost over
£4,000,000. After crediting receipts, the net cost to the London rates up to
1956 is estimated at £3,500,000. By 1986 it is expected that this will be
written off out of revenue (Dr. W. A. Robson, *Government and Misgovern-
ment of London*, 1939). But this cheerful calculation of course ignores
loss of interest on the ratepayers' huge 'investment'. *Ed.*

machinery can be used on an extended scale to *give* employment as well as to *take it away*—to *implace* labour as well as to *displace* it—to free men as well as to *enslave* them. There will be plenty of work to be done in Garden City. That is obvious. It is also obvious that, until a large number of houses and factories are built, many of these things cannot be done, and that the faster the trenches are dug, the subways finished, the factories and the houses built, and the light and the power turned on, the sooner can this town, the home of an industrious and a happy people, be built, and the sooner can others start the work of building other towns, not like it, but gradually becoming as much superior to it as our present locomotives are to the first crude attempts of the pioneers of mechanical traction.[80]

THE PATH FOLLOWED UP

There is, however, a type of reformers who push the land question very much to the front, though, as it appears to me, in a manner little likely to commend their views to society. Mr. Henry George, in his well-known work, *Progress and Poverty*, urges with much eloquence, if not with complete accuracy of reasoning, that our land laws are responsible for all the economic evils of society, and that as our landlords are little better than pirates and robbers, the sooner the State forcibly appropriates their rents the better, for when this is accomplished the problem of poverty will, he suggests, be entirely solved. But is not this attempt to throw the whole blame of and punishment for the present deplorable condition of society on to a single class of men a very great mistake? In what way are landlords as a class less honest than the average citizen? Give the average citizen the opportunity of becoming a landlord and of appropriating the land values created by his tenants, and he will embrace it to-morrow. If then, the average man is a potential landlord, to attack landlords as individuals is very like a nation drawing up an indictment against itself, and then making a scape-goat of a particular class.[7]

[7] I hope it is not ungrateful in one who has derived much inspiration from *Progress and Poverty* to write thus.

But to endeavour to change our land system is a very different matter from attacking those individuals who represent it. But how is this change to be effected? I reply: By the force of example, that is, by setting up a better system, and by a little skill in the grouping of forces and manipulation of ideas. . . .[136]

Petr Aleksíeevich Kropotkin_____
FIELDS, FACTORIES AND WORKSHOPS

Petr Aleksíeevich Kropotkin, *Fields, Factories and Workshops; or, Industry Combined with Agriculture and Brain Work with Manual Work* [1898], rev. and enl. ed. (London, Thomas Nelson and Sons, [1912]).*

THE DECENTRALISATION OF INDUSTRIES

Who does not remember the remarkable chapter by which Adam Smith opens his inquiry into the nature and causes of the wealth of nations? Even those of our contemporary economists who seldom revert to the works of the father of political economy, and often forget the ideas which inspired them, know that chapter almost by heart, so often has it been copied and re-copied since. It has become an article of faith; and the economical history of the century which has elapsed since Adam Smith wrote has been, so to speak, an actual commentary upon it.[17]

"Division of labour" was its watchword. And the division and subdivision—the permanent subdivision—of functions has been pushed so far as to divide humanity into castes which are almost as firmly established as those of old India. We have, first, the broad division into producers and consumers: little-consuming producers on the one hand, little-producing consumers on the other hand. Then, amidst the former, a series of further sub-divisions: the manual worker and the intellectual worker, sharply separated from one another to the detriment of both; the agri-

° Reprinted by permission of Messrs. Hutchinson & Co., Ltd.

cultural labourers and the workers in the manufacture; and, amidst the mass of the latter, numberless subdivisions again— so minute, indeed, that the modern ideal of a workman seems to be a man or a woman, or even a girl or a boy, without the knowledge of any handicraft, without any conception whatever of the industry he or she is employed in, who is only capable of making all day long and for a whole life the same infinitesimal part of something: who from the age of thirteen to that of sixty pushes the coal cart at a given spot of the mine or makes the spring of a penknife, or "the eighteenth part of a pin." Mere servants to some machine of a given description; mere flesh-and-bone parts of some immense machinery; having no idea how and [18] why the machinery performs its rhythmical movements.

Skilled artisanship is being swept away as a survival of a past condemned to disappear. The artist who formerly found æsthetic enjoyment in the work of his hands is substituted by the human slave of an iron slave. Nay, even the agricultural labourer, who formerly used to find a relief from the hardships of his life in the home of his ancestors—the future home of his children—in his love of the field and in a keen intercourse with nature, even he has been doomed to disappear for the sake of division of labour. He is an anachronism, we are told; he must be substituted, in a Bonanza farm, by an occasional servant hired for the summer, and discharged as the autumn comes: a tramp who will never again see the field he has harvested once in his life. "An affair of a few years," the economists say, "to reform agriculture in accordance with the true principles of division of labour and modern industrial organisation."

Dazzled with the results obtained by a century of marvellous inventions, especially in England, our economists and political men went still farther in their dreams of division of labour. They proclaimed the necessity of dividing the whole of humanity into national workshops having each of them its own specialty. We [19] were taught, for instance, that Hungary and Russia are predestined by nature to grow corn in order to feed the manufacturing countries; that Britain had to provide the world-market with cottons, iron goods, and coal; Belgium with woollen cloth; and so on. Nay, within each nation, each region had to have its own specialty. So it has been for some time since; so

it ought to remain. Fortunes have been made in this way, and
will continue to be made in the same way. It being proclaimed
that the wealth of nations is measured by the amount of profits
made by the few, and that the largest profits are made by means
of a specialisation of labour, the question was not conceived
to exist as to whether human beings *would* always submit to
such a specialisation; whether nations could be specialised like
isolated workmen. The theory was good for to-day—why should
we care for to-morrow? To-morrow might bring its own theory!

And so it did. The narrow conception of life which consisted
in thinking that *profits* are the only leading motive of human
society, and the stubborn view which supposes that what has
existed yesterday would last for ever, proved in disaccordance
with the tendencies of human life; and life took another direction. Nobody will deny the high pitch of production [20] which
may be attained by specialisation. But, precisely in proportion
as the work required from the individual in modern production
becomes simpler and easier to be learned, and, therefore, also
more monotonous and wearisome—the requirements of the individual for varying his work, for exercising all his capacities,
become more and more prominent. Humanity perceives that there
is no advantage for the community in riveting a human being
for all his life to a given spot, in a workshop or a mine; no gain
in depriving him of such work as would bring him into free
intercourse with nature, make of him a conscious part of the
grand whole, a partner in the highest enjoyments of science and
art, of free work and creation.

Nations, too, refuse to be specialised. Each nation is a compound aggregate of tastes and inclinations, of wants and resources, of capacities and inventive powers. The territory occupied
by each nation is in its turn a most varied texture of soils and
climates, of hills and valleys, of slopes leading to a still greater
variety of territories and races. Variety is the distinctive feature,
both of the territory and its inhabitants; and that variety implies
a variety of occupations. Agriculture calls manufactures into
existence, and manufactures support agriculture. Both are in-
separable; and the combination, the integration [21] of both brings
about the grandest results. In proportion as technical knowledge
becomes everybody's virtual domain, in proportion as it becomes

international, and can be concealed no longer, each nation acquires the possibility of applying the whole variety of her energies to the whole variety of industrial and agricultural pursuits. Knowledge ignores artificial political boundaries. So also do the industries; and the present tendency of humanity is to have the greatest possible variety of industries gathered in each country, in each separate region, side by side with agriculture. The needs of human agglomerations correspond thus to the needs of the individual; and while a *temporary* division of functions remains the surest guarantee of success in each separate undertaking, the *permanent* division is doomed to disappear, and to be substituted by a variety of pursuits—intellectual, industrial, and agricultural—corresponding to the different capacities of the individual, as well as to the variety of capacities within every human aggregate.

When we thus revert from the scholastics of our text-books, and examine human life as a whole, we soon discover that, while all the benefits of a temporary division of labour must be maintained, it is high time to claim those of the *integration of labour*. Political economy [22] has hitherto insisted chiefly upon *division*. We proclaim *integration;* and we maintain that the ideal of society—that is, the state towards which society is already marching—is a society of integrated, combined labour. A society where each individual is a producer of both manual and intellectual work; where each able-bodied human being is a worker, and where each worker works both in the field and the industrial workshop; where every aggregation of individuals, large enough to dispose of a certain variety of natural resources —it may be a nation, or rather a region—produces and itself consumes most of its own agricultural and manufactured produce.

Of course, as long as society remains organised so as to permit the owners of the land and capital to appropriate for themselves, under the protection of the State and historical rights, the yearly surplus of human production, no such change can be thoroughly accomplished. But the present industrial system, based upon a permanent specialisation of functions, already bears in itself the germs of its proper ruin. The industrial crises, which grow more acute and protracted, and are rendered still worse and still more acute by the armaments and wars implied by the present system, are rendering its maintenance more and more difficult. Moreover, the workers plainly manifest their intention to [23] support no longer patiently the misery occasioned by each crisis. And each crisis accelerates the day when the present institutions of individual property and production will be shaken to their foundations with such internal struggles as will depend upon the more or less good sense of the now privileged classes.

But we maintain also that any socialist attempt at remodelling the present relations between Capital and Labour will be a failure, if it does not take into account the above tendencies towards integration. These tendencies have not yet received, in our opinion, due attention from the different socialist schools—but they must. . . .

Each nation—her own agriculturist and manufacturer; each individual working in the field and in some industrial art; each individual [24] combining scientific knowledge with the knowledge of a handicraft—such is, we affirm, the present tendency of civilised nations. . . .[25]

But enough! I have before me so many figures, all telling the same tale, that examples could be multiplied at will. It is time to conclude, and, for every unprejudiced mind, the conclusion is self-evident. Industries of all kinds decentralise and are scattered all over the globe; and everywhere a variety, an integrated variety, of trades grows, instead of specialisation. Such are the prominent features of the times we live in. Each nation becomes in its turn a manufacturing nation; and the time is not far [74] off when each nation of Europe, as well as the United States, and even the most backward nations of Asia and America, will themselves manufacture nearly everything they are in need of. Wars and several accidental causes may check for some time the scattering of industries: they will not stop it; it is unavoidable. For each new-comer the first steps only are difficult. But, as soon as any industry has taken firm root, it calls into existence hundreds of other trades; and as soon as the first steps have been made, and the first obstacles have been overcome, the industrial growth goes on at an accelerated rate.

The fact is so well felt, if not understood, that the race for colonies has become the distinctive feature of the last twenty

years. Each nation will have her own colonies. But colonies will
not help. There is not a second India in the world, and the
old conditions will be repeated no more. Nay, some of the
British colonies already threaten to become serious competitors
with their mother country; others, like Australia, will not fail
to follow the same lines. As to the yet neutral markets, China
will never be a serious customer to Europe: she can produce
much cheaper at home; and when she begins to feel a need for
goods of European patterns, she will produce them herself.
Woe to Europe, if on the day that the steam engine invades
China she is still relying on [75] foreign customers! As to the
African half-savages, their misery is no foundation for the
well-being of a civilised nation.

Progress must be looked for in another direction. *It is in producing for home use.* The customers for the Lancashire cottons
and the Sheffield cutlery, the Lyons silks and the Hungarian
flour-mills, are not in India, nor in Africa. The true consumers
of the produce of our factories must be our own populations.
And they *can* be that, once we organise our economical life so
that they might issue from their present destitution. No use to
send floating shops to New Guinea with British or German
millinery, when there are plenty of would-be customers for
British millinery in these very islands, and for German goods
in Germany. Instead of worrying our brains by schemes for
getting customers abroad, it would be better to try to answer the
following questions: Why the British worker, whose industrial
capacities are so highly praised in political speeches; why the
Scotch crofter and the Irish peasant, whose obstinate labours
in creating new productive soil out of peat bogs are occasionally
so much spoken of, are no customers to the Lancashire weavers,
the Sheffield cutlers and the Northumbrian and Welsh pitmen?
Why the Lyons weavers not only do not wear silks, but sometimes [76] have no food in their attics? Why the Russian peasants
sell their corn, and for four, six, and sometimes eight months
every year are compelled to mix bark and auroch grass to a
handful of flour for baking their bread? Why famines are so
common amidst the growers of wheat and rice in India?

Under the present conditions of division into capitalists and
labourers, into property-holders and masses living on uncertain

wages, the spreading of industries over new fields is accompanied
by the very same horrible facts of pitiless oppression, massacre
of children, pauperism, and insecurity of life. The Russian
Fabrics Inspectors' Reports, the Reports of the Plauen Handels-
kammer, the Italian inquests, and the reports about the growing
industries of India and Japan are full of the same revelations
as the Reports of the Parliamentary Commissions of 1840 to
1842, or the modern revelations with regard to the "sweating
system" at Whitechapel and Glasgow, London pauperism, and
York unemployment. The Capital and Labour problem is thus
universalised; but, at the same time, it is also simplified. To
return to a state of affairs where corn is grown, and manufactured
goods are fabricated, *for the use of those very people who grow
and produce them*—such will be, no doubt, the problem to be
solved during the [77] next coming years of European history.
Each region will become its own producer and its own consumer of manufactured goods. But that unavoidably implies that,
at the same time, it will be its own producer and consumer of
agricultural produce; and that is precisely what I am going
to discuss next.[78]

THE POSSIBILITIES OF AGRICULTURE

And yet the Paris gardener is not our ideal of an agriculturist.
In the painful work of civilisation he has shown us the way to
follow; but the ideal of modern civilisation is elsewhere. He toils,
with but a short interruption, from three in the morning till
late in the night. He knows no leisure; he has no time to
live the life of a human being; the commonwealth does not
exist for him; his world is his garden, more than his family.
He cannot [130] be our ideal; neither he nor his system of
agriculture. Our ambition is, that he should produce even *more*
than he does with *less* labour, and should enjoy all the joys of
human life. And this is fully possible.

As a matter of fact, if we put aside those gardeners who
chiefly cultivate the so-called *primeurs*—strawberries ripened in
January, and the like—if we take only those who grow their
crops in the open field, and resort to frames exclusively for

the earlier days of the life of the plant, and if we analyse their system, we see that its very essence is, first, to create for the plant a nutritive and porous soil, which contains both the necessary decaying organic matter and the inorganic compounds; and then to keep that soil and the surrounding atmosphere at a temperature and moisture superior to those of the open air. The whole system is summed up in these few words. If the French *maraîcher* spends prodigies of labour, intelligence, and imagination in combining different kinds of manure, so as to make them ferment at a given speed, he does so for no purpose but the above: a nourishing soil, and a desired equal temperature and moisture of the air and the soil. All his empirical art is devoted to the achievement of these two aims. But both can also be achieved in another and much easier [131] way. The soil can be *improved* by hand, but it need not be *made* by hand. Any soil, of any desired composition, can be made by machinery. We already have manufactures of manure, engines for pulverising the phosphorites, and even the granites of the Vosges; and we shall see manufactures of loam as soon as there is a demand for them.[132]

. . . The resources of science, both in enlarging the circle of our production and in new discoveries, are inexhaustible. And each new branch of activity calls into existence more and more new branches, which steadily increase the power of man over the forces of nature.

If we take all into consideration; if we realise the progress made of late in the gardening culture, and the tendency towards spreading its methods to the open field; if we watch the [135] cultural experiments which are being made now—experiments to-day and realities to-morrow—and ponder over the resources kept in store by science, we are bound to say that *it is utterly impossible to foresee at the present moment the limits as to the* maximum *number of human beings who could draw their means of subsistence from a given area of land,* or as to what a variety of produce they could advantageously grow in any latitude. . . .[136]

We know that a crowded population is a necessary condition for permitting man to increase the productive powers of his labour. We know that highly productive labour is impossible

The Collective Mechanical Assault on Nature for Food and Money. A phenomeno new enough in the history of agriculture to be of interest to the readers of *Harper*

eekly, where this drawing by W. A. Rogers appeared in 1891, and to Prince opotkin, who in *Fields, Factories and Workshops* often alludes to Bonanza farms.

so long as men are scattered, few in numbers, over wide territories, and are thus unable to combine together for the higher
achievements of civilisation. We know what an amount of labour
must be spent to scratch the soil with a primitive plough, to
spin and weave by hand; and we know also how much less
labour it costs to grow the same amount of food and weave the
same cloth with the help of modern machinery.

We also see that it is infinitely easier to grow 200,000 lb. of
food on one acre than to grow them on ten acres. It is all very
well to imagine that wheat grows by itself on the Russian steppes;
but those who have seen how the peasant toils in the "fertile"
black [137] earth region will have one desire: that the increase
of population may permit the use of the steam-digger and
gardening culture in the steppes; that it may permit those who
are now the beasts of burden of humanity to raise their backs
and to become at last men. . . .[138]

The other country which must especially be recommended
to the attention of horticulturists is America. When we see the
mountains of [198] fruit imported from America we are inclined
to think that fruit in that country grows by itself. "Beautiful
climate," "virgin soil," "immeasurable spaces"—these words continually recur in the papers. The reality, however, is that horticulture—that is, both market-gardening and fruit culture—has been
brought in America to a high degree of perfection. Prof. Baltet,
a practical gardener himself, originally from the classical *marais*
(market-gardens) of Troyes, describes the "truck farms" of Nor-
folk in Virginia as real "model farms." A highly complimentary
appreciation from the lips of a practical *maraîcher* who has
learned from his infancy that only in fairyland do the golden
apples grow by the fairies' magic wand. As to the perfection to
which apple-growing has been brought in Canada, the aid
which the apple-growers receive from the Canadian experimental farms, and the means which are resorted to, on a truly
American scale, to spread information amongst the farmers and
to supply them with new varieties of fruit trees—all this ought
to be carefully studied in this country, instead of inducing
Englishmen to believe that the American supremacy is due to
the golden fairies' hands. If one tenth part of what is done in
the States and in Canada for favouring agriculture and horti-

culture were done in this country, English fruit would not [199] have been so shamefully driven out of the market as it was a few years ago.

The extension given to horticulture in America is immense. The "truck farms" alone—that is, the farms which work for export by rail or steam—covered in the States in 1892 no less than 400,000 acres. At the very doors of Chicago one single market-gardening farm covers 500 acres, and out of these, 150 acres are given to cucumbers, 50 acres to early peas, and so on. During the Chicago Exhibition a special "strawberry express," composed of thirty waggons, brought in every day 324,000 quarts of the freshly gathered fruit, and there are days that over 10,000 bushels of strawberries are imported in New York —three-fourths of that amount coming from the "truck farms" of Virginia by steamer.

This is what can be achieved by an intelligent combination of agriculture with industry, and undoubtedly will be applied on a still larger scale in the future. . . .[200]

SMALL INDUSTRIES AND INDUSTRIAL VILLAGES

The two sister arts of agriculture and industry were not always so estranged from one another as they are now. There was a time, and that time is not so far back, when both were thoroughly combined; the villages were then the seats of a variety of industries, and the artisans in the cities did not abandon agriculture; many towns were nothing else but industrial villages. If the mediæval city was the cradle of those industries which bordered upon art and were intended to supply the wants of the richer classes, still it was the rural manufacture which supplied the wants of the million, as it does until the present day in Russia, and to a very great extent in Germany and France. But then came the water-motors, steam, the [241] development of machinery, and they broke the link which formerly connected the farm with the workshop. Factories grew up and they abandoned the fields. They gathered where the sale of their produce was easiest, or the raw materials and fuel could be obtained with the greatest advantage. New cities rose, and the old ones rapidly enlarged; the fields were deserted. Millions of labourers, driven away by sheer force from the land, gathered in the cities in search of labour, and soon forgot the bonds which formerly attached them to the soil. And we, in our admiration of the prodigies achieved under the new factory system, overlooked the advantages of the old system under which the tiller of the soil was an industrial worker at the same time. We doomed to disappearance all those branches of industry which formerly used to prosper in the villages; we condemned in industry all that was not a big factory.

True, the results were grand as regards the increase of the productive powers of man. But they proved terrible as regards the millions of human beings who were plunged into misery and had to rely upon precarious means of living in our cities. . . .[242]

The facts which we have briefly passed in review show, to some extent, the benefits which could be derived from a combination of agriculture with industry, if the latter could come to the village, not in its present shape of a capitalist factory, but in the shape of a socially organised industrial production, with the full aid of machinery and technical knowledge. In fact, the most prominent feature of the petty trades is that a relative well-being is found only where they are combined with agriculture: where the workers have remained in possession of the soil and continued to cultivate it. Even amidst the weavers of France or Moscow, who have to reckon with the competition of the factory, relative well-being prevails so long as they are not compelled to part with the soil. On the contrary, as soon as high taxation or the impoverishment during a [349] crisis has compelled the domestic worker to abandon his last plot of land to the usurer, misery creeps into his house. The sweater becomes all-powerful, frightful overwork is resorted to, and the whole trade often falls into decay.

Such facts, as well as the pronounced tendency of the factories towards migrating to the villages, which becomes more and more apparent nowadays, and found of late its expression in the 'Garden Cities' movement, are very suggestive. Of course, it would be a great mistake to imagine that industry ought to return to its hand-work stage in order to be combined with agriculture. Whenever a saving of human labour can be obtained by means of a machine, the machine is welcome and will be resorted to; and there is hardly one single branch of industry into which machinery work could not be introduced with great advantage, at least at some of the stages of the manufacture. In the present chaotic state of industry, nails and cheap pen-knives can be made by hand, and plain cottons be woven in the hand-loom; but such an anomaly will not last. The machine will supersede handwork in the manufacture of plain goods. But at the same time, handwork very probably will extend its domain in the artistic finishing of many things which are now made entirely [350] in the factory; and it will always remain an important factor in the growth of thousands of young and new trades.

But the question arises, Why should not the cottons, the woollen cloth, and the silks, now woven by hand in the villages, be woven by machinery in the same villages, without ceasing to remain connected with work in the fields? Why should not hundreds of domestic industries, now carried on entirely by hand, resort to labour-saving machines, as they already do in the knitting trade and many others? There is no reason why the small motor should not be of a much more general use than it is now, wherever there is no need to have a factory; and there is no reason why the village should not have its small factory, wherever factory work is preferable, as we already see it occasionally in certain villages in France.

More than that. There is no reason why the factory, with its motive force and machinery, should not belong to the community, as is already the case for motive power in the above-mentioned workshops and small factories in the French portion of the Jura hills. It is evident that now, under the capitalist system, the factory is the curse of the village, as it comes to overwork children and to make [351] paupers out of its male inhabitants; and it is quite natural that it should be opposed by all means by the workers, if they have succeeded in maintaining their olden trades' organisations (as at Sheffield, or Solingen), or if they have not yet been reduced to sheer misery (as in the Jura). But under a more rational social organisation the factory would find no such obstacles: it would be a boon to the village. And

there is already unmistakable evidence to show that a move in
this direction *is being made* in a few village communities.

The moral and physical advantages which man would derive
from dividing his work between the field and the workshop are
self-evident. But the difficulty is, we are told, in the necessary
centralisation of the modern industries. In industry, as well as in
politics, centralisation has so many admirers! But in both spheres
the ideal of the centralisers badly needs revision. In fact, if we
analyse the modern industries, we soon discover that for some
of them the co-operation of hundreds, or even thousands, of workers gathered at the same spot is really necessary. The great iron
works and mining enterprises decidedly belong to that category;
oceanic steamers cannot be built in village factories. But very
many of [352] our big factories are nothing else but agglomerations
under a common management, of several distinct industries;
while others are mere agglomerations of hundreds of copies of
the very same machine; such are most of our gigantic spinning
and weaving establishments. . . .[353]

That all the industries find an advantage in being carried on in
close contact with a great variety of other industries the reader
has seen already from numerous examples. Every industry requires *technical surroundings*. But the same is also true of
agriculture.

Agriculture cannot develop without the aid of machinery, and
the use of a perfect machinery cannot be generalised without
industrial surroundings: without mechanical workshops, easily
accessible to the cultivator of the soil, the use of agricultural
machinery is not possible. The village smith would not do. If the
work of a thrashing-machine has to be stopped for a week or
more, because one of the cogs in a wheel has been broken, and
if to obtain a new wheel one must send a special messenger to
the next province—then the use of a thrashing-machine is not
possible. . . .[358]

CONCLUSION

Readers who have had the patience to follow the facts accumulated in this book, especially those who have given them a thoughtful attention, will probably feel convinced of the immense powers over the productive forces of Nature that man has acquired within the last half a century. Comparing the achievements indicated in this book with the present state of production, some will, I hope, also ask themselves the question which will be ere long, let us hope, the main object of a scientific political economy: Are the means now in use for satisfying human needs, under the present system of permanent division of functions and production for profits, really *economical?* Do they really lead to economy in the expenditure of human forces? Or, are they not mere wasteful survivals from a past that was plunged into darkness, ignorance and oppression, and never [410] took into consideration the economical and social value of the human being?

In the domain of agriculture it may be taken as proved that if a small part only of the time that is now given in each nation or region to field culture was given to well thought out and socially carried out permanent improvements of the soil, the duration of work which would be required afterwards to grow the yearly bread-food for an average family of five would be less than a fortnight every year; and that the work required for that purpose would not be the hard toil of the ancient slave, but work which would be agreeable to the physical forces of every healthy man and woman in the country.

It has been proved that by following the methods of intensive market-gardening—partly under glass—vegetables and fruit can be grown in such quantities that men could be provided with a rich vegetable food and a profusion of fruit, if they simply devoted to the task of growing them the hours which everyone willingly devotes to work in the open air, after having spent most of his day in the factory, the mine, or the study. Provided, of course, that the production of food-stuffs should not be the work of the isolated individual, but the planned-out and combined action of human groups.

It has also been proved—and those who care [411] to verify it by themselves may easily do so by calculating the real expenditure for labour which was lately made in the building of workmen's houses by both private persons and municipalities [1]—that under a proper combination of labour, twenty to twenty-four months of one man's work would be sufficient to secure for ever, for a family of five, an apartment or a house provided with all the comforts which modern hygiene and taste could require.

And it has been demonstrated by actual experiment that, by adopting methods of education, advocated long since and partially applied here and there, it is most easy to convey to children of an average intelligence, before they have reached the age of fourteen or fifteen, a broad general comprehension of Nature, as well as of human societies; to familiarise their minds with sound methods of both scientific research and technical work, and inspire their hearts with a deep feeling of human solidarity and justice; and that it is extremely easy to convey during the next four or five years a reasoned, scientific [412] knowledge of Nature's laws, as well as a knowledge, at once reasoned and practical, of the technical methods of satisfying man's material needs. Far from being inferior to the "specialised" young persons manufactured by our universities, the *complete* human being, trained to use his brain and his hands, excels them, on the contrary, in all respects, especially as an initiator and an inventor in both science and technics.

All this has been proved. It is an acquisition of the times we live in—an acquisition which has been won despite the innumerable obstacles always thrown in the way of every initiative mind. It has been won by the obscure tillers of the soil, from whose hands greedy States, landlords and middlemen snatch the fruit of their labour even before it is ripe; by obscure teachers who

---

[1] These figures may be computed, for instance, from the data contained in "The Ninth Annual Report of the Commissioner of Labour of the United States, for the year 1893: Building and Loan Associations." In this country the cost of a workman's cottage is reckoned at about £200, which would represent 700 to 800 days of labour. But we must not forget how much of this sum is a toll raised by the capitalists and the landlords upon everything that is used in building the cottage: the bricks and tiles, the mortar, the wood, the iron, etc.

only too often fall crushed under the weight of Church, State, commercial competition, inertia of mind and prejudice.

And now, in the presence of all these conquests—what is the reality of things?

Nine-tenths of the whole population of grain-exporting countries like Russia, one-half of it in countries like France which live on home-grown food, work upon the land—most of them in the same way as the slaves of antiquity did, only to obtain a meagre crop from a soil, and with a machinery which they cannot improve, because [413] taxation, rent and usury keep them always as near as possible to the margin of starvation. In this twentieth century, whole populations still plough with the same plough as their mediæval ancestors, live in the same incertitude of the morrow, and are as carefully denied education as their ancestors; and they have, in claiming their portion of bread, to march with their children and wives against their own sons' bayonets, as their grandfathers did hundreds of years ago.

In industrially developed countries, a couple of months' work, or even much less than that, would be sufficient to produce for a family a rich and varied vegetable and animal food. But the researches of Engel (at Berlin) and his many followers tell us that the workman's family has to spend one full half of its yearly earnings—that is, to give six months of labour, and often more— to provide its food. And what food! Is not bread and dripping the staple food of more than one-half of English children?

One month of work every year would be quite sufficient to provide the worker with a healthy dwelling. But it is from 25 to 40 per cent. of his yearly earnings—that is, from three to five months of his working time every year—that he has to spend in order to get a dwelling, in most cases unhealthy and far too small; and [414] this dwelling will never be his own, even though at the age of forty-five or fifty he is sure to be sent away from the factory, because the work that he used to do will by that time be accomplished by a machine and a child.

We all know that the child ought, at least, to be familiarised with the forces of Nature which some day he will have to utilise; that he ought to be prepared to keep pace in his life with the steady progress of science and technics; that he ought to study science and learn a trade. Everyone will grant thus much; but what do we do? From the age of ten or even nine we send the child to push a coal-cart in a mine, or to bind, with a little monkey's agility, the two ends of threads broken in a spinning gin. From the age of thirteen we compel the girl—a child yet—to work as a "woman" at the weaving-loom, or to stew in the poisoned, over-heated air of a cotton-dressing factory, or, perhaps, to be poisoned in the death chambers of a Staffordshire pottery. As to those who have the relatively rare luck of receiving some more education, we crush their minds by useless overtime, we consciously deprive them of all possibility of themselves becoming producers; and under an educational system of which the motive is "profits," and the means "specialisation," we simply work to death the women teachers who take [415] their educational duties in earnest. What floods of useless sufferings deluge every so-called civilised land in the world!

When we look back on ages past, and see there the same sufferings, we may say that perhaps then they were unavoidable on account of the ignorance which prevailed. But human genius, stimulated by our modern Renaissance, has already indicated new paths to follow.

For thousands of years in succession to grow one's food was the burden, almost the curse, of mankind. But it need be so no more. If you make yourselves the soil, and partly the temperature and the moisture which each crop requires, you will see that to grow the yearly food of a family, under rational conditions of culture, requires so little labour that it might almost be done as a mere change from other pursuits. If you return to the soil, and co-operate with your neighbours instead of erecting high walls to conceal yourself from their looks; if you utilise what experiment has already taught us, and call to your aid science and technical invention, which never fail to answer to the call—look only at what they have done for warfare—you will be astonished at the facility with which you can bring a rich and varied food out of the soil. You will admire the amount of sound knowledge which your children will [416] acquire by your side, the rapid growth of their intelligence, and the facility with which they will grasp the laws of Nature, animate and inanimate.

Have the factory and the workshop at the gates of your fields and gardens, and work in them. Not those large establishments, of course, in which huge masses of metals have to be dealt with and which are better placed at certain spots indicated by Nature, but the countless variety of workshops and factories which are required to satisfy the infinite diversity of tastes among civilised men. Not those factories in which children lose all the appearance of children in the atmosphere of an industrial hell, but those airy and hygienic, and consequently economical, factories in which human life is of more account than machinery and the making of extra profits, of which we already find a few samples here and there; factories and workshops into which men, women and children will not be driven by hunger, but will be attracted by the desire of finding an activity suited to their tastes, and where, aided by the motor and the machine, they will choose the branch of activity which best suits their inclinations.

Let those factories and workshops be erected, not for making profits by selling shoddy or useless and noxious things to enslaved Africans, but [417] to satisfy the unsatisfied needs of millions of Europeans. And again, you will be struck to see with what facility and in how short a time your needs of dress and of thousands of articles of luxury can be satisfied, when production is carried on for satisfying real needs rather than for satisfying shareholders by high profits or for pouring gold into the pockets of promoters and bogus directors. Very soon you will yourselves feel interested in that work, and you will have occasion to admire in your children their eager desire to become acquainted with Nature and its forces, their inquisitive inquiries as to the powers of machinery, and their rapidly developing inventive genius.

Such is the future. . . .[418]

Patrick Geddes————————————————

CITIES IN EVOLUTION

Patrick Geddes, *Cities in Evolution* [1915] ed. by Edinburgh Outlook Tower Association and London Association for Plannng and Regional Reconstruction (London, Knapp, Drewett and Sons, 1949).*

So bookish has been our past education, so strict our school drill of the "three R's," and so wellnigh complete our lifelong continuance among them, that nine people out of ten, sometimes even more, understand print better than pictures, and pictures better than reality. Thus, even for the few surviving beautiful cities of the British Isles, their few marvellous streets—for choice the High Street of Oxford and the High Street of Edinburgh—a few well-chosen picture postcards will produce more effect upon most people's minds than does the actual vision of their monumental beauty—there colleges and churches, here palace, castle, and city's crown. Since for the beauty of such streets, and to their best elements of life and heritage, we have become half-blind, so also for their deteriorated ones. . . .

Happily the more regional outlook of science is beginning to counteract this artificial blindness. The field-naturalist has of course always been working in this direction. So also the photographer, the painter, the architect; their public also are following, and may soon lead. Even open-air games have been for the most part too confined and subjective: it is but yesterday that the campers-out went afield; to-day (1910) the boy-scouts are abroad; to-morrow our young airmen will be recovering the synoptic vision. Thus education, at all its levels, begins to tear away those blinkers of many print-layers which so long have been strapped over our eyes. . . .[7]

* Reprinted by permission of Ernest Benn Ltd.

THE STUDY OF CITIES

We have seen that many, and in all countries, are awakening to deal with the practical tasks of citizenship. Indeed, never, since the golden times of classic or mediæval cities, has there been so much interest, so much goodwill as now. Hence the question returns, and more and more frequently, how best can we set about the study of cities? How organise speedily in each, in all, and therefore here and there among ourselves to begin with, a common understanding as to the methods required to make observations orderly, comparisons fruitful and generalisations safe? It is time for sociologists—that is for all who care for the advance of science into the social world—to be bringing order into these growing inquiries, these limitless fields of knowledge.

The writer has no finally formulated answer, since his own inquiries are far from concluded; and, since no bureaucrat, he has not a cut-and-dried method to impose meanwhile: nor can he cite this from others: he may best describe his own experience. The problem of city study has occupied his mind for thirty years and more: indeed his personal life, as above all things a wandering student, has been largely determined and spent in restless and renewed endeavours towards searching for the secrets of the evolution of cities, towards making out ways of approach towards their discovery. And his interests and experiences are doubtless those of many.

The nature lover's revolt from city life, even though in youth strengthened and reinforced by the protest of the romantics and the moralists, of the painters and the poets, may be sooner or later overpowered by the attractions, both cultural and practical, which city life exerts. Studies of economics and statistics, of history and social philosophy in many schools, though each [109] fascinating for a season, come to be felt inadequate. An escape from libraries and lecture-rooms, a return to direct observation is needed; and thus the historic culture-cities—classic, mediæval, renaissance—with all their treasures of the past—museums, galleries, buildings and monuments—come to renew their claim to dominate attention, and to supply the norms of civic thought.

Again the view-points of contemporary science renew their promise—now doctrines of energetics, or theories of evolution, at times the advance of psychology, the struggle towards vital education, the renewal of ethics—each in its turn may seem the safest clue with which to penetrate the city's labyrinth. Geographer and historian, economist and æsthete, politician and philosopher have all to be utilised as guides in turn; and from each of these approaches one learns much, yet never sufficient; so that at times the optimist, but often also the pessimist, has seemed entitled to prevail.

Again, as the need of co-ordination, of all these and more constantly makes itself felt, the magnificent prosynthetic sketch of Comte's sociology or the evolutionary effort of Spencer reasserts its central importance, and with these also the historic Utopias. But all such are too abstract constructions, and have as yet been lacking in concrete applications, either to the interpretation or to the improvement of cities; they are deficient in appreciation of their complex activities. Hence the fascination of those transient but all the more magnificent museums of contemporary industry which we call International and Local Exhibitions, centring round those of Paris on 1878, '89 and 1900, with their rich presentments of the material and artistic productivity of their present, alike on its Paleotechnic and Neotechnic levels, and in well-nigh all substages and phases of these.

As we return from these, at one time the roaring forges of industrial activity of Europe and America must seem world-central, beyond even the metropolitan cities which dominate and exploit them. Yet at another time the evolutionary secret [110] seems nearer through the return to nature; and we seek the synoptic vision of geography with Reclus, or of the elemental occupations with Le Play and Demolins, with their sympathetic study of simple peoples, and of the dawn of industry and society with the anthropologists.

And thus we return once more, by way of family unit and family budget, to modern life; and even to its statistical treatments, to Booth and Rowntree for poverty, to Galton and the eugenists, and so on. In such ways and more, ideas accumulate, yet the difficulties of dealing with them also; for to leave out any aspect or element of the community's life must so far lay us open to that reproach of crudely simplified theorising, for which we blame the political economist.

One of the best ways in which a man can work towards this clearing up of his own ideas is through the endeavour of communicating them to others: in fact to this the professoriate largely owe and acknowledge such productivity as they possess. Well-nigh every writer will testify to a similar experience: and the inquirer into sociology and civics may most courageously of all take part in the propaganda for these studies.

Another of the questions—one lying at the very outset of our social studies, and constantly reappearing—is this: what is to be our relation to practical life? The looker-on sees most of the game; a wise detachment must be practised; our observations cannot be too comprehensive or too many-sided. Our meditations too must be prolonged and impartial; and how all this if not serene?

Hence Comte's "cerebral hygiene," or Mr. Spencer's long and stoutly maintained defence of his hermitage against the outer world, his abstention from social responsibilities and activities, even those faced by other philosophers.

Yet there is another side to all this: we learn by living; and as the naturalist, beside his detached observations, and even to aid these, cannot too fully identify himself with the life and activities of his fellow-men in the simple natural environments he wishes [111] to investigate, so it may be for the student of societies. From this point of view, "when in Rome let us do as the Romans do"; let us be at home as far as may be in the characteristic life and activity, the social and cultural movements, of the city which is our home, even for the time being—if we would understand its record or its spirit, its qualities and defects, its place in civilisation.

Still more must we take our share in the life and work of the community if we would make this estimate an active one; that is, if we would discern the possibilities of place, of work, of people, of actual groupings and institutions or of needed ones, and thus leave the place in some degree the better of our life in it; the richer, not the poorer, for our presence. Our activity may in some measure interrupt our observing and philosophising; indeed must often do so; yet with no small compensations in the long run. For

here is that experimental social science which the theoretic political economists were wont to proclaim impossible; but which is
none the less on parallel lines and of kindred experimental value
to the practice which illuminates theory, criticising it or advancing it, in many simpler fields of action—say, engineering or medicine for choice. It is with civics and sociology as with these. The
greatest historians, both ancient and modern, have been those
who took their part in affairs. Indeed with all sciences, as with
the most ideal quests, the sample principle holds good; we must
live the life if we would know the doctrine. Scientific detachment
is but one mood, though an often needed one; our quest cannot
be attained without participation in the active life of citizenship.

In each occupation and profession there is a freemasonry,
which rapidly and hospitably assimilates the reasonably sympathetic newcomer. Here is the advantage of the man of the world,
of the artist and art-lover, of the scholar, the specialist of every
kind; and, above all of the citizen, who is alive to the many-
sidedness of the social world, and who is willing to help and to
work with his fellows.[112]

Moreover, though the woof of each city's life be unique, and
this it may be increasingly with each throw of the shuttle, the
main warp of life is broadly similar from city to city. The family
types, the fundamental occupations and their levels may thus be
more readily understood than are subtler resultants. Yet in practice this is seldom the case, because the educated classes everywhere tend to be specialised away from the life and labour of the
people. Yet these make up the bulk of the citizens; even their
emergent rulers are often but people of a larger growth, for better
and for worse. Hence a new demand upon the student of cities,
to have shared the environment and conditions of the people, as
far as may be their labour also; to have sympathised with their
difficulties and their pleasures, and not merely with those of the
cultured or the governing classes.

Here the endeavour of the University Settlements has gone far
beyond the "slumming" now happily out of fashion, but the civic
student and worker needs fuller experiences than these commonly
supply. Of the value of the settlement alike to its workers, and
to the individuals and organisations they influence much might
be said, and on grounds philanthropic and educational, social

and political; but to increase its civic value and influence a certain advance is needed in its point of view, analogous to that made by the medical student when he passes from his dispensary experience of individual patients to that of the public health department.

In all these various ways, the writer's ideas on the study of cities have been slowly clearing up, throughout many years of civic inquiries and endeavours. These have been largely centred at Edinburgh (as for an aggregate of reasons one of the most instructive of the world's cities, alike for survey and for experimental action), also at the great manufacturing town and seaport of Dundee, with studies and duties in London and in Dublin, and especial sympathies and ties in Paris, and in other continental cities and also American ones—and from among all these interests and occupations a method of civic study and research, a [113] mode of practice and application, have gradually been emerging.

Each of these is imperfect, embryonic even, yet a brief indication may be at least suggestive to other students of cities. The general principle is the synoptic one, of seeking as far as may be to recognise and utilise all points of view—and so to be preparing for the Encyclopædia Civica of the future. For this must include at once the scientific and, as far as may be, the artistic presentment of the city's life: it must base upon these an interpretation of the city's course of evolution in the present: it must increasingly forecast its future possibilities; and thus it may arouse and educate citizenship, by organizing endeavours towards realising some of these worthy ends. . . .[114]

Our survey, then, is a means towards the realisation of our community's life-history. This life-history is not past and done with; it is incorporated with its present activities and character. All these again, plus such fresh influences as may arise or intervene, are determining its opening future. From our survey of facts we have to prepare no mere material record, economic or structural, but to evoke the social personality, changing indeed so far with every generation, yet ever expressing itself in and through these.

Here, in fact, is the higher problem of our surveys, and to these the everyday purposes of our previous chapters will all be found to converge. He is no true town planner, but at best a too simple engineer, who sees only the similarity of cities, their common network of roads and communications. He who would be even a sound engineer, doing work to endure, let alone an artist in his work, must know his city indeed, and have entered into its soul —as Scott and Stevenson knew and loved their Edinburgh; as Pepys and Johnson and Lamb, as Besant and Gomme their London. Oxford, Cambridge, St. Andrews, Harvard, have peculiarly inspired their studious sons; but Birmingham and Glasgow, New York or Chicago, have each no small appeal to observant and active minds. In every city there is much of beauty and more of possibility; and thus for the town planner as an artist, the very worst of cities may be the best.[137]

Andrew Jackson Downing
OUR COUNTRY VILLAGES

Andrew Jackson Downing, "Our Country Villages" [1850], in *Rural Essays*, ed. by George William Curtis (New York, Leavitt and Allen, 1857).

Without any boasting, it may safely be said, that the natural features of our common country (as the speakers in Congress call her), are as agreeable and prepossessing as those of any other land—whether merry England, *la belle France,* or the German fatherland. We have greater lakes, larger rivers, broader and more fertile prairies than the old world can show; and if the Alleghanies are rather dwarfish when compared to the Alps, there are peaks and summits, "castle hills" and volcanoes, in our great back-bone range of the Pacific—the Rocky Mountains— which may safely hold up their heads along with Mont Blanc and the Jungfrau.

Providence, then, has blessed this country—our country—with "natural born" features, which we may look upon and be glad. But how have we sought to deform the fair landscape here and there by little, miserable shabby-looking towns and villages; not miserable and shabby-looking from the poverty and wretchedness of the inhabitants—for in no land is there more peace and plenty—but miserable and shabby-looking from the absence of taste, symmetry, order, space, proportion,—all that constitutes beauty. Ah, well and truly did Cowper say,

"God made the country, but *man* made the town."

For in the one, we every where see utility and beauty harmoniously [236] combined, while the other presents us but too often the reverse; that is to say, the marriage of utility and deformity.

Some of our readers may remind us that we have already preached a sermon from this text. No matter; we should be glad to preach fifty; yes, or even establish a sect,—as that seems the only way of making proselytes now,—whose duty it should be to convert people living in the country towns to the true faith; we mean the true rural faith, viz., that it is immoral and uncivilized to live in mean and uncouth villages, where there is no poverty, or want of intelligence in the inhabitants; that there is nothing laudable in having a piano-forte and mahogany chairs in the parlor, where the streets outside are barren of shade trees, destitute of side-walks, and populous with pigs and geese.

We are bound to admit (with a little shame and humiliation,—being a native of New-York, the "Empire State"), that there is one part of the Union where the millennium of country towns, and good government, and rural taste has not only commenced, but is in full domination. We mean, of course, Massachusetts. The traveller may go from one end of that State to the other, and find flourishing villages, with broad streets lined with maples and elms, behind which are goodly rows of neat and substantial dwellings, full of evidences of order, comfort and taste. Throughout the whole State, no animals are allowed to run at large in the streets of towns and villages. Hence so much more cleanliness than elsewhere; so much more order and neatness; so many more pretty rural lanes; so many inviting flower-gardens and orchards —only separated from the passerby by a low railing or hedge, instead of a formidable board fence. Now, if you cross the State line into New-York—a State of far greater wealth than Massachusetts, as long settled and nearly as populous—you feel directly

that you are in the land of "pigs and poultry," in the least agreeable sense of the word. In passing through villages and towns, the
truth is still more striking, as you go to the south and west; and
you feel little or nothing of that sense, of "how pleasant it must
be to live here," which the traveller through Berkshire, or the
Connecticut valley, or the pretty villages about Boston, feels
moving his heart within him. You are rather inclined to wish there
were two new commandments, viz.: thou shalt plant [237] trees,
to hide the nakedness of the streets; and thou shalt not keep pigs
—except in the back yard! [1]

Our more reflective and inquiring readers will naturally ask,
why is this better condition of things—a condition that denotes
better citizens, better laws, and higher civilization—confined almost wholly to Massachusetts? To save them an infinite deal of
painstaking research and investigation, we will tell them in a
few words. *That State is better educated than the rest.* She sees
the advantage, morally and socially, of orderly, neat, tasteful
villages; in producing better citizens, in causing the laws to be
respected, in making homes dearer and more sacred, in making
domestic life and the enjoyment of property to be more truly and
rightly estimated.

And these are the legitimate and natural results of this kind of
improvement we so ardently desire in the outward life and
appearance of rural towns. If our readers suppose us anxious for
the building of good houses, and the planting of street avenues,
solely that the country may look more beautiful to the eye, and
that the taste shall be gratified, they do us an injustice. This is
only the external sign by which we would have the country's
health and beauty known, as we look for the health and beauty
of its fair daughters in the presence of the rose on their cheeks.
But as the latter only blooms lastingly there, when a good constitution is joined with healthful habits of mind and body, so the
tasteful appearance which we long for in our country towns, we

[1] We believe we must lay this latter sin at the doors of our hard-working
emigrants from the Emerald Isle. Wherever they settle, they cling to their
ancient fraternity of porkers; and think it "no free country where pigs
can't have their liberty." Newburgh is by no means a well-planned village,
though scarcely surpassed for scenery; but we believe it may claim the
credit of being the only one among all the towns, cities and villages of New-
York, where pigs and geese have not the freedom of the streets.

seek as the outward mark of education, moral sentiment, love of home, and refined cultivation, which makes the main difference between Massachusetts and Madagascar.

We have, in a former number, said something as to the practical manner in which "graceless villages" may be improved. We have urged the force of example in those who set about improving [238] their own property, and shown the influence of even two or three persons in giving an air of civilization and refinement to the streets and suburbs of country towns. There is not a village in America, however badly planned at first, or ill-built afterwards, that may not be redeemed, in a great measure, by the aid of shade trees in the streets, and a little shrubbery in the front yards, and it is never too late or too early to project improvements of this kind. Every spring and every autumn should witness a revival of associated efforts on the part of select-men, trustees of corporations, and persons of means and influence, to adorn and embellish the external condition of their towns. Those least alive to the result as regards beauty, may be roused as to the effects of increased value given to the property thus improved, and villages thus rendered attractive and desirable as places of residence.

But let us now go a step further than this. In no country, perhaps, are there so many *new* villages and towns laid out every year as in the United States. Indeed, so large is the number, that the builders and projectors are fairly at a loss for names,—ancient and modern history having been literally worn threadbare by the godfathers, until all association with great heroes and mighty deeds is fairly beggared by this re-christening going on in our new settlements and future towns, as yet only populous to the extent of six houses. And notwithstanding the apparent vastness of our territory, the growth of new towns and new States is so wonderful—fifteen or twenty years giving a population of hundreds of thousands, where all was wilderness before—that the plan and arrangement of new towns ought to be a matter of national importance. And yet, to judge by the manner in which we see the thing done, there has not, in the whole duration of the republic, been a single word said, or a single plan formed, calculated to embody past experience, or to assist in any way the laying out of a village or town.

We have been the more struck by this fact in observing the
efforts of some companies who have lately, upon the Hudson,
within some twenty or more miles of New-York, undertaken to
lay out rural villages, with some pretension to taste and comfort;
and aim, at least, at combining the advantages of the country
with easy railroad access to them.[239]

Our readers most interested in such matters as this (and, taking
our principal cities together, it is a pretty large class), will be
interested to know what is the beau-ideal of these companies,
who undertake to buy tracts of land, lay them out in the best
manner, and form the most complete and attractive rural villages,
in order to tempt those tired of the wayworn life of sidewalks,
into a neighborhood where, without losing society, they can see
the horizon, breathe the fresh air, and walk upon elastic greensward.

Well, the beau-ideal of these newly-planned villages is not
down to the zero of dirty lanes and shadeless roadsides; but it
rises, we are sorry to say, no higher than streets, lined on each
side with shade-trees, and bordered with rows of houses. For the
most part, those houses—cottages, we presume—are to be built
on fifty-feet lots; or if any buyer is not satisfied with that amount
of elbow room, he may buy two lots, though certain that his
neighbor will still be within twenty feet of his fence. And this is
the sum total of the rural beauty, convenience, and comfort, of
the latest plan for a rural village in the Union.[2] The buyer gets
nothing more than he has in town, save his little patch of back
and front yard, a little peep down the street, looking one way at
the river, and the other way at the sky. So far from gaining any
thing which all inhabitants of a village should gain by the combination, one of these new villagers actually loses; for if he were
to go by himself, he would buy land cheaper, and have a fresh
landscape of fields and hills around him, instead of houses on all
sides, almost as closely placed as in the city, which he has en-
deavored to fly from.

Now a rural village—newly planned in the suburbs of a great
city, and planned, too, specially for those whose circumstances

[2] We say *plan*, but we do not mean to include in this such villages as
Northampton, Brookline, &c., beautiful and tasteful as they are. But they
are in Massachusetts!

will allow them to own a tasteful cottage in such a village—should present attractions much higher than this. It should aim at something higher than mere rows of houses upon streets crossing each other at right angles, and bordered with shade-trees. Any one may find as good shade-trees, and much better houses, in certain streets of the city which he leaves behind him; and if he is to give up fifty conveniences [240] and comforts, long enjoyed in town, for the mere fact of fresh air, he had better take board during the summer months in some snug farmhouse as before.

The indispensable desiderata in rural villages of this kind, are the following: 1st, a large open space, common, or park, situated in the middle of the village—not less than twenty acres; and better, if fifty or more in extent. This should be well planted with groups of trees, and kept as a lawn. The expense of mowing it would be paid by the grass in some cases; and in others, a considerable part of the space might be inclosed with a wire fence, and fed by sheep or cows, like many of the public parks in England.

This park would be the nucleus or *heart of the village*, and would give it an essentially rural character. Around it should be grouped all the best cottages and residences of the place; and this would be secured by selling no lots fronting upon it of less than one-fourth of an acre in extent. Wide streets, with rows of elms or maples, should diverge from the park on each side, and upon these streets smaller lots, but not smaller than one hundred feet front, should be sold for smaller cottages.

In this way, we would secure to our village a permanent rural character; first, by the possession of a large central space, always devoted to park or pleasure-ground, and always held as joint property, and for the common use of the whole village; second, by the imperative arrangement of cottages or dwellings around it, in such a way as to secure in all parts of the village sufficient space, view, circulation of air, and broad, well-planted avenues of shade-trees.

After such a village was built, and the central park planted a few years, the inhabitants would not be contented with the mere meadow and trees, usually called a park in this country. By submitting to a small annual tax per family, they could turn the whole park, if small, or considerable portions, here and there, if large, into pleasure-grounds. In the latter, there would be collected, by the combined means of the village, all the rare, hardy shrubs, trees, and plants, usually found in the private grounds of any amateur in America. Beds and masses of ever-blooming roses, sweet-scented climbers, and the richest shrubs, would thus be open to the enjoyment of all during the whole growing season. Those who had [241] neither the means, time, nor inclination, to devote to the culture of private pleasure-grounds, could thus enjoy those which belonged to all. Others might prefer to devote their own garden to fruits and vegetables, since the pleasure-grounds, which belonged to all, and which all would enjoy, would, by their greater breadth and magnitude, offer beauties and enjoyments which few private gardens can give.

The next step, after the possession of such public pleasure-grounds, would be the social and common enjoyment of them. Upon the well-mown glades of lawn, and beneath the shade of the forest-trees, would be formed rustic seats. Little arbors would be placed near, where in midsummer evenings ices would be served to all who wished them. And, little by little, the musical taste of the village (with the help of those good musical folks— the German emigrants) would organize itself into a band, which would occasionally delight the ears of all frequenters of the park with popular airs.

Do we overrate the mental and moral influences of such a common ground of entertainment as this, when we say that the inhabitants of such a village—enjoying in this way a common interest in flowers, trees, the fresh air, and sweet music, daily—would have something more healthful than the ordinary life of cities, and more refining and elevating than the common gossip of country villages!

"Ah! I see, Mr. Editor, you are a bit of a communist." By no means. On the contrary, we believe, above all things under heaven, in the power and virtue of the *individual home*. We devote our life and humble efforts to raising its condition. But people *must* live in towns and villages, and therefore let us raise the condition of towns and villages, and especially of rural towns and villages, by all possible means!

But we are *republican;* and, shall we confess it, we are a little vexed that as a people generally, we do not see how much in

America we lose by not using the advantages of republicanism. We mean now, for refined culture, physical comfort, and the like. Republican *education* we are now beginning pretty well to understand the value of; and it will not be long before it will be hard to find a native citizen who cannot read and write. And this comes by [242] making every man see what a great moral and intellectual good comes from cheerfully bearing a part in the burden of popular education. Let us next take up popular refinement in the arts, manners, social life, and innocent enjoyments, and we shall see what a virtuous and educated republic can really become.

Besides this, it is the proper duty of the state—that is, *the people* —to do in this way what the reigning power does in a monarchy. If the kings and princes in Germany, and the sovereign of England, have made magnificent parks and pleasure-gardens, and thrown them wide open for the enjoyment of all classes of the people (the latter, after all, having to pay for it), may it not be that our sovereign *people* will (far more cheaply, as they may) make and support these great and healthy sources of pleasure and refinement for themselves in America? We believe so; and we confidently wait for the time when public parks, public gardens, public galleries, and tasteful villages, shall be among the peculiar features of our happy republic.[243]

SHADE-TREES IN CITIES

Andrew Jackson Downing, "Shade-Trees in Cities" [1852], in *Rural Essays*, ed. by George William Curtis (New York, Leavitt and Allen, 1857).

"Down with the ailanthus!" is the cry we hear on all sides, town and country,—now that this "tree of heaven" (as the catalogues used alluringly to call it) has penetrated all parts of the Union, and begins to show its true character. Down with the ailanthus! "Its blossoms smell so disagreeably that my family are made ill by it," says an old resident on one of the squares in New York, where it is the only shade for fifty contiguous houses. "We must positively go to Newport, papa, to escape these horrible ailan-thuses," exclaim numberless young ladies, who find that even their best *Jean Maria Farina* affords no permanent relief, since their front parlors have become so celestially embowered. "The vile tree comes up all over my garden," say fifty owners of sub-urban lots who have foolishly been tempted into bordering the outside of their "yards" with it—having been told that it grows so "surprisingly fast." "It has ruined my lawn for fifty feet all round each tree," say the country gentlemen, who, seduced by the oriental beauty of its foliage, have also been busy for years dot-ting it in open places, here and there, in their pleasure-grounds. In some of the cities southward, the authorities, taking the matter more seriously, have voted the entire downfall of the whole species, and the Herods who wield the besom of sylvan destruc-tion, have probably made a clean sweep of the first born of celes-tials, in more towns than one south of Mason and Dixon's line this season.

Although we think there is picturesqueness in the free and luxuriant [311] foliage of the ailanthus, we shall see its downfall without a word to save it. We look upon it as an usurper in rather bad *odor* at home, which has come over to this land of liberty, under the garb of utility,[1] to make foul the air, with its pestilent breath, and devour the soil, with its intermeddling roots —a tree that has the fair outside and the treacherous heart of the Asiatics, and that has played us so many tricks, that we find we have caught a Tartar which it requires something more than a Chinese wall to confine within limits.

Down with the ailanthus! therefore, we cry with the populace. But we have reasons beside theirs, and now that the favorite has fallen out of favor with the sovereigns, we may take the oppor-unity to preach a funeral sermon over its remains, that shall not, like so many funeral sermons, be a bath of oblivion-waters to wash out all memory of its vices. For if the Tartar is not laid violent hands upon, and kept under close watch, even after the

---

[1] The ailanthus, though originally from China, was first introduced into this country from Europe, as the "Tanner's sumac"—but the mistake was soon discovered, and its rapid growth made it a favorite with planters.

The **Ailanthus Tree** in its various humors. This tree is known to some as *Ailanthus altissima*, to others as the Tree of Heaven, to still others as the Stink Tree. See the warm passages by Downing and the Goodmans on this city dweller.

spirit has gone out of the old trunk, and the coroner is satisfied that he has come to a violent end—lo, we shall have him upon us tenfold in the shape of suckers innumerable—little Tartars that will beget a new dynasty, and overrun our grounds and gardens again, without mercy.

The vices of the ailanthus—the incurable vices of the by-gone favorite—then, are twofold. In the first place, it *smells horribly*, both in leaf and flower—and instead of sweetening and purifying the air, fills it with a heavy, sickening odor; [2] in the second place, it *suckers* abominably, and thereby overruns, appropriates, and reduces to beggary, all the soil of every open piece of ground where it is planted. These are the mortifications which every body feels sooner or later, who has been seduced by the luxuriant outstretched welcome of its smooth round arms, and the waving and beckoning of its graceful plumes, into giving it a place in their home circle. For a few years, while the tree is growing, it has, to be sure, a fair [312] and specious look. You feel almost, as you look at its round trunk shooting up as straight, and almost as fast as a rocket, crowned by such a luxuriant tuft of verdure, that you have got a young palm-tree before your door, that can whisper tales to you in the evening of that "Flowery Country" from whence you have borrowed it, and you swear to stand by it against all slanderous aspersions. But alas! you are greener in your experience than the Tartar in his leaves. A few years pass by; the sapling becomes a tree—its blossoms fill the air with something that looks like curry-powder, and smells like the plague. You shut down the windows to keep out the *unbalmy* June air, if you live in town, and invariably give a wide berth to the *heavenly* avenue, if you belong to the country.

But we confess openly, that our crowning objection to this petted Chinaman or Tartar, who has played us so falsely, is a patriotic objection. It is that he has drawn away our attention from our own more noble native American trees, to waste it on this miserable pigtail of an Indiaman. . . .[313]

More than forty species of oak are there in North America (Great Britain has only two species—France only five), and we are richer in maples, elms, and ashes, than any country in the old

[2] Two acquaintances of ours, in a house in the upper part of the city of New-York, are regularly driven out by the ailanthus malaria every season.

world. Tulip-trees and magnolias from America, are the exotic glories of the princely grounds of Europe. But (saving always the praiseworthy partiality in New England for our elms and maples), who plants an American tree—in America? And who, on the contrary, that has planted shade-trees at all in the United States, for the last fifteen years, has not planted either ailanthuses or abele poplars? We should like to see that discreet, sagacious individual, who has escaped the national ecstasy for foreign suckers. . . .[314]

Frederick Law Olmsted and
Calvert Vaux
DESCRIPTION OF A PLAN FOR THE
IMPROVEMENT OF THE CENTRAL PARK

Frederick Law Olmsted and Calvert Vaux [both "Greensward"], *Description of a Plan for the Improvement of the Central Park* [1858] (New York, Aldine, 1868).

A general survey of the ground allotted to the park, taken with a view to arrive at the leading characteristics which present themselves as all-important to be considered in adapting the actual situation to its purpose, shows us, in the first place, that it is very distinctly divided into two tolerably equal portions, which, for convenience sake, may be called the upper and lower parks.

The horizon lines of the upper park are bold and sweeping and the slopes have great breadth in almost every aspect in which they may be contemplated. As this character is the highest ideal that can be aimed at for a park under any circumstances, and as it is in most decided contrast to the confined and formal lines of the city, it is desirable to interfere with it, by cross-roads and other constructions, as little as possible.[5] Formal planting and

Central Park, 1864. A bird's-eye lithograph view from about the junction of Fifth Avenue and 59th Street, drawn by Martel and H. Geissler. Traffic underpasses (and overpasses), distinctly seen in this view of the Park, have become an increasingly prominent element in city design with the advent of the automobile. See the references to them by Olmsted and Vaux, Stein, Wright and Gruen.

The Same View of **Central Park**, not quite a century later. In new urban contexts, new meanings.

architectural effects, unless on a very grand scale, must be
avoided. . . .

The lower park is far more heterogeneous in its character and
will require a much more varied treatment. . . .[6]

Our instructions call for four transverse roads. Each of these
will be the sole line of communication between one side of the
town and the other, for a distance equal to that between Chambers street and Canal street. If we suppose but one crossing of
Broadway to be possible in this interval, we shall realize what
these transverse roads are destined to become. Inevitably they
will be crowded thoroughfares, having nothing in common with
the park proper, but every thing at variance with those agreeable
sentiments which we should wish the park to inspire. It will not
be possible to enforce the ordinary police regulations of public
parks upon them. They must be constantly open to all the legitimate traffic of the city, to coal carts and butchers' carts, dust
carts and dung carts; engine companies will use them, those on
one side the park rushing their machines across it with frantic
zeal at every alarm from the other; ladies and invalids will need
special police escort for crossing them, as they do in lower
Broadway: eight times [9] in a single circuit of the park will they
oblige a pleasure drive or stroll to encounter a turbid stream of
coarse traffic, constantly moving at right angles to the line of the
park movement.

The transverse roads will also have to be kept open, while the
park proper will be useless for any good purpose, after dusk, for
experience has shown that even in London, with its admirable
police arrangements, the public cannot be secured safe transit
through large open spaces of ground after nightfall.

These public thoroughfares will then require to be well lighted
at the sides and, to restrain marauders pursued by the police from
escaping into the obscurity of the park, strong fences or walls,
six or eight feet high, will be necessary. A public road thus
guarded passes through the Regent's Park of London, at the
Zoological Gardens. It has the objection that the fence, with its
necessary gates at every crossing of the park drives, roads or
paths, is not only a great inconvenience but a disagreeable object
in the landscape.

To avoid a similar disfigurement an important passage across the garden of the Tuileries is closed by gates at night, forcing all who would otherwise use it to go a long distance to the right or left.

The form and position of the Central Park are peculiar in respect to this difficulty, and such that precedent in dealing with it is rather to be sought in the long and narrow Boulevards of some of the old [10] Continental cities of Europe, than in the broad parks with which, from its area in acres, we are most naturally led to compare it. The Boulevards referred to are, however, generally used only as walks, not as drives or places of ceremony. In frequent instances, in order not to interrupt their alleys, the streets crossing them are made in the form of causeways and carried over on high arches. This, of course, destroys all landscape effect, since it puts an abrupt limit to the view. Some expedient is needed for the Central Park by which the convenience of the arrangement may be retained, while the objection is as far as possible avoided.

In the plan herewith offered to the Commission, each of the transverse roads is intended to be sunk so far below the general surface that the park drives may, at every necessary point of intersection, be carried entirely over it, without any obvious elevation or divergence from their most attractive routes. The banks on each side will be walled up to the height of about seven feet, thus forming the protective barrier required by police considerations, and a little judicious planting on the tops or slopes of the banks above these walls will, in most cases, entirely conceal both the roads and the vehicles moving in them, from the view of those walking or driving in the park.[1] . . .[11]

Vista Rock, the most prominent point in the landscape of the lower park, here first comes distinctly into view, and fortunately in a direction diagonal to the boundary lines, from which it is desirable to withdraw attention in every possible way. We therefore accept this line of view as affording an all-sufficient motive to our further procedure. Although averse on general principles to a symmetrical arrangement of trees, we consider it an essential feature of a metropolitan park, that it should contain a grand promenade, level, spacious, and thoroughly shaded. This result

---

[1] NOTE, 1868.—In execution, the four traffic roads have been carried through the Park in the manner suggested.

can in no other way be so completely arrived at, as by an avenue,
which in itself even, exclusive of its adaptability for this purpose,
contains so many elements of grandeur and magnificence, that
it should be recognized as an essential feature in the arrangement
of any large park. The objection to which it is liable is that it
divides the landscape into two parts, and it is therefore
desirable [17]   to decide at what point this necessity can be
submitted to with the least sacrifice to the general effect. The
whole topographical character of the park is so varied, so suggestive of natural treatment, so picturesque, so individual in its
characteristics, that it would be contrary to common sense to
make the avenue its leading feature, or to occupy any great
extent of ground for this special purpose. It must be subservient
to the general design, if that general design is to be in accordance
with the present configuration of the ground, and we have therefore thought that it should, so far as possible, be complete in
itself, and not become a portion of any of the leading drives.
There is no dignity of effect to be produced by driving through
an avenue a quarter of a mile long, unless it leads to, and becomes
an accessory of, some grand architectural structure, which itself,
and not the avenue, is the ultimatum of interest. An avenue for
driving in should be two or three miles long, or it will be petite
and disappointing. We have therefore thought it most desirable
to identify the idea of the avenue with the promenade, for which
purpose a quarter of a mile is not insufficient, and we can
find no better place for such a grand mall, or open air hall
of reception, as we desire to have, than the ground before
us.[2] [18]

    . . . Many elegant buildings may be appropriately erected for
desirable purposes in a public park, but we conceive that all such
architectural structures should be confessedly subservient to the
main idea, and that nothing artificial should be obtruded on the
view as an ultimatum of interest. The idea of the park itself
should always be uppermost in the mind of the beholder. Holding
this general principle to be of considerable importance, we have
preferred to place the avenue where it can be terminated appropriately at one end with a landscape attraction of considerable

_____

[2] Note, 1868.—In execution, this avenue has been planted with elms, as
suggested later in the report, and is now called "The Mall."

extent, and to relieve the south entrance with only so much
architectural treatment as may give the idea that due regard has
been paid to the adornment of this principal promenade, without
interfering with its real character.

This avenue may be considered the central feature in our plan
for laying out the lower park, and the other details of arrangement are more or less designed in connection with it.[19]

. . . [T]he most attractive view of a flower-garden is from
some point above it, that will [23] enable the visitor to take in at
a glance a general idea of the effect aimed at.

The garden is located in low ground to the northeast of the
promenade, and close upon the line of Fifth avenue, the grade
of which opposite the centre of the garden is about twenty feet
above the present level of the ground; this, for the reasons above
stated, we consider a desideratum, and have suggested that over
the arcade or veranda that we propose should be built against the
east wall of the park in connection with the garden, a structure
should be erected, with an entrance on a level with the avenue,
so as to give an opportunity for a view of the garden, both from
this level and from another story above it. This idea is not, of
course, necessary to the design, and the sketch submitted is
merely a suggestion to show what may be done at some future
time.

The plan of the flower-garden itself is geometrical; and it is
surrounded by an irregular and less formal plantation of shrubs,
that will serve to connect it with the park proper. . . .[24]

The plan does not show any brooks, except a small one in connection with the pool at the foot of Bogardus Hill, which can
always be kept full by the waste of water from the New Reservoir. Mere rivulets are uninteresting, and we have preferred to
collect the ornamental water in large [35] sheets, and to carry off
through underground drains the water that at present runs
through the park in shallow brooks.

As a general rule, we propose to run footpaths close to the
carriage roads, which are intended to be 60 feet wide, allowing
a space of four feet of turf as a barrier between the drive and the
path. Other more private footpaths are introduced, but it is
hardly thought that any plan would be popular in New York,
that did not allow of a continuous promenade along the line of

the drives, so that pedestrians may have ample opportunity to look at the equipages and their inmates.

It will be perceived that no long straight drive has been provided on the plan; this feature has been studiously avoided, because it would offer opportunities for trotting matches. The popular idea of the park is a beautiful open space, in which quiet drives, rides, and strolls may be had. This cannot be preserved if a race-course, or a road that can readily be used as a race-course, is made one of its leading attractions.[36]

Frederick Law Olmsted

PUBLIC PARKS AND THE ENLARGEMENT OF TOWNS

Frederick Law Olmsted, "Public Parks and the Enlargement of Towns," in *Journal of Social Science*, III (1870).

It used to be a matter of pride with the better sort of our country people that they could raise on their own land or manufacture within their own households almost everything needed for domestic consumption. But if now you leave the rail, at whatever remote station, the very advertisements on its walls will manifest how greatly this is changed. Push out over the prairie and make your way to the house of any long-settled and prosperous farmer, and the intimacy of his family with the town will constantly appear, in dress, furniture, viands, in all the conversation. If there is a piano, they will be expecting a man from town to tune it. If the baby has outgrown its shoes, the measure is to be sent to town. If a tooth is troublesome, an appointment is to be arranged by telegraph with the dentist. The railway time-table hangs with the almanac. The housewife complains of her servants. There is no difficulty in getting them from the intelligence offices in town, such as they are; but only the poorest, who cannot find employment in the city, will come to the country, and these as soon as they have got a few dollars ahead, are crazy to get back to town. It is much the same with the men, the farmer will add; he has to run up in the morning and get some one to take "Wolf's" place. You will find, too, that one of his sons is in a lawyer's office, another at a commercial college, and his oldest daughter at an "institute," all in town. I know several girls who travel eighty miles a day to attend school in Chicago. . . . [2]

There can be no doubt then, that, in all our modern civilization, as in that of the ancients, there is a strong drift townward. But some seem to regard the class of symptoms I have referred to as those of a sort of moral epidemic, the crisis and reaction of which they constantly expect to see. They even detect already a growing disgust with the town and signs of a back-set towards rural simplicity. To avoid prolonged discussion of the question thus suggested I will refer but briefly to the intimate connection which is evident between the growth of towns and the dying out of slavery and feudal customs, of priestcraft and government by divine right, the multiplication of books, newspapers, schools, and other means of popular education and the adoption of improved methods of communication, transportation, and of various labor-saving inventions. No nation has yet begun to give up schools or newspapers, railroads or telegraphs, to restore feudal rights or advance rates of postage. King-craft and priestcraft are nowhere gaining any solid ground. On the contrary, considered as elements of human progress, the more apparent forces under which men have [4] thus far been led to gather together in towns are yet growing; never more rapidly than at this moment. It would seem then more rational to prepare for a continued rising of the townward flood than to count upon its subsidence. Examining our own country more particularly, it is to be considered that we have been giving away our public lands under a square form of division, as if for the purpose of preventing the closer agricultural settlement which long and narrow farms would have favored, and that we have used our mineral deposits as premiums for the encouragement of wandering and of forms of enterprise, individual, desultory and sequestered in character, in distinction from those which are organized, systematized and public. This policy has had its day; the choicest lands have been taken up; the most prominent and easiest worked metallic veins have been seized, the richest placers are abandoned to Chinamen, and the only reaction that we can reasonably anticipate is one from, not toward, dispersion. . . . [5]

It should be observed that possession of the various advantages of the town to which we have referred, and, indeed, of all the advantages which are peculiar to large towns, while it very certainly cannot be acquired by people living in houses a quarter or a half a mile apart, does not, on the other hand, by any means involve an unhealthy density of population. Probably the advantages of civilization can be found illustrated and demonstrated under no other circumstances so completely as in some suburban neighborhoods where each family abode stands fifty or a hundred feet or more apart from all others, and at some distance from the public road. And it must be remembered, also, that man's enjoyment of rural beauty has clearly increased rather than diminished with his advance in civilization. There is no reason, except in the loss of time, the inconvenience, discomfort, and expense of our present arrangements for short travel, why suburban advantages should not be almost indefinitely extended. Let us have a cheap and enjoyable method of conveyance, and a building law like that of old Rome, and they surely will be. . . . [9]

We come then to the question: what accommodations for recreation can we provide which shall be so agreeable and so accessible as to be efficiently attractive to the great body of citizens, and which, while giving decided gratification, shall also cause those who resort to them for pleasure to subject themselves, for the time being, to conditions strongly counteractive to the special enervating conditions of the town?

In the study of this question all forms of recreation may, in the first place, be conveniently arranged under two general heads. One will include all of which the predominating influence is to stimulate exertion of any part or parts needing it; the other, all which cause us to receive pleasure without conscious exertion. Games chiefly of mental skill, as chess, or athletic sports, as baseball, are examples of means of recreation of the first class, which may be termed that of *exertive* recreation; music and the fine arts generally of the second or *receptive* division.

Considering the first by itself, much consideration will be needed in determining what classes of exercises may be advantageously provided for. In the Bois de Boulogne there is a race-course; in the Bois de Vincennes a ground for artillery target-practice. Military parades are held in Hyde Park. A few cricket clubs are accommodated in most of the London parks, and swimming is permitted in the lakes at certain hours. In the New York Park, on the other hand, none of these exercises are provided for or permitted, except that the boys of the public schools are given the use on holidays of certain large spaces for ball playing. It is considered that the advantage to individuals which would be gained in providing for them would not compensate for the general inconvenience and expense they would cause.

I do not propose to discuss this part of the subject at present, as it is only necessary to my immediate purpose to point out that if recreations requiring large spaces to be given up to the use of a comparatively small number, are not considered essential, numerous small grounds so distributed through a large town that some one of them could be easily reached by a short walk from every house, would be more desirable than a single area of great extent, however rich in landscape attractions it might be. Especially would this be the case if the numerous local grounds were connected and supplemented by a series of trunk-roads or boulevards such as has already been suggested.[17]

Proceeding to the consideration of receptive recreations, it is necessary to ask you to adopt and bear in mind a further subdivision, under two heads, according to the degree in which the average enjoyment is greater when a large congregation assembles for a purpose of receptive recreation, or when the number coming together is small and the circumstances are favorable to the exercise of personal friendliness.

The first I shall term *gregarious;* the second, *neighborly.* Remembering that the immediate matter in hand is a study of fitting accommodations, you will, I trust, see the practical necessity of this classification.

Purely gregarious recreation seems to be generally looked upon in New England society as childish and savage, because, I suppose, there is so little of what we call intellectual gratification in it. We are inclined to engage in it indirectly, furtively, and with complication. Yet there are certain forms of recreation, a large share of the attraction of which must, I think, lie in the gratification of the gregarious inclination, and which, with those who can afford to indulge in them, are so popular as to establish the importance of the requirement.

If I ask myself where I have experienced the most complete gratification of this instinct in public and out of doors, among trees, I find that it has been in the promenade of the Champs Elysées. As closely following it I should name other promenades of Europe, and our own upon the New York parks. I have studiously watched the latter for several years. I have several times seen fifty thousand people participating in them; and the more I have seen of them, the more highly have I been led to estimate their value as means of counteracting the evils of town life.

Consider that the New York Park and the Brooklyn Park are the only places in those associated cities where, in this eighteen hundred and seventieth year after Christ, you will find a body of Christians coming together, and with an evident glee in the prospect of coming together, all classes largely represented, with a common purpose, not at all intellectual, competitive with none, disposing to jealousy and spiritual or intellectual pride toward none, each individual adding by his mere presence to the pleasure of all others, all helping to the greater happiness of each. You may thus often see vast numbers of persons brought closely together, poor and rich, young and old, Jew and Gentile. I have seen a hundred thousand thus congregated, and I assure you that though there have been not a few that seemed a little dazed, as if they did [18] not quite understand it, and were, perhaps, a little ashamed of it, I have looked studiously but vainly among them for a single face completely unsympathetic with the prevailing expression of good nature and light-heartedness.

Is it doubtful that it does men good to come together in this way in pure air and under the light of heaven, or that it must have an influence directly counteractive to that of the ordinary hard, hustling working hours of town life?

You will agree with me, I am sure, that it is not, and that opportunity, convenient, attractive opportunity, for such congregation, is a very good thing to provide for, in planning the extension of a town. . . .

I have next to see what opportunities are wanted to induce people to engage in what I have termed *neighborly* receptive

recreations, under conditions which shall be highly counteractive to the prevailing bias to degeneration and demoralization in
large towns. To make clearer what I mean, I need an illustration
which I find in a familiar domestic gathering, where the prattle
of the children mingles with the easy conversation of the more
sedate, the bodily requirements satisfied with good cheer, fresh
air, agreeable [19] light, moderate temperature, snug shelter, and
furniture and decorations adapted to please the eye, without calling for profound admiration on the one hand, or tending to
fatigue or disgust on the other. The circumstances are all favorable to a pleasurable wakefulness of the mind without stimulating exertion; and the close relation of family life, the association
of children, of mothers, of lovers, or those who may be lovers,
stimulate and keep alive the more tender sympathies, and give
play to faculties such as may be dormant in business or on the
promenade; while at the same time the cares of providing in detail for all the wants of the family, guidance, instruction, reproof,
and the dutiful reception of guidance, instruction, and reproof,
are, as matters of conscious exertion, as far as possible laid aside.

There is an instinctive inclination to this social, neighborly,
unexertive form of recreation among all of us. In one way or
another it is sure to be constantly operating upon those millions
on millions of men and women who are to pass their lives within
a few miles of where we now stand. To what extent it shall
operate so as to develop health and virtue, will, on many occasions, be simply a question of opportunity and inducement. And
this question is one for the determination of which for a thousand
years we here to-day are largely responsible. . . .

Consider how often you see young men in knots of perhaps
half a dozen in lounging attitudes rudely obstructing the sidewalks, chiefly led in their little conversation by the suggestions
given to their minds by what or whom they may see passing in
the street, men, women, or children, whom they do not know,
and for whom they have no respect or sympathy. There is nothing among them or about them which is adapted to bring into
play a spark of admiration, of delicacy, manliness, or tenderness.
You see them presently descend in search of physical comfort to
a brilliantly [20] lighted basement, where they find others of their
sort, see, hear, smell, drink, and eat all manner of vile things.

Whether on the curb-stones or in the dram-shops, these young men are all under the influence of the same impulse which some satisfy about the tea-table with neighbors and wives and mothers and children, and all things clean and wholesome, softening and refining.

If the great city to arise here is to be laid out little by little, and chiefly to suit the views of land-owners, acting only individually, and thinking only of how what they do is to affect the value in the next week or the next year of the few lots that each may hold at the time, the opportunities of so obeying this inclination as at the same time to give the lungs a bath of pure sunny air, to give the mind a suggestion of rest from the devouring eagerness and intellectual strife of town life, will always be few to any, to many will amount to nothing.

But is it possible to make public provision for recreation of this class, essentially domestic and secluded as it is?

It is a question which can, of course, be conclusively answered only from experience. And from experience in some slight degree I shall answer it. . . .

There will be room enough in the Brooklyn Park, when it is finished, for several thousand little family and neighborly parties to bivouac at frequent intervals through the summer, without discommoding one another, or interfering with any other purpose, to say nothing of those who can be drawn out to make a day of it, as many thousand were last year. . . . [21]

When the arrangements are complete, I see no reason why thousands should not come every day where hundreds come now to use them; and if so, who can measure the value, generation after generation, of such provisions for recreation to the overwrought, much-confined people of the great town that is to be?

For this purpose neither of the forms of ground we have heretofore considered are at all suitable. We want a ground to which people may easily go after their day's work is done, and where they may stroll for an hour, seeing, hearing, and feeling nothing of the bustle and jar of the streets, where they shall, in effect, find the city put far away from them. We want the greatest possible contrast with the streets and the shops and the rooms of the town which will be consistent with convenience and the preservation of good order and neatness. We want, especially, the greatest possible contrast with the restraining and confining conditions of the town, those conditions which compel us to walk circumspectly, watchfully, jealously, which compel us to look closely upon others without sympathy. Practically, what we most want is a simple, broad, open space of clean greensward, with sufficient play of surface and a sufficient number of trees about it to supply a variety of light and shade. This we want as a central feature. We want depth of wood enough about it not only for comfort in hot weather, but to completely shut out the city from our landscapes. . . . [22]

A Promenade may, with great advantage, be carried along the outer part of the surrounding groves of a park; and it will do no harm if here and there a broad opening among the trees discloses its open landscapes to those upon the promenade. But recollect that the object of the latter for the time being should be to see *congregated human life* under glorious and necessarily artificial conditions, and the natural landscape is not essential to them; though there is no more beautiful picture, and none can be more pleasing incidentally to the gregarious purpose, than that of beautiful meadows, over which clusters of level-armed sheltering trees cast broad shadows, and upon which are scattered dainty cows and flocks of black-faced sheep, while men, women, and children are seen sitting here and there, forming groups in the shade, or moving in and out among the woody points and bays.

It may be inferred from what I have said, that very rugged ground, abrupt eminences, and what is technically called picturesque in distinction from merely beautiful or simply pleasing scenery, is not the most desirable for a town park. Decidedly not in my opinion. The park should, as far as possible, complement the town. Openness is the one thing you cannot get in buildings. Picturesqueness you can get. Let your buildings be as picturesque as your artists can make them. This is the beauty of a town. Consequently, the beauty of the park should be the other. It should be the beauty of the fields, the meadow, the prairie, of the green pastures, and the still waters. What we want to gain is tranquillity and rest to the mind. . . . [23]

Benton MacKaye_____

THE NEW EXPLORATION

Benton MacKaye, *The New Exploration: A Philosophy of Regional Planning*
(New York, Harcourt, Brace, 1928).*

. . . Look over yonder there at the Hudson Highlands (you do
not even need your field glasses). In those hills there lives a man
who recently made his first visit to New York. He had lived a long
life within fifty miles from Times Square, and in spite of the
Sunday supplement had no real notion of a metropolis. Yonder
in the Appalachian hinterland there dwells another world. This
world is the indigenous America. It is being invaded (but is not
yet captured) by metropolitan America. . . .

In brief, we have discovered two worlds in surveying the landscape from the Times Building—just as Huxley discovered two
worlds from London Bridge. Immediately beneath us, we observed the streams of traffic, passing through Manhattan, streams
which flow and mingle with all the great traffic and goods
streams of the earth. Here is the realm of the metropolis, the
mouth that receives the industrial flow, the domain of standardized existence. It is a transient and ever-changing environment.
In the hinterland of the great metropolis, we have visualized the
industrial watershed, the parts of the country where the traffic
streams take rise, first in small trickles and runnels, in farms,
served the streams of traffic, passing through Manhattan, streams
of raw materials which go, as food or as basic products, into the
homes and workshops of the [14] world. Here is the realm of the
indigenous, the realm of the soil, the ores, the forests, the water-
power forces, and of the other sources of life and industry. If the
metropolitan environment presents us typically with what flows
and passes and changes, the indigenous environments provide

* Reprinted by permission of the author, copyright 1928 by Harcourt,
Brace, renewed 1956 by the author.

us with what stays. A railway may stop running, or a city may disappear: but the earth itself, as a receiver and storer of solar energy, as a hoarder and container of soils and metals and potential vegetation—that does not alter: it can never basically alter. . . . [15]

The metropolitan world . . . may be considered as an exotic intrusion or "flow" into certain portions of the innate or indigenous world. Considered thus, and not merely as a static framework, it becomes the dominant part of the flow of population and of the industrial migration to which we have referred in a previous chapter. The control and guidance of this flow and migration we have stated to be the fundamental problem of regional engineering toward the goal set up by Governor Smith of New York, which was "the making of the mold in which future generations shall live." The particular aspect of this problem treated of in this Philosophy of Regional Planning is the strategy of the indigenous world with respect to its contact with this metropolitan flow. This strategy consists, roughly speaking, in developing the indigenous environments (primeval, rural, and communal) and in confining the encroachments of the metropolitan environment. As applied to this country, therefore, it consists in developing the Indigenous America and in confining the Metropolitan America. . . . [74]

. . . Of first concern in any regional industrial situation is an exact vision of the ends to be achieved. These for our purposes may be placed within two classes: the geographic and the nongeographic. The tangible objectives of the second class consist of food, clothing, shelter, and leisure *time*. The tangible objectives of the first class consist of these plus the further (and complemental) goal of [117] environment and leisure *space*. The attainment of this goal is intimately entwined in the contention which we have termed "indigenous vs. metropolitan." Here is a dormant but vital and specific conflict in men's minds: it is the subconscious effort to preserve and to develop the inherent human values of a country (on the part of all the members of a society) against that other subconscious effort to develop the mundane values of an exotic mechanized iron civilization (on the part of the proprietors of that civilization). It is a fight for space, for a place in the sun, for an environment unshadowed by the smoke-

clouds of iron metropolitan industrialism—whether in China or
America. Here is the *most* immediate function of the regional
planner: it is for him to "take sides" in this coming conflict, and
to fight, with the sharp weapon of visualization, for the intrinsic
human values of his country and his world.

Appalachian America promises to be a strenuous battleground.
It looms large on the map of the world. Here is the nucleus of
what seems to be, potentially, the mightiest industrial empire on
earth. The next generation may see in this region the greatest
eruption ever of iron civilization: the "Backflows" from our metropolitan centers, big and little, may coalesce into a laval flow, or
else (to change the figure) into a modern glacier whose iron
fabric may do to human life and aspiration what the ice-sheet did
to life in other forms. Against this world-wide movement of the
"material fact," near-cosmic in its apparent fatefulness, there
stands what seems to be a puny force indeed. Its tiny evidences
are seen in the tame little movements to establish National Parks
and Forests, to restore the realm of nature as Thoreau glimpsed
it for us, to develop the realm of art through local drama, and
otherwise to invoke the [118] "spiritual form," in our society. But
within this funny little seed there also lies a cosmic force. "It is
a faint intimation, yet so are the first streaks of morning." It is the
first lisping perhaps of the next endeavor of that eternal determination of man to win a land and world wherein to lead a life
for carrying out a human evolution in lieu of an existence for
satisfying the external routine of the machine. There is a dormant
barbarian thrill for freedom beating beneath the waistcoat of
the average citizen, and it is beginning to awaken. The immediate job of the regional planner is to prepare for this awakening
—not through unconstructive and chimerical efforts on the metropolitan "Bottle-Neck," but through a synthetic creative effort
back on the crestline sources where an indigenous world of intrinsic human values (and specifically an Indigenous America)
awaits its restoration and development as a *land in which to
live.* . . . [119]

. . . The confusion in men's minds regarding the underlying
nature of the indigenous and metropolitan worlds is entertaining, but it is tragic. These worlds, these environments, represent
in their essence the antipodes of human experience: one is in-

The almost untamed wilderness, the "indigenous environment" of Benton MacKaye's world. From this ridge of the **Appalachian Mountains**, looking westward toward the Poconos in Pennsylvania, one has the site of Azilum about three hours by automobile ahead, metropolitan New York less than two hours behind. The rocks in the foreground lie athwart the Appalachian Trail, a footpath conceived by MacKaye, now running from Maine to Georgia.

herent, the other is intrusive; one is natural, the other is mechanized; one is art, the other is artifice; one is symphonic, the other
is cacophonous.

But unfortunately it is not in their essence that we experience
these environments; we experience them instead in what might
be called in very truth a "complex." We get the two essences in
combination. The titanic turreted skyscraper viewed through
evening lights from New York harbor combines national power
in repose and majesty with imperialistic affront and sinister con-
temptuousness. The down-town shopping district of the average
small American city, with its left-over shade trees, combines the
home-coming thrill of the stately elm-lined village roadway and
common meeting-ground with the rotary excitement of the typical Main Street. The journey by motor [150] through the American countryside combines the elixir of the stage-coach drive
through hill and dale with the melancholia inflicted by a wayside
architecture glorying in the heydey of its drabness. . . . [151]

DEVELOPING THE INDIGENOUS ENVIRONMENT

. . . By practicing strenuously the *act*, we can in time develop
the full *art* of "living in the open."

The primeval environment we have placed as one of the so-
called "elemental environments," the communal and the urban
being the others. Together these form the indigenous environment—that which innately belongs to the soil and the human
mind in contrast to the intrusive influence of the metropolis
which does "not belong." The primeval environment, as already
pointed out, is seen to form, on close analysis, the one environment which is truly elemental; for out of this come all the others.
It is the mother of the indigenous environment: it forms the outward setting for the contact of man and nature, but in it lies the
seed also of the relation—man and man. Let us set up the three
elemental human contacts which go, roughly speaking, with the
three elemental settings. They are:

The contact of man and nature—capable of permanent development in the primeval setting.

The all-round symmetric contact of man and man—capable

presumably of highest development in the communal setting, the "neighborhood." [205]

The specialized contact of man and man—which has developed for the most part in the urban setting, the city proper.

The communal setting grows out of the primeval, while the urban is a compound of the communal. The notion of the "regional city," whose specifications we have already crudely sketched, would combine all three of these. I have in mind, for illustration, a certain small city in New England whose tributary territory (that embraced within an hour's drive by motor) contains potentially the settings and contacts named. A small mountainous and pastoral area in the northwest corner provides the primeval (or near-primeval) contact; each one of some forty typical New England villages within the territory provides a base for developing the communal contact; the totality of such villages connected by a framework of intervillage highways would form a compound community providing for the urban (or group) contacts. This is not a "plan," it is a physical possibility; it might or might not be revealed as of innate consequence.

Each one of the three settings and contacts just named constitutes the subject for developing a definite portion of the art of "living in the open." Three distinct situations are provided for developing definite lines of activity. Each line of action would emanate naturally from a specific site.

One line of action would spread outward from the *camp fire.* Speaking geographically, the zone covered by this action would embrace . . . a "wilderness area" or open way. Through the instrumentality of cabin and trail, the wilderness area would be developed as a primeval (or near-primeval) environment. This line of work would (and does) constitute the primary [206] step perhaps in developing the "act" or "sport" or "art" of living in the open. This particular field of endeavor is being developed, in the several regions of America, by various outing and outdoor groups like those represented in such gatherings as the New England Trail Conference.

Another line of action would radiate from the *village green.* The zone covered would embrace the village Common and community and the surrounding rural area which is naturally tributary thereto. This area would be developed as a communal en-

vironment. In the case of New England the innate setting would
be revealed most likely as some form of the colonial mold. Dealing with the outward general life of the community, and not
with the inner particular life of the individual, the activity involved would constitute an extension of the art of living in the
open. Certain activities, literally speaking, must be carried on
under roof: the home folks might gather in the town hall just as
the campers would gather in the mountain cabin. This particular
field of endeavor is now making its beginnings in various parts
of America. I do not mean the dogmatic attempts, of long-time
standing, toward village improvement and civic betterment; I
refer to the keen attempts toward revealing and dramatizing the
indigenous communal life made by such groups as the Little
Country Theater of North Dakota and the Carolina Players.

A third line of action would emanate from the *wayside*. The
zone here covered would consist of the abutting land and aspects
along the inter-village highways; in other words, the intertown.
This zone would be developed as a fitting and suitable link in the
framework of the "regional city." This does not mean that it
would be an urban environment; on the contrary it would be a
rural environment.[207] *By no means* would it be a suburban environment. The zone would be developed as far as possible as an
attractive passageway between one village and another, and in
this sense would become a part of the total environment of the
regional city. The purpose of the work involved would be as far
as possible to complete the setting for a life "in the open." The
first steps in this endeavor are now being taken by those rising
strenuous groups of general "appreciators" who are beginning to
wage a dogged war on billboards, "hot-dog kennels," and the
other metropolitan personifications of wayside desecration. I
refer to protectors of the countryside such as are represented in
the various local and State committees on the billboard nuisance;
I refer also to those revealers of the latent countryside who by
visualizing and establishing artistic settings for tea houses and
other intertown utilities, in harmony with local surroundings and
picturesque tradition, are developing, in positive manner, the
potential resource of the wayside environment.

The job to do in each one of these developments is not to
"plan" but to *reveal*—to seek the innate design of forces higher

than our limited powers. We have taken a whole chapter to explain that planning is fundamentally revelation. Let us never forget this. The true planner is a seeker—a revealer: he must guard himself from dogma as he would from poison. This is a special admonition to the technical planner. And the best guard he can procure is the amateur planner. The point may be made that the technician unsupported by the people and a public consciousness is a head without a body, and that the public at large, unguided by technical advice, is a body without a head. The amateur in any line is a representative of the [208] best thought of the public at large—he is the forerunner of the ultimate conviction of an advancing public opinion: for this reason he is the ally *par excellence* of the technician. Let the technical planner or "revealer" ally himself closely with a body of amateur revealers: then shall we have a body *with* a head. . . . [209]

There is one class of revealer whose field of activity emanates from all three environments—that of the camp fire, that of the village green, and that of the wayside. This is the artist proper— the landscape painter or even the amateur photographer. He brings the comprehensive notion to the eye as the musical artist brings it to the ear. Each of the revealers we have mentioned— naturalist, historian, dramatist, artist—is engaged in the imaging, on paper or canvas or other vicarious medium, of the vital forces, rhythms, and aspects of definite desirable environments. Could their efforts, properly mobilized and focused, achieve a revelation of these selfsame forces in a medium more vital and more real? This apparently was the query in the back of Thoreau's head when he pointed out the latent consummation which in these chapters has been emphasized. He says:

It is something to be able to paint a particular picture, or to carve a statue, and so to make a few objects beautiful; but it is far more glorious to carve and paint the very atmosphere and medium through which we look. . . . To affect the quality of the day, that is the highest of arts. [212]

"The very atmosphere and medium through which we look." Here is the common mind which we have called *environment;* it is the "quality of the day": to "affect" it is the "highest of arts." Such is the consummation awaiting the combined vision and sensibility of the various classes of "revealers" we have mentioned.

The art of the drama came about as a synthesis of the other arts. The "art" of developing environment, of "living in the open," of "affecting the quality of the day," seems by natural and inevitable steps to be forthcoming as another and greater synthesis. . . . [213]

Lewis Mumford . . . has pointed out to us two distinct types of utopia: the utopia of escape and the utopia of reconstruction. Here is our choice: between the make-believe and the real. Shall we go to the play and for the time being become a big vicarious Cyrano and let it go at that?—or shall we, in addition, capture the spirit of our hero and resolve to become real, if diminutive, Cyranos? Our job in the new exploration is nothing short of making a utopia of reconstruction—the remodeling of an unshapen and cacophonous environment into a humanized and well-ordered one. This is something which the technical "planner" cannot do alone: he requires the close alliance of the amateur revealer of life's setting, and above all of human life itself. To remodel our house properly, we must live in it. To remodel "the open," we must learn the art of "living in the open." This art is in the making. It is the coming synthetic art—call it outdoor culture or what you will—which, from camp fire and village and wayside, is even now radiating its vital influence and beginning to find itself. And so we begin to realize Thoreau's dream and prophecy, and to take part each in our humble path in affecting the quality itself of our common mind and day.[214]

Clarence Arthur Perry ————————
HOUSING FOR THE MACHINE AGE

Clarence Arthur Perry, *Housing for the Machine Age* (New York, Russell Sage Foundation, 1939).*

Thus it is plain that the family occupying a city dwelling is [17] vitally affected by the appearance and uses of adjacent struc-

* Reprinted by permission of the Russell Sage Foundation.

tures; by the location of the public school, retail stores, and play-grounds; and by the traffic conditions encountered in making use of these facilities and services. Through zoning and other meas-ures most municipalities are doing something to control environ-mental troubles. . . . The fact is, however, that as yet their methods are not adequate for the purpose. In particular, there are two shortcomings in residential environment which still grievously afflict families living in city apartments houses, namely, lack of play space and of the conditions that create neighbor-liness.

DWELLINGS WITHOUT YARDS

When a builder loads a single plot with so many families that their children are forced to obtain their play opportunities and character development from the street, from the yards of neigh-bors, or from the public playground—then his conduct is not un-like that of the cuckoo which lays eggs in other birds' nests, for strangers to hatch. Probably he, like the bird, follows his instincts and therefore we should not blame him too severely. But even the apartment builder, completely governed by his instincts, would no doubt be amazed if he realized the injury his product had wrought—and was still working—upon human development.

If you asked him where the children of his apartment families could play, he would undoubtedly point to the public parks and playgrounds. You would have to admit that indeed most munic-ipalities have set aside large spaces for recreation and have trained men and women to conduct wholesome games and sports upon them. But we should not let that circumstance blind us to the fact that the public recreation movement—extensive and progressive as it is—has not as yet been able to fill the breach in the environment of child-life that was made when homes were shorn of yards by the institution of multi-family dwellings.

While it is true that the extent of public play space varies in different localities, it is still, even in the most progressive munici-palities, patently insufficient in two respects: (1) Many apart-ment families are more than a quarter of a mile from a play-ground (experience shows that few children will travel farther).

(2) Children [18] of the pre-school age, who cannot go alone to a playground, are served only in a very limited degree by existing public facilities.

To appreciate what the apartment child has lost we have only to recall what the children in a single-family dwelling still enjoy. Take the most common type of home yard—that with a small grass plot and a garden space. In digging, climbing, teetering, and throwing at targets children develop strength and muscular co-ordination. In building slides and bird and chicken houses they gain manual skill and whet the constructive impulse. In caring for dogs, rabbits, and other pets they exercise their parental impulses and learn the value of kindness. In team games, involving the neighbors' children, they begin to practice fairness and to place the interests of the team before those of the individual. And all of this activity, which is so instrumental in the development of the child's various capacities and behavior patterns, is self-driven and carried on with joyous satisfaction.

Moreover, one of the important aspects of home-yard play is that it is carried under parental oversight. If a child's baseball goes through a neighbor's window, his mother leads him to face the owner while she pays for the damage. The emotions the boy experiences are more wholesome and more promising for his future than would have been occasioned had the property damage happened away from his home and resulted in an exciting chase in which he filled in the eyes of his comrades the role of a "wild west" outlaw. The thrills of anti-social acts have an extraordinary efficacy in moulding behavior patterns, in creating an appetite for the forbidden.

Students of crime have often speculated on why it is that large cities, with elaborate park and playground systems, still show a high delinquency rate. Some of it may be due to the wide unprotected gulf which lies between the apartment home and the play field. When the youngster tells his mother he is going to the public playground, how can she be certain that he actually reaches it? He may play there on some occasions and on others meet his gang in their hideouts. To watch the doings of her offspring and prevent their taking the wrong form is an arduous task for the tenement mother.

When one reads the current crime statistics, it is difficult to convince oneself that the public playground system has, in any high [19] degree, compensated the city boy for the loss of the traditional playground—his own yard.

URBAN ISOLATION

There is another kind of defect in city life that is also due mainly to the multi-family dwelling. Urbanites may live close together physically and yet be miles apart socially. A striking instance was related to the writer some years ago by the late George B. Ford, eminent architect and city planner. Lunching one day at the Harvard Club, he fell into conversation with the man seated next to him at the "general" table. Ford had an enjoyable chat with his table neighbor and at the door they bade each other goodbye with the fervor of old friends, but immediately discovered that they were going in the same direction. Three times they started to part, only to find they were continuing the same way. Finally they entered the same apartment house, on different floors of which they had dwelt for a year and a half!

It is true that families living in the same apartment house do often become acquainted, although a large number actually do not. In the main we associate with those people who have ways like our own. If we put our waste paper in a bag, tie a string around its neck, and carefully place it out where the garbage collectors can get it, we are likely to feel suspicious of the housekeeper who puts her papers out in an open basket, leaving them to become the sport of idle winds. What people are like can easily in village districts be determined by the neighbors. The day and hour when the new family puts out its wash, how often the postman calls, what time the husband goes to work, how often a fire is built in the front room, who the callers are, the children's actions while at play, the way they are dressed for school, the hour the family retires, the hour it gets up—these will all be known in a single-family district.

Contrast that situation with the one that obtains in the ordinary apartment house. Here residents come and go for months without even seeing the people who live under the same roof. If the solitary dweller is held in bed by illness there is no signal—

such as absence of the smoke that usually issues from the chimney, to apprise neighbors and bring their willing aid. The very congestion of family compartments, their lack of a distinctive and personal atmosphere,[20] their anonymity—all these conditions are hostile to the neighborly life.

DECLINE IN URBAN PROPERTY VALUES

When tenants stay only a short time in a dwelling its income begins to shrink and its value as property to decline. Diminishing values in a residential district are evidence of incipient blight and a matter of serious concern to all taxpayers.

It is a significant fact that families in large numbers are abandoning the central portions of our large cities, and this movement is having heavy consequences. . . . [21]

THE HUMAN CONSEQUENCES

Is there any evidence that defects of city environment have affected the welfare of its residents? A person well equipped to answer this question is William F. Ogburn, director of the country-wide investigation of social trends. In *You and Machines,* he says:

The city has done things to us. More crimes are committed in the city than in the country. Not so many people get married. Families have [22] fewer children. More women are employed outside the home. Suicides are more frequent in cities. City people are more nervous and more of them go insane. There is more wealth in the cities, more conveniences. We don't know many of our neighbors in the cities. There is not so much gossip. There is more music, more books, more education. All these differences between city and country life, the machine has caused.[1]

Crimes, insanity, suicides! Have you ever gazed on a picture more grim? And within the same frame, more music, more books, more education! What supreme irony!

Ogburn says that this state of affairs is due to the machine.

[1] *You and Machines.* (Chicago, University of Chicago Press, 1934), p. 33.

Undoubtedly it is, but the statement needs explaining. Just standing by a motor-driven lathe all day would not ordinarily lead to murder. But the use of machines in industry leads workers to live crowded around the factory. It is a main cause for the piling up of populations in a congested city. The modern apartment house is the answer to the swollen demand for shelter near one's work.

When we look for the immediate cause of the conditions which Professor Ogburn enumerates, there is perhaps no more plausible one than the kind of home environment which we find in the large city. For thousands of youngsters the most exciting play opportunity which it provides is that of being chased by the "cop," a circumstance that certainly has a relationship to crime. The multi-family way of life has reduced the opportunities for vigorous games, for wholesome companionship, for securing neighborly help and advice. Does this fact help to explain the city's insanity and suicides? When the need of people is for warm personal sympathy, just how much consolation can they find in a rich supply of books and education?

The truth is that the natural nest of the human family is not merely six solid walls, but this box plus a surrounding medium through which sunshine and air can penetrate and in which social activities of vital import to its members can be carried on. When we consider how ruthlessly the city has disrupted the family nest, it is easy to understand the misery peculiar to present urban living.

In our search for a sound basis upon which to erect a national housing policy, we have now discovered a promising lead. To cure the present housing evils it is necessary to provide not only new [23] dwellings but new dwellings set in the environment that is required for the proper development of family life. . . . [24]

THE NEIGHBORHOOD UNIT FORMULA

. . . [T]hat area which embraces all the public facilities and conditions required by the average family for its comport and proper development within the vicinity of its dwelling . . . is called [in this study] the family's "neighborhood." The facilities it should contain are apparent after a moment's reflection. They include at the least (1) an elementary school; (2) retail stores; and (3) public recreation facilities.

The conditions surrounding the dwelling which a family most consciously seeks come under the head of residential character. This quality depends upon many and varied features. In an apartment house district, it may rest upon location of the site, architecture of the building, or the character of its courts. In a single-family district, harmony in the style of dwellings, amount of yard devoted to lawns and planting, and comprehensiveness and excellence of the entire development plan govern residential quality. Most important in this day of swift-moving automobiles is street safety. This can best be achieved by constructing a high-way system that reduces the points where pedestrians and vehicles cross paths and that keeps through traffic entirely out of a residential district.

The formula for a city neighborhood, then, must be such that when embodied in an actual development all its residents will be taken care of as respects the following points: They will all be within convenient access to an elementary school, adequate common play spaces, and retail shopping districts. Furthermore, their district will enjoy a distinctive character, because of qualities pertaining visibly to its terrain and structure, not the least of which will be a reduced risk from vehicular accidents.

NEIGHBORHOOD UNIT PRINCIPLES

A formula which, it is believed, meets all the above requirements was elaborated and published in volume 7—Neighborhood and [50] Community Planning—of the Regional Survey of New York and Its Environs.[2] In that publication, "the neighborhood unit—a scheme of arrangement for the family-life community" is set forth in detail. Essentially, it consists of six principles:

  1. *Size.* A residential unit development should provide

[2] Perry, Clarence Arthur, The Neighborhood Unit, Monograph 1 in vol. 7, Neighborhood and Community Planning, of the Regional Survey of New York and Its Environs. Published by Committee on Regional Plan of New York and Its Environs, New York, 1929. (To be found in most public libraries.)

Photo by the editor

Clarence A. Perry's Idea of a Neighborhood Realized at Radburn (at Fair Lawn, near Passaic) in New Jersey. In this photograph, taken in October, 1961, children of the small Radburn community play on the large inner lawn enclosed on three sides by private homes. The neighborhood school building is out of sight to the right, about a two-minute walk from the scene shown here.

housing for that population for which one elementary school is ordinarily required, its actual area depending upon its population density.

2. *Boundaries.* The unit should be bounded on all sides by arterial streets, sufficiently wide to facilitate its by-passing, instead of penetration, by through traffic.

3. *Open Spaces.* A system of small parks and recreation spaces, planned to meet the needs of the particular neighborhood, should be provided.

4. *Institution Sites.* Sites for the school and other institutions having service spheres coinciding with the limits of the unit should be suitably grouped about a central point, or common.

5. *Local Shops.* One or more shopping districts, adequate for the population to be served, should be laid out in the circumference of the unit, preferably at traffic junctions and adjacent to similar districts of adjoining neighborhoods.

6. *Internal Street System.* The unit should be provided with a special street system, each highway being proportioned to its probable traffic load, and the street net as a whole being designed to facilitate circulation within the unit and to discourage its use by through traffic.

The six principles above enumerated do not constitute the description of a real estate development or of urban neighborhoods in general. Together they do not make a plan. They are principles which a professional planner—if so disposed—can observe in the making of a development plan. If they are complied with, there [51] will result a neighborhood community in which the fundamental needs of family life will be met more completely, it is believed, than they are now by the usual residential sections in cities and villages.

In this scheme, the neighborhood is regarded both as a unit of a larger whole and as an entity. It is not held, however, that in an ideal city plan the whole municipality could be laid out in neighborhood units. It is recognized that a city is composed of various areas each of which is devoted to a dominant function. There are industrial districts, business districts, and large areas used as parks and cemeteries. A neighborhood unit would have local retail business areas, but besides these there would also be downtown or main business districts, and subsidiary business centers serving large sections.

It is apparent that the unit scheme can be fully applied only to *new* developments. Thus it is limited to the unbuilt areas around the urban fringe and to central deteriorated sections, large enough and sufficiently blighted to warrant reconstruction. Nor is it expected that the whole of a residential section, in any practical plan, could be laid out in unit districts. There would generally be irregular areas set off by main highways, railways, streams, quarries, or parks, of a size or location that would make them unsuited for inclusion in a unit plan. . . . [52]

THE REGIONAL PLAN OF NEW YORK AND ITS ENVIRONS

. . . On May 10, 1922, it was formally announced that the Russell Sage Foundation would promote a "Regional Plan of New York and Its Environs" and that definite studies in that field had been in progress for more than a year. In the final setup of this project the writer, by virtue of his connection with the Recreation Department of the Foundation, became a member of the Social Division of the Regional Plan. . . . [208]

It was evident that a neighborhood playground could not be treated by itself. Consideration had to be given to the other elements of a neighborhood. But what were these and how should they be arranged? In a word, if one had the wealth of a Midas and the power of a Fascist dictator, how would one build an urban neighborhood?

FOREST HILLS GARDENS

The answer to this broad question came to the writer in a simple but unexpected way. When he had first reflected upon the problems put to him by the Regional Plan it had looked as if answers could be found only by wide surveys and much investigation. The solution of the problem, however, was near at hand. He himself already lived in a highly satisfactory neighborhood and had watched it grow ever since 1912, when with his family he had moved into it. He had only to analyze the factors responsible for its success and reduce them to general principles.

The development referred to is Forest Hills Gardens, located in [209] the Borough of Queens, New York City, which had been promoted and financed by the Russell Sage Foundation as a residential development modeled after developments that had been impressive in England. Frederick Law Olmsted had laid out these streets and done the landscaping, while Grosvenor Atterbury was the architect in charge of design and building construction. The Foundation believed that the development would provide healthful and attractive homes to many people and demonstrate that tasteful surroundings and open spaces would pay in suburban housing. It hoped to encourage imitation. The project was organized therefore as a commercial rather than philanthropic enterprise.

When the writer analyzed the Gardens development into its essential elements, he found that they constituted the main principles of an ideal neighborhood. . . . [211]

FUNCTION OF THE FACE-TO-FACE COMMUNITY

In the opening chapter attention was called to the difficulty with which the neighborly atmosphere, common to the long-settled village, is reproduced in cities, particularly in multi-family districts. Vast numbers of urban dwellers are not acquainted with the people living next door. When, however, residents are brought together through the use of common recreational facilities, they come to know one another and friendly relations ensue. Existing developments with neighborhood unit features have consistently produced the face-to-face social condition, and that is the reason for introducing the subject in the discussion.

Certain individuals with adequate mental and social resources and craving for independence object to living in a state in which their daily comings and goings are carried on under the scrutiny of neighbors. No doubt many rural persons with this view have fled to the city for the sake of its anonymity. There is evidence, however, that the face-to-face condition is a normal feature of the environment of society and that man tends to degenerate when it is missing. Just what this social mechanism is, how it acts, and how far back in human history it goes, can best be revealed to us by psychologists and students of society. . . . [215]

So far in this section we have dealt with the effects of environment only in bringing about conformity with the social code. An important aspect of life, it is true, but a negative one. We might have a state in which there was never any infraction of the law— where nobody ever used a knife except to cut bread or meat crosswise [219]—and yet have a dull and unprogressive society. That which makes existence bright, exciting, and colorful is variation, not conformity; difference, rather than sameness. When an individual rises to a hitherto unattained professional height, achieves an unexcelled proficiency in an art, or masters a personal situation of unusual poignancy—then he has made progress and life becomes richer than it was. In these positive aspects of the growth of personality the neighborhood community also plays a unique and important role.

In the case of the actor, musician, painter, or playwright individual development depends largely upon the environment in which fate has placed him. His peculiar talent never emerges full blown. The youngster's ability to sketch or fiddle may seem only mildly significant to his immediate family. In less well-to-do homes it is generally when persons outside the home circle begin to comment upon a boy's ability that his elders are impressed and consideration is given to ways of providing him with further training. Actors and actresses often first discover their histrionic abilities in some chance local production, and many an individual with latent dramatic talent has never discovered it at all, or not until it was too late to develop it. Every art that entertains requires an audience in all the stages of development. The critical period for the novice is usually the stage between fireside appreciation and professional box-office recognition. It is that gap in one's development that a neighborhood audience is so well constituted to fill.

The artist, however, is not the only type whose personality is nourished by a primary group environment. An individual aspiring to any kind of public leadership can find in the organized activities of a neighborhood community center many opportunities for learning and practice, chances to speak in public, to serve on committees, to organize the programs of formal meetings. If he wants to promote a cause he can there acquire the art of propagandism. Young men, fresh from college, who look forward to a public career can begin their apprenticeship at once in the neighborhood community. Any business man occupying a position in which the ability to organize entertainments would be a valuable asset can attain that gift easily by joining the executive board of a community center. The ease with which a novice, desiring to pursue an evening vocational [220] course, can join with others in getting an instructor and forming a class has already been mentioned.

In the avocational sphere, there are also many opportunities. Any pursuit that is furthered by joining with others, whether it be learning a foreign language, studying photography, making stamp collections, practicing tap dancing, trimming hats, or playing badminton—can be followed with greater facility in a district where neighbors know one another, and there is a common structure in which they can meet. The "friction of distance" that takes the energy out of so many citywide societies of special interests is absent.

It is commonly believed that it was the machine which dehumanized the city. If so, a kind of poetic justice would be served if now the machine, in the process of rebuilding the city, should restore its friendly atmosphere. [221]

Clarence S. Stein_____
RADBURN, NEW JERSEY (1928–1933)
GREENBELT, MARYLAND (1935–1937)

Clarence S. Stein, *Toward New Towns for America* (Liverpool, University Press of Liverpool, 1951).*

RADBURN

The Site

After examining some 50 possible sites [for Radburn, we chose] a large tract of undeveloped fertile farm land in the Borough of Fairlawn, New Jersey, only sixteen miles from New York. . . . There was an area sufficient for three neighborhoods, for a population of about 25,000.[39]

Elements of the Radburn Plan

'The Radburn Idea,' to answer the enigma 'How to live with the auto': or, if you will, 'How to live in spite of it,' met these difficulties with a radical revision of relation of houses, roads, paths, gardens, parks, blocks, and local neighborhoods. For this purpose it used these elements:

1. THE SUPERBLOCK in place of the characteristic narrow, rectangular block.

2. SPECIALIZED ROADS PLANNED AND BUILT FOR ONE USE INSTEAD OF FOR ALL USES: service lanes for direct access to buildings; secondary collector roads around superblocks; main through roads, linking the traffic of various sections, neighborhoods and districts; express highways or parkways, for connection

---

* Reprinted by permission of the author and the Liverpool University Press, copyright 1957 by the author.

with outside communities. (Thus differentiating between movement, collection, service, parking, and visiting).

3. COMPLETE SEPARATION OF PEDESTRIAN AND AUTOMOBILE, or as complete separation as possible. Walks and paths routed at different places from roads and at different levels when they cross. For this purpose overpasses and underpasses were used.[42]

4. HOUSES TURNED AROUND. Living and sleeping rooms facing toward gardens and parks; service rooms toward access roads.

5. PARK AS BACKBONE of the neighborhood. Large open areas in the center of superblocks, joined together as a continuous park. . . .[44]

NEIGHBORHOODS.—At Radburn, I believe, the modern neighborhood conception was applied for the first time and, in part, realized in the form that is now generally accepted.[47]

The neighborhoods were laid out with a radius of half a mile, centering on elementary schools and playgrounds. Each was to have its own shopping center. The size of the neighborhood was determined by the number of children cared for by a single school. . . .

The neighborhoods were planned for 7,500 to 10,000—this to depend on the most desirable number of pupils in a school—a matter that was then,[49] and I believe still is, open to a wide diversity of opinions. . . .[50]

How the Radburn Plan Worked

Those who live in Radburn and have lived there for any great length of time find that it has served its objective of making home and community life more reposeful, pleasant and safe— and particularly safe for children. The physical plan of central parks, superblocks without through traffic, safe walks, houses facing on gardens and parks along with the convenience of service have, they find, given them a quality of living that, as medium-income folks, they could not find elsewhere. . . .[51]

GREENBELT, MARYLAND

In the end [three] towns were constructed: [Greenbelt, Maryland, 13 miles from the center of the National Capital;] Greendale, Wisconsin, seven miles from the business center of Milwaukee; and Greenhills, Ohio, five miles north of Cincinnati.

Although these three are among America's outstanding demonstrations of New Towns, it must be admitted that they all missed out on the score of industry. Cincinnati, Milwaukee, and Washington have grown as centers of industry, business or government. But the Greenbelt Towns have not yet drawn in factories or offices. They have continued in the role of suburbs, near [103] but yet too expensively far from employment. All this shows the difficulty and the importance of co-ordinating broad physical planning with industrial planning.

In the location of the fourth project, Warren Vinton did prove to be an industrial prophet; the New Brunswick area of New Jersey has of late had a fantastic industrial growth. The town of Greenbrook, of which Henry Wright was planner and Albert Mayer and Henry Churchill the architects, would probably have been a complete garden city. But it was never built because of local opposition and the threat of court action. . . .[104]

Three Basic Planning Ideas

The Greenbelt Towns are the first experiments in the combined development of the three basic ideas of the modern community: the Garden City, the Radburn Idea, and the Neighborhood Unit. These three conceptions in greater or less degree from the essential basis of the plans for New Towns that are being discussed, planned, or constructed in various parts of the Western World. In Sweden, in Poland, in Great Britain, the planners are starting out on the great voyage of discovery of the form and operation of new communities that will fit today's living, practically, economically, and at the same time spaciously, beautifully, and safely.

For over a decade Greendale, Greenhills, and Greenbelt have in embryo form been trying out the various elements of the evolving city. All too little is known of how these ideas really work. . . .[106]

The General Plan

If you are fortunate you will first see Greenbelt from the air while flying between New York and Washington. The town is formed in the shape of a graceful crescent set on a vast background of green. For a moment its attractive flowing curves remind you of the Crescent at Bath, England. But the Greenbelt crescent is much bigger and bolder; it is much freer—though no less rhythmic. It is not so monumentally formal. The Bath crescent is a closed wall of masonry with landscape foreground and background; at Greenbelt most of the principal buildings are at right angles rather than parallel to the great curve.

The Greenbelt crescent is marked mainly by the graceful sweep of the two main highways, and the shade and shadow of lower land that surrounds the natural plateau that suggested and gave it its form.

The essential shape of the Greenbelt town plan was indicated by nature. Here, as in many other great plans, the planners' job was primarily to discover, not invent. As Benton MacKaye says:

'Planning is a scientific charting and picturing of the thing . . . which man desires and which the eternal forces will permit. The basic achievement of planning is to make potentialities visible . . . Planning is revelation.' [1]

The planners of Greenbelt revealed the potentialities of the great curved plateau as a beautiful place for good living. . . .

The inner crescent sweeps round the spacious community center, some 1,500 feet wide and, including the athletic field, quite as deep. This forms the heart of Greenbelt. Here is the focus for the common life of the town, and here, in its physical center, are located in logical and beautiful arrangement the various elements for community activities. Here is the seat of government and management; the focus of cultural, religious, and educational life; the main recreational and entertainment center; and the market place. [109]

. . . The space is . . . divided into superblocks of about 14 acres each. . . .

[1] *The New Exploration,* pp. 147 and 188.

The People

The first settlers of Greenbelt moved in as the homes were completed between October 1937 and the summer of 1938. . . .

Greenbelt started as a young community in every way; fathers and mothers were practically all under 30, and most of the children, although two or three to a family, were still under school age.

An effort was made to populate the town with an average cross-section of residents. Proportions found in the nearby District of Columbia were applied. Among the first residents, therefore, 70 per cent of the wage-earners were government workers, 30 per cent non-government; 30 per cent were Catholic, 7 per cent Jewish, and 63 per cent Protestant.

The families were fairly homogeneous in respect to education. Most were high-school graduates, a small percentage professionally trained, and a small proportion had had little schooling. The government workers represented the white-collar clerical group; the other 30 per cent were professional or manual workers. . . .[110]

Greenbelt as a Garden City

Rex Tugwell and his associates were apparently more deeply influenced by Ebenezer Howard's Garden City than any other idea in their conception of the New Towns they proposed to create. To what extent was Howard's program realized? What were the causes and what the effects of the variations from Howard's conception?

The accepted definition of a Garden City is:

'A garden city is a town planned for industry and healthy living, of a size that makes possible a full measure of social life, but no larger, surrounded by a permanent rural belt, the whole of the land being in public ownership, or held in trust for the community.'

PLANNED FOR LIVING. All of the Greenbelt Towns are exceptionally well planned for healthy living. They meet the requirements of good living in these days, and they do it at a moderate

Some thirty-five years after Ebenezer Howard's little book: **Greenbelt, Maryland.** No
is toward the top of the photograph, somewhat to the left. A library, elementary scho

Fairchild Aerial Surveys, Inc.

mmunity center, swimming pool, youth center, nursery school, and recreation field are
ated within the horseshoe curve. The Washington-Baltimore Boulevard lies to the west.

cost, so that people of limited means can secure these advantages. That they enjoy them is attested by the inquiry that we made at Greenbelt and by similar investigations in the other two towns.

PLANNED FOR INDUSTRY they have not been—and none of the three towns have had any industry worth considering within its boundaries. Although all of them were located in regions in which employment has grown, they have all had serious difficulties because of travel to work—caused by time consumed and the cost of transportation. . . .[113]

PERMANENT GREENBELT. Greenbelts have continued to form an essential part of the three towns since the beginning. . . . In this tract to create a community, protected by an encircling greenbelt . . .' formed part of the statement of the objectives of the Resettlement program, which also proposed 'a system of rural economy co-ordinate with the land use plan for the rural portions of the tract surrounding the suburban community.' The importance of the greenbelts was accentuated by the names of the towns. In all three towns there is still a predominance of open land; the developed areas form a very small part of the total tracts.

In Greenbelt the land has not been used for agricultural purposes, unless you call the allotment gardens agriculture. These have been located in five places, more or less near the residential areas. Here 500 families have grown food on 50-feet x 50-feet plots. Up to a short time ago these were ploughed and fertilized by the town for a charge of $1 each.

The two other towns have been much more successful in using their open land for farming. At Greenhills about 4,000 acres are in agricultural use. There are 34 old farms used as suburban residences with one to 20 acres each, but [115] the greater part of the land is occupied by 28 full-time farmers, whose products are chiefly dairy. Although a farmers' market was originally proposed, the dairymen have tended almost entirely to market their milk, eggs, poultry, and vegetables in the bigger center at Cincinnati.

At Greendale there are about 3,000 acres in 18 farms or dairies of 100 to 240 acres each, as well as rural homes and 25 acres of allotment gardens.

In Greendale and Greenhills the unity of town and country

has been of mutual advantage to the urban and rural population. Farms, dairies, and forests form a familiar part of the daily life of the town children and their parents. Town and farm folks have come to know each other as neighbors, friends and associates. They gather together in town meetings, at church, social parties, and lectures, at the movies, the co-operative stores, or, in Greendale, at the tavern. This association has broken down barriers of misunderstanding between farmer and factory workers at Greendale, and in Greenhills.

At Greenbelt the great open area that surrounds it has served for recreation and free contact with the out-of-doors, rather than agriculture. Groups of little ones explore it without restraint; they are pioneers and Indians in their own wilderness. In the picturesque rugged section to the south, areas have been set aside for both Boy Scouts and Girl Scouts. On weekends the whole family is united in hiking and picnicking in the woods. At the side of the lake are picnic tables and benches as well as fireplaces on which to prepare hot meals. At the lake, young and old fish for striped bass. From the lake can be heard the crack of rifles from the nearby Greenbelt Gun Club. Although swimming in the lake has been temporarily prohibited because of lack of sufficient town funds to pay guards, sunbathing and boating are favorite forms of relaxation. There is horseback riding also, for a more limited number who rent their horses from nearby stables.

Large portions of the surrounding greenbelt at Greendale and Greenhills have been dedicated to permanent use as parks and recreation areas, by putting them in the hands of the County Park Departments. At Greenbelt this method of perpetuating the protection is not yet accomplished. However, the National Capital Park and Planning Commission is considering a large tract in the southern portion as a regional park. This land, which is in large part rough and well-wooded, and cut by a meandering brook some 50 feet below the higher plateaus, would make an excellent semi-wilderness recreation area. As a public park it would be a permanent protective greenbelt to the south, as the National Agricultural Center is along the northern boundary. The narrow green natural wall along the future Washington-Baltimore Superhighway, with only one point of access to Greenbelt, will protect the eastern boundary. Only a park to the west is required to complete the greenbelt. . . .[116]

The Neighborhood Unit

At the present time the neighborhood unit is generally accepted as a basis for the purposeful design of new communities. But the Neighborhood less consciously influenced the planning of the Greenbelt Towns than the Garden City or the Radburn Idea. Yet the three towns are among the best applications of the principles laid down by Clarence Perry, which we would have carried out at Radburn, had its growth not been stunted.

Each Greenbelt Town in the beginning was, in effect, a single neighborhood. The focus of each is a planned neighborhood center consisting of school, community buildings, shopping center, government and management offices, and principal recreation activities. They are each built around such a planned center. However, only in Greenbelt have we an opportunity to study the effect of growth and changing size on the neighborhood. . . .[129]

An Unfinished Story

The Greenbelt Towns are often referred to as *demonstrations*. Perhaps it would be better to say that they have been *indicators*. They have indicated that certain unusual policies and practices in the planning, organization and operation of communities are both attractive and highly practical. They have indicated very strongly that certain development methods and forms that have been followed in the past are obsolete, unnecessarily wasteful and ugly. One illustration is the contrast between the concentrated Greenbelt shopping center and nearby roadside sprawl.

Perhaps the co-operative shopping center is the appropriate place to leave Greenbelt. For physically this marketplace, with the nearby related community buildings and recreation fields, is the heart of Greenbelt, and the dominant spirit of Greenbelt is that of doing things together—or co-operation. . . [160]

Lewis Mumford_____

REGIONS—TO LIVE IN

Lewis Mumford, "Regions—To Live In," *Survey Graphic*, LIV (May 1, 1925).

The hope of the city lies outside itself. Focus your attention on the cities—in which more than half of us live—and the future is dismal. But lay aside the magnifying glass which reveals, for example, the hopelessness of Broadway and Forty-second Street, take up a reducing glass and look at the entire region in which New York lies. The city falls into focus. Forests in the hill-counties, water-power in the mid-state valleys, farmland in Connecticut, cranberry bogs in New Jersey, enter the picture. To think of all these acres as merely tributary to New York, to trace and strengthen the lines of the web in which the spider-city sits unchallenged, is again to miss the clue. But to think of the region as a whole and the city merely as one of its parts—that may hold promise.

Not merely a wistful hope of a better environment, but sheer necessity, leads us thus to change our approach to the problem. For cities, as the foregoing articles show, are becoming too big; as they grow they fall behind in the barest decencies of housing; they become more expensive to operate, more difficult to police, more burdensome to work in, and more impossible to escape from even in the hours of leisure that we achieve. The forces that have created the great cities make permanent improvement within them hopeless; our efforts to plan them lag pitifully behind the need when indeed they do not foster the very growth that is becoming insupportable. We are providing, in Professor Geddes' sardonic phrase, more and more of worse and worse.

Not so with regional planning. Regional planning asks not how wide an area can be brought under the aegis of the

metropolis, but how the population and civic facilities can
be distributed so as to promote and stimulate a vivid, creative life throughout a whole region—a region being any geographic area that possesses a certain unity of climate, soil,
vegetation, industry and culture. The regionalist attempts to
plan such an area so that all its sites and resources, from forest
to city, from highland to water level, may be soundly developed,
and so that the population will be distributed so as to utilize,
rather than to nullify or destroy, its natural advantages. It sees
people, industry and the land as a single unit. Instead of trying,
by one desperate dodge or another, to make life a little more
tolerable in the congested centers, it attempts to determine what
sort of equipment will be needed for the new centers. It does not
aim at urbanizing automatically the whole available countryside;
it aims equally at ruralizing the stony wastes of our cities. In
a sense that will become clear to the reader as he follows the
later articles in this number, the civic objective of the regional
planning movement is summed up with peculiar accuracy in
the concept of the garden-city.

There are a hundred approaches to regional planning; it
brings to a head, in fact, a number of movements and methods
which have been gathering momentum during the last twenty
or thirty years. But each approach has this in common with
the others; it attempts to promote a fuller kind of life, at every
point in the region. No form of industry and no type of city
are tolerable that take the joy out of life. Communities in
which courtship is furtive, in which babies are an unwelcome
handicap, in which education, lacking the touch of nature and
of real occupations, hardens into a blank routine, in which people
achieve adventure only on wheels and happiness only by having
their minds "taken off" their daily lives—communities like these
do not sufficiently justify our modern advances in science and
invention.

Now the impulse that makes the prosperous minority build
country estates, that causes the well-to-do professional man to
move out into the suburbs, the impulse that is driving the family
of small means out upon the open road, there to build primitive
bungalows regardless of discomfort and dangers to health, seems
to us to be a pretty common one. These people are in the

vanguard of a general effort to get a little joy back into life. At present this exodus is undertaken blindly and, as Mr. Wright shows, all its promises are [151] illusory, since a helter-skelter development such as is now going on in the countryside around our big cities promises only to spoil the landscape without permanently satisfying the hungry urbanites. The community planning movement in America, and the garden-cities movement in England are definite attempts to build up a more exhilarating kind of environment—not as a temporary haven of refuge but as a permanent seat of life and culture, urban in its advantages, permanently rural in its situation. This movement toward garden cities is a movement towards a higher type of civilization than that which has created our present congested centers. It involves a change in aim as well as a change of place. Our present congested districts are the results of the crude applications of the mechanical and mathematical sciences to social development; our garden cities represent fuller development of the more humane arts and sciences—biology and medicine and psychiatry and education and architecture. As modern engineering has made Chicago or New York physically superior to Athens, whilst the labyrinth of subways and high buildings is more deficient for complete living than a Stone Age cave, so we may expect that the cities of tomorrow will not merely embody all that is good in our modern mechanical developments, but also all that was left out in this one-sided existence, all the things that fifth century Athens or thirteenth century Florence, for all their physical crudity, possessed.

On its economic side, this movement towards a fuller human environment goes hand in hand with what has been aptly called the industrial counter revolution. For a hundred years in America business has been concentrating financial resources, concentrating factories and urban districts, attempting to create material prosperity by producing goods which could be quickly "turned over." The paper values have increased enormously even in the brief period from 1900 to 1920; but most statisticians seem agreed that the real wages of the majority of workers have remained nearly stationary. The new industrial revolution is an attempt to spread the real income of industry by decentralizing industry, by removing some of the burden of the business overhead and sales-promotion, ground rents in congested districts, and so forth. Far-sighted industrialists like Dennison and Ford are already planning this move, and business men like Edward Filene feel that business is at an impasse unless decentralization is followed as "The Way Out." Regional planning is an attempt to turn industrial decentralization—the effort to make the industrial mechanism work better—to permanent social uses. It is an attempt to realize the gains of modern industry in permanent houses, gardens, parks, playgrounds and community institutions.

Finally, regional planning is the New Conservation—the conservation of human values hand in hand with natural resources. Regional planning sees that the depopulated countryside and the congested city are intimately related; it sees that we waste vast quantities of time and energy by ignoring the potential resources of a region, that is, by forgetting all that lies between the terminal points and junctions of our great railroads. Permanent agriculture instead of land-skinning, permanent forestry instead of timber mining, permanent human communities, dedicated to life, liberty and the pursuit of happiness, instead of camps and squatter-settlements, and to stable building, instead of the scantling and falsework of our "go-ahead" communities— all this is embodied in regional planning.

It follows pretty plainly from this summary that, unlike city planning, regional planning is not merely the concern of a profession: it is a mode of thinking and a method of procedure, and the regional plan itself is only a minor technical instrument in carrying out its aims. The planners of the Ontario power project are genuine regional planners; Mr. Ford in his schemes for industrial decentralization is a regional planner; the Pennsylvania State Power Commission, as Mr. Bruère makes clear, is handling an essential element in regional planning. The Chicago Regional Planning Commission with its emphasis on transportation, power and industrial development over wide areas, the Sage Foundation Study in New York with parts of three states included in its "environs" mark the break with our old method of treating the city as a unit by itself. The New York State Housing and Regional Planning Commission has made a series of important preliminary studies which radically cut loose from the older tradition and employ the whole commonwealth rather than the large city as their base.

Moreover the aim of regional planning is not confined to those who are interested in the development of industries and resources. The cultural forces that have begun to challenge the dominance of the big city are plainly working in the same direction. So the little theater movement, by building local centers of culture instead of waiting patiently for the crumbs dropped from our metropolitan table, is essential to regionalism; and in the same way our new experimental schools, which have showed the rich educational opportunities that come from exploring and utilizing the whole living environment rather than sticking to the pallid routine of books, find themselves handicapped in the existing centers and demand a new environment patterned on the human scale, in which the school may work intimately in touch with the home and with industry and with the surrounding world of nature.

In sum, regional planning does not mean the planning of big cities beyond their present areas; it means the reinvigoration and rehabilitation of whole regions so that the products of culture and civilization, instead of being confined to a prosperous minority in the congested centers, shall be available to everyone at every point in a region where the physical basis for a cultivated life can be laid down. The technical means of achieving this new distribution of power and culture are at hand. The question before us is whether the automatic operation of physical and financial forces is to burke our rising demand for a more vital and happy kind of existence, or whether, by coordinating our efforts and imaginatively grasping our opportunity, we can remold our institutions so as to promote a regional development— development that will eliminate our enormous economic wastes, give a new life to stable agriculture, set down fresh communities planned on a human scale, and, above all, restore a little happiness and freedom in places where these things have been pretty well wrung out. This is a question that cuts diametrically across a large part of our current political and social problems; some of these it places in a new light, and some of them it makes meaningless. Regionalism or super-congestion? Will man in America learn the art of mastering and ordering his environment, to promote his own fuller purposes, or will he be mastered by his environment, and presently, as in Samuel Butler's picture in Erewhon, or in Zamiatin's We, find himself without any purposes other than those of the Machine? [152]

WHAT IS A CITY?

Lewis Mumford, "What Is a City?" *Architectural Record*, LXXXII (November, 1937).*

Most of our housing and city planning has been handicapped because those who have undertaken the work have had no clear notion of the social functions of the city. They sought to derive these functions from a cursory survey of the activities and interests of the contemporary urban scene. And they did not, apparently, suspect that there might be gross deficiencies, misdirected efforts, mistaken expenditures here that would not be set straight by merely building sanitary tenements or straightening out and widening irregular streets.

The city as a purely physical fact has been subject to numerous investigations. But what is the city as a social institution? The earlier answers to these questions, in Aristotle, Plato, and the Utopian writers from Sir Thomas More to Robert Owen, have been on the whole more satisfactory than those of the more systematic sociologists: most contemporary treatises on "urban sociology" in America throw no important light upon the problem.

One of the soundest definitions of the city was that framed by John Stow, an honest observer of Elizabethan London, who said: "Men are congregated into cities and commonwealths for honesty and utility's sake, these shortly be the commodities that do come by cities, commonalties, and corporations. First, men by this nearness of conversation are withdrawn from barbarous fixity and force, to certain mildness of manners, and to humanity and justice. . . . Good behavior is yet called *urbanitas*

° Reprinted by permission of the author and *Architectural Record*.

because it is rather found in cities than elsewhere. In sum, by often hearing, men be better persuaded in religion, and for that they live in the eyes of others, they be by example the more easily trained to justice, and by shamefastness restrained from injury.

"And whereas commonwealths and kingdoms cannot have, next after God, any surer foundation than the love and good will of one man towards another, that also is closely bred and maintained in cities, where men by mutual society and companying together, do grow to alliances, commonalties, and corporations."

It is with no hope of adding much to the essential insight of this description of the urban process that I would sum up the sociological concept of the city in the following terms:

The city is a related collection of primary groups and purposive associations: the first, like family and neighborhood, are common to all communities, while the second are especially characteristic of city life. These varied groups support themselves through economic organizations that are likewise of a more or less corporate, or at least publicly regulated, character; and they are all housed in permanent structures, within a relatively limited area. The essential physical means of a city's existence are the fixed site, the durable shelter, the permanent facilities for assembly, interchange, and storage; the essential social means are the social division of labor, which serves not merely the economic life but the cultural processes. The city in its complete sense, then, is a geographic plexus, an economic organization, an institutional process, a theater of social action, and an esthetic symbol of collective unity. The city fosters art and *is* art; the city creates the theater and *is* the theater. It is in the city, the city as theater, that man's more purposive activities are focused, and work out, through conflicting and cooperating personalities, events, groups, into more significant culminations.

Without the social drama that comes into existence through the focusing and intensification of group activity there is not a single function performed in the city that could not be performed —and has not in fact been performed—in the open country. The physical organization of the city may deflate this drama or make it frustrate; or it may, through the deliberate efforts of art, politics, and education, make the drama more richly significant, as a stage-set, well-designed, intensifies and underlines the gestures of the actors and the action of the play. It is not for nothing that men have dwelt so often on the beauty or the ugliness of cities: these attributes qualify men's social activities. And if there is a deep reluctance on the part of the true city dweller to leave his cramped quarters for the physically more benign environment of a suburb—even a model garden suburb!—his instincts are usually justified: in its various and many-sided life, in its very opportunities for social disharmony and conflict, the city creates drama: the suburb lacks it.

One may describe the city, in its social aspect,[59] as a special framework directed toward the creation of differentiated opportunities for a common life and a significant collective drama. As indirect forms of association, with the aid of signs and symbols and specialized organizations, supplement direct face-to-face intercourse, the personalities of the citizens themselves become many-faceted: they reflect their specialized interests, their more intensively trained aptitudes, their finer discriminations and selections: the personality no longer presents a more or less unbroken traditional face to reality as a whole. Here lies the possibility of personal disintegration; and here lies the need for reintegration through wider participation in a concrete and visible collective whole. What men cannot imagine as a vague formless society, they can live through and experience as citizens in a city. Their unified plans and buildings become a symbol of their social relatedness; and when the physical environment itself becomes disordered and incoherent, the social functions that it harbors become more difficult to express.

One further conclusion follows from this concept of the city: social facts are primary, and the physical organization of a city, its industries and its markets, its lines of communication and traffic, must be subservient to its social needs. Whereas in the development of the city during the last century we expanded the physical plant recklessly and treated the essential social nucleus, the organs of government and education and social service, as mere afterthought, today we must treat the social nucleus as the essential element in every valid city plan: the spotting and inter-relationship of schools, libraries, theaters, community centers, is the first task in defining the urban neighborhood and laying down the outlines of an integrated city.

In giving this sociological answer to the question: What is a City? one has likewise provided the clue to a number of important other questions. Above all, one has the criterion for a clear decision as to what is the desirable size of a city—or may a city perhaps continue to grow until a single continuous urban area might cover half the American continent, with the rest of the world tributary to this mass? From the standpoint of the purely physical organization of urban utilities—which is almost the only matter upon which metropolitan planners in the past have concentrated—this latter process might indeed go on indefinitely. But if the city is a theater of social activity, and if its needs are defined by the opportunities it offers to differentiated social groups, acting through a specific nucleus of civic institutes and associations, definite limitations on size follow from this fact.

In one of Le Corbusier's early schemes for an ideal city, he chose three million as the number to be accommodated: the number was roughly the size of the urban aggregate of Paris, but that hardly explains why it should have been taken as a norm for a more rational type of city development. If the size of an urban unit, however, is a function of its productive organization and its opportunities for active social intercourse and culture, certain definite facts emerge as to adequate ratio of population to the process to be served. Thus, at the present level of culture in America, a million people are needed to support a university. Many factors may enter which will change the size of both the university and the population base; nevertheless one can say provisionally that if a million people are needed to provide a sufficient number of students for a university, then two million people should have two universities. One can also say that, other things being equal, five million people will not provide a more effective university than one million people would. The alternative to recognizing these ratios is to keep on overcrowding and overbuilding a few existing institutions, thereby limiting, rather than expanding, their genuine educational facilities.

What is important is not an absolute figure as to population

or area: although in certain aspects of life, such as the size of
city that is capable of reproducing itself through natural fertility, one can already lay down such figures. What is more
important is to *express size always as a function of the social
relationships to be served.* There is an optimum numerical size,
beyond which each further increment of inhabitants creates difficulties out of all proportion to the benefits. There is also an optimum area of [60] expansion, beyond which further urban growth
tends to paralyze rather than to further important social relationships. Rapid means of transportation have given a regional area,
with a radius of from forty to a hundred miles, the unity that
London and Hampstead had before the coming of the underground railroad. But the activities of small children are still
bounded by a walking distance of about a quarter of a mile; and
for men to congregate freely and frequently in neighborhoods
the maximum distance means nothing, although it may properly
define the area served for a selective minority by a university, a
central reference library, or a completely equipped hospital.

The area of potential urban settlement has been vastly increased by the motor car and the airplane; but the necessity for
solid contiguous growth, for the purposes of intercourse, has in
turn been lessened by the telephone and the radio. In the Middle
Ages a distance of less than a half a mile from the city's center
usually defined its utmost limits. The block-by-block accretion of
the big city, along its corridor avenues, is in all important respects a denial of the vastly improved type of urban grouping
that our fresh inventions have brought in. For all occasional
types of intercourse, the region is the unit of social life: but
the region cannot function effectively, as a well-knit unit, if
the entire area is densely filled with people—since their very
presence will clog its arteries of traffic and congest its social
facilities.

Limitations on size, density, and area are absolutely necessary
to effective social intercourse; and they are therefore the most
important instruments of rational economic and civic planning.
The unwillingness in the past to establish such limits has been
due mainly to two facts: the assumption that all upward changes
in magnitude were signs of progress and automatically "good
for business," and the belief that such limitations were essentially

No doubt the very idea of a city-centered region is clarified and strengthened through aerial photography. A great many relationships of city to country are suggested by this view of **Buffalo, New York.**

arbitrary, in that they proposed to "decrease economic opportunity"—that is, opportunity for profiting by congestion—and to halt the inevitable course of change. Both these objections are superstitious.

Limitations on height are now common in American cities; drastic limitations on density are the rule in all municipal housing estates in England: that which could not be done has *been* done. Such limitations do not obviously limit the population itself: they merely give the planner and administrator the opportunity to multiply the number of centers in which the population is housed, instead of permitting a few existing centers to aggrandize themselves on a monopolistic pattern.

These limitations are necessary to break up the functionless, hypertrophied urban masses of the past. Under this mode of planning, the planner proposes to replace the "mononucleated city," as Professor Warren Thompson has called it, with a new type of "polynucleated city," in which a cluster of communities, adequately spaced and bounded, shall do duty for the badly organized mass city. Twenty such cities, in a region whose environment and whose resources were adequately planned, would have all the benefits of a metropolis that held a million people, without its ponderous disabilities: its capital frozen into unprofitable utilities, and its land values congealed at levels that stand in the way of effective adaptation to new needs.

Mark the change that is in process today. The emerging sources of power, transport, and communication do not follow the old highway network at all. Giant power strides over the hills,[61] ignoring the limitations of wheeled vehicles; the airplane, even more liberated, flies over swamps and mountains, and terminates its journey, not on an avenue, but in a field. Even the highway for fast motor transportation abandons the pattern of the horse-and-buggy era. The new highways, like those of New Jersey and Westchester, to mention only examples drawn locally, are based more or less on a system definitively formulated by Benton Mac-Kaye in his various papers on the Townless Highway. The most complete plans form an independent highway network, isolated both from the adjacent countryside and the towns that they by-pass: as free from communal encroachments as the railroad system. In such a network no single center will, like the metropolis of old, become the focal point of all regional advantages: on the contrary, the whole region becomes open for settlement. Even without intelligent public control, the likelihood is that within the next generation this dissociation and decentralization of urban facilities will go even farther. The Townless Highway begets the Highwayless Town in which the needs of close and continuous human association on all levels will be uppermost. This is just the opposite of the earlier mechanocentric picture of Roadtown, as pictured by Edgar Chambless and the Spanish projectors of the Linear City. For the highwayless town is based upon the notion of effective zoning of functions through initial public design, rather than by blind legal ordinances. It is a town in which the various functional parts of the structure are isolated topographically as urban islands, appropriately designed for their specific use: with no attempt to provide a uniform plan of the same general pattern for the industrial, the commercial, the domestic, and the civic parts.

The first systematic sketch of this type of town was made by Messrs. Wright and Stein in their design for Radburn in 1929; a new type of plan that was repeated on a limited scale—and apparently in complete independence—by planners in Köln and Hamburg at about the same time. Because of restrictions on design that favored a conventional type of suburban house and stale architectural forms, the implications of this new type of planning were not carried very far in Radburn. But in outline the main relationships are clear: the differentiation of foot traffic from wheeled traffic in independent systems, the insulation of residence quarters from through roads; the discontinuous street pattern; the polarization of social life in specially spotted civic nuclei, beginning in the neighborhood with the school and the playground and the swimming pool. This type of planning was carried to a logical conclusion in perhaps the most functional and most socially intelligent of all Le Corbusier's many urban plans: that for Nemours in North Africa, in 1934.

Through these convergent efforts, the principles of the polynucleated city have been well established. Such plans must result in a fuller opportunity for the primary group, with all its habits of frequent direct meeting and face-to-face intercourse: they must also result in a more complicated pattern and a more comprehensive life for the region, for this geographic area can only now, for the first time, be treated as an instantaneous whole for all the functions of social existence. Instead of trusting to the mere massing of population to produce the necessary social concentration and social drama, we must now seek these results through deliberate local nucleation and a finer regional articulation. The words are jargon; but the importance of their meaning should not be missed. To embody these new possibilities in city life, which come to us not merely through better technical organization but through acuter sociological understanding, and to dramatize the activities themselves in appropriate individual and urban structures, forms the task of the coming generation.[62]

Paul and Percival Goodman
COMMUNITAS

Paul and Percival Goodman, *Communitas: Means of Livelihood and Ways of Life* [1947], rev. ed., Vintage Books (New York, Random House and Alfred A. Knopf, 1960).*

A NEW COMMUNITY: THE ELIMINATION OF THE DIFFERENCE BETWEEN PRODUCTION AND CONSUMPTION

Quarantining the Work, Quarantining the Homes

Men like to make things, to handle the materials and see them take shape and come out as desired, and they are proud of the products. And men like to work and be useful, for work has a rhythm and springs from spontaneous feeling just like play, and to be useful makes people feel right. Productive work is a kind of creation, it is an extension of human personality into nature. But

---

* Reprinted by permission of Paul and Percival Goodman.

it is also true that the private or state capitalist relations of production, and machine industry as it now exists under whatever
system, have so far destroyed the instinctive pleasures of work
that economic work is what all ordinary men dislike. (Yet unemployment is dreaded, and people who don't like their work
don't know what to do with their leisure.) In capitalist or state-
socialist economies, efficiency is measured by profits and expansion rather than by handling the means. Mass production, analyzing the acts of labor into small steps and distributing the products far from home, destroys the sense of creating anything.
Rhythm, neatness, style belong to the machine rather than to the
man.

The division of economy into production and consumption as
two opposite poles means that we are far from the conditions
in which work could be a way of life. A way of life requires
merging the means in the end, and work would [153] have to be
thought of as a continuous process of satisfying activity, satisfying in itself and satisfying in its useful end. Such considerations
have led many moralist-economists to want to turn back the
clock to conditions of handicraft in a limited society, where the
relations of guilds and small markets allow the master craftsmen
a say and a hand in every phase of production, distribution, and
consumption. Can we achieve the same values with modern technology, a national economy, and a democratic society? With this
aim, let us reanalyze efficiency and machine production.

Characteristic of American offices and factories is the severe
discipline with regard to punctuality. (In some states the law requires time clocks, to protect labor and calculate the insurance.)
Now no doubt in many cases where workers cooperate in teams,
where business is timed by the mails, where machines use a temporary source of power, being on time and on the same time as
everybody else is essential to efficiency. But by and large it would
make little difference at what hour each man's work began and
ended, so long as the job itself was done. Often the work could
be done at home or on the premises indifferently, or part here
part there. Yet this laxity is never allowed, except in the typical
instances of hack-writing or commercial art—typical because
these workers have an uneasy relation to the economy in any
case. (There is a lovely story of how William Faulkner asked

M-G-M if he could work at home, and when they said, "Of course," he went back to Oxford, Mississippi.)

Punctuality is demanded not primarily for efficiency but for the discipline itself. Discipline is necessary because the work is onerous; perhaps it makes the idea of working even more onerous, but it makes the work itself much more tolerable, for it is a structure, a decision. Discipline establishes the work in an impersonal secondary environment where, once one has gotten out of bed early in the morning, the rest easily follows. Regulation of time, separation from the personal environment: these are signs that work is not a way of life; they are the methods by which, for better or [154] worse, work that cannot be energized directly by personal concern can get done, unconfused by personal concern.

In the Garden City plans, they "quarantined the technology" from the homes; more generally, we quarantine the work from the homes. But it is even truer to say that we quarantine the homes from the work. For instance, it is calamitous for a man's wife or children to visit him at work; this privilege is reserved for the highest bosses.

Reanalyzing Production

In planning a region of satisfying industrial work, we therefore take account of four main principles:

1. A closer relation of the personal and productive environments, making punctuality reasonable instead of disciplinary, and introducing phases of home and small-shop production; and vice versa, finding appropriate technical uses for personal relations that have come to be considered unproductive.

2. A role for all workers in all stages of the production of the product; for experienced workers a voice and hand in the design of the product and the design and operation of the machines; and for all a political voice on the basis of what they know best, their specific industry, in the national economy.

3. A schedule of work designed on psychological and moral as well as technical grounds, to give the most well-rounded employment to each person, in a diversified environment. Even in technology and economics, the men are ends as well as means.

4. Relatively small units with relative self-sufficiency, so that

each community can enter into a larger whole with solidarity and independence of viewpoint.

These principles are mutually interdependent.

1. To undo the present separation of work and home environments, we can proceed both ways: (a) Return certain parts of production to home-shops or near home; and [155] (b) Introduce domestic work and certain productive family-relations, which are now not considered part of the economy at all, into the style and relations of the larger economy.

(a) Think of the present proliferation of machine-tools. It could once be said that the sewing machine was the only widely distributed productive machine; but now, especially because of the last war, the idea of thousands of small machine shops, powered by electricity, has become familiar; and small power-tools are a best-selling commodity. In general, the change from coal and steam to electricity and oil has relaxed one of the greatest causes for concentration of machinery around a single driving-shaft.

(b) Borsodi, going back to the economics of Aristotle, has proved, often with hilarious realism, that home production, such as cooking, cleaning, mending, and entertaining has a formidable economic, though not cash, value. The problem is to lighten and enrich home production by the technical means and some of the expert attitudes of public production, but without destroying its individuality.

But the chief part of finding a satisfactory productive life in homes and families consists in the analysis of personal relations and conditions: e.g., the productive cooperation of man and wife as it exists on farms, or the productive capabilities of children and old folk, now economically excluded. This involves sentimental and moral problems of extreme depth and delicacy that could only be solved by the experiments of integrated communities.

2. A chief cause of the absurdity of industrial work is that each machine worker is acquainted with only a few processes, not the whole order of production. And the thousands of products are distributed he knows not how or where. Efficiency is organized from above by expert managers who first analyze production into its simple processes, then synthesize these into combinations built

into the machines, then arrange the logistics of supplies, etc., and then assign the jobs.

As against this efficiency organized from above, we must [156] try to give this function to the workers. This is feasible only if the workers have a total grasp of all the operations. There must be a school of industry, academic and not immediately productive, connected with the factory. Now let us distinguish apprentices and graduates. To the apprentices, along with their schooling, is assigned the more monotonous work; to the graduates, the executive and coordinating work, the fine work, the finishing touches. The masterpiece that graduates an apprentice is a new invention, method, or other practical contribution advancing the industry. The masters are teachers, and as part of their job hold free discussions looking to basic changes.

Such a setup detracts greatly from the schedule of continuous production; but it is a question whether it would not prove more efficient in the long run to have the men working for themselves and having a say in the distribution. By this we do not mean merely economic democracy or socialist ownership. These are necessary checks but are not the political meaning of industrialism as such. What is needed is the organization of economic democracy on the basis of the productive units, where each unit, relying on its own expertness and the bargaining power of what it has to offer, cooperates with the whole of society. This is syndicalism, simply an industrial town meeting. To guarantee the independent power of each productive unit, it must have a relative regional self-sufficiency; this is the union of farm and factory.

3. Machine work in its present form is often stultifying, not a "way of life." The remedy is to assign work on psychological and moral as well as technical and economic grounds. The object is to provide a well-rounded employment. Work can be divided as team work and individual work, or physical work and intellectual work. And industries can be combined in a neighborhood to give the right variety. For instance, cast glass, blown glass, and optical instruments; or more generally, industry and agriculture, and factory and domestic work. Probably most important, but difficult to [157] conjure with, is the division in terms of faculties and powers, routine and initiation, obeying and commanding.

The problem is to envisage a well-rounded schedule of jobs for each man, and to arrange the buildings and the farms so that the schedule is feasible.

4. The integration of factory and farm brings us to the idea of regionalism and regional relative autonomy. These are the following main parts:

(a) Diversified farming as the basis of self-subsistence and, therefore, small urban centers (200,000).

(b) A number of mutually dependent industrial centers, so that an important part of the national economy is firmly [158] controlled. (The thought is always to have freedom secured by real power.)

(c) These industries developed around regional resources of field, mine, and power.

Diversified farmers can be independent, and small farms have therefore always been a basis of social stability, though not necessarily of peasant conservatism. On the other hand, for the machines now desirable, the farmer needs cash and links himself with the larger economy of the town.

The political problem of the industrial worker is the reverse, since every industry is completely dependent on the national economy, for both materials and distribution. But by regional interdependence of industries and the close integration of factory and farm work—factory workers taking over in the fields at peak seasons, farmers doing factory work in the winter; town people, especially children, living in the country; farmers domestically making small parts for the factories—the industrial region as a whole can secure for itself independent bargaining power in the national whole.

The general sign of this federal system is the distinction of the local regional market from the national market. In transport, the local market is served by foot, bicycle, cart, and car; the national market by plane and trailer-truck.

(Now all of this—decentralized units, double markets, the selection of industries on political and psychological as well as economic and technical grounds—all this seems a strange and roundabout way of achieving an integrated national economy, when at present this unity already exists with a tightness that leaves nothing to be desired, and an efficiency that is even excessive. But we are aiming at a different standard of efficiency,

one in which invention will flourish and the job will be its own
incentive; and most important, at the highest and nearest ideals
of external life: liberty, responsibility, self-esteem as a workman,
and initiative. Compared with these aims the present system has
nothing to offer us.) [160]

A Piazza in the Town

With us at present in America, a man who is fortunate enough
to have useful and important work to do that is called for and
socially accepted, work that has initiative and exercises his best
energies—such a man (he is one in a thousand among us) is
likely to work not only very hard but too hard; he finds himself,
as if compulsively, always going back to his meaningful job, as
if the leisurely pursuits of society were not attractive. But we
would hope that where every man has such work, where society
is organized only to guarantee that he has, that people will have
a more good-humored and easygoing attitude. Not desiring to
get away from their work to a leisure that amounts to very little
(for where there is no man's work there is no man's play), people will be leisurely about their work—it is all, one way or another, making use of the time.

Now, the new community has *closed squares* like those described by Camillo Sitte. Such squares are the *definition* of a
city.

Squares are not avenues of motor or pedestrian traffic, but are
places where people remain. Place of work and [162] home are
close at hand, but in the city square is what is still more interesting—the other people.

The easygoing leisure of piazzas is a long simple interim,
just as easygoing people nowadays are often happiest on train
trips or driving to work, the time in-between. Conscience is clear
because a useful task will begin at a set time (not soon). The
workers of the new community give themselves long lunchtimes
indeed. For, supposing ten men are needed on a machine or a
line for four hours' work: they arrange to start sometime in mid-
afternoon, and where should they find each other, to begin, but in
the piazza? [163]

On one side of the piazza opens the factory; another entrance is a small library, provided with ashtrays. As in all other squares, there is a clock with bells; it's a reminder, not a tyrant.

The leisure of piazzas is made of repetitive small pleasures like feeding pigeons and watching a fountain. These are ways of being with the other people and striking up conversations. It is essential to have outdoor and indoor tables with drinks and small food.

There is the noise of hammering, and the explosions of tuning a motor, from small shops a little way off. But if it's a quieter square, there may be musicians. Colored linen and silk are blowing on a line—not flags but washing! For everything is mixed up here. At the same time, there is something of the formality of a college campus.[164]

Another face of the piazza is an apartment house, where an urban family is making a meal. They go about this as follows. The ground floor of the building is not only a restaurant but a foodstore; the farmers deliver their produce here. The family cooks upstairs, phones down for their uncooked meat, vegetables, salad, and fixings, and these are delivered by dumbwaiter, cleaned and peeled—the potatoes peeled and spinach washed by machine. They dress and season the roast to taste and send it back with the message: "Medium rare about 1845." The husband observes, unfortunately for the twentieth time, that when he was a student in Paris a baker on the corner used to roast their chickens in his oven. Simpler folk, who live in smaller row houses up the block, consider this procedure a lot of foolishness; they just shop for their food, prepare it themselves, cook it, and eat it. But they don't have factory jobs: they run a lathe in the basement.

The main exit from the square is almost cut off by a monument with an inscription. But we cannot decipher the future inscription. The square seems enclosed.

In the famous piazzas described and measured in all their [165] asymmetry by Camillo Sitte, the principal building, the building that gives its name to the place, as the Piazza San Marco or the Piazza dei Signori, is a church, town hall or guild hall. What are such principal buildings in the squares we are here describing? We don't know.

The windmill and water tower here, that work the fountain

and make the pool, were put up gratuitously simply because such an ingenious machine is beautiful.

A Farm and Its Children

Let us rear all the children in the natural environment where they are many and furnish a society for one another. This has an immense pedagogic advantage, for the business of the country environment is plain to the eyes, it is not concealed in accounts and factories. The mechanism of urban production is clear to adult minds; the nature of farm production is not much clearer to the adults than to the children of ten or eleven.

Integrating town and country, we are able to remedy the present injustice whereby the country bears the burden of rearing and educating more than its share of the population, then loses 50% of the investment at maturity. (And then the cities complain that the youth have been educated on rural standards!) If the city children go to the country schools, the city bears its pro rata share of the cost and has the right to a say in the policy.

The parents who work in the city live in small houses on nearby farms: that is home for the children. But when they leave for work, the children are not alone but are still at home on the farm. Some such arrangement is necessary, for it is obvious that we cannot, as the urban home continues to break down, be satisfied with the pathos of crèches, nursery-schools, and kindergartens.

To the farmers, the city families are the most valuable source of money income.

The best society for growing children, past the age of [166] total dependency, is other children, older and younger by easy grades. It is a rough society but characterized at worst by conflict rather than by loving, absolute authority. These children, then, no longer sleep with their parents, but in a dormitory.

From quite early, children are set to work feeding the animals and doing chores that are occasionally too hard for them. Perhaps urban sentiment can here alleviate the condition of farm and city children both.

Everybody praises diversified farming as a way of life. Yet the farm youth migrate to the city when they can. (Just as everybody praises lovely Ireland, but the young Irish leave in droves.) This is inevitable when all the advertised [167] social values, broadcast by radio and cinema, are urban values. It is universally admitted that these values are claptrap; but they are more attractive than nothing. To counteract this propaganda, the farm-sociologists try to establish a social opinion specifically rural, they revive square dances and have 4-H clubs and contests, organized by the farmers' collectives and cooperatives.

But is it necessary for "farm" and "city" to compete? All values are human values.[168]

Regional and National Economy

The large number of diversified farms means, on the one hand, that the region is self-subsistent, but on the other that the farmers have little crop to export outside the region. Their cash comes, however, from the city market, from domestic industry, from some industrial agriculture, and from housing the city folk. If farmers have a specialized crop, such as grapes or cotton, it is processed in the town. All this guarantees a tight local economy.

Now, even apart from political freedom, such a tight local economy is essential if there is to be a close relation between production and consumption, for it means that prices and the value of labor will not be so subject to the fluctuations of the vast general market. A man's work, meaningful during production, will somewhat carry through the distribution and what he gets in return. That is, within limits, the nearer a system gets to simple household economy, the more it is an economy of specific things and services that are bartered, rather than an economy of generalized money.

"Economy of things rather than money"—this formula is the essence of regionalism. The persons of a region draw on their local resources and cooperate directly, without the intermediary of national bookkeeping with its millions of clashing motives never resoluble face-to-face. The regional development of the TVA brought together power and fertilizer for farms, navigation and the prevention of erosion, the control of floods and the processing of foods, national recreation, and in this natural co-operation it produced a host of ingenious inventions. All of this (in its inception) was carried on in relative autonomy, under the loose heading of "general welfare."

The kind of life looked for in this new community depends on the awareness of local distinctness, and this is also the condition of political freedom as a group of industries [170] and farm co-operatives, rather than as a multitude of abstract votes and consumers with cash.

Yet every machine economy *is* a national and international economy. The fraction of necessary goods that can be produced in a planned region is very substantial, but it is still a fraction. And this fact is the salvation of regionalism! For otherwise regionalism succumbs to provincialism—whether we consider art or literature, or the characters of the people, or the fashions in technology. The regional industrialists in their meeting find that, just because their region is strong and productive, they are subject to wide circles of influence, they have to keep up.

Refinement

Let us try to envisage the moral ideal of such a community as we are describing.

In the luxury city of consumers' goods, society was geared to an expanding economy—capital investment and consumption [171] had to expand at all costs, or even especially at all costs. In the third community that we shall describe in this book, "maximum security, minimum regulation," we shall find that, in order to achieve the aim of social security and human liberty, a part of the economy must never be allowed to expand at all.

But in this present, middle-of-the-road, plan there is no reason why the economy either must expand or must not expand. Every issue is particular and comes down to the particular question: "Is it worthwhile to expand along this new line? Is it worth the trouble to continue along that old line?"

This attitude is a delicate one, hard for us Americans to grasp clearly: we always like to do it bigger and better, or we jump to something new, or we cling. But when people are accustomed to knowing what they are lending their hands to, when they know the operations and the returns, when they don't have to prove something competitively, then they are just in the business, so to speak, of judging the relation of means and ends. They are all efficiency experts. And then, curiously, they may soon hit on a new conception of efficiency itself, very unlike that of the engineers of Veblen. When they can say, "It would be more efficient to make it this way," they may go on to say, "And it would be even *more* efficient to forget it altogether."

Efficient for what? For the way of life as a whole. Now in all times honorable people have used this criterion as a negative check: "*We* don't do that kind of thing, even if it's convenient or profitable." But envisage doing it positively and inventively: "Let's do it, it becomes us. Or let's omit it and simplify, it's a lag and a drag."

Suppose that one of the masters, away on his two months of individual work, drafting designs for furniture, should, having studied the furniture of the Japanese, decide to dispense with chairs. Such a problem might create a bitter struggle in the national economy, one thing leading to another.

The economy, like any machine economy, would expand,[172] for it creates a surplus. It would expand into refinement. The Japanese way is a powerful example. They cover the floor with deep washable mats and dispense with chairs and dispense with the floor. It is too much trouble to clutter the room with furniture. It is not too much trouble to lavish many days' work on the minute carving on the inside of a finger pull of a shoji. They dispense with the upholstery but take pains in arranging the flowers. They do not build permanent partitions in a room because the activities of life are always varying.

When production becomes an integral part of life, the workman becomes an artist. It is the definition of an artist that he follows the medium, and finds new possibilities of expression in it. He is not bound by the fact that things have always been made in a certain way, nor even by the fact that it is these things that have been made. Our industrialists—even International Business Machines—are very [173] much concerned these days to get "creative" people, and they make psychological studies on how to foster an "atmosphere of creativity"; but they don't sufficiently conjure with the awful possibility that truly creative people might tell them to shut up shop. They wish to use creativity in just the way that it cannot be used, for it is a process that also generates its own ends.

Notes on Neo-Functionalism:
the Ailanthus and the Morning-Glory

In the Introduction to this book, we called this attitude neo-functionalism, a functionalism that subjects the function to a formal critique. The neo-functionalist asks: Is the use as simple, ingenious, or clear as the efficient means that produce it? Is the *using* a good experience? For instance, these days they sell us machines whose operation is not transparent and that an intelligent layman cannot repair. Such a thing is ugly in itself, and it enslaves us to repairmen.

There is one abuse of present-day production, however, that is not only ugly and foolish but morally outrageous, and the perpetrators should be ostracized from decent society. This is building obsolescence into a machine, so it will wear out, be discarded, and replaced. For instance, automobile-repair parts are now stocked for only five years, whereas previously they were stocked for ten. Does this mean that the new cars, meant to last a shorter time, are cheaper? On the contrary, they are more expensive. Does it mean that there are so many new improvements that there is no point in keeping the older, less efficient models running? There are no such improvements; the new models are characterized merely by novel gimmicks to induce sales—just as the difficulty of repair and the obsolescence are built in to enforce sales.

Neo-functionalists are crotchety people, for they are in love with the goddess of common sense, and the way we do things catches them by the throat. They take exception [174] to much that is universally accepted, because it doesn't add up; they stop to praise many things universally disregarded, such as the custom of sitting on slum stoops and sidewalks, with or without chairs: Park Avenue does not provide this amenity. To a neo-functionalist, much that is insisted on seems not worth all that bother, and he is often easygoing; his attitude is interpreted as laziness, but he sees no reason to be busy if he is not bored. He praises the ailanthus.

Of all trees and shrubs it seems to be only the locust and especially the ailanthus that flourish of themselves in the back alleys and yard-square plots of dirt that are the gardens of Manhattan Island. They bloom from the mouths of basements. But the maple saplings and the elms that are transplanted there at large expense and are protected from pests with doses of a nauseating juice, languish and die in that environment of motor fumes and pavements.

Should our native city not, out of simple respect and piety, exalt the ailanthus to be our chief ornamental scenery, and make places for it everywhere? For the ailanthus loves *us* and thrives in our balance of nature. Our city is rich enough, it could become elegant enough, to flaunt a garden [175] of native weeds. There is everywhere a prejudice against the luxuriating plantain weed, which as abstract design is as lovely as can be. Why should not this weed be raised to the dignity of a grass—it is only a matter of a name—and then carefully be weeded in, in rows and stars, to decorate the little sidewalk plots?

The Rivers of New York

Trained in the New Commune, the neo-functionalist mentions also the ludicrous anomaly of New York's bathing-places. During the heat of summer tens of thousands of Manhattanites daily travel from two to three hours to go swimming and boating on far-off shores. Many millions of dollars were spent in developing a bathing place no less [176] than 40 miles from midtown Manhattan, and this place—it is the darling of our notorious Park Commissioner—has been connected with the city by remarkable highways on which at peak hours the traffic creeps at four miles an hour, while the engines boil.

Meantime the venturesome poor boys of the city swim daily, as they always have, in the Hudson River and the East River—under the sidelong surveillance of usually reasonable police; it is quite illegal. It is illegal because the water is polluted. No strenuous effort is made by the Park Commissioner to make it unpolluted; and the shore is not developed for bathing. Yet to the boys it seems the obvious thing to do on a hot day, to dive into the nearest water, down the hill at the end of the street, into

> Our lordly Hudson hardly flowing
> under the green-grown cliffs
> —and has no peer in Europe or the East.[177]

The Museum of Art

Suppose again, says our neo-functionalist friend, that a number of mighty masterpieces of painting and statuary were decentralized from the big museum and placed, one in this neighborhood church (as in Rome one encounters astounded, *Moses*), and one on this fountain in a local square, wherever there is a quiet place to pause. A few of the neighbors would come to have a friendly and perhaps somewhat proprietary acquaintance with their masterpiece. Are they not to be trusted so close to the treasure?

One cannot help but think of Florence that has come down to us not as a museum city (like Venice), but as a bustling modern town, yet still a continuous home for those strange marble and bronze monsters of the Renaissance, in the squares. It would be very interesting for a sociologist to study, with his questionnaires, the effect of those things on the Florentines. They have had an effect.

When there is such a work in a neighborhood, a stranger, who from afar has heard of its fame, will come to visit the local square where he would otherwise never have ventured. Then the children notice how carefully and reverently he is looking at the statue they climb on. . . . [178]

The Theory of Home Furnishings

The furniture of a home expresses, in its quantity and kind, the division of the concerns of the soul; in different community arrangements this division falls in different places.

On the principle of neo-functionalism, the place where the chief material outlay is made should give the chief satisfaction, otherwise why bother? If this rule is neglected, the material outlay becomes a dead weight, discouraging by its initial cost and even more by its continuing presence.

Now except in the woods, the chief material outlay we see

about us is the public city with its services. But in America these streets, squares, and highways do not pretend to compete in satisfaction with the private homes or the theaters of fantasy. They are a dead weight on these other satisfactions. One emerges from the theater into an environment that is less exciting, and one emerges from home into an environment that is quite impersonal and uninteresting. In late medieval times, they spent no effort on the streets, but burgher and baron adorned their homes.

Let us rather take a lesson from the Greeks who were often practical in what concerned the chief end and did not complicate their means. An Athenian, if free and male, experienced in the public places, the market, the law court, the porticoes, the gymnasia, most of the feelings of ease, intimacy, and personal excitement that we reserve for home and private clubs. He lived in the city more than at home. He had for his public objects the affairs of empire, civic duties, and passions of friendship. There was no sharp distinction between public and private affairs.

On the civic places and public institutions, then, they lavished an expense of architecture, mulcted from an empire and slaves in the silver mines, that with us would be quite deadening in its pretentiousness. But the thousands of free men were at home there.

An Athenian's domestic home was very simple; it was not [183] an asylum for his personality. It did not have to be filled with furniture, mirrors, keepsakes, curiosa, and games.

But a bourgeois gentleman, when he is about to leave his home in the morning, kisses his wife and daughter, steps before a mirror and adjusts his tie, and then, the last thing before emerging, puts on a public face.

The most curious examples of heavily furnished homes that are the insane asylums of the spirit frozen and rejected in the city square can be found among the middle classes at the beginning of the twentieth century. And the most curious room of this most curious home was not the bedroom, the dining room, or the parlor, where after all there existed natural and social satisfactions, but the master's den, the jungle and the cavern of his reveries. In our decade, this den of nostalgic revery is in print in the stories of *The New Yorker* magazine.

Public Faces in Private Places

It is always a question whether the bourgeois den is worse or better than no private home at all, the norm of the states ancient and modern which consider men as public animals, and homes as army barracks.

But it has remained for our own generation to perfect the worst possible community arrangement, the home of the average American. This home is liberally supplied with furniture and the comforts of private life, but these private things are neither made nor chosen by personal creation or idiosyncratic taste, but are made in a distant factory and distributed by unresisted advertising. At home they exhaust by their presence—a bare cell would give more peace or arouse restlessness. They print private life with a public meaning. But if we turn to read this public meaning, we find that the only moral aim of society is to provide private satisfactions called the Standard of Living. This is remarkable. The private places have public faces, as Auden said, but the public faces are supposed to imitate private faces. What a booby trap! [184]

VI
From Europe:
Bold Conservatism

Camillo Sitte———————————————————

THE ART OF BUILDING CITIES

Camillo Sitte, *The Art of Building Cities* [orig. publ. as *Der Städtebau,*
1889], trans. by Charles T. Stewart (New York, Reinhold, 1945).*

Memory of travel is the stuff of our fairest dreams. Splendid
cities, plazas, monuments, and landscapes thus pass before our
eyes, and we enjoy again the charming and impressive spectacles
that we have formerly experienced. If we could but stop again
at those places where beauty never satiates, we could bear many
dreary hours with a light heart and pursue life's long struggle
with new energies. Assuredly the imperturbable lightheartedness
of the South, on the Hellenic coast, in lower Italy and other favored climes, is above all a gift of nature. And the old cities of
these countries, built after the beauty of nature itself, continue
to augment nature's gentle and irresistible influence upon the
soul of man. Only the person who has never understood the
beauty of an ancient city could contradict this assertion.

Let him go ramble on the ruins of Pompeii to convince himself

* Reprinted by permission of the Reinhold Publishing Corporation.

249

of it. If, after a day of patient investigation there, he walks across the bare Forum, he will be drawn, in spite of himself, to the summit of the monumental staircase toward the terrace of Jupiter's temple. On this platform, which dominates the entire place, he will sense, rising within him, waves of harmony like the pure, full tones of sublime music. Under this influence he will truly understand the words of Aristotle, who thus summarized all principles of city building: "A city should be built to give its inhabitants security and happiness."

The science of the technician will not suffice to accomplish this. We need, in addition, the talent of the artist. Thus it was in ancient times, in the Middle Ages, and in the Renaissance, wherever fine arts were held in esteem. It is only in our mathematical century that the construction and extension of cities has become a purely technical matter. Perhaps, then, it is not beside the point to recall that these problems have diverse aspects, and that he who has been given the least attention in our time is perhaps not the least important.

The object of this study, then, is clear. It is not our purpose to republish ancient and trite ideas, nor to reopen sterile complaints against the already proverbial banality of modern streets. It is useless to hurl general condemnations and to put everything that has been done in our time and place once more to the pillory. That kind of purely negative effort should be left to the critic who is never satisfied and who [1] can only contradict. Those who have enough enthusiasm and faith in good causes should be convinced that our own era can create works of beauty and worth. We shall examine the plans of a number of cities, but neither as historian nor as critic. We wish to seek out, as technician and artist, the elements of composition which formerly produced such harmonious effects, and those which today produce only loose and dull results. Perhaps this study will permit us to find the means of satisfying the three principal requirements of practical city building: to rid the modern system of blocks and regularly aligned houses; to save as much as possible of that which remains from ancient cities; and in our creation to approach more closely the ideal of the ancient models. . . .[2]

Technicians of today take more trouble than is necessary to create interminable rectangular streets and public squares of impeccable symmetry. These efforts seem misdirected to those who are interested in good city appearance. Our forebears had ideas on this subject quite different to ours. Here is some evidence of it: the Piazza dei Eremitani and the Piazza del Duomo at Padua, the Cathedral Square at Syracuse, and the Piazza S. Francesco at Palermo.

The typical irregularity of these old squares indicates their gradual historical development. We are rarely mistaken in attributing the existence of these windings to practical causes— the presence of a canal, the lines of an old roadway, or the form of a building. Everyone knows from personal experience that these disruptions in symmetry are not unsightly. On the contrary, they arouse our interest as much as they appear natural, and preserve a picturesque character. Few people, however, understand why irregularity can avoid giving an unpleasant appearance. We must study a map to understand it. Any city can offer a good example of this, for the eye is inclined to overlook slight irregularities and is incapable of evaluating angles. We are willing to see more regularity in forms than actually exists.

Whoever studies a map of his own city can be convinced that violent irregularities, shown on the map, do not in the least seem to be striking irregularities when seen on the ground. . . . [30]

The difference between a graphic representation and an actual view of the Piazza S. Maria Novella at Florence is equally surprising. In fact, the square has five sides, but, in the memory of many travelers, it has only four. For on the ground only three sides of it can be seen at one time, and the angle formed by the two other sides is always behind the observer's back. Furthermore, we are easily mistaken in calculating by sight the angle formed by these two sides. Perspective makes this calculation difficult even for engineers if they use only their eyes. This is truly a square of surprises, for in it we are subjected to so many varied [31] optical illusions. It is a far cry indeed from the rigorous symmetry so dear to modern city builders.

It is strange that the slightest irregularity in modern city plans upsets us, although those of ancient public squares do not have a displeasing appearance. In fact, their irregularities are such that they are seen only on paper. On the ground they escape us.

The ancients did not conceive their plans on drawing boards. Their buildings rose bit by bit *in natura*. Thus they were readily governed by that which struck the eye in reality. . . .

We know how little symmetry and absolute geometrical regularity contributed to the picturesque beauty of medieval castles. In spite of their tormented structures, these old castles achieved an harmonious impression because their architecture clearly explained what was in them. Each individual structural mass has a kind of counterbalance which assures an overall equilibrium, boldly conceived and composed of patterns that were varied but not confusing. There is much of this in the art of building cities. Here the liberty of the artist is a still greater factor, for the realm of applied artistic resources is much vaster, and the methods at his disposal are so numerous that they may all be used without infringing on each other. Why then should we be content with the stiff regularity, the useless symmetry, and the tiresome uniformity of modern city plans? In parts of old country houses and in the architecture of castles we perceive a certain picturesque abandon. Why must the straightedge and the compass be the all powerful masters of city building?

The notion of symmetry is propagating itself today like the spread of an epidemic. The least cultivated are familiar with it, and each one feels called upon to [32] have his say about the involved artistic matters that concern the building of cities, for each thinks he has at his finger tips the single criterion—symmetry. . . .

When Gothic masters began to form architectural patterns and became more concerned with the axes of symmetry in the modern sense of the term, the notion of similarity of figures to the left and right of a principal line was established in theory. An ancient name, with its meaning altered, was given to this idea. Writers of the Renaissance were using it in this sense. Since then, the axes of symmetry have become continually more frequent in plans for buildings, as they have in plans for cities. Aided by this alone, the modern architect undertakes to perform all the tasks that are thrust on him. Our self-styled esthetic principles of building are at hand to prove the deficiency of this unfortunate principle. Everybody insists that a rule governing the building of cities cannot completely ignore the laws of beauty, but, since the problem is one of moving from theory to practice, initial enthusiasm gives way to utter confusion. The mouse brought forth by the mountain is universal, inevitable, indisputable, essential *symmetry!* Thus a syrupy law of 1864 sought to satisfy the artistic requirements of the country by enjoining the architects to avoid everything that "could offend symmetry and morality" in the design of façades. It remains to be learned which of the two offenses was considered the graver.

In modern cities irregularity in plan is unsuccessful because it has been created [33] artificially with the straightedge. It most often takes the form of triangular public places—the fatal dregs of drawing board plotting. They nearly always have a bad effect. There is no illusion to the eye, for the clashing intersection[s] of building lines are always in view. The sole means of remedying the defects of such places would be to make each side irregular in itself. That would bring about numerous recesses, partially symmetrical, and open spaces removed from traffic where monuments and statues might be advantageously situated. Unfortunately, that is impossible today, for since each of the three sides of a triangular "square" is rigorously straight, all efforts toward pleasing treatment are in vain. From this springs the legend of regular and irregular squares which holds that the first class are beautiful and suitable for monuments located, it is needless to say, in the geometrical center. If we limit ourselves to modern squares, this assertion is true, but when we begin to examine those of past epochs we see that irregular squares can be more readily adorned with statues and monuments, for they do not lack suitable places for them.[34]

. . . Obviously the model of the ancient forum was followed by the builders of northern cities. They produced original results out of old principles by choosing the most natural solutions to their practical problems. This simplified matters for them, for they undertook to judge the effect of their projected buildings on the particular sites [46] and in the natural settings intended for them, and their determinations were made accordingly. Modern architects often design structures for sites that they have never seen. That inevitably leads to banal work, for the building conceived for construction on just any site goes up, through the workings of a perverse fate, in the midst of an empty expanse without the slightest correlation to its surroundings, and without balance between its height and that of neighboring structures.

Our era is marked by the mass production of buildings stamped out according to some accepted standard. The old builders, on the contrary, knew how to place their most important structures around a plaza in a way that could give character to an entire city despite the fact that the direct effect of such groupings was necessarily exercised in a single place. . . .[47]

Modern systems! That, indeed, is the appropriate term! We set up rigid *systems*, and then grow fearful of deviating from them by as much as a hair's breadth. Suppression, or sacrifice to system, of every ingenious touch that might give real expression to the joy of living, is truly the mark of our times.

We have three dominant systems for building cities, and a number of variations of them. They are: the rectangular system, the radial system, and the triangular system. Generally speaking, the variations are bastard offspring of these three. From an artistic point of view the whole tribe is worthless, having exhausted the last drop of art's blood from its veins. These systems accomplish nothing except a standardization of street pattern. They are purely mechanical in conception. They reduce the street system to a mere traffic utility, never serving the purposes of art. They make no appeal to the sense of perception, for we can see their features only on a map.

For that reason we have thus far avoided the term "street pattern" in discussing ancient Athens, Rome, Nuremburg, or Venice. It is really beside the point, as far as art is concerned, for artistic worth can be expected only in that which we can see, like a single street or plaza. This obvious fact will suggest that under certain circumstances almost any kind of street pattern can lend itself to artistic results, unless it has been designed with brutal heedlessness, as happened in the cities of the new world according to the dictates of the *genius loci*, and, unfortunately, as has become common in our cities.

Even the rectangular system could be used to form pleasing plazas and streets if the technician would permit the artist to look over his shoulder and change the position of his compass and T-square now and then. The two might even achieve a neat division of labor, for the artist could accomplish his purpose by de-

signing a few of the principal streets and plazas, willingly ceding
the remainder to the necessities of traffic movement and other
utilitarian considerations. In work areas of the community, the
city would display its working clothes, but the principal streets
and plazas could be arrayed in their best for sunshine to the
stimulation and pleasure of those who use them. Thus these outstanding streets and plazas could serve to foster civic pride and
to fire the ambition of maturing youth.

That is exactly what we find in the old cities. Their numerous
secondary [59] streets, as a matter of fact, have little artistic significance. Only the traveler, the exceptional onlooker, finds special beauty in them, as he does in everything. Critical appraisal
finds only a few principal streets and plazas in the center of the
city where the old builders have achieved a rich accumulation
of their clever talents in works of civic art.

This leads us to a vantage point that we must reach if, despite
these modern city building systems, we are to preserve a modi-
cum of the artistic in our cities. There is need for compromise,
for if we are too exacting in what we demand for art, we will
make little headway among those who are concerned with utilitarian requirements. Whoever is to succeed in upholding esthetic
considerations in urban development must, first, realize that
practical solutions to traffic problems are not necessarily rigid,
unalterable remedies; and, secondly, he must be prepared to
demonstrate that practical requirements of modern living need
not necessarily obstruct artful development.

The most common modern system is the rectangular plan. It
was established with inflexible permanence at Mannheim many
years ago, resulting in a perfect chess board pattern for the City.
Rectangularity is so completely dominant that it has even discouraged distinctive names for streets. An array of cubes extending in one direction is designated by a letter, while those files of
similar cubes running in perpendicular directions are given numbers for names. Thus, the last vestiges of old city building forms,
with their undertones of imagination and fancy, have been
pushed into oblivion. Mannheim boasts of having created this
system. *Volenti non fiat injuria.*[1] Whoever bothers to compile all
of the condemnation and scorn inspired by the invention will be

---

[1] No injury is done to a consenting party.

able to fill volumes with it. Surprisingly enough, however, this very system has virtually taken the whole world. No matter where we go we find that newly developed city areas have followed the rectangular plan, for even where the radial or triangular systems are in evidence, the lesser streets in the pattern are designed as closely as possible to the chess-board motif. This is especially surprising because such combinations have long been in disrepute even among those who are interested solely in the circulation of traffic. To the inconveniences in the system that these people have pointed out, we add another, which seems to have been overlooked heretofore, and that is the traffic difficulty created by intersecting streets. . . .[60]

Obviously a planner cannot plan a new city area in an artful manner without a definite idea of what it is to be, what public buildings will be in it, and what plazas it is to have. He cannot begin work until he has taken probabilities of use into full account. Only in that way can his plan conform to the topography, fulfill the essential requirements, and permit an artistic development of the area. To proceed in any other way would be like expecting an architect to begin work after being told to "build something to cost about one hundred thousand dollars." Residential investment property, the architect might ask. "No." A villa? "No." A factory perhaps. "No." And so on. That kind of procedure would be ridiculous, even insane, and it doesn't happen because nobody builds a building without some purpose in mind, and consequently nobody commissions an architect without having a building program.

Only in city building, apparently, is it considered sane to prepare a building plan without a definite building program. In this field it is quite usual to go ahead with the plan but without any idea as to how the new district is to be developed. The city block with its monotonous lot plotting is the striking expression of this uncertainty. Planning attempts of this kind simply say, in their barren way, "We could certainly do something useful and beautiful, but we don't know what, and so we humbly lay aside the problem which was never stated in sufficient detail to suit us, and neatly divide the surface into regular parcels so that sales by the square foot may begin."

What a departure this is from the ideal of the ancients! And we have not been indulging in caricature. This little scene is a true portrayal of the facts. A block system of this kind has been ruled for a new district in Vienna and stands now as the plan for the so called new Danube City. It is as poor and as awkward a plan as could be devised.

The division of North America into states was a gigantic block plan that illustrates the unfortunate results of planning without a program. This vast country was divided by straight lines according to degrees of latitude and longitude, and its consequent imperfections are striking. At the time it was done the country was unknown. Having no past, and representing but so many square miles of land to civilization, America's future development could not be foreseen. This same rectangular system of dividing land, when applied to cities, was perhaps satisfactory for the cities of America, Australia, and other new countries. The inhabitants of those cities were primarily concerned with survival. They lived only [84] for gainful production, and produced only to live. It mattered little to them that they were packed up in barracks like herring in casks. . . .[85]

Le Corbusier
A CONTEMPORARY CITY OF THREE MILLION INHABITANTS (1922) THE VOISIN PLAN (1924)

Le Corbusier [Charles Édouard Jeanneret-Gris], *The City of To-morrow and Its Planning* [orig. publ. as *Urbanisme,* 1924], trans. by Frederick Etchells (New York, Payson and Clarke, 1929).*

THE PACK-DONKEY'S WAY AND MAN'S WAY

Man walks in a straight line because he has a goal and knows where he is going; he has made up his mind to reach some particular place and he goes straight to it.

* Reprinted by permission of The Architectural Press, Ltd.

The pack-donkey meanders along, meditates a little in his scatter-brained and distracted fashion, he zigzags in order to avoid the larger stones, or to ease the climb, or to gain a little shade; he takes the line of least resistance.

But man governs his feelings by his reason; he keeps his feelings and his instincts in check, subordinating them to the aim he has in view. He rules the brute creation by his intelligence. His intelligence formulates laws which are the product of [5] experience. His experience is born of work; man works in order that he may not perish. In order that production may be possible, a line of conduct is essential, the laws of experience must be obeyed. Man must consider the result in advance.

But the pack-donkey thinks of nothing at all, except what will save himself trouble.

The Pack-Donkey's Way is responsible for the plan of every continental city; including Paris, unfortunately.

In the areas into which little by little invading populations filtered, the covered wagon lumbered along at the mercy of bumps and hollows, of rocks or mire; a stream was an intimidating obstacle. In this way were born roads and tracks. At cross roads or along river banks the first huts were erected, the first houses and the first villages; the houses were planted along the tracks, along the Pack-Donkey's Way. The inhabitants built a fortified wall round and a town hall inside it. They legislated, they toiled, they lived, and always they respected the [6] Pack-Donkey's Way. Five centuries later another and larger enclosure was built, and five centuries later still a third yet greater. The places where the Pack-Donkey's Way entered the town became the City Gates and the Customs officers were installed there. The village has become a great capital; Paris, Rome, and Stamboul are based upon the Pack-Donkey's Way.

The great capitals have no arteries; they have only capillaries: further growth, therefore, implies sickness or death. In order to survive, their existence has for a long time been in the hands of surgeons who operate constantly.

The Romans were great legislators, great colonizers, great administrators. When they arrived at a place, at a cross roads or at a river bank, they took a square and set out the plan of a rectilinear town, so that it should be clear and well arranged, easy to

police and to clean, a place in which you could find your way
about and stroll with comfort—the working town or the pleasure
town (Pompeii). The square plan was in conformity with the
dignity of the Roman citizen.

But at home, in Rome itself, with their eyes turned towards [7]
the Empire, they allowed themselves to be stifled by the Pack-
Donkey's Way. What an ironical situation! The wealthy, however, went far from the chaos of the town and built their great
and well-planned villas, such as Hadrian's villa.

They were, with Louis XIV, the only great town-planners of
the West.

In the Middle Ages, overcome by the year 1000, men accepted the leading of the pack-donkey, and long generations
endured it after. Louis XIV, after trying to tidy up the Louvre
(i.e. the Colonnade), became disgusted and took bold measures:
he built Versailles, where both town and chateau were created
in every detail in a rectilinear and well-planned fashion; the
Observatoire, the Invalides and the Esplanade, the Tuileries
and the Champs Élysées, rose far from the chaos, outside the
town;—all these were ordered and rectilinear.

The overcrowding had been exorcised. Everything else followed, in a masterly way: the Champ de Mars, l'Étoile, the
avenues de Neuilly, de Vincennes, de Fontainebleau, etc., for
succeeding generations to exploit.

But imperceptibly, as a result of carelessness, weakness and
anarchy, and by the system of "democratic" responsibilities, the
old business of overcrowding began again.

And as if that were not enough, people began to desire it;
they have even created it in invoking the laws of beauty! The
Pack-Donkey's Way has been made into a religion.

The movement arose in Germany as a result of a book by
Camille Sitte on town-planning, a most wilful piece of work;
a glorification of the curved line and a specious demonstration
of its unrivalled beauties. Proof of this was advanced by the
example of all the beautiful towns of the Middle Ages; the
author confounded the picturesque with the conditions vital
to the existence of a city. Quite recently whole quarters have
been constructed in Germany based on this *æsthetic*. . . .[8]

The great city expresses man's power and might; the houses

which shelter such an active ardour should follow a noteworthy plan. At least, this seems to my mind the logical conclusion of a quite simple reasoning.

Antiquity has left us, in its various remains, a demonstration of this fact. There have been golden moments when the power of the mind dominated the rabble. We have already seen it clearly in regard to Babylon and Pekin, and they are but examples among many; great cities and smaller ones, even quite small ones, which during certain noble periods were illumined by talent, science and experience. Everywhere there are remains, or units still intact, which provide us with a model: Egyptian temples, the rectilinear cities of North Africa (*e.g.* Kairouan), the sacred cities of India, the Roman cities of the Empire, or those built in the great tradition: Pompeii, Aigues-Mortes, Monpazier.

The structure of cities reveals two possibilities; a progressive growth, subject to chance, with resultant characteristics of slow accumulation and a gradual rise; once it has acquired its gravitational pull it becomes a centrifugal force of immense power, bringing the rush and the mob. Such was Rome; such are now Paris, London or Berlin.

Or on the other hand, the construction of a city as the [91] expression of a preconceived and predetermined plan embodying the then known principles of the science; such is Pekin and such are the fortified cities of the Renaissance (*e.g.* Palmanova), or the colonial cities set by the Romans amongst their barbarian subjects. . . .[92]

We struggle against chance, against disorder, against a policy of drift and against the idleness which brings death; we strive for order, which can be achieved only by appealing to what is the fundamental basis on which our minds can work: geometry. In the general confusion there appear crystallizations of pure forms which bring strength and reassurance and give to beauty the material support it must have. At such moments, man has reflected well, he has employed the means proper to him and has produced works of a human order. . . .[93]

A CONTEMPORARY CITY

The use of technical analysis and architectural synthesis enabled me to draw up my scheme for a contemporary city of three million inhabitants. The result of my work was shown in November 1922 at the Salon d'Automne in Paris. It was greeted with a sort of stupor; the shock of surprise caused rage in some quarters and enthusiasm in others. The solution I put forward was a rough one and completely uncompromising. There were no notes to accompany the plans, and, alas! not everybody can read a plan. I should have had to be constantly on the spot in order to reply to the fundamental questions which spring from the very depths of human feelings. Such questions are of profound interest and cannot remain unanswered. When at a later date it became necessary [163] that this book should be written, a book in which I could formulate the new principles of Town Planning, I resolutely decided *first of all* to find answers to these fundamental questions. I have used two kinds of argument: first, those essentially human ones which start from the mind or the heart or the physiology of our sensations as a basis; secondly, historical and statistical arguments. . . .

A CONTEMPORARY CITY OF
THREE MILLION INHABITANTS

Proceeding in the manner of the investigator in his laboratory, I have avoided all special cases, and all that may be accidental, and I have assumed an ideal site to begin with. My object was not to overcome the existing state of things, but *by constructing a theoretically water-tight formula to arrive at the fundamental principles of modern town planning.* Such fundamental principles, if they are genuine, can serve as the skeleton of any system of modern town planning; being as it were the *rules* according to which development will take place. We shall then be in a position to take a special case, no matter what: whether it be Paris, London, Berlin, New York or some small town.

Then, as a result of what we have learnt, we can take control
and decide in what direction the forthcoming battle is to be
waged. For the desire to rebuild any great city in a modern way
is to engage in a formidable battle. Can you imagine people
engaging in a battle without knowing their objectives? Yet that
is exactly what is happening. The authorities are compelled [164]
to do something, so they give the police white sleeves or set
them on horseback, they invent sound signals and light signals,
they propose to put bridges over streets or moving pavements
under the streets; more garden cities are suggested, or it is
decided to suppress the tramways, and so on. And these decisions
are reached in a sort of frantic haste in order, as it were, to
hold a wild beast at bay. That BEAST is the great city. It is
infinitely more powerful than all these devices. And it is just
beginning to wake. What will to-morrow bring forth to cope
with it?

We must have some rule of conduct.[1]

We must have fundamental principles for modern town
planning.

Site

A level site is the ideal site. In all those places where traffic
becomes over-intensified the level site gives a chance of a normal
solution to the problem. Where there is less traffic, differences
in level matter less. . . .

---

[1] New suggestions shower on us. Their inventors and those who believe
in them have their little thrill. It is so easy for them to believe in them. But
what if they are based on grave errors? How are we to distinguish between
what is reasonable and an over-poetical dream? The leading newspapers
accept everything with enthusiasm. One of them said, "The cities of to-
morrow must be built on new virgin soil." But no, this is not true! We must
go to the old cities, all our inquiries confirm it. One of our leading papers
supports the suggestion made by one of our greatest and most reasonable
architects, who for once gives us bad counsel in proposing to erect round
about Paris a ring of sky-scrapers. The idea is romantic enough, but it cannot be defended. The sky-scrapers must be built *in the centre* and not on the
periphery.

Population

This consists of the citizens proper; of suburban dwellers; and of those of a mixed kind.[165]

(a) Citizens are of the city: those who work and live in it.

(b) Suburban dwellers are those who work in the outer industrial zone and who do not come into the city: they live in garden cities.

(c) The mixed sort are those who work in the business parts of the city but bring up their families in garden cities.

To classify these divisions (and so make possible the transmutation of these recognized types) is to attack the most important problem in town planning, for such a classification would define the areas to be allotted to these three sections and the delimitation of their boundaries. This would enable us to formulate and resolve the following problems:

1. The *City*, as a business and residential centre.

2. The *Industrial City* in relation to the *Garden Cities* (*i.e.* the question of transport).

3. The *Garden Cities* and the *daily transport* of the workers.

Our first requirement will be an organ that is compact, rapid, lively and concentrated: this is the City with its well-organized centre. Our second requirement will be another organ, supple, extensive and elastic; this is *the Garden City* on the periphery.

Lying between these two organs, we must *require the legal establishment* of that absolute necessity, a protective zone which allows of extension, *a reserved zone* of woods and fields, a fresh-air reserve.

Density of Population

The more dense the population of a city is the less are the distances that have to be covered. The moral, therefore, is that we must *increase the density of the centres of our cities, where business affairs are carried on.*

Lungs

Work in our modern world becomes more intensified day by day, and its demands affect our nervous system in a way [166] that grows more and more dangerous. Modern toil demands quiet and fresh air, not stale air.

The towns of to-day can only increase in density at the expense of the open spaces which are the lungs of a city.

We must *increase the open spaces and diminish the distances to be covered*. Therefore the centre of the city must be constructed *vertically*.

The city's residential quarters must no longer be built along "corridor-streets," full of noise and dust and deprived of light.

It is a simple matter to build urban dwellings away from the streets, without small internal courtyards and with the windows looking on to large parks; and this whether our housing schemes are of the type with "set-backs" or built on the "cellular" principle.

The Street

The street of to-day is still the old bare ground which has been paved over, and under which a few tube railways have been run.

The modern street in the true sense of the word is a new type of organism, a sort of stretched-out workshop, a home for many complicated and delicate organs, such as gas, water and electric mains. It is contrary to all economy, to all security, and to all sense to bury these important service mains. They ought to be accessible throughout their length. The various storeys of this stretched-out workshop will each have their own particular functions. If this type of street, which I have called a "workshop," is to be realized, it becomes as much a matter of *construction* as are the houses with which it is customary to flank it, and the bridges which carry it over valleys and across rivers.

The modern street should be a masterpiece of civil engineering and no longer a job for navvies.

The "corridor-street" should be tolerated no longer, for it

poisons the houses that border it and leads to the construction of small internal courts or "wells." . . . [167]

THE PLAN OF THE CITY

The basic principles we must follow are these:
1. We must de-congest the centres of our cities.
2. We must augment their density.
3. We must increase the means for getting about.
4. We must increase parks and open spaces.

At the very centre we have the STATION with its landing stage for aero-taxis.

Running north and south, and east and west, we have the [170] MAIN ARTERIES for fast traffic, forming elevated roadways 120 feet wide.

At the base of the sky-scrapers and all round them we have a great open space 2,400 yards by 1,500 yards, giving an area of 3,600,000 square yards, and occupied by gardens, parks and avenues. In these parks, at the foot of and round the sky-scrapers, would be the restaurants and cafes, the luxury shops, housed in buildings with receding terraces: here too would be the theatres, halls and so on; and here the parking places or garage shelters.

The sky-scrapers are designed purely for business purposes. . . .

All round the city is the *protected zone* of woods and green fields.

Further beyond are the *garden cities,* forming a wide encircling band. . . . [171]

The City

Here we have twenty-four sky-scrapers capable each of housing 10,000 to 50,000 employees; this is the business and hotel section, etc., and accounts for 400,000 to 600,000 inhabitants.

The residential blocks, of the two main types already mentioned, account for a further 600,000 inhabitants.

The garden cities give us a further 2,000,000 inhabitants, or more. . . . [172]

A Contemporary City, as envisioned by Le Corbusier. A part of the caption from the
English edition of *Urbanisme* reads as follows: "We are in the very centre of the city

From The City of Tomorrow

...ie point of greatest density of population and traffic; there is any amount of room for
oth. . . . Theatres, public halls, etc., are scattered in the open spaces between the
ky-scrapers and are surrounded by trees."

GARDEN CITIES

A simple phrase suffices to express the necessities of to-morrow: WE MUST BUILD IN THE OPEN. The lay-out must be of a purely geometrical kind, with all its many and delicate implications.

The city of to-day is a dying thing because it is not geometrical. To build in the open would be to replace our present haphazard arrangements, *which are all we have to-day,* by a *uniform* lay-out. Unless we do this *there is no salvation.*

The result of a true geometrical lay-out is *repetition.*

The result of repetition is a *standard,* the perfect form (*i.e.* the creation of standard types). A geometrical lay-out means that mathematics play their part. There is no first-rate human production but has geometry at its base. It is of the very essence of Architecture. To introduce uniformity into the building of the city we must *industrialize building.* Building is the one economic activity which has so far resisted industrialization.[175] It has thus escaped the march of progress, with the result that the cost of building is still abnormally high.

The architect, from a professional point of view, has become a twisted sort of creature. He has grown to love irregular sites, claiming that they inspire him with original ideas for getting round them. Of course he is wrong. For nowadays the only building that can be undertaken must be either for the rich or built at a loss (as, for instance, in the case of municipal housing schemes), or else by jerry-building and so robbing the inhabitant of all amenities. A motor-car which is achieved by mass production is a masterpiece of comfort, precision, balance and good taste. A house built to order (on an "interesting" site) is a masterpiece of incongruity—a monstrous thing.

If the builder's yard were reorganized on the lines of standardization and mass production we might have gangs of workmen as keen and intelligent as mechanics.

The mechanic dates back only twenty years, yet already he forms the highest caste of the working world.

The mason dates . . . from time immemorial! He bangs away

with feet and hammer. He smashes up everything round him, and the plant entrusted to him falls to pieces in a few months. The spirit of the mason must be disciplined by making him part of the severe and exact machinery of the industrialized builder's yard.

The cost of building would fall in the proportion of 10 to 2.

The wages of the labourers would fall into definite categories; to each according to his merits and service rendered.

The "interesting" or erratic site absorbs every creative faculty of the architect and wears him out. What results is equally erratic: lopsided abortions; a specialist's solution which can only please other specialists.

We must build *in the open:* both within the city and around it.

Then having worked through every necessary technical stage and using absolute ECONOMY, we shall be in a position to experience the intense joys of a creative art which is based on geometry.[176]

THE CITY AND ITS ÆSTHETIC

(The plan of a city which is here presented is a direct consequence of purely geometrical considerations.)

A new unit *on a large scale* (400 yards) inspires everything. Though the gridiron arrangement of the streets every 400 yards (sometimes only 200) is uniform (with a consequent ease in finding one's way about), no two streets are in any way alike. This is where, in a magnificent contrapuntal symphony, the forces of geometry come into play.

Suppose we are entering the city by way of the Great Park. Our fast car takes the special elevated motor track between the majestic sky-scrapers: as we approach nearer there is seen the repetition against the sky of the twenty-four sky-scrapers; to our left and right on the outskirts of each particular area are the municipal and administrative buildings; and enclosing the space are the museums and university buildings.

Then suddenly we find ourselves at the feet of the first sky-scrapers. But here we have, not the meagre shaft of sunlight which so faintly illumines the dismal streets of New York, but

an immensity of space. The whole city is a Park. The terraces
stretch out over lawns and into groves. Low buildings of a horizontal kind lead the eye on to the foliage of the trees. Where are
now the trivial *Procuracies?* Here is the CITY with its crowds
living in peace and pure air, where noise is smothered under the
foliage of green trees. The chaos of New York is overcome. Here,
bathed in light, stands the modern city.

Our car has left the elevated track and has dropped its speed
of sixty miles an hour to run gently through the residential quarters. The "set-backs" [2] permit of vast architectural perspectives.
There are gardens, games and sports grounds. And sky everywhere, as far as the eye can see. The square silhouettes of the
terraced roofs stand clear against the sky, bordered with the
verdure of the hanging gardens. The [177] uniformity of the units
that compose the picture throw into relief the firm lines on which
the far-flung masses are constructed. Their outlines softened by
distance, the sky-scrapers raise immense geometrical façades all
of glass, and in them is reflected the blue glory of the sky. An
overwhelming sensation. Immense but radiant prisms.

And in every direction we have a varying spectacle: our
"gridiron" is based on a unit of 400 yards; but it is strangely
modified by architectural devices! (The "set-backs" are in coun-
terpoint, on a unit of 600 × 400.)

The traveller in his airplane, arriving from Constantinople or
Pekin it may be, suddenly sees appearing through the wavering
lines of rivers and patches of forests that clear imprint which
marks a city which has grown in accordance with the spirit of
man: the mark of the human brain at work.

As twilight falls the glass sky-scrapers seem to flame.

This is no dangerous futurism, a sort of literary dynamite flung
violently at the spectator. It is a spectacle organized by an Architecture which uses plastic resources for the modulation of
forms seen in light. . . . [178]

---

[2] As before, this refers to set-backs *on plan;* buildings "à redents," *i.e.*
with projecting salients.—F.E.

THE URBAN SCENE

. . . This new lay-out enables us to introduce trees into our city. Leaving hygienic considerations on one side for the moment, it may be admitted, æsthetically speaking, that the proximity of geometrical forms of dwellings to the picturesque forms of vegetation produces a much-needed and satisfying combination in our urban scene. Indeed, having got so far with our rich variety of plastic forms, the clear-cut shapes of the buildings, the rounded forms of the foliage and the arabesques of the branches, hardly anything remains to be done except to continue to develop these good things. To illustrate what I mean I will give a concrete example. The *Tuileries* might be continued over whole quarters of Paris in the form of parks, whether of the formal French kind or in the undulating English manner, and could be combined with purely geometrical architecture. I conclude with this reassuring statement: no matter how rigidly uniform the façades of our dwellings with "set-backs" may be, they will form a sort of grill or trellis against which the trees will display themselves to advantage, and this whether they are seen close at hand or from a distance; they will make a sort of draught-board which will harmonize well with the formal flower-beds. To go back to the conclusions of an earlier chapter: uniformity in detail is at the base of all architectural practice; but uniformity in detail implies variety in the general effect. The problem is now put on a wider basis: the house is no longer a fraction of façade 50 or 75 feet in length, it extends to 600 or 1,200 feet, and it is varied by the lively incidence of its recessions and salients. Think of the Procuracies, the Place des Vosges or the Place Vendôme, and it will be clear that the architectural "frills" of these famous places are not for one [236] moment their only claim to beauty. And the economist will conclude: Here is a plan which permits us to standardize building by a full use of machinery, industrial organization and the creation of standards. Out of the earth spring up the shrubs and foliage, the lawns stretch away into the distance, and the beds of flowering plants. A ring of geometrical forms encloses this charming and picturesque scene, and the silhouette seen against the sky is an architectural one. The old corridor-street has given way to wide, noble and cheerful spaces.

THE HUMAN SCALE

Now, all these considerations apply to functions which appertain to *man* and man's height varies between, say, 5 feet 6 inches and 6 feet 2 inches. And when man finds himself alone in vast empty spaces he grows disheartened. We must learn how to tighten up the urban landscape and discover units of measurement to our own scale. This problem is essentially one of architecture. Architecture is able to make great play with contrasts, to harmonize simple elements with complex ones and small with great, to blend the forcible with the graceful. The vast buildings which the town planning of the future will bring about would crush us if there were no common measure between them and ourselves. We have already seen how a tree is a thing that pleases us all, since, however remotely, we are still children of Nature; and we have seen that an urban manifestation which completely ignored Nature would soon find itself at odds with our deepest primeval impulses. The tree modifies a scene that is too vast, and its casual forms contrast with the rigid forms which we have conceived and made by the machinery of our epoch. It would seem that the tree is an element essential to our comfort, and its presence in the city is a sort of caress, a kindly thing in the midst of our severe creations. . . .[237]

THE CENTRE OF PARIS

The "Voisin Plan" [3] for Paris is the result of combining two new essential elements: *a commercial city* and *a residential city*.

The *commercial city* would occupy 600 acres of a particularly

[3] As it is the motor-car which has completely overturned all our old ideas of town planning, I thought of interesting the manufacturers of cars in the construction of the *Esprit Nouveau* Pavilion at the Paris International Exhi-

antiquated and unhealthy part of Paris, *i.e.* from the Place [277] de la République to the Rue du Louvre, and from the Gare de l'Est to the Rue de Rivoli.

The *residential city* would extend from the Rue des Pyramides to the circus on the Champs Élysées, and from the Gare Saint-Lazare to the Rue de Rivoli, and would involve the destruction of areas which for the most part are overcrowded, and covered with middle-class houses now used as offices.[278]

The central station would be between the business city and the residential city, and would be underground.

The principal axis of the new plan of the centre of Paris would lie east to west, from Vincennes to Levallois-Perret. It would re-create one of the indispensable great transversal arteries which no longer exist to-day. It would serve as the principal artery for fast traffic; it would be nearly 400 feet wide, and would have a speedway for one-way traffic without cross roads. The effect of this vital artery would be to empty the Champs Élysées, which quite clearly cannot continue to serve as a main thoroughfare for fast traffic, since it ends in a blank wall: *i.e.* at the Jardin des Tuileries.[279]

The "Voisin" scheme for Paris means regaining possession of the eternal centre of the city. I showed in a former chapter how it was impossible in practice to displace the settled centres of

---

bition of Decorative Art, since this Pavilion was planned as a dwelling and as a unit of modern town planning.

I saw the heads of the Peugeot, Citroën and Voisin Companies and said to them:

"The motor has killed the great city.

"The motor must save the great city.

"Will you endow Paris with a Peugeot, Citroën or Voisin scheme of re-building; a scheme whose sole object would be to concentrate public notice on the true architectural problem of this era, a problem not of decoration but of architecture and town planning; a sane reconstruction of the dwelling unit and the creation of urban organs which would answer to our conditions of living which have been so profoundly affected by machinery?"

Messrs. Peugeot would not risk themselves on our venturesome scheme.

M. Citroën very amiably replied that he did not know what I was talking about, and did not see what the motor-car had to do with the problem of the centre of Paris.

M. Mongermon, of the Voisin Company, without any hesitation agreed to finance my researches into the question of the centre of Paris, and so the resulting scheme is called the "Voisin" scheme for Paris.

great cities and to create an adequate new city at the side of the
old one.[4]

This plan makes a frontal attack on the most diseased quarters
of the city, and the narrowest streets: it is not "opportunist" or
designed to gain a yard or two at odd points in over-congested
roads. Its aim is rather to open up in the strategic heart of Paris
a splendid system of communication. As against streets ranging
from 20 to 35 feet in width with cross roads every 20, 30 or 50
yards, its aim is to establish a plan on the "gridiron" system with
roads 150, 250, to 400 feet in width, with cross roads every 350
or 400 yards; and on the vast island sites thus formed to build
immense cruciform sky-scrapers, so creating a *vertical* city, a city
which will pile up the cells which have for so long been crushed
on the ground, and set them high above the earth, bathed in
light and air.

Thenceforward, instead of a flattened-out and jumbled city
such as *the airplane reveals to us for the first time,* terrifying
in its confusion . . . our city rises vertical to the sky, open
to light and air, clear and radiant and sparkling. The soil,
of whose surface 70 to 80 per cent. has till now been [280] en-
cumbered by closely packed houses, is now built over to the extent of a mere 5 per cent. The remaining 95 per cent. is devoted
to the main speedways, car parks and open spaces. The avenues
of trees are doubled and quadrupled, and the parks at the foot
of the sky-scrapers do, in fact, make the city itself one vast
garden.

The density, which is too great as things are at present, of the
districts affected by the "Voisin" plan would not be reduced. It
would be *quadrupled.*

Instead of those terible districts with which we are so little
acquainted,[5] which have a density of population of 320 to the
acre, these new quarters would allow of 1,400 to the same area.

I wish it were possible for the reader, by an effort of imagina-

---

[4] It is true that during the Renaissance new cities were constructed contiguous to an old one. The reason was entirely military, and the ancient
city being extremely small there would have been no gain in rebuilding
the centre.

[5] I should like any of my readers who may find themselves able to do so
to take a walk in the daytime, and another at night, in the districts of
Paris covered by the "Voisin" plan. They would be surprised!

This model by Le Corbusier and Pierre Jeanneret is of the **Voisin Plan for Paris.** It was exhibited in 1925 at the Pavillon de L'Esprit Nouveau and was a bold idea for Paris at that time. Currents of architectural and city-planning thought were beginning to run both ways across the Atlantic Ocean. Le Corbusier early admired American skyscrapers and came in turn to be admired by many American planners.

tion, to conceive what such a vertical city would be like; imagine all this junk, which till now has lain spread out over the soil like a dry crust, cleaned off and carted away and replaced by immense clear crystals of glass, rising to a height of over 600 feet; each at a good distance from the next and all standing with their bases set among trees. Our city, which has crawled on the ground till now, suddenly rises to its feet in the most natural way, even for the moment going beyond the powers of our imaginations, which have been constrained by age-long habits of thought.

For the Pavilion of the *Esprit Nouveau* at the International Exhibition of Decorative Art held in Paris, and in which the "Voisin" plan was on view, I painted a panorama whose aim was to make evident *to the eye* this new conception, so unfamiliar to us as yet. The panorama was most carefully executed and showed Paris as it is to-day, from Notre-Dame to the Étoile, including those monuments which are our imperishable heritage. Behind it rose the new city. But one is no longer confronted with the spires and campaniles of a wild Manhattan,[281] jostling against one another and mutually robbing each other of light and air, but the majestic rhythm of vertical surfaces receding into the distance in a noble perspective and outlining pure forms. From one skyscraper to another a relationship of voids and solids is established. At their feet the great open spaces are seen. The city is once more based on axes, as is every true architectural creation. Town planning enters into architecture and architecture into town planning. If the "Voisin" plan is studied there can be seen to west and southwest the great openings made by Louis XIV, Louis XV and Napoleon: the Invalides, the Tuileries, the Place de la Concorde, the Champ de Mars and the Étoile. These works are a signal example of *creation,* of that spirit which is able to dominate and compel the mob. Set in juxtaposition the new *business city* does not seem an anomaly, but rather gives the [282] impression of being in the same tradition and following the normal laws of progress. . . .[283]

THE "VOISIN" SCHEME AND THE PAST

In this scheme the historical past, our common inheritance, is respected. More than that, it is *rescued*. The persistence of the present state of crisis must otherwise lead rapidly to the destruction of that past.

First of all I must make a distinction, of a sentimental nature, but one of great importance; in these days the past has lost something of its fragrance, for its enforced mingling with the life of to-day has set it in a false environment. My dream is to see the Place de la Concorde empty once more, silent and lonely, and the Champs Élysées a quiet place to walk in. The "Voisin" scheme would isolate the whole of the ancient city and bring back peace and calm from Saint-Gervais to the Étoile.

The districts of the *Marais*, the *Archives*, the *Temple*, etc., would be demolished. But the ancient churches would be preserved.[6] They would stand surrounded by verdure; what could be more charming! And even if we must admit that their original environment has thus been transformed, we must agree that their present setting is not only an unreal one, but is also dreary and ugly.

Similarly the "Voisin" plan shows, still standing among the masses of foliage of the new parks, certain historical monuments, arcades, doorways, carefully preserved because they are pages out of history or works of art.

Thus one might find, surrounded by green grass, an exciting and delightful relic such as, say, some fine Renaissance house, now to be used as a library, lecture hall or what not.

The "Voisin" scheme covers 5 per cent. only of the ground with buildings, it safeguards the relics of the past and enshrines them harmoniously in a framework of trees and woods. For material things too must die, and these green parks with their relics are in some sort cemeteries, carefully tended, in which people may breathe, dream and learn. In this way the past [287] becomes

[6] This was not one of the objects of the plan, but was merely the result of their falling into the architectural composition of the scheme.

no longer dangerous to life, but finds instead its true place within it.

The "Voisin" scheme does not claim to have found a final solution to the problem of the centre of Paris; but it may serve to raise the discussion to a level in keeping with the spirit of our age, and to provide us with reasonable standards by which to judge the problem. It sets up *principles* as against the medley of silly little reforms with which we are constantly deceiving ourselves.[288]

VII
The New Centrifuge

Ralph Borsodi

FLIGHT FROM THE CITY

Ralph Borsodi, *Flight from the City: The Story of a New Way to Family Security* (New York, Harper and Brothers, 1933).

FLIGHT FROM THE CITY

In 1920 the Borsodi family—my wife, my two small sons, and myself—lived in a *rented* home. We *bought* our food and clothing and furnishings from retail stores. We were *dependent* entirely upon my income from a none too certain white-collar job.

We lived in New York City—the metropolis of the country. We had the opportunity to enjoy the incredible variety of food-stuffs which pour into that great city from every corner of the continent; to live in the most luxurious apartments built to house men and women in this country; to use the speedy subways, the smart restaurants, the great office buildings, the libraries, theaters, public schools—all the thousand and one conveniences which make New York one of the most fantastic creations in the history of man. Yet in the truest sense, we could not enjoy any of them.

How could we enjoy them when we were financially insecure and never knew when we might be without a job; when we lacked the zest of living which comes from real health and suffered all the minor and sometimes major ailments which come from too much excitement, too much artificial food,[1] too much sedentary work, and too much of the smoke and noise and dust of the city; when we had to work just as hard to get to the places in which we tried to entertain ourselves as we had to get to the places in which we worked; when our lives were barren of real beauty—the beauty which comes only from contact with nature and from the growth of the soil, from flowers and fruits, from gardens and trees, from birds and animals?

We couldn't. Even though we were able for years and years, like so many others, to forget the fact—to ignore it amid the host of distractions which make up city life.

And then in 1920, the year of the great housing shortage, the house in which we were living was sold over our heads. New York in 1920 was no place for a houseless family. Rents, owing to the shortage of building which dated back to the World War, were outrageously high. Evictions were epidemic—to enable rapacious landlords to secure higher rents from new tenants—and most of the renters in the city seemed to be in the courts trying to secure the protection of the Emergency Rent Laws. We had the choice of looking for an equally endurable home in the city, of reading endless numbers of classified advertisements, of visiting countless real estate agents, of walking weary miles and climbing endless flights of steps, in an effort to rent another home, or of flight from the city. And while we were trying to prepare ourselves for the struggle with this typical [2] city problem, we were overcome with longing for the country—for the security, the health, the leisure, the beauty we felt it must be possible to achieve there. Thus we came to make the experiment in living which we had often discussed but which we had postponed time and again because it involved so radical a change in our manner of life.

Instead, therefore, of starting the irritating task of house and apartment hunting, we wrote to real estate dealers within commuting distance of the city. We asked them for a house which could be readily remodeled; a location near the railroad station

because we had no automobile; five to ten acres of land with
fruit trees, garden space, pasturage, a woodlot, and if possible a
brook; a location where electricity was available, and last but
not least, a low purchase price. Even if the place we could afford
only barely complied with these specifications, we felt confident
that we could achieve economic freedom on it and a degree of
comfort we never enjoyed in the city. All the other essentials of
the good life, not even excepting schooling for our two sons, we
decided we could produce for ourselves if we were unable to buy
in a neighborhood which already possessed them.

We finally bought a place located about an hour and three-
quarters from the city. It included a small frame house, one and
a half stories high, containing not a single modern improvement—
there was no plumbing, no running water, no gas, no electricity,
no steam heat. There were an old barn, and a [3] chicken-house
which was on the verge of collapse, and a little over seven acres
of land. There was a little fruit in the orchard—some apples,
cherries, and plums, but of the apples at least there were plenty.
. . . "Sevenacres," as we called the place, was large enough for
our initial experiment. Four years later we were able to select a
more suitable site and begin the building of the sort of home we
really wanted.

We began the experiment with three principal assets, courage
—foolhardiness, our city friends called it; a vision of what modern
methods and modern domestic machinery might be made to do
in the way of eliminating drudgery, and the fact that my wife
had been born and had lived up to her twelfth year on a ranch
in the West. She at least had had childhood experience of life in
the country.

But we had plenty of liabilities. We had little capital and only
a modest salary. We knew nothing about raising vegetables, fruit,
and poultry. All these things we had to learn. While I was a
handy man, I had hardly ever had occasion to use a hammer and
saw (a man working in an office rarely does), and yet if our experiment was to succeed it required that I should make myself
a master of all trades. We cut ourselves off from the city comforts to which we had [4] become so accustomed, without the
countryman's material and spiritual compensations for them.

We went to the country with nothing but our city furniture.

We began by adding to this wholly unsuitable equipment for pioneering, an electric range. This was the first purchase in the long list of domestic machines with which we proposed to test our theory that it was possible to be more comfortable in the country than in the city, with security, independence, and freedom to do the work to which we aspired thrown in for good measure.

Discomforts were plentiful in the beginning. The hardships of those early years are now fading into a romantic haze, but they were real enough at the time. A family starting with our handicaps had to expect them. But almost from the beginning there were compensations for the discomforts.

Before the end of the first year, the year of the depression of 1921 when millions were tramping the streets of our cities looking for work, we began to enjoy the feeling of plenty which the city-dweller never experiences. We cut our hay; gathered our fruit; made gallons and gallons of cider. We had a cow, and produced our own milk and butter, but finally gave her up. By furnishing us twenty quarts of milk a day she threatened to put us in the dairy business. So we changed to a pair of blooded Swiss goats. We equipped a poultry-yard, and had eggs, chickens, and fat roast capons. We ended the year with plenty not only for our own needs but for a [5] generous hospitality to our friends—some of whom were out of work—a hospitality which, unlike city hospitality, did not involve purchasing everything we served our guests.

To these things which we produced in our first year, we have since added ducks, guineas, and turkeys; bees for honey; pigeons for appearance; and dogs for company. We have in the past twelve years built three houses and a barn from stones picked up on our place; we weave suitings, blankets, carpets, and draperies; we make some of our own clothing; we do all of our own laundry work; we grind flour, corn meal, and breakfast cereals; we have our own workshops, including a printing plant; and we have a swimming-pool, tennis-court, and even a billiard-room.

In certain important respects our experiment was very different from the ordinary back-to-the-land adventure. We quickly abandoned all efforts to raise anything to sell. After the first year, during which we raised some poultry for the market, this became an inviolable principle. We produced only for our own consumption. If we found it difficult to consume or give away any surplus, we cut down our production of that particular thing and devoted the time to producing something else which we were then buying. We used machinery wherever we could, and tried to apply the most approved scientific methods to small-scale production. We acted on the theory that there was always some way of doing what we wanted to do,[6] if we only sought long enough for the necessary information, and that efficient machinery would pay for itself in the home precisely as it pays for itself in the factory.

The part which domestic machinery has played in making our adventure in homesteading a success cannot be too strongly emphasized. Machinery enabled us to eliminate drudgery; it furnished us skills which we did not possess, and it reduced the costs of production both in terms of money and in terms of labor. Not only do we use machines to pump our water, to do our laundry, to run our refrigerator—we use them to produce food, to produce clothing, to produce shelter.

Some of the machines we have purchased have proved unsatisfactory—something which is to be expected since so little real thought has been devoted by our factory-dominated inventors and engineers to the development of household equipment and domestic machinery. But taking the machines and appliances which we have used as a whole, it is no exaggeration to say that we started our quest of comfort with all the discomforts possible in the country, and, because of the machines, we have now achieved more comforts than the average prosperous city man enjoys.

What we have managed to accomplish is the outcome of nothing but a conscious determination to use machinery for the purpose of eliminating drudgery from the home and to produce for ourselves [7] enough of the essentials of living to free us from the thralldom of our factory-dominated civilization.

What are the social, economic, political, and philosophical implications of such a type of living? What would be the consequence of a widespread transference of production from factories to the home?

If enough families were to make their homes economically productive, cash-crop farmers specializing in one crop would have to abandon farming as a business and go back to it as a way of life. The packing-houses, mills, and canneries, not to mention the railroads, wholesalers, and retailers, which now distribute agricultural products would find their business confined to the production and distribution of exotic foodstuffs. Food is our most important industry. A war of attrition, such as we have been carrying on all alone, if extended on a large enough scale, would put the food industry out of its misery, for miserable it certainly is, all the way from the farmers who produce the raw materials to the men, women, and children who toil in the canneries, mills, and packing-towns, and in addition reduce proportionately the congestion, adulteration, unemployment, and unpleasant odors to all of which the food industry contributes liberally.

If enough families were to make their homes economically productive, the textile and clothing industries, with their low wages, seasonal unemployment,[8] cheap and shoddy products, would shrink to the production of those fabrics and those garments which it is impractical for the average family to produce for itself.

If enough families were to make their homes economically productive, undesirable and non-essential factories of all sorts would disappear and only those which would be desirable and essential because they would be making tools and machines, electric light bulbs, iron and copper pipe, wire of all kinds, and the myriad of things which can best be made in factories, would remain to furnish employment to those benighted human beings who prefer to work in factories.

Domestic production, if enough people turned to it, would not only annihilate the undesirable and non-essential factory by depriving it of a market for its products. It would do more. It would release men and women from their present thralldom to the factory and make them masters of machines instead of servants to them; it would end the power of exploiting them which ruthless, acquisitive, and predatory men now possess; it would free them for the conquest of comfort, beauty and understanding.[9]

DOMESTIC PRODUCTION

With Newton, it was the falling of an apple which led to the discovery of gravitation. With Watts, it was the popping of the lid of a boiling kettle which led to the invention of the steam-engine. With the Borsodi family, it was the canning of tomatoes which led to the discovery of domestic production. Out of that discovery came not only an entirely new theory of living; it led to my writing several books dealing with various phases of the discovery—*National Advertising vs. Prosperity* was the first; then came *The Distribution Age*, finally *This Ugly Civilization.*

In the summer of 1920—the first summer after our flight from the city—Mrs. Borsodi began to can and preserve a supply of fruits and vegetables for winter use. I remember distinctly the pride with which she showed me, on my return from the city one evening, the first jars of tomatoes which she had canned. But with my incurable bent for economics, the question "Does it really pay?" instantly popped into my head. Mrs. Borsodi had rather unusual equipment for doing the work efficiently. She cooked on an electric range; she used a steam-pressure cooker; she had most of the latest gadgets for reducing the labor to a minimum.[10] I looked around the kitchen, and then at the table covered with shining glass jars filled with tomatoes and tomato juice.

"It's great," I said, "but does it really pay?"

"Of course it does," was her reply.

"Then it ought to be possible to prove that it does—even if we take into consideration every cost—the cost of raw materials, the value of the labor put into the work yourself, the fuel, the equipment."

"That ought to be easy," she maintained.

It didn't prove as easy as we anticipated. We spent not only that evening, but many evenings, trying to arrive at a fairly accurate answer to the question. It wasn't even easy to arrive at a satisfactory figure on the cost of raw materials she had used. Some of the tomatoes had been grown in our own garden; some had been purchased. How much had it cost us to produce the tomatoes we had raised? We had kept no figures on gardening costs. Even if we had kept track of all the odd times during which we had worked in the garden, that would have helped little without a record of the time put into caring for the single row of tomato plants we had planted.

It proved equally difficult to determine how much time should be charged to the actual work of canning—since several different kinds of household tasks in addition to canning were often performed at the same time. While the jars were processing in the pressure cooker, work having nothing to do with canning was often performed.[11]

And when it came to determining how much electric current had been used—how much to charge for salt, spices, and other supplies—the very smallness of the quantities used made it difficult to arrive at a figure which approximated the facts. However, by abandoning the effort to determine gardening costs, and labor costs, and substituting the market value for both raw materials and for labor, we did finally come to figures which I felt we might use.

Then we still had the problem of determining what it had cost to buy canned tomatoes; we had to buy canned goods in a number of different stores so as to get a fair average price on the cannery-made product; of making certain that they were of a quality similar to those which we had produced at home, and of reducing the quantity in each can and each jar to some unit which would make comparison possible quantitatively as well as qualitatively. *When we finally made the comparison, the cost of the home-made product was between 20 per cent and 30 per cent lower than the price of the factory-made merchandise.*

The result astonished me. . . .[12]

It cost the Campbell Soup Company much less to produce a can of tomatoes in their great factories than it cost Mrs. Borsodi to produce one in her kitchen. But after they had produced theirs, all the costs of getting it from their factory to the ultimate consumer had to be added. In Mrs. Borsodi's case the first cost was the final cost. No distribution costs had to be added because the point of production and the point of consumption was the same.

All the orthodox economic teachings to which I had subscribed underwent a complete transformation as soon as I fully digested the implications of this discovery.

I discovered that more than two-thirds of the things which the average family now buys could be [16] produced more economically at home than they could be bought factory made;

—that the average man and woman could earn more by producing at home than by working for money in an office or factory and that, therefore, the less time they spent working away from home and the more time they spent working at home, the better off they would be;

—finally, that the home itself was still capable of being made into a productive and creative institution and that an investment in a homestead equipped with efficient domestic machinery would yield larger returns per dollar of investment than investments in insurance, in mortgages, in stocks and bonds.

The most modern and expensive domestic machinery need not, therefore, be a luxury. It can be a productive investment, in spite of the fact that most manufacturers of appliances still sell their machines on the basis of a luxury appeal. Even appliances like vacuum cleaners can be made paying investments, if the time they save is used productively in the garden, the kitchen, the sewing and loom room.

These discoveries led to our experimenting year after year with domestic appliances and machines. We began to experiment with the problem of bringing back into the home, and thus under our own direct control, the various machines which the textile-mill, the cannery and packing house, the flour-mill, the clothing and garment factory, had taken over from the home during the past two hundred years.[17]

. . . As long as the only available form of power was *centralized* power, the transfer of machinery and production from the home and the individual, to the factory and the group, was inevitable. But with the development of the gas-engine and the electric motor, power became available in *decentralized* forms. The home, so far as power was concerned, had been put in position to compete with the factory. . . .[18]

The average factory, no doubt, does produce food and clothing cheaper than we produce them even with our power-driven machinery on the Borsodi homestead. But factory costs, because of the problem of distribution, are only first costs. They cannot, therefore, be compared with home costs, which are final costs. The final cost of factory products, after distribution costs have been added, make the great bulk of consumer goods actually more expensive than home-made products of the same quality.

This is what we learned from Mrs. Borsodi's adventure with the tomatoes.[19]

SECURITY *VERSUS* INSECURITY

The essence of the matter is that when the farmer [124] shifted his productive activities from production for his own use to production for sale, he subjected himself to economic insecurities of a type roughly comparable in nature to the insecurities to which the wage-worker and the office-worker are now subjected. The farmer at one time was self-sufficient. He not only produced his own foodstuffs; he produced his own fabrics and clothing. Weaving and knitting were as much the activities of the homestead as farming. Sheep furnished him wool; the cattle he slaughtered furnished him leather; a wood lot furnished him fuel for heat and cooking. The farmer of the past, in most instances, spent the part of the year when farming operations could not be performed because of the season, operating grist-mills or lumber-mills, or working at some craft or trade. Such a life had only the insecurities which nature itself seems to impose upon human activities, and the possible damage from storm and drought, from locusts and hail, was reduced by storage of supplies and diversification of production. The threat of dispossession and unemployment which the dependence of the farmer upon the cash market has brought into farming was then unknown. Today farmers have abandoned not only the production of fabrics and clothing, but on about 20 per cent of the farms in this country there is not even a cow or a chicken; on 30 per cent there is not a single hog, and on approximately 90 per cent not even one sheep. What is more, on many of the farms in our banner agricultural states no gardens are kept [125] and almost every article of food is purchased at the store. If the unemployed of the cities turn to that kind of farming, they will merely have exchanged one kind of economic insecurity for another.

What is called subsistence farming, however, is a step, though only a step, in the right direction. . . .[126]

INDEPENDENCE *VERSUS* DEPENDENCE

Compare the position of the millions of men who are today unemployed to the position of our pioneer forefathers of a hundred years ago. At the beginning of the last century, Brillat-Savarin, the famous Frenchman who wrote *The Physiology of Taste,* made a long visit to the United States. In the fourth chapter of his book he tells the story of a visit of several weeks which he made to a farm which is now within the densely populated region of Hartford, Connecticut. As he was leaving, his host took him aside and said:

"You behold in me, my dear sir, a happy man, if there is one on earth; everything you see around you, and what you have seen at my house, is produced on my farm. These stockings have been knitted by my daughters; my shoes and clothes came from my herds; they, with my garden and my farmyard, supply me with plain and substantial [148] food. The greatest praise of our government is that in Connecticut there are thousands of farmers quite as content as myself, and whose doors, like mine, are never locked."

Today the farm on which that happy man once lived is cut up into city streets and covered with city buildings. The men and women of Hartford no longer produce their own food, clothing, and shelter. They work for them in stores and offices and factories. And in that same city, descendants of that pioneer farmer are probably walking the streets, not knowing what to do in order to be able to secure food, clothing and shelter.[149]

Twelve Southerners[*]
A STATEMENT OF PRINCIPLES

Twelve Southerners, *I'll Take My Stand: The South and the Agrarian Tradition* (New York, Harper and Brothers, 1930).[†]

INTRODUCTION: A STATEMENT OF PRINCIPLES

The authors contributing to this book are Southerners, well acquainted with one another and of similar tastes, though not necessarily living in the same physical community, and perhaps only at this moment aware of themselves as a single group of men. By conversation and exchange of letters over a number of years it had developed that they entertained many convictions in common, and it was decided to make a volume in which each one should furnish his views upon a chosen topic. This was the general background. But background and consultation as to the various topics were enough; there was to be no further collaboration. And so no single author is responsible for any view outside his own article. It was through the good fortune of some deeper agreement that the book was expected to achieve its unity. All the articles bear in the same sense upon the book's title-subject: all tend to support a Southern way of life against what may be called the American or prevailing way; and all as much as agree that the best terms in which to represent the distinction are contained in the phrase, Agrarian *versus* Industrial.

* [John Crowe Ransom, Donald Davidson, Frank Lawrence Owsley, John Gould Fletcher, Lyle H. Lanier, Allen Tate, Herman Clarence Nixon, Andrew Nelson Lytle, Robert Penn Warren, John Donald Wade, Henry Blue Kline and Stark Young—Ed.]

† Excerpts from "Introduction" and chapter "The Hind Tit" by Andrew Nelson Lytle from *I'll Take My Stand* by Twelve Southerners. Copyright 1930, by Harper and Brothers. Reprinted by permission of Harper and Brothers.

But after the book was under way it seemed a pity if the contributors, limited as they were within their special subjects, [ix] should stop short of showing how close their agreements really were. On the contrary, it seemed that they ought to go on and make themselves known as a group already consolidated by a set of principles which could be stated with a good deal of particularity. This might prove useful for the sake of future reference, if they should undertake any further joint publication. It was then decided to prepare a general introduction for the book which would state briefly the common convictions of the group. This is the statement. To it every one of the contributors in this book has subscribed.

Nobody now proposes for the South, or for any other community in this country, an independent political destiny. That idea is thought to have been finished in 1865. But how far shall the South surrender its moral, social, and economic autonomy to the victorious principle of Union? That question remains open. The South is a minority section that has hitherto been jealous of its minority right to live its own kind of life. The South scarcely hopes to determine the other sections, but it does propose to determine itself, within the utmost limits of legal action. Of late, however, there is the melancholy fact that the South itself has wavered a little and shown signs of wanting to join up behind the common or American industrial ideal. It is against that tendency that this book is written. The younger Southerners, who are being converted frequently to the industrial gospel, must come back to the support of the Southern tradition. They must be persuaded to look very critically at the [x] advantages of becoming a "new South" which will be only an undistinguished replica of the usual industrial community. . . .

Industrialism is the economic organization of the collective American society. It means the decision of society to invest its economic resources in the applied sciences. But the word science has acquired a certain sanctitude. It is out of order to quarrel with science in the abstract, or even with the applied sciences when their applications are made subject to criticism and intelligence. The capitalization of the applied sciences has now become extravagant and uncritical; it has enslaved our human energies to a degree now clearly felt to be burdensome. . . .[xi]

Opposed to the industrial society is the agrarian, which does not stand in particular need of definition. An agrarian society is hardly one that has no use at all for industries, for [xviii] professional vocations, for scholars and artists, and for the life of cities. Technically, perhaps, an agrarian society is one in which agriculture is the leading vocation, whether for wealth, for pleasure, or for prestige—a form of labor that is pursued with intelligence and leisure, and that becomes the model to which the other forms approach as well as they may. But an agrarian regime will be secured readily enough where the superfluous industries are not allowed to rise against it. The theory of agrarianism is that the culture of the soil is the best and most sensitive of vocations, and that therefore it should have the economic preference and enlist the maximum number of workers. . . .[xix]

. . . This much is clear: If a community, or a section, or a race, or an age, is groaning under industrialism, and well aware that it is an evil dispensation, it must find the way to throw it off. To think that this cannot be done is pusillanimous. And if the whole community, section, race, or age thinks it cannot be done, then it has simply lost its political genius and doomed itself to impotence.[xx]

Andrew Nelson Lytle_____

THE HIND TIT

Andrew Nelson Lytle, "The Hind Tit," in *I'll Take My Stand: The South and the Agrarian Tradition* (New York, Harper and Brothers, 1930).

When we remember the high expectations held universally by the founders of the American Union for a more perfect order of society, and then consider the state of life in this country today, it is bound to appear to reasonable people that somehow the experiment has proved abortive, and that in some way a great commonwealth has gone wrong.

There are those among us who defend and rejoice in this miscarriage, saying we are more prosperous. They tell us—and we are ready to believe—that collectively we are possessed of enormous wealth and that this in itself is compensation for whatever has been lost. But when we, as individuals, set out to find and enjoy this wealth, it becomes elusive and its goods escape us. We then reflect, no matter how great it may be collectively, if individually we do not profit by it, we have lost by the exchange. This becomes more apparent with the realization that, as its benefits elude us, the labors and pains of its acquisition multiply.

To be caught unwittingly in this unhappy condition is calamitous; but to make obeisance before it, after learning how barren is its rule, is to be eunuched. For those who are Southern farmers this is a particularly bitter fact to consider.[201] We have been taught by Jefferson's struggles with Hamilton, by Calhoun's with Webster, and in the woods at Shiloh or along the ravines of Fort Donelson where the long hunter's rifle spoke defiance to the more accelerated Springfields, that the triumph of industry, commerce, trade, brings misfortune to those who live on the land.

Since 1865 an agrarian Union has been changed into an industrial empire bent on conquest of the earth's goods and ports to sell them in. This means warfare, a struggle over markets, leading, in the end, to actual military conflict between nations. But, in the meantime, the terrific effort to manufacture ammunition—that is, wealth—so that imperialism may prevail, has brought upon the social body a more deadly conflict, one which promises to deprive it, not of life, but of living; take the concept of liberty from the political consciousness; and turn the pursuit of happiness into a nervous running-around which is without the logic, even, of a dog chasing its tail.

This conflict is between the unnatural progeny of inventive genius and men. It is a war to the death between technology and the ordinary human functions of living. The rights to these human functions are the natural rights of man, and they are threatened now, in the twentieth, not in the eighteenth, century for the first time. Unless man asserts and defends them he is doomed, to use a chemical analogy, to hop about like sodium on water, burning up in his own energy.

But since a power machine is ultimately dependent upon human control, the issue presents an awful spectacle: men, run mad by their inventions, supplanting themselves with [202] inanimate objects. This is, to follow the matter to its conclusion, a moral and spiritual suicide, foretelling an actual physical destruction.

The escape is not in socialism, in communism, or in sovietism—the three final stages industrialism must take. These change merely the manner and speed of the suicide; they do not alter its nature. Indeed, even now the Republican government and the Russian Soviet Council pursue identical policies toward the farmer. The Council arbitrarily raises the value of its currency and forces the peasant to take it in exchange for his wheat. This is a slightly legalized confiscation, and the peasants have met it by refusing to grow surplus wheat. The Republicans take a more indirect way—they raise the tariff. Of the two policies, that of the Russian Soviet is the more admirable. It frankly proposes to make of its farmers a race of helots.

We have been slobbered upon by those who have chewed the mad root's poison, a poison which penetrates to the spirit and rots the soul. And the time is not far off when the citizens of this one-time Republic will be crying, "What can I do to be saved?" If the farmers have been completely enslaved by that time, the echo to their question will be their only answer. If they have managed to remain independent, the answer lies in a return to a society where agriculture is practiced by most of the people. It is in fact impossible for any culture to be sound and healthy without a proper respect and proper regard for the soil, no matter how many urban dwellers think that their victuals come from groceries and delicatessens and their milk from tin cans. This ignorance does not release them from a final [203] dependence upon the farm and that most incorrigible of beings, the farmer. Nor is this ignorance made any more secure by Mr. Haldane's prognostication that the farm's ancient life will become extinct as soon as science rubs the bottle a few more times. The trouble is that already science has rubbed the bottle too many times. Forgetting in its hasty greed to put the stopper in, it has let the genius out.

But the resumption by the farmer of his place of power in the present order is considered remote. Just what political pressure he will be able to bring upon the Republicans to better his lot is, at the moment, unknown. Accepting the most pessimistic view, the continued supremacy of this imperialism and his continued dependency upon it, his natural enemy, the wealth-warrior who stands upon the bridge of high tariff and demands tribute, he is left to decide upon immediate private tactics. How is the man who is still living on the land, and who lives there because he prefers its life to any other, going to defend himself against this industrial imperialism and its destructive technology?

One common answer is heard on every hand: Industrialize the farm; be progressive; drop old-fashioned ways and adopt scientific methods. These slogans are powerfully persuasive and should be, but are not, regarded with the most deliberate circumspection, for under the guise of strengthening the farmer in his way of life they are advising him to abandon it and become absorbed. Such admonition coming from the quarters of the enemy is encouraging to the landowner in one sense only: it assures him he has something left to steal. Through its philosophy of Progress it is committing [204] a mortal sin to persuade farmers that they can grow wealthy by adopting its methods. A farm is not a place to grow wealthy; it is a place to grow corn.

It is telling him that he can bring the city way of living to the country and that he will like it when it gets there. His sons and daughters, thoroughly indoctrinated with these ideas at state normals, return and further upset his equilibrium by demanding the things they grew to like in town. They urge him to make the experiment, with threats of an early departure from his hearth and board. Under such pressure it is no wonder that the distraught countryman, pulled at from all sides, contemplates a thing he by nature is loath to attempt . . . experimentation.

If it were an idle experiment, there would be no harm in such an indulgence; but it is not idle. It has a price and, like everything else in the industrial world, the price is too dear. In exchange for the bric-à-brac culture of progress he stands to lose his land, and losing that, his independence, for the vagaries of its idealism assume concrete form in urging him to overproduce his money crop, mortgage his land, and send his daughters to town to clerk in ten-cent stores, that he may buy the products of the Power Age and keep its machines turning. That is the nigger in the woodpile . . . keep the machines turning!

How impossible it is for him to keep pace with the procession is seen in the mounting mortgages taken by banks, insurance companies, and the hydra-headed loan companies which have sprung up since the World War. In spite of these acknowledged facts, the Bureau of Agriculture, the State Experimental Stations, farm papers, and county [205] agents, all with the best possible intentions, advise him to get a little more progressive, that is, a little more productive. After advising this, they turn around and tell him he must curtail his planting. They also tell him that he (meaning his family) deserves motor-cars, picture shows, chain-store dresses for the women-folks, and all the articles in Sears-Roebuck catalogues. By telling him how great is his deserving, they prepare the way to deprive him of his natural deserts.

He must close his ears to these heresies that accumulate about his head, for they roll from the tongues of false prophets. He should know that prophets do not come from cities, promising riches and store clothes. They have always come from the wilderness, stinking of goats and running with lice and telling of a different sort of treasure, one a corporation head would not understand. Until such a one comes, it is best for him to keep to his ancient ways and leave the homilies of the tumble-bellied prophets to the city man who understands such things, for on the day when he attempts to follow the whitewash metaphysics of Progress, he will be worse off than the craftsman got to be when he threw his tools away. If that day ever comes, and there are strong indications that it may, the world will see a new Lazarus, but one so miserable that no dog will lend sympathy enough to lick the fly dung from his sores. Lazarus at least groveled at the foot of the rich man's table, but the new Lazarus will not have this distinction. One cannot sit at the board of an insurance company, nor hear the workings of its gargantuan appetite whetting itself on its own digestive processes.[206]

He must close his ears because an agrarian culture and industrial warfare are sustained through the workings of two different economies. Nothing less than confusion can follow the attempt of one economy to react to the laws of another. The progressive-farmer ideal is a contradiction in terms. A stalk of cotton grows. It does not progress. In 50,000 years it may evolve into something different, but for us and our four score and ten, it grows.

This error is also seen in the works of those highly respectable historians who, pointing to the census returns and the mounting wealth of the industrial states during the early decades of the nineteenth century, declared that the Southern culture was then already doomed, and that the Civil War merely hastened its demise. This view holds that industrialism is *manifest destiny*, that it would have supplanted agriculture in the South even if the Confederacy had maintained its withdrawal from the already disrupted Union. It strangely argues that the victorious planter and the small yeoman farmer would have abandoned what they had waged a desperate war to preserve from others; and what, in spite of defeat, survived in its essential features until the second decade of the twentieth century; and what still possesses sufficient strength to make a desperate fight for its inherited way of life.

If an abundance of those things which a people considers the goods and the riches of the earth defines wealth, then it follows that that particular culture is wealthy in proportion to the production and distribution of just those things and no others; and it does not depend upon what another people may consider the goods and riches, no matter how [207] greatly those things have multiplied for them, nor how many individuals they have to possess them. What industrialism counts as the goods and riches of the earth the agrarian South does not, nor ever did.

It is true that the planting aristocracy bought freely from England and the North. It is also true that the Cotton Kingdom was hastened into being by the invention of the cotton gin, an apparatus of the Machine Age; but because of this, it did not assume the habits and conduct of a factory town. Stocks and bonds and cities did not constitute wealth to the planter. Broad acres and increasing slaves, all tangible evidence of possession, were the great desiderata of his labors; and regardless of their price fluctuation on the world market, if they were paid for, their value remained constant in the planting states.

But the farming South, the yeoman South, that great body of free men, had hardly anything to do with the capitalists and their merchandise. In the upland country, the pine barrens, in the hills and mountains, and interspersed between the large plantations or lying on their fringe, and in the bad-road districts wherever they lay, communication with the main arteries of trade was so difficult that the plain people were forced into a state of self-sufficiency. And those who could reach the main turnpikes or the rivers and those who owned a few slaves in the planting districts, when they sold their cotton in New Orleans, were even less dependent than the planters, for they kept their looms going and fed their stock home-grown feed. Even the planters were beginning to say in the middle 'fifties that horses do not fatten on bought corn.[208]

By 1860 these broad, as yet somewhat flexible, outlines marked the structural formation of the Confederacy: belonging to the planting body, in round numbers, 3,000,000; slaves and free negroes, 4,000,000; townsmen, 1,000,000; plain people, including those who owned a few slaves, 4,000,000. By 1830 the lower South, leavened by Tennessee and Kentucky, became dominant in the agrarian stronghold below the line; and the lower South at this time was largely the plain people. From them the planter class was made.

After 1860 there would have been no fundamental economic rivalry between the yeoman farmer and the great landowner. The struggle before that time had been to determine who would rule, and the planters who emerged had done so because they were the more vigorous, the more intelligent, the more fortunate —the strong men of their particular culture. Jackson, demanding for the talented obscure the chance to grow rich and distinguished, expressed their demands politically. Jacksonian Democracy was, therefore, no Democracy; and although it claimed to be sired by Jefferson, his self-sufficient republic of freeholders did not contemplate any such leadership. "Down here, men like me and Gineral Jackson and Colonel Davy Crockett always demands our rights; and if we don't git 'em, somebody else is mighty liable to git Hell" is not the assertion of one contented to live easily and at peace on a fifty-acre steading. Cotton had changed the connotation of the demand.

In a society which recognizes the supremacy of nature and man's frailty each individual enjoys or subdues nature [209] according to his capacity and desires, and those who accumulate great estates deserve whatever reward attends them, for they have striven mightily. This is the common way a ruling class establishes itself. The South, and particularly the plain people, has never recovered from the embarrassment it suffered when this class was destroyed before the cultural lines became hard and fast.

The Whig Party was evidence of the painful readjustment between the static East and the dynamic West, and it pointed to the metamorphosis of the two into Calhoun's Feudal Aristocracy. It is significant that when the Western states were changing their constitutions to deliver universal suffrage into the hands of the farmer and artisan, Dew from Virginia and Harper from South Carolina were publishing tracts defending the strictest sort of society.

The force of Jackson's character introduced tragedy into the drama. His fight with Calhoun divided the house with an internecine struggle and so confused the agrarian states that they were unable to stand united before the irrepressible conflict. Calhoun, a philosopher as well as a logician, could see beyond his times the conclusion to the premises; but Jackson and Clay, men of action, one a soldier, the other a politician, could only act the parts their periods gave them. It was impossible for them, living pleasantly on their country estates, to foresee the impending dominion of technology.

The story of these strong men and their negro slaves has been told and mistold; but the farming South has had few to tell of its virtues, and it has left fewer written records to tell its story. Oblivion has almost covered it in a generation.[210] The planters whom it looked to in the days of its strength to defend their common life have busied themselves after the migration to the towns with a defense of their own part in the story, ignoring or referring to the yeomanry as the pore white trash.

Travellers have remembered the bedbugs, greasy food, rough cribs found in some places, and all those disagreeable elements which in the midst of the fatigues and worries of travel overemphasize the virtue of clean sheets and native food. Fresh linen has too often been mistaken for culture by people who scrub all the oil from their skins in the articles of the plumbing industry.

The most unique example of a garbled interpretation is found in the journals of one Olmstead [sic], [1] who traveled through the South in the early 'fifties. In the hill country he called to a young ploughman to inquire the way, and when not one, but several, ambled over and seemed willing to talk as long as he cared to linger, his time-ordered attitude was shocked at their lazy indifference to their work. Others who were mixed in their geography, who thought, for example, that New York lay to the south of Tennessee, amazed him. Although he could never know it, it was the tragedy of these people that they ever learned where New York lay, for such knowledge has taken them from a place where they knew little geography but knew it well, to places where they see much and know nothing.

This will be the most difficult task industrialism has undertaken, and on this rock its effort to urbanize the farm will probably split—to convince the farmer that it is time, not space, which has value. It will be difficult because the [211] farmer knows that he cannot control time, whereas he can wrestle with space, or at least with that particular part which is his orbit. He can stop, set, chaw, and talk, for, unable to subdue nature, it is no great matter whether he gets a little more or a little less that year from her limitless store. He has the choice of pleasant conversation, the excitement of hunting, fishing, hearing the hounds run, or of the possibility of accumulating greater spoils. Olmstead's young ploughmen did well to stop and talk with the "quair strangy"; ask "whare he's bin"; "whare he's aimin' to go"; and "air he bin to see his kin in Texas?" for by so doing they exchanged an uncertain physical satisfaction for a certain mental pleasure.

But those records which have been left, some few in writing, some through the patronage of journalists like Olmstead, through folk-games, songs, and ballads, particularly in the bad-road districts, and scattered more generally than is supposed upon the farms of the South, make it clear just how Southern life, and that part of it which was the plain people, was crystallizing when the war came.

One of these records comes from C. C. Henderson's *Story of*

[1] [The very Olmsted whose arguments on behalf of city parks are presented elsewhere in the present volume.—Ed.]

Murfreesboro. Martin Van Buren, when he was Chief Executive, made a speech from the court-house balcony. Everybody who could travel was there, for no Southern man ever missed, or misunderstood, a speech. Among those who had come to town that day was one Abner L., a squatter living on a large farm near the town. The landowner had promised Abner that he would introduce him to the President. After the speaking the planter moved through the crowd to keep his promise. This gentleman [212] understood thoroughly the honor he was about to receive. In a becoming, if somewhat nervous, manner he received the hand of the New-Yorker, squeezed it damply, then turned and presented Abner. Unlike the planter, Abner stepped up with perfect composure, pressed His Excellency's hand deliberately down, and said in a calm, even tone:

"Mr. Buren, the next time you come down here I want you to come out my way and ra'r around some with us boys."

This man worked a little truck patch on somebody else's land; hunted at night for pelts; fished in Stone's River; and ra'red around when he was a mind to. He possessed nature as little as possible, but he enjoyed it a great deal, so well that he felt the President might be satisfied with what hospitality he had to offer. Whenever a society has at its base people so contented with their lot, it may not be perfect ideally, but it is the best politicians will ever effect and maintain.

When Confederate defeat destroyed the planter as a class, it upset the balance of the whole. The yeomanry, who had had little to do with the money crop before, moved down from the hills and bought for a song the planter's dismembered plantations. As this was done, it only prepared the way to undermine the Southern culture, for the destruction of the rulers did not mean its destruction. The plain man brought from his isolation his ways and habits, and the impoverished state which had fallen upon the country after war and reconstruction forced him to rely upon home manufactures. In the great exodus to Texas in 1873 all the [213] emigrants wore homespun. It looked as if conditions were preparing to produce another set of rulers.

Unfortunately, the plain man did a thing which prevented this. When he took over the planter's land, he took over the worst of his habits, the furnishing system. Whereas with the planter it had been the factor of the great ports, with him it became the merchant of the county towns, the villages, and even the crossroads. The high price of cotton was responsible for this. When the prices broke in 1870, the small farmer was faced with a new experience: his reliance upon a money economy made him responsible to its laws. So long as they paid him well for his labors, it was profitable; but he learned that there was no assurance that this would continue. Something he could not understand was beginning to control his life. He could only hope for better days, and in the meantime mortgage next year's crop. Because it was the money crop, the merchant forced him to grow only cotton and buy the feed for his stock. This caused over-production, a drop in prices, more mortgages, and still greater over-production.

Such conditions broke many, and for the first time in the Cotton Kingdom, white tenantry developed. This was a definite social loss. With an entirely different race to serve the rich men as in slavery, the small white man could feel no very strong social inequality, and those who lived in isolation none at all. Now, economic dependence brought about social lines drawn, not upon a comparative use and enjoyment of nature, but upon a possession of cash.

This turned the plain man, for he had lost his independence, into something he had never been before, the pore [214] white, the hookwormed illiterate. Formerly, no matter how wealthy or how powerful a neighbor might grow, or how many slaves he might own, the small farmer who lived next to his plantation was still a free man so long as he paid his taxes and provided his family with food, clothes and shelter. He was economically and politically independent.

The uses of fertilizers, making for a quicker maturity, spread cotton culture northward and into Texas. Railroads ended the isolation of those places which bad roads had cut off from the markets, and the plain people who remained at home were brought into the money economy. The Cotton Kingdom before 1860 was supported by black backs. It now changed its nature. The small white farmer, from raising 12 per cent gradually worked and picked the greatest part of the crop. This spread of cotton meant the spread of a false set of economics.

He had been misled, and he was to wander farther afield under false doctrine. His former leaders, the generals and colonels and lawyer-statesmen, moved into the towns and cities and entered the industrial world. This move deprived them of any right to lead or rule the farmer, for no longer would his problems and theirs be the same. Nevertheless, for a long time after the war, from habit and affection, and because of the menace of the free negro, they still followed the counsel of these men. The time came when they realized their betrayal, for railroad and corporation presidents as they spoke of chivalry and pure womanhood did not put sow-belly in the pantry, nor meal in the barrel. This protest expressed itself politically through Private John Allen from [215] Mississippi, Tom Watson in Georgia, and Bob Taylor in Tennessee, and farmer candidates everywhere.

But he had listened too long. He himself began to think more and more of money, and his inability to take much of it from the industrial scheme produced a feeling of moral defeat. His ambitious sons, instead of becoming the leaders of the farm communities, went North and West and to the growing Southern cities to make their fortunes, and as they left he did not protest. Those who remained, caught by the furnishing system, could not rise to lead. They were bound hand and foot—so firmly bound that the high price of cotton during the World War led them deeper into the money economy instead of freeing them.

As a result, up to the entrance of the United States into this war the farmer was trying unconsciously to live by two antithetical economies. In spite of his dual existence he managed to secure many good things from the soil, for his life was still largely ordered after his agrarian inheritance. The next, the fatal step, is to become a progressive farmer, for then he must reverse this dualism and think first of a money economy, last of a farmer's life. The new emphasis puts him in a critical condition; the precedence of the money economy means the end of farming as a way of life. . . .[216]

Frank Lloyd Wright_____
BROADACRE CITY:
A NEW COMMUNITY PLAN (1935)

Frank Lloyd Wright, "Broadacre City: A New Community Plan," Architectural Record, LXXVII (April, 1935).*

Given the simple exercise of several inherently just rights of man, the freedom to decentralize, to redistribute and to correlate the properties of the life of man on earth to his birthright—the ground itself—and Broadacre City becomes reality.

As I see Architecture, the best architect is he who will devise forms nearest organic as features of human growth by way of changes natural to that growth. Civilization is itself inevitably a form but not, if democracy is sanity, is it necessarily the fixation called "academic." All regimentation is a form of death which may sometimes serve life but more often imposes upon it. In Broadacres all is symmetrical but it is seldom obviously and never academically so.

Whatever forms issue are capable of normal growth without destruction of such pattern as they may have. Nor is there much obvious repetition in the new city. Where regiment and row serve the general harmony of arrangement both are present, but generally both are absent except where planting and cultivation are naturally a process or walls afford a desired seclusion. Rhythm is the substitute for such repetitions everywhere. Wherever repetition (standardization) enters, it has been modified by inner rhythms either by art or by nature as it must, to be of any lasting human value.

The three major inventions already at work building Broadacres, whether the powers that over-built the old cities otherwise like it or not, are:

* Reprinted by permission of *Architectural Record*.

(1) The motor car: general mobilization of the human being.

(2) Radio, telephone and telegraph: electrical intercommunication becoming complete.

(3) Standardized machine-shop production: machine invention plus scientific discovery.

The price of the major three to America has been the exploitation we see everywhere around us in waste and in ugly scaffolding that may now be thrown away. The price has not been so great if by way of popular government we are able to exercise the use of three inherent rights of any man: [244]

(1) His social right to a direct medium of exchange in place of gold as a commodity: some form of social credit.

(2) His social right to his place on the ground as he has had it in the sun and air: land to be held only by use and improvements.

(3) His social right to the ideas by which and for which he lives: public ownership of invention and scientific discoveries that concern the life of the people.

The only assumption made by Broadacres as ideal is that these three rights will be the citizen's so soon as the folly of endeavoring to cheat him of their democratic values becomes apparent to those who hold (feudal survivors or survivals), as it is becoming apparent to the thinking people who are held blindly abject or subject against their will.

The landlord is no happier than the tenant. The speculator can no longer win much at a game about played out. The present success-ideal placing, as it does, premiums upon the wolf, the fox and the rat in human affairs and above all, upon the parasite, is growing more evident every day as a falsity just as injurious to the "successful" as to the victims of such success.

Well—sociologically, Broadacres is release from all that fatal "success" which is after all, only excess. So I have called it a new freedom for living in America. It has thrown the scaffolding aside. It sets up a new ideal of success.

In Broadacres, by elimination of cities and towns the present curse of petty and minor officialdom, government, has been reduced to one minor government for each county. The waste motion, the back and forth haul, that today makes so much idle business is gone. Distribution becomes automatic and direct; taking place mostly in the region of origin. Methods of distribution of everything are simple and direct. From the maker to the consumer by the most direct route.

Coal (one third the tonnage of the haul of our railways) is eliminated by burning it at the mines and transferring that power, making it easier to take over the great railroad rights of way; to take off the cumbersome [245] rolling stock and put the right of way into general service as the great arterial on which truck traffic is concentrated on lower side lanes, many lanes of speed traffic above and monorail speed trains at the center, continuously running. Because traffic may take off or take on at any given point, these arterials are traffic not dated but fluescent. And the great arterial as well as all the highways become great architecture, automatically affording within their structure all necessary storage facilities of raw materials, the elimination of all unsightly piles of raw material.

In the hands of the state, but by way of the county, is all redistribution of land—a minimum of one acre going to the childless family and more to the larger family as effected by the state. The agent of the state in all matters of land allotment or improvement, or in matters affecting the harmony of the whole, is the architect. All building is subject to his sense of the whole as organic architecture. Here architecture is landscape and landscape takes on the character of architecture by way of the simple process of cultivation.

All public utilities are concentrated in the hands of the state and county government as are matters of administration, patrol, fire, post, banking, license and record, making politics a vital matter to every one in the new city instead of the old case where hopeless indifference makes "politics" a grafter's profession.

In the buildings for Broadacres no distinction exists between much and little, more and less. Quality is in all, for all, alike. The thought entering into the first or last estate is of the best. What differs is only individuality and extent. There is nothing poor or mean in Broadacres.

Nor does Broadacres issue any dictum or see any finality in the matter either of pattern or style.

Organic character is style. Such style has myriad forms inherently good. Growth is possible to Broadacres as a fundamental form: not as mere accident of change but as integral pattern unfolding from within.

Here now may be seen the elemental units of our social structure: The correlated farm, the factory—its smoke and gases eliminated by burning coal at places of origin, the decentralized school, the various conditions of residence, the home offices, safe traffic, simplified government.[246] All common interests take place in a simple coordination wherein all are employed: *little* farms, *little* homes for industry, *little* factories, *little* schools, a *little* university going to the people mostly by way of their interest in the ground, *little* laboratories on their own ground for professional men. And the farm itself, notwithstanding its animals, becomes the most attractive unit of the city. The husbandry of animals at last is in decent association with them and with all else as well. True farm relief.

To build Broadacres as conceived would automatically end unemployment and all its evils forever. There would never be labor enough nor could under-consumption ever ensue. Whatever a man did would be done—obviously and directly—mostly by himself in his own interest under the most valuable inspiration and direction: under training, certainly, if necessary. Economic independence would be near, a subsistence certain; life varied and interesting.

Every kind of builder would be likely to have a jealous eye to the harmony of the whole within broad limits fixed by the county architect, an architect chosen by the county itself. Each county would thus naturally develop an individuality of its own. Architecture—in the broad sense—would thrive.

In an organic architecture the ground itself predetermines all features; the climate modifies them; available means limit them; function shapes them.

Form and function are one in Broadacres. But Broadacres is no finality. The model shows four square miles of a typical countryside developed on the acre as unit according to conditions in the temperate zone and accommodating some 1,400 families. It

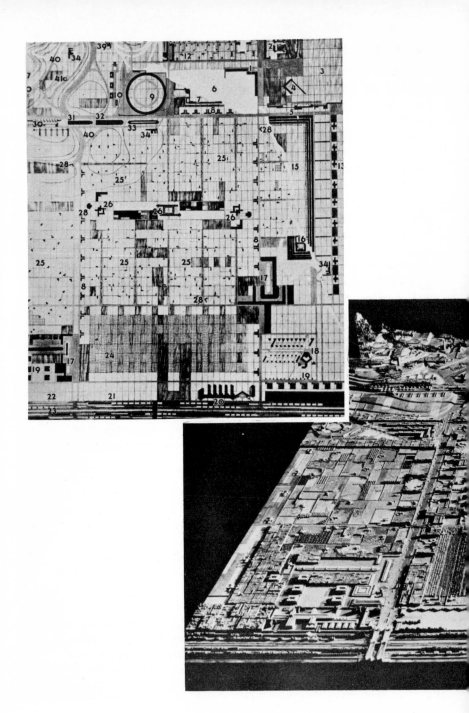

t first glance the model and diagram of **Broadacre City** do not reveal as much natural
rrain as Frank Lloyd Wright's descriptions of the plan lead one to expect. A close
rutiny of both, together with the details furnished in the text, is necessary to discover
the geographical and architectural principles on which this community is built.

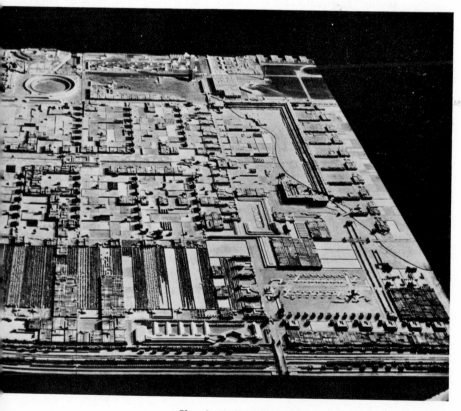

Photo by Highton and Jensen from F. S. Lincoln; from American
Architect, May, 1935, courtesy, Architectural Record

would swing north or swing south in type as conditions, climate and topography of the region changed.

In the model the emphasis has been placed upon diversity in unity, recognizing the necessity of cultivation as a need for formality in most of the planting. By a simple government subsidy certain specific acres or groups of acre units are, in every generation, planted to useful trees,[247] meantime beautiful, giving privacy and various rural divisions. There are no rows of trees alongside the roads to shut out the view. Rows where they occur are perpendicular to the road or the trees are planted in groups. Useful trees like white pine, walnut, birch, beech, fir, would come to maturity as well as fruit and nut trees and they would come as a profitable crop meantime giving character, privacy and comfort to the whole city. The general park is a flowered meadow beside the stream and is bordered with ranks of trees, tiers gradually rising in height above the flowers at the ground level. A music-garden is sequestered from noise at one end. Much is made of general sports and festivals by way of the stadium, zoo, aquarium, arboretum and the arts.

The traffic problem has been given special attention, as the more mobilization is made a comfort and a facility the sooner will Broadacres arrive. Every Broadacre citizen has his own car. Multiple-lane highways make travel safe and enjoyable. There are no grade crossings nor left turns on grade. The road system and construction is such that no signals nor any lamp-posts need be seen. No ditches are alongside the roads. No curbs either. An inlaid purfling over which the car cannot come without damage to itself takes its place to protect the pedestrian.

In the affair of air transport Broadacres rejects the present airplane and [249] substitutes the self-contained mechanical unit that is sure to come: an aerotor capable of rising straight up and by reversible rotors able to travel in any given direction under radio control at a maximum speed of, say, 200 miles an hour, and able to descend safely into the hexacomb from which it arose or anywhere else. By a doorstep if desired.

The only fixed transport trains kept on the arterial are the long-distance monorail cars traveling at a speed (already established in Germany) of 220 miles per hour. All other traffic is by motor car on the twelve lane levels or the triple truck lanes on the lower levels which have on both sides the advantage of delivery direct to warehousing or from warehouses to consumer. Local trucks may get to warehouse-storage on lower levels under the main arterial itself. A local truck road parallels the swifter lanes.

Houses in the new city are varied: make much of fireproof synthetic materials, factory-fabricated units adapted to free assembly and varied arrangement, but do not neglect the older nature-materials wherever they are desired and available. Householders' utilities are nearly all planned in prefabricated utility stacks or units, simplifying construction and reducing building costs to a certainty. There is the professional's house with its laboratory, the minimum house with its workshop, the medium house ditto, the larger house and the house of machine-age-luxury. We might speak of them as a one-car house, a two-car house, a three-car house and a five-car house. Glass is extensively used as are roofless rooms. The roof is used often as a trellis or a garden. But where glass is extensively used it is usually for domestic purposes in the shadow of protecting overhangs.

Copper for roofs is indicated generally on the model as a permanent cover capable of being worked in many appropriate ways and giving a general harmonious color effect to the whole.

Electricity, oil and gas are the only popular fuels. Each land allotment has a pit near the public lighting fixture where access to the three and to water and sewer may be had without tearing up the pavements.

The school problem is solved by segregating a group of low buildings [253] in the interior spaces of the city where the children can go without crossing traffic. The school building group includes galleries for loan collections from the museum, a concert and lecture hall, small gardens for the children in small groups and well-lighted cubicles for individual outdoor study: there is a small zoo, large pools and green playgrounds.

This group is at the very center of the model and contains at its center the higher school adapted to the segregation of the students into small groups.

This tract of four miles square, by way of such liberal general allotment determined by acreage and type of ground, including apartment buildings and hotel facilities, provides for about 1,400 families at, say, an average of five or more persons to the family.

To reiterate: the basis of the whole is general decentralization as an applied principle and architectural reintegration of all units into one fabric; free use of the ground held only by use and improvements; public utilities and government itself owned by the people of Broadacre City; privacy on one's own ground for all and a fair means of subsistence for all by way of their own work on their own ground or in their own laboratory or in common offices serving the life of the whole.

There are too many details involved in the model of Broadacres to permit complete explanation. Study of the model itself is necessary study. Most details are explained by way of collateral models of the various types of construction shown: highway construction, left turns, crossovers, underpasses and various houses and public buildings.

Any one studying the model should bear in mind the thesis upon which the design has been built by the Taliesin Fellowship, built carefully not as a finality in any sense but as an interpretation of the changes inevitable to our growth as a people and a nation.

Individuality established on such terms must thrive. Unwholesome life would get no encouragement and the ghastly heritage left by over-crowding in overdone ultra-capitalistic centers would be likely to disappear in three or four generations. The old success ideals having no chance at all, new ones more natural to the best in man would be given a fresh opportunity to develop naturally.[254]

WHEN DEMOCRACY BUILDS

Frank Lloyd Wright, When Democracy Builds, rev. ed. (Chicago, University of Chicago Press, 1945).*

EARTH

The value of earth as man's heritage is gone far from him in cities centralization has built. Centralization has overbuilt them all. Urban happiness of the properly citified citizen consists in the hypnotic warmth and pressure or the approbation of the crowd. The surge and mechanical uproar of the city turns the citified head, fills citified ears as the song of birds, wind in the trees, animal cries, or voices and songs of his loved ones once filled his heart.

But where and as he now stands, out of the Machine that his city has become, no citizen can create more than more machinery.

The properly citified citizen is a broker, vendor of gadgetry; a salesman dealing for profit in human frailties or a speculator in the ideas and inventions of others. This puller of levers is presser of the buttons of vicarious power: power his only by way of mechanical craft or graft.

A parasite of the spirit is here; this whirling dervish in a whirling vortex. Yes; enamored of the whirl.

Perpetual to-and-fro excites this citified citizen, robs him of the deeper meditation and reflection once his as he lived and walked under clean sky among the greenery to which he was born companion.

He has traded the Book of Creation for emasculation by way of the Substitute.

He has traded native pastimes with streams, woods, fields, and

animals for the taint of carbon monoxide rising to a rented aggregate of cells upended on hard pavements. "Paramounts,"
"Roxies," night clubs, speakeasies, such as these are his recourse.
For all this he lives in some cubicle among other cubicles under
a landlord who himself probably lives up there above him in
some penthouse, the apotheosis of rent in some form. All are
parasitic if not quite parasites.[1]

So the properly citified citizen, still slave to the herd instinct, is
fatally committed to vicarious power—just as the medieval laborer, not so long before him, was slave to king or state. A cultural weed grows rank in the cultural field.

The weed goes to seed. Children grow up, herded by thousands in schools built like factories, run like factories: schools
systematically turning out herd-struck morons as machinery turns
out shoes.

When our commercial men of genius succeed, they become
more than ever vicarious. Soon these very men sink in the sham
luxury of their city to produce, but *create* nothing. Impotent.
Fixation has them where it wants them.

Life itself is become restless "tenant" in the big city. Yes. . . .
above the belt, the citizen if properly citified has lost sight of the
true aims of human existence and accepted substitute aims. His
unnaturally gregarious life tends toward the promiscuous, blind
adventure of a crafty animal; some form of graft, the febrile
pursuit of sex as "relief" from factual routine in prevailing uproar
of mechanical conflict. Meantime struggling to artificially maintain, as he can, teeth, hair, muscles, and sap, his sight is growing
dim; hearing is chiefly by telephone. He goes against or across
the tide of traffic, as he must, at the risk of damage or death to
himself or others. His own good time is inevitably, regularly, and
increasingly wasted by others because he is as determined to
waste theirs. All go in different directions to various ugly scaffold-
ings over concrete or down underground, only to get into some
other cubicle occupied by some other parasite-of-rent higher up
under some other landlord. The citizen's entire life is *exaggerated* on wheels and by telephone instead of *expanded*. His is a
vicarious life virtually sterilized by machinery. And medicine.

Were motor oil and castor oil to dry up, the great city would
cease to function and the citizen promptly perish.

This monster exaggeration of the Renaissance City today, machine-made, is become the form universal of anxious rent. The citizen's very life rented in a rented world; he and his family evicted if in arrears, or the whole "system" goes to smash. He must soon make his choice! All is founded upon renting, or being rented, until the man himself is finally no more than an anxious form of inhumane rent. . . .[2]

Having done all it can do for Humanity, the centralization we call the city has become centripetal force beyond control, increasingly exaggerated by continually additional vicarious powers. The "system" is steadily increasing in man his animal fear of being turned out of the hole from which he has been accustomed to crawl out again each morning. Natural horizontality—the line of human freedom on earth—is going or gone. The citizen condemns himself to unnatural pig-piling—aspiring to a sterile verticality. He is upended and suspended by his own excess. He is calling his prone fixability success.

Notwithstanding slum clearance and the profit-sharing of sporadic "housing," all unwittingly designed by himself to build himself permanently into bondage, he is more and more helpless now. Still cursed by the primitive cave-dwelling instinct, were it not for the involuntary running-away [3] of the mechanical factors of the industrial revolution that made him what he is today—he stays where he is doomed. . . .[4]

Already it is evident that modern life must be more naturally conserved by far more space and light, by much greater freedom of movement, and by a more general freedom of the individual in the ideal practice of what we call civilization. A new space-concept is needed. It is evident that it has come in what we are calling organic architecture: the architecture of democracy.

Modern autobility, as one of the leading factors of our valid modernity (alongside glass and steel), is having characteristic effect upon the surviving nature of the cave-dweller through modern means of transport: this city brother who submits obedience to man in order to be well saved by his faith but not so much by his faith in his own works. But these scientific future-liberating forces-of-the-machine are potential of means of self-realization returning to the descendant of the wandering tribe: the adventurer. He will use them for human freedom.

And directly contrary to human intent the "machine" is continuously at work molding, remolding, or driving human character in that more mobile direction. The question is becoming more and more one of grass or goods? Men or Man.[6]

In our cities today terms of feudal thinking are changed only in name to terms of diplomatic commerce and commercial diplomacy. But the city has nothing substantial to give citizens above wagery and the belt.

New York appears the prime example, leading universal urban conspiracy to beguile men away from their birthright (the good ground), to hang above pavements by their eyebrows from skyhooks for "employment." Such high priests of such culture as we have set up in professorial armchairs with their enormous flocks meantime sing false hymns to vicarious power by jazzing a dreary dirge. High priests of religion or education have seldom understood or ever dared teach the freedom that is the life-basis and the life-blood of militant democracy. . . .

Human values are life-giving.

None are life-taking.

When man builds his buildings, builds his very life, builds his society inspired by nature in this interior sense which we shall call organic—meantime training imagination to see life as an architect should train his own imagination to see the nature of glass as Glass; see a board as Board; see a brick as Brick; see the nature of steel as Steel, and seeing the nature of Time, Place, and Hour; always eager to be honest with himself and to others, deeply desiring to live harmonious with nature, to live in nature as the trees are native to the wood or grass is to the field—only then can the individual arise as the safe citizen in the communal life of the only safe, free, and creative civilization. We are calling it democracy. . . .[7]

But, although with no corresponding revisions of traditional, therefore Romish or feudal, property rights or much, if any, consideration given to an appropriate new economy, the new country *was* founded upon a more just freedom for the individual than any known before in all the world: a government that should be "best government because least government." And a Thomas Jefferson crossing an Alexander Hamilton, a George Washington weighing upon a Thomas Paine; an Abraham Lincoln, a William

Lloyd Garrison, a John Brown, Emerson, Whitman, Thoreau, a Henry George, Louis Sullivan, their kind to the rescue— such were her sons. In them the original ideal was held still clear. . . .[17]

ORGANIC ARCHITECTURE

If you can see the design of the farm itself (little or big) in its true relation to adjoining farms and to you; if you see the sizes and shapes of fields all well laid out in good proportion each to each and to one and all—and can see the whole man-built occupation adapted to natural contours—tillage itself becoming a charming feature of the landscape; hedgeways, ravines, and waterways themselves becoming boundaries. If you can see all this [54] completely rhythmic in relation to well-considered buildings; all related to well-placed roads. If you can see *"horizontal farming"* contour plowing, properly applied to crops, pastures, animals, and all such well related to the people; if you can see the varied, various parts contributing to a great dramatic whole in which you sense the repose of contentment and the exuberance of plenty—aesthetic, truly, in the over-all view from where you stand: well—then you are getting a glimpse of the country-loving life of the Usonian [1] city of our democratic future. The culture of the nation our forefathers had some right to expect of what they were pleased to call democracy.

And you will see the people of this future Usonian countryside hating, more than all beside, waste or any exaggeration of any human power. You will see a whole people suspicious of any too easy opportunity to live by the life vicarious that is everywhere now being forced upon human beings by the mechanical reiterations of rent: exaggerations more and more empty of all human significance.

Broadacre buildings would naturally be adapted to the lives of people who would no longer build or consent to live in the prettified cavern or take any pleasure at all in any glorified cave, however "stylized." . . .[55]

[1] Samuel Butler's suggestion of a name for a nameless nation (see his *Erewhon*).

BROADACRE CITY

We are going to call our legacy from the past "Broadacre City."
This, the greater free city for the individual, simply because it is
broadly based upon the minimum spacing of an acre (or several) to the individual. But, more important, because when
democracy builds—this is also the natural city of the reflex:
democracy. . . .[61]

ARCHITECTURE AND ACREAGE ARE LANDSCAPE

Architectural features of true democratic ground-freedom would
rise naturally from topography; which means that buildings
would all take on the nature and character of the ground on
which in endless variety they would stand and be component
part. And, wherever possible, be integral, organic features.

Therefore, no two districts of the city could ever be precisely
alike except as the new city might spread to some featureless
plain which, too, has a certain natural beauty of its own, and
might well bear repetitions of the appropriate patterns then
characteristic of tillage and forestation. Broadacres would be so
built in sympathy with nature that a deep feeling for the beauty
of the terrain would be a fundamental qualification in the new
city-builders. They would be seeking for beauty of feature in
the landscape not so much to build *upon* as to build *with*. Endless unity-in-variety would thus become inevitable. Indigenous
character would be as inevitable. Both endless variety and indigenous character would be the inevitable [63] effect of terrain
and individuality coming together, and a naturally varied topography would naturally vary all forms of organic architecture
wherever they might arise naturally. . . .

So, from economic basis to great buildings and good government, the various features of the free city which we have now
reached and are about to describe in detail are primarily architecture. From great road systems which are natural veins and
arteries of the great city to the various buildings that are its

cellular tissue; to parks and gardens that are its pleasure places,
its smile; to factories and fields that are its subsistence and health,
this new city of democracy—Broadacres—would be great architecture. . . .

The good ground should determine the fundamental shape,
even the style, of every building, road, or institution in the city.
To see where the ground leaves off and the building begins would
require careful attention. But this proper "ground-motive," once
established in general practice, variety in unity would be infinite.
The ideal of organic unity thus held firmly in mind, the architect
would himself gradually become more equal to vast opportunities. The ever growing intelligence of the artifex together with
a universal desire for a whole life for everyone, all free to grow—
these [64] impulses would make of the new city into which the
old one will gradually disappear a great work of art. Petty partitions of property, wilful deformations of natural beauty by utilities, the perpetual defacements in the name of sordid self-interest
everywhere so irritating would no longer be possible. Unpardon-
able crimes against the landscape of so-called "utilities service"
and conscienceless advertising of goods and chattels along the
roads by universal shopkeeping disappear. Mankind would go
on a more normal way, without mechanical screams, sobs, roars,
shrieks, or smoke! . . . no longer perpetually endangered. No
more glaring abortionists would be free to set up or set down
their work by the wayside to blind the desired eye, while garish
posters fight it out with each other to sell the helpless passer-by
anything and everything that can be posted or imagined. . . .

THE USONIAN VISION

Imagine, now, spacious, well-landscaped highways, grade crossings eliminated by a new kind of integrated by-passing or over-
or underpassing all traffic in cultivated or living areas: these
great highways devoid of ugly scaffolding, telegraph and telephone poles and wires, free of glaring billboards, and free especially from ugly fencing—ditching and hedging now taking its
place. Imagine these great highways of generous safe width and
always easy grade, bright with wayside flowers or cool with

shade trees, joined at intervals with modern aer-rotor fields from which self-contained mechanical units—safe, noiseless transport planes, radio-controlled [65] carrying neither engines nor fuel— take off from convenient stations and land anywhere. Giant roads, themselves great architecture, pass public service stations now no longer eyesores but expanded as good architecture to include all kinds of roadside service for the traveler, charm and comfort throughout. These great roads unite and separate, separate and unite, in endless series of diversified units passing by farm units, roadside markets, garden schools, dwelling places, each on its acres of individually adorned and cultivated ground, developed homes all places for pleasure in work or leisure. And imagine man-units so arranged and integrated each to the other that every citizen as he chooses may have all forms of production, distribution, self-improvement, enjoyment, within the radius of, say, ten to twenty miles of his own home. And speedily available by means of his private car or plane or public conveyance. This integrated distribution of living related to ground composes the great city that I see embracing this country. This would be the Broadacre City of tomorrow that is the nation. Democracy realized. . . .

Strong but light and appropriate houses, spacious convenient workplaces to which all would be tributary, each item would be solidly and sympathetically built out of materials native to Time, Place, and Man. Building construction would be so designed as to take full advantage of the nature of the ground. Farmers and factory workers in the new city would work in environment no less superior than they would live in in their homes. All would live within walking distance from work or pleasures and live a short ride, in time, away from the now interesting, attractive factories. Smokeless, of course, and noiseless. Of course. No longer the farmer [66] envying the urban dweller his mechanical improvements while the latter in turn covets the farmer's green pastures.

Normally each factory, farm, or dwelling would be within a ten-mile radius of vast, variegated wayside fresh-food and manufacturers' markets so that each might serve the other units simply and effectively, all directly serving population living or working in its particular neighborhood. No need would exist for futile

racing to and from a common center, tired out but racing back
and forth again. No more stalling of time and crucifying of life
just to keep things congested and "big" for the pacing of some
money-maker's patent money-making system eventuating into the
present money trust. Instead of big fixations a multiplicity of
fluid units.

Without fresh air, fresh food, sunlight, good green land under-
foot, and appropriate spaciousness everywhere, human life cannot develop. No, nor even go on living! Recognizing these facts
as we are all beginning to do, all except the banker and the university, Usonian home life will not eliminate the gadgetry of
modern comforts, and yet, it will come back to keep alive the
ageless health-giving comforts which are due to ground. Modern
steel, glass, and the plastics will be sensibly called upon to ra-
tionally fulfil their natural uses. Steel for strength, durability,
and lightness; translucent glass inclosing interior space to give
privacy and yet make of living in any Usonian house a delightful
association with light; sun, sky, surrounding gardens. Yes, and
the neighbors. The home should be an outdoor garden; the garden an outdoor home.

Tall buildings need not be barred. But, forever leaving all interior walled courts, they would be impelled to stand free of
neighbors in small green parks or in the countryside in natural
parks, where desirable. "Cooperative" apartment houses might
be erected for immured but untrained urbanites desiring the
beauty of the country but yet unable to participate in creating
it. Apartment houses, say eighteen stories tall, tier on tier of
glass used as screen-walls, golden with sun on the shining steel
of copper-sheathed frames, each tier with its flower- and vine-
festooned balcony terraces. Such tall buildings would stand in
iridescence of vivid color in the landscape, set up in spacious blossoming grounds in the midst of a neighborhood of varied activities all similarly independent—*each presentable to all!* . . .[67]

The sense of space *within* as the reality of any building is a
new concept wherever architecture is concerned. But it is essential ancient principle just the same and is not only necessary now
but implied by the ideal of democracy itself. Inherent in the
philosophy of Laotze and of Jesus, it is of today as it was then.

And it is time to implement this eternal principle with our

modern mechanical equipment, thereby making life *actual* instead of allowing it to grow more and more vicarious. This, too, is a profound architectural problem.

Along with steel and the use of a great variety of indestructible thin insulated sheets of metal or plastics comes a demand for the economic and appropriate use of all materials whether new or old. This demand is for lightly, widely spanned spaces closed in against the elements but not closed in except at will to light and air.

Here, then, enter the significance and liberating uses of the new super-material we call glass.

Architecture as heavy inclosure for human life or as any survival of the cave-dwelling instinct such as desire for fortification, for instance, vanishes. A new kind of building comes to view—like magic. A modern building more natural to the modern man whose modern home it is. The man living in it—in spite of all untoward circumstances—is to be less separated from nature. The man living in it is to be, in every way, a broader, stronger man in the life of his own spirit. Hard and fast lines between outside and inside (where he is concerned) tend to disappear. The outside of any building may now come inside and the inside go outside, each seen as part of the other. Continuity, plasticity, and all the new simplicity they imply have at last come home to him—a miraculous release. The democratic reflex is to be his in place of the stricture of monarchic major and minor axis in which he was imprisoned by the "classic."

This difference to life is fundamental.[78]

Baker Brownell——————————————————
THE HUMAN COMMUNITY

Baker Brownell, *The Human Community: Its Philosophy and Practice for a Time of Crisis* (New York, Harper and Brothers, 1950).*

THE COMMUNITY AND RURAL LIFE

Though rural life usually is assumed to be the normal context in which the human community emerges and survives, it really is different things to different people. Its central meaning no doubt is the functional cooperation of human beings with vegetable and animal life. It is thus the context of human ecology. Rural life is not the lonely conquest of a hostile wilderness. It is not the life of the hunter or trapper or old-time lumberman killing or capturing his prey. It is a cooperative alliance with Nature in which the survival and abundance of life of many species, including man, are mutually dependent. Rural life, on the other hand, is not a life in cities removed from growing things, nor is it residence in a park or suburb, or visiting a country estate. It is a functional relationship with Nature and is found for the most part in agriculture and husbandry. It may include many members of that increasing group called "rural, non-farm," but only if they are productively close to the life of the country. A country grocer or banker, a small manufacturer, an artificer, a country doctor, or a village housewife may well be as much a part of the rural context of life as a farmer. If they partake of the rhythmic processes associated with the growth of plants and animals and participate in the variegated pattern of rural living, they belong.

This symbiotic relationship of man and growing things called rural life is normally the seat of the small community and, as I shall try to show, of the true community. All human life, of

* Reprinted by permission of Harper and Brothers.

course, is eventually dependent on this relationship, though some men and women live remotely from it. They learn to remove themselves from the close, compelling influences of natural things. They abstract their thoughts and interests and even their activities from the green context and spiritual milieu of life in Nature, and reside in massive aggregations or in other ways remote from rural interests. But they have not taken with them into those aggregations the stable human community or the naturally integrated life. They have renounced Nature at a price. That price would seem to be something close to spiritual impoverishment and phyletic discontinuity and decadence.[6]

In this age of wonders and defeat it is conceivable at least that men might dissolve entirely their alliance with living Nature, reject their symbiotic ecology, and live entirely by artifice and material technology. Scientists may find ways to substitute completely an artificial process for the green chemistries, the native photosynthesis, the animal assimilative processes, of the natural world on which we now live. They thus would release men wholly from the rhythms and compulsions of the fields. It would be a senseless procedure, no doubt; it would be economically and socially inefficient, I am told, but that might not greatly limit its large-scale development. It has in fact already been accomplished in part.

The limiting principle in such a substitutive procedure is less the physical and technological restrictions, or those of common sense, than the psychological, social, and deeply cultural cast of a man's nature. The pattern of his living, as it were, has been laid out through millions of years in association with living animals and plants and the vast music and movement of the natural world. The form of human life and the structure of its activities are involved in these natural forms and structures. The values that men have, the accents, the appreciations, the criteria of morals, even the insistence on living survival itself, were derived initially in this milieu, given form there, and now evolve—if they evolve at all—as part of that great order. To abstract human beings by some technological procedure from this functional relationship with the life and creative persistence of the natural world around them would be literally to abstract them from life itself. They would be no longer men in a complete or formal sense. Their communities would disintegrate; their values disappear. That indeed is already happening in part, as their relations with Nature becomes more indirect. The decline of the human community as we see it today corresponds to the decline of rural culture and economy.

The beasts and the plants participate primevally in our communities. They enter our philosophies; mold our natures; help make us fully human. They are among our greatest teachers. Through the mutuality and interlocking functions of men and plants and animals we and they domesticate each other, and create severally characters, modes of life, and human communities unattainable alone. We still hold to our totems—or the phyletic identification with animals—though not in the totemistic faith. When men are deprived of these associations something secure and primitively creative in their lives is lost. When they rebel, like some rural Lucifer, against the order of things within which they were created, they lose somehow the wisdom and the pace of Nature, and invent, as he did,[7] disunity and conflict. They invent disorder. For animals and plants bind us functionally to the sun and seasons. Our life and work among them indenture us to wordless patterns of the four winds and the summer solstice. We are more fully unified through them with the sources and sustenance of our lives. We are continuous with Nature and the world. This sense of functional unity with the natural world is a basic condition, we may assume, of what is called a meaningful and stable life.

On the child this revolt against nature, or, to say it more quietly, this removal of our life from the rural community of animals, plants, and human beings, is particularly harmful. John Dewey has pointed it out: when life in the main was rural, the child came into contact with natural things. He knew the care of domestic animals, the cultivation of the soil, the raising of crops. The home was the center of industry and in it all the child took a functional part. His mental and moral training was here. The development here of hand and eye, of skill and deftness, and, above all, his "initiation into self-reliance, independence of judgment and action" were the stimulus to habits of regular and continuous work. In the city these educative influences usually are absent. "Just at the time," Dewey says, "when a child is subjected to a great increase in stimulus and pressure from his environment, he loses the practical and motor training necessary to balance his intellectual development. Facility in acquiring information is gained: the power of using it is lost." [1]

What is this value in the relationship with Nature? It is the working continuity of men with other living things and natural processes. Though an Otis elevator or a subway train is also a natural thing subject to natural processes and in its way as wonderful as a wild rose in June, there is still a difference. The elevator lacks the evaluative continuity and spiritual response in the minds of men that native things possess. It is an artifice without organic continuity and without versatility of value. It forces its design of action on our lives but has no meaning otherwise. Our use of it involves little responsibility and no traditional concern, still it imposes its authority upon us. The elevator has no joy nor thrust of life like that of the maple sapling, the redwing, or the child. It is an instrument to go up and down. The difference from natural things is indefinable perhaps, but in the life of man critically important.

Beyond all that is the fact that rural life is the normal milieu of the human community. Thousands of years of human culture confirm it. I do not know whether the community must be rural to exist, but the evidence [8] of centuries seems to indicate it. Cities have come and gone. Their cultures and philosophies have been epiphenomenal, as it were, upon the deep permanence of their rural background. But the human community as a sustaining, many-functioned, organic pattern of life has rarely, if ever, been in them. The community is rural. It belongs to rural culture, philosophy, and life. . . .[9]

LITTLE PLACES

A little town is a drama that moves on from climax to climax through the years. It is as original as life and as crowded with color and character, action and conflict, as human nature can be. It is a drama of men and women, of youth and age, of spring and

[1] John Dewey, "The Primary Education Fetish," *Education Today* (New York, G. P. Putnam's Sons, 1940), Chap. 2, p. 23.

autumn. All the people of the place are players. They move
through harvests and hog-killing time, the cold mornings in winter, through blizzards and Christmas, through the family prayers,
it may be, or the dancing, gaming, quarreling, and singing of
people at home with each other. There is house cleaning, making
garden, the basketball games toward spring. There is swimming,
the canning and freezing, the early morning and the slow, reti-
cent twilight in summer. No auditors or spectators are in this
little place except those justified by their part in the process.
Mere listening and mere watching, and paying for the privilege,
are relatively uncommon. The people all take part and in their
parts may find a synthesis of doing things and enjoying them
that usually is quite unknown in functionally more segregated
cultures.

Some may say that small communities are dull, monotonous.
They do indeed lack the artificial coloration of New York. They
lack the shocks, the feverish discontinuity and delirium, the dis-
plays, the fictions of significance and attention-getting, that make
so much in the city that is called interesting. They express more
often the continuities of living, the lifelong drama with its beginning, its middle, and its end, and the deep stability and balance
of movement that human life sometimes can attain.

If we are interested mainly in human beings, the little places
are the most interesting area of experience in the world. I say
this perhaps dogmatically. The statement is made in the belief
that human beings, not parts of human beings in fragmented
jolts and thrills, are the most important to us of all things. Not
solely hands to work, or feet to dance, or brains to direct a bank
or a laboratory; not solely athletic skill, or beauty of face and
body, or sex lure; not solely this perfected skill or that narrowly
limited job, or some other specialized functional relation; these
are not human relations in any full or complete sense, nor can
they be substituted for them. They are fragments, and in spite of
scientific codes and philosophies designed to put them together
again, in spite of over-all organizational efforts and totalitarian
plans, they remain—so far as [31] human beings are concerned—
fragments. They lack essential human wholeness. Human beings,
I believe, are found in this enormous world only in the small
community. . . .[32]

LONEPINE, MONTANA

Lonepine is a little place in Sanders County in western Montana. The people there are farmers. In the crossroads store a corner is set aside for the post office, and around this combination store and post office in a desultory cluster are a few buildings. These stand more or less as monuments to the common functions of the community. The frame school where the elementary and high school pupils are housed is crowded and lively. The community church and the graveyard adjoin a large and rather bare community building. The one-man cheese factory just back of Ted Van der Ende's home makes up the industrial section. A seed storage building, a garage and repair shop across the road from Freeman Halverson's store, are the rest of the business district. The Halverson house is down the road a bit and there are one or two other farm homes near the crossroads.

A single pine tree grows on the little prairie, the lone pine. The quiet valley is a cup set in the mountains, rimmed around by tawny slopes, forests, and high pastures. The Little Bitterroot River flows southward across the plain, and water in the irrigated valley, or the lack of it, limits the community to its present area and productiveness. Lonepine probably cannot expand. In the short hot summers the dust blows. In the winters the snow scatters down unevenly over the valley floor and piles up on the hills. Every spring the question is heard: Has the lake filled? Is the west reservoir up to the mark? How deep is the snow in the mountains? Last year the irrigation water ran low. There was worry and questioning toward the end of June. The crops, the alfalfa seed, the cheese, the cream, the beef that Lonepine produces, were at stake.

But the water assessments are all paid up. The soil is good, the climate mild and healthful. The valley is secure, happy, and fairly prosperous. The ninety families of Lonepine make a go of it with hard work, but [33] without the grind and fear of poverty. They own their farms, pay their bills, and give their children good educations.

Lonepine, not incorporated, was settled for the most part between 1910 and 1913. The old families, some of them now in the third generation, came then. Their names alone are an American social document. There are the Von Segens, the Howsers, the Dondanvilles, the Halversons, the Van der Endes, the Hillmans, the McCoys, the Brases, the Casons, Cooks, McHenrys. Here are families whose background or even nativity may be French, German, Norwegian, English, Dutch, Scotch, Irish, and even— on a remote creek in the canyon—original American. They are not killing one another, however, deporting one another, starving, enslaving, raping, or irresponsibly building tariff walls against one another. They are not trying to absorb or defeat one another in business, or competing violently with one another in sport, art, and other professions. Though Lonepiners are decidedly human and therefore not all is sunshine and sweet breezes, the community is as friendly as a human community can well be. The conflicts and tensions find normal release, if not always productive adjustment, in the simple pattern of the little place. They do not build up into wars and assassinations and rarely into neuroses, juvenile delinquencies, or divorce.

By luck or good will or perhaps the fortune of being little, Lonepine has escaped the divisive chemistries that corrode the solidarity of many groups. These corrosive influences, such as competing churches, race aloofness, the arrogance of national origins, the snobbery of the educated or miseducated, the cultural exclusiveness and privilege, or the economic coercion of one segment of the group by another have not been active in Lonepine. The cultural distances between man and man in Lonepine are not great.

At a community dinner last spring, Ted Van der Ende, who learned to make cheese in the Frisian Islands off Holland, was called on for a speech. He rose, said he had no speech, but would sing a song. He sang a boyhood song of Holland, first in Dutch, then translated into English. That started things: Freeman Halverson rose and sang a boyhood song of Norway. Another tried a boyhood Czech song, but forgot it midway. There were Germans there who could sing the folk songs of Germany. They hesitated at first, but were urged on by the others. Then four college students back for vacation rose and sang American songs.

For thirty-four years without interruption, the Lonepine community has held a Thanksgiving dinner. For the last decade or so it has been held in the basement of the community church. Last year they borrowed the [34] Reverend Baty from Missoula for the day, listened to a brief sermon and song service, and then the men cooked and served the dinner. Great was its reputation in the region. A scholar, were he competent, could well study the work, peace, and relative serenity in the little community of Lonepine. Amid the worthy sentiments relating to a United World it might be pointed out that only here, in these little places, where men are known not as symbols but as men, can there be significant unity.

Freeman Halverson is the downtown population of Lonepine, he and perhaps Ted Van der Ende, the cheesemaker. Free Halverson is postmaster and the owner and operator of the general store. His place is the rendezvous. The tiny post office, not much larger than a telephone booth, is on the dry-goods side of the big room. For a time the public library also was housed here. Below are freeze lockers. The butcher shop with its big refrigerator is at the back. In this rambling frame building with its somewhat informal front porch may be bought a modern cream separator or a pair of overalls, a pound of cheese or a tube of lip stick, a silken, western neckerchief, a saddle or a pound of old fashioned chocolate creams. Brisk bargains are announced in the weekly mimeographed sheet of news and market items, and the prices paid for local eggs and poultry, vegetables, seeds, potatoes, and fruit are revised to suit the season.

A blackboard nailed to the outside wall tells in scribbled chalk the socials, the study group meetings, 4-H club evenings and contests, band rehearsals, and all the goings on of the little place. Through the doors of the store—it is named The Hub—come and go the people of Lonepine, old and young, men and women, with their leisurely business, their gossip and laughter. Down the road a piece the Halverson dog, Major, greets the guest at the white gate of the farmstead. One of Halverson's good-looking daughters now goes to the university eighty-five miles away. His two sons, back from the armed service, are taking over the farm and the garage repair shop across the street.

Freeman Halverson is tall, fast on his feet, and works hard. On his slender shoulders are laid many of the responsibilities of the

little community. He is postmaster, storekeeper, driver of the
school bus. He is chairman of the community study group, head
of the newly organized conservation unit, president of the state
alfalfa seed growers' association, editor of the *Hub News*. He is
on the citizens' advisory board of the state agricultural college.
He leads the Lonepine band. At times he trains the girls' chorus.
And then toward the evening he plays the clarinet at home in the
family ensemble.

Meanwhile his wife and daughters can or freeze hundreds of
quarts [35] of fruit and vegetables. They manipulate the modern
pressure cooker and the quick-freeze techniques with economy
and skill. They care for Freeman's old father, now pretty feeble.
They keep the house spick-and-span, teach a Sunday-school class,
design smart dresses for themselves, sew, cook with ample art
and joy to all the family, and regularly take prizes in the Extension Service projects led by the county agent.

The Halverson family is a productive unit of no mean significance. It is mutually cooperative in a dynamic, effective, going
process. To city and suburban folk the most remarkable aspect
of it perhaps is the spiritual joy and solidarity with which the
members go about their work. There is work to do together and
they know how to do it without psychic resistance or complaint.
Here where their pattern of life is set in a modern technology,
here with a good car and a truck, a vacuum cleaner and a flush
toilet, an electric mixer and a pressure cooker, a modern washing
machine, an electric range and a radio, their productive process
is still identified inextricably with the ends and consummations of
action.

The Halversons are busy but never burdened. Their tasks are
not designed for escape or to be escaped, or through purchase
to be replaced by "sit-down" substitutes. They live in the sunshine of this moment. They bring the past and future to bear
intimately—and eternally—in this living present of their communal life. They have somehow assimilated, at least for their
vivid moment here, the technologies of our modern culture into
truly human values. In this their success surpasses by far that of
most city and suburban folk.

Freeman Halverson supplies that ingredient so important in
the little place: friendly, democratic leadership by a person liv-

ing in the community. He would make a wise and progressive senator, not because he is above his community, but because he is of it and for it. But I am glad that he stays where he is. . . .[36]

I could name dozens more in the rural communities of America, in Montana, Illinois, Kansas, Wisconsin, Alabama, Florida, Vermont, and Rhode Island. I do not say that all rural communities are like Lonepine or that all rural communities have people like those in Lonepine. Rural communities are on many different levels economically, educationally, culturally. Their diversity as groups and within groups is as great or greater than the diversity of classes in the great cities. Nor do I say that there are no good people, no functional families, and no communal groups in cities. The picture is not all black or white.

The Lonepiners, however, are characteristic as rural people. Their level of ability, intelligence, and social responsibility is probably not exceeded by any large group in the entire country. Lonepine withal has [37] remained a community. In the cities, on the other hand, the people usually are organized on a piecework basis, not as human beings, but as functional fragments coordinated in a great machine. . . .[38]

The true community is thus built to the human scale. Its range is limited to men's capacity for integrated experience. Beyond that limit it breaks down. The human being, on the other hand, is limited by the community. He is keyed to its capacity to coordinate the functions of his life as a whole with other whole persons. At the point where interpersonal relationships are solely between the isolated functions of different persons, the human being disintegrates.

This principle of limitation in the human being and his community is critically important. In Part VIII of this book I shall try to show that it is interlocked with other essential characteristics of communal life and thus makes unacceptable the concept, held by many sociologists, that the community may be an extensive, more or less wide-ranging group. It is not extensive, nor is it entirely identical, on the other hand, with what rural sociologists call the neighborhood. This of course is partly a matter of the terms used; still the community should be defined, I think, more by its structure and function and by the nature of the human stuff in it than by its geography. That structure and function in human affairs I shall try to clarify in the course of the book. The community in this sense will apply to many families, many neighborhoods, many villages and towns, but not to all of them. . . .[41]

THE SYNTHESIS OF ENDS AND MEANS

In Lonepine this coordination of functions in the human being and his community takes place without much theorizing. It is a natural order of life and the folk of Lonepine take it for granted. They live in a milieu of human beings, and somehow they are human beings—if I may use the words as a term of approbation— more securely than are most city people.

One reason for this is their spiritual unity. Not only are Lonepine people functionally coordinated; they have what may be called spiritual wholeness as well. This is a poetic term for something in human life that rises from below the levels of language and articulate symbol. This solidarity of values, this intimate coherence of values within a man's life, gives him whatever wholeness the human spirit may have.

In this is the synthesis of ends and means in human life. Lonepine is a culture where productive activities are likely to be taken as appreciatively final as well. The cleavage in values, so marked in urban culture, between work and play, industry and art, flesh and spirit, labor and pleasure seeking, becoming and being, and so on in innumerable variations and degrees of evaluative divergence, very likely in Lonepine do not take place at all. Freeman Halverson, for example, works hard, but his work, or at least a great deal of it, has also a high appreciative worth to him. It is worth-while now, in this moment. It is worth-while in this brisk realm of action; the values usually assigned to the future and past are caught together in a timeless present. Ted Van der Ende and his sons produce cheese, but in the economic and social pattern of the community, where he is master of the whole procedure, from eighty acres of pasture land to the storage [42] of the cool, fat loaves of cheese, production has the rhythmic form and thrill of art. It is organic production, as it were; it is identified with the richly functional and appreciative pattern of a human life.

Ferdinand Tönnies uses this unity of ends and means in a formal sense as one of the ways of distinguishing *Gemeinschaft*— or roughly village culture—from *Gesellschaft*—or the culture more commonly of cities. Contrariwise the rationalization of the means of human activity whereby they are separated in quality completely from the ends, and are valued solely in reference to those ends, underlies the specialization of productive processes. They are divorced from intrinsic values. They are set up in urban cultures in vast assembly lines of manufacturing, sales procedures, market techniques, and the machinery of mass civilization.

Though urban professional men, executives, and some others may find a synthesis of extrinsic and intrinsic values in their work, it is at a heavy cost. That cost is their relative isolation as a privileged group and their adherence to a cult of so-called objectivity that removes from their activities some or all of the social responsibility for the consequences of their work.

The solidarity of values, or what I have called tentatively the spiritual life, is found in small communities and among people known well. Beyond those human limits the spiritual life is likely to become morbidly specialized and remote from concrete living. In such abstraction there is eventually spiritual death. . . . [43]

LABOR, THE COMMUNITY, AND
INDUSTRIAL TECHNOLOGY

. . . No thoughtful person expects to see large centers of production and population disappear even under such violent influences toward decentralization as the atom bomb. Nor does he contemplate a time when all industries will be decentralized. Some industries—a heavy industry such as steel, for example— must continue to be rather highly centralized both in their productive technique and their financing. Some cities must be rather large to be efficient as centers of commerce, banking, research, and other services. Nevertheless the overwhelming urbanism of today is unnecessary. Certainly the newer technology does not require it. The industrial massing of power, production, and population in centers such as New York, Chicago, London, Moscow, and Pittsburgh is no longer justified. Two thirds to three fourths of our industry, according to economists such as Montgomery of Texas, might well be decentralized in the interests of efficiency.

DIFFERENTIAL DECENTRALIZATION

The best answer to this problem is a differential one. Granting that centralization is desirable in some fields and should be even increased [92] under some conditions, it is important to recognize that decentralization in most fields is the pressing need of this time. The criteria should be the welfare of the human community on the one hand and technological efficiency on the other. In terms of a modern technology these need not be in conflict.

The Tennessee Valley Authority is the first major effort—the only one thus far—to join the efficiencies of large-scale operations and planning with a diffused enrichment of life on regional, community, and family levels. This project covers the 40,600 square miles of the Tennessee Valley, an area about four fifths the size of England, in a multiple-purpose, closely integrated structure which includes navigation, flood control, and hydroelectric power as primary functions and an entire complex of ecological and cultural factors, such as soil and forest conservation, the manufacture of fertilizer, refrigeration, designing farm machinery, farm demonstration, recreation, library service, and rural electrification, as coordinate functions in a socially organic whole.

From the point of view of the community the unique characteristic of the TVA is its emphasis on decentralized administration. Though the TVA has the centralized authority necessary to a great regional program, the administration of that authority usually is limited to the appropriate level involved. Decisions on local matters are made, not by a central authority, but by the local people concerned, and so on across the different levels of interest.

The TVA, in contrast to totalitarian patterns of authority, is administratively a structure of integrated decisions at different levels, from the farmer and his family to the community, school district, village, county, state, region, and on to the authority of Congress at Washington. All are free on their level to decide on matters relevant to that level. A local group of farmers, for example, decides whether they want a demonstration farm. They choose the demonstration farmer themselves. If he accepts, he receives free metaphosphate fertilizer, except for freight, on condition that he take the advice of the agent as to its use. As his alfalfa grows greener and his stock heavier, the other neighboring farmers make their own decisions as to this farm practice. Within six years after the beginning of the TVA there were 23,000 demonstration farms in the Valley and elsewhere.

Today the TVA is a worldwide model of applied intelligence. In 1947, for example, the dams saved Chattanooga alone $42,000,000 in flood damage, according to careful estimate, and more millions on the lower rivers. In that same year the navigational system of the TVA carried [93] 350,000,000 ton-miles of freight at a saving in freight rates of $3,000,000. Power revenues in that year were $48,000,000, with a net of $17,176,000, and electric rates in the area averaged 1.57 cents per kilowatt hour, as compared with the 3.03 cents national average. Enormous amounts of phosphate and nitrate fertilizers were produced, soil conservation programs were carried out, and 200,000,000 seedling trees have been planted on eroded and abandoned lands during the course of the project. Malaria has been reduced from as high as 25 per cent in 1934 in some areas to less than 1 per cent in 1948. Private interests have invested there more than $13,000,000 in recreational facilities.

In 1933 the per capita income in the Valley was 40 per cent of the national average. Today it is 60 per cent of that average. Since 1933 the seven valley states have doubled their share of the income taxes paid to the federal government. The accumulated total of this increased contribution, says James Rorty,[2] is about two billion dollars. This alone is more than the total government investment to date. In growth of trade, of bank deposits, of cash farm income, and total income payments the Valley led the nation between 1933 and 1939. Farm income in 1945 was 149 per cent of that of 1933, or 10 per cent above the

[2] James Rorty, "The TVA Idea," *The Survey*, June, 1949.

national average. In 1946, nonagricultural employment was up 122 per cent, as compared with the national average of 73 per cent, and wages were up 250 per cent, as compared with 145 per cent for the nation as a whole.

By joining the native, local interests of the community with regional and national needs the TVA has brought about a pattern of development unique in this era of modern technology. It is almost alone in recognizing through a widespread system of action the neotechnical vision of a Patrick Geddes and the basic balance between the little places and the larger order that is so fundamental in Jefferson's political philosophy. Of this latter John Dewey says (in a letter to me): "Some years ago I edited a small volume of selections from Thomas Jefferson. I was surprised as well as much stimulated by his plan for local communities, with his vast respect for the New England town meeting which was his *constructive counterpart* of his 'states rights' theory. From his own point of view the latter, *without* the rest of his scheme, which never caught on, was I am confident, a one-legged political device—though very little is said about it in writings about Thomas Jefferson." [3]

On the decentralization of centralized authority David Lilienthal, [94] former chairman of the TVA, says, "The distinction between authority and its administration is a vital one. For a long time all of us—administrators, citizens, and politicians—have been confused on this point. We have acted on the assumption that because there was an increasing need for centralized authority, the centralized execution of that authority was likewise inevitable. . . . Out of lethargy and confusion we have taken it for granted that the price of federal action was a top-heavy, cumbersome administration. Clearly this is nonsense. The *problem is to divorce the two ideas of authority and administration of authority.*"

The original thesis of the TVA, as worked out largely by Senator Norris and the first chairman, Arthur E. Morgan, and by Harcourt Morgan and President Roosevelt, was to develop through modern technology the magnificent resources of the Valley and

---

[3] John Dewey, in a letter to me, May 16, 1950. See also David Lilienthal, *TVA, Democracy on the March* (New York, Harper and Brothers, 1944), p. 142.

make them available to the people within the frame of their normal community and family life. This had not been done before, and the TVA became the great sociotechnological experiment of the century.

It challenges our fate. It repudiates man's unique kind of failure, which is to build structures beyond human limits. It leads not to distortion of the human pattern but to an enrichment of it. In accepting a social objective it has become preeminent as a guide at this critical time.[95]

Louis Bromfield———————————————
OUT OF THE EARTH

Louis Bromfield, *Out of the Earth* (New York, Harper and Brothers, 1950).*

OUT OF THE SEA

. . . The good farmer is the man who learns as much as he can about the vast range of things which the good farmer must know concerning veterinary science, economics, chemistry, botany, animal husbandry, nutrition and countless other fields, all of which are tied into the ancient, complex and varied profession of agriculture, and then knows how to apply this knowledge to his own problems.

Perhaps no stupider human saying has ever been formulated than the one that "anybody can farm." Anyone can go through the motions, but not 10 per cent of our agricultural population today could be seriously called "good farmers." Thirty per cent are pretty good, and the remaining 60 per cent do not, through ignorance or laziness or sometimes through the misfortune of living on wretched land fit only for forests, deserve the dignified title of "farmer." Most of them still remain within the range of

* Reprinted by permission of Harper and Brothers and The Estate of the late Louis Bromfield.

a completely primitive [5] agriculture confined to plowing, scattering seed and harvesting whatever crops with luck turn up at the end of the season. That they perform these operations with the aid of modern machinery does not make them either good or modern farmers. Tragically, a great many of them actually hate the soil which they work, the very soil which, if tended properly, could make them prosperous and proud and dignified and happy men. . . .

In the beginning we all came from the sea, and the elements of the sea—its oxygen, its nitrogen, its infinite range and variety of mineral wealth—are still as necessary to us as the proteins and carbohydrates which they make possible and by which we sustain life. Some of them we are able to live without as we are able to live without gills. Some of the organs and glands once necessary to existence and procreation have become atrophied and useless and will doubtless disappear one day as our gills have disappeared, but we are, like the plants themselves, still dependent upon a remarkable range of minerals for the structure of our bodies, for the vigor and health and the maintenance of that metabolic system which permits us to utilize the complex proteins and carbohydrates which give us energy and brains, and for the fertility which permits us to reproduce ourselves and so [6] continue the future of a species which is still in the process of change and adaptivity.

Once not very long ago it was believed that only phosphorus and calcium and one or two other major elements were necessary to the development, birth and growth of a living human organism. Today we are becoming aware that in the functioning of a normal and healthy metabolism producing a healthy, vigorous human, or even an animal or a plant of the same category, an infinitely greater range of elements and minerals is necessary; and constantly, almost day by day as new discoveries are being made, the range is growing larger to include more and more of the minerals from the sea out of which that first spark of life was born.

The relation of iodine to goiter and cretinism is perhaps the oldest and longest-established case. A child born in a wholly iodine-deficient area stands one chance in ten of being an idiot, one in five of dying of goiter and virtually one in one of suffering from all the maladies and handicaps that come of the disorder of the thyroid gland, all because he and his mother before him did not have daily as much iodine as could be smeared on the head of a pin. The function of fluorine in the most minute quantities in the creation and maintenance of good teeth and bone has long been established, or that of cobalt, copper and manganese in relation to acute anemia and the capacity to breed. Cobalt in exquisitely minute quantities plays its part in the creation of one of the most recently discovered and important of all vitamins, B-12, a vitamin by which it indeed could be said that we live.

But as the physiologists and men of medicine are beginning to discover, the story of life, complicated as it is, contains still greater complexities, many of them still undiscovered. One may suffer from thyroid derangement through the lack of infinitesimal amounts of iodine, but the thyroid derangement may make it impossible for the human metabolism to absorb sufficient amounts of calcium or phosphorus, no matter the amount taken into the body, or impossible to absorb the infinitesimal amounts of zinc which may be the safeguard against leukemia. The pattern is intricate and extremely difficult to unravel—this pattern of nutrition and the relation of minerals to our health, growth, intelligence and vitality, and to the intricate workings and interdependence of all our glands. We have only begun to unravel the fringes of the whole pattern of metabolism, of minerals and vitamins and enzymes and hormones and the nutrition which, it appears, runs back and back into the steam and fogs of the [7] primeval world in which the first tiny spark, born of the minerals and elements themselves, came into existence.

Why, you might well ask again, should this concern the farmer? It concerns the farmer because the chief concern of the farmer is his soil. Out of it comes the health, intelligence and vitality of his animals and his family and, in a broader sense, of his fellow citizens. Out of it also comes his economic prosperity, his independence of banks and of government subsidies and regimentation. If his soil is good and minerally balanced and well managed and productive up to the optimum (which means simply that he is getting maximum potential production in quantity and quality without loss of fertility) he is the most independent man in the world, a world which has never been able to do without him and which becomes daily and hourly and by the minute less and less able to do without him. Slaves do not produce great quantities of food (as Soviet Russia has discovered) nor do they produce, except by accident of Nature, good and highly nutritious foods. The good independent successful farmer produces both. Better than any man he knows, through his plants and animals and his daily contact and struggles with the weather, that out of the earth we come and to the earth we return. Out of the sea, one might almost say. . . .[8]

THE NEW WORLD IN AGRICULTURE

. . . At Malabar Farm we have been led by our own soil, by the results we have obtained and by the factors we have observed, virtually to assume that the laws which govern good soil and optimum production are perhaps as exact and immutable as the laws of chemistry, physics or any of the natural sciences which play so important a part in the creation of such soils. We are inclined to believe that there are a series of balances, absolute in character, which, when attained, produce optimum production, which is simply maximum production both in quantity and nutritional quality without reducing and possibly even augmenting the fertility factor.

We are inclined to believe that production of soils, both in terms of quantity and quality, mounts or declines in exact ratio to the degree with which their absolute balances are established and maintained. Any intelligent farmer is well aware that when his major elements—calcium, phosphorus, potash and nitrogen— are out of proper balance for any given crop, lowered yields and poor quality results. Sometimes the unbalance leads to actual deformation of the plants and to all manner of signs, as clear as the spots of measles on a child, of deficiencies, or in the case of excess nitrogen to a growth which is rank enough but inferior in quality and in seed and reproductive capacity. . . .[17]

To the layman without experience in agriculture or soils, the phrase "virgin soil" implies a rich, well-balanced and productive soil. Few implications could be less true, for Nature laid down her soils in a haphazard fashion without regard to the balances

Photo by Joe Munroe, courtesy, The Farm Quarterly

Louis Bromfield placed this photograph and the following one next to each other in his book, *Out of the Earth*. Of the **Mason Place** in spring he wrote, "the desolation which follows bad agriculture on good land."

Photo by Joe Munroe, courtesy, The Farm Quarterly

Malabar Farm, "over the hill in the next valley from the Mason place."

in question. Very few soils contain the major elements, the organic material and the trace elements in any degree approaching the balance which results in optimum production. Perhaps only in the sea itself does every element exist because *all* elements, through erosion and run-off water, eventually reach the sea from which life itself came. Yet even in the sea there are serious *un*balances in relation to given vegetations. Salt marshes are infertile save for a narrow range of specially adapted and qualified plants, largely because their soils and the waters which feed them contain *too much* chlorine and *too much* sodium—a notable case of exaggerated balance. Indeed, sea water cannot be used for irrigation purposes because of the notable unbalances which actually render it destructive and even toxic to most plant life. Yet we know today how, by complicated chemical processes, to rearrange the balances of minerals existing in sea water to a point where it may actually behave as fertilizer.[18]

Specifically the expression "virgin soil" means simply soil which has never been put under cultivation by the hand of man, and some of our "virgin soils" are among the worst in the world through deficiencies and *unbalances* for which Nature herself was responsible in the process of laying them down. Areas of Wisconsin and Michigan and Minnesota were deforested or drained with the idea of putting them to agricultural production, only to be discovered to be of such poor balance, or so depleted by leaching caused by their sandy quality, that they could not raise crops decent enough to pay taxes or interest, and the cost of artificially creating out of them soils which could be even moderately productive was economically prohibitive. Those areas have been rapidly reforested or restored to a swampy condition as refuges for wild life or have been allowed, uneconomically, to grow back as second-growth, low-quality forest.

There are areas in Florida and along the whole of the Gulf Coast [19] where one can see cattle walking about all day in rich-looking grass up to their knees with their ribs and hip bones sticking out. These wretched animals are a notable example of the results of unbalances in soils and of the deceptiveness of a lush growth which appears to the eye of the untutored to be nutritive but is not because of deficiencies of almost everything but nitrogen, carbon and water. . . .

An exact contrast and the converse of the Gulf Plain conditions exists only a little way off in the almost arid regions of the Great Plains where cattle, wandering over land sparsely covered by tufty grasses which appear, both in winter or summer, far from lush or green, remain fat and sleek and healthy because the Great Plains as a whole is an area notable for the fine mineral balance of its soils and, despite a rainfall which is only a fraction of that on the damp Gulf [20] Coast Plain, produces in its grasses and legumes a much higher level of mineral and vitamin nutrition. In bulk, an animal need consume on the Great Plains only a fraction of the weight of the Gulf Plain forage in order to remain sleek, healthy and in good flesh.[21]

EPILOGUE: A PHILOSOPHICAL EXCURSION

At Malabar when the shadows grow longer across the Valley and each day the Big House falls earlier beneath the deep shadow of the low sandstone cliffs, we know that winter is closing in. On a still day when we hear the whistles of the big Diesels on the Pennsylvania Railroad six miles away we know that we shall have fine clear weather, and when the sound comes from the opposite direction from the Baltimore and Ohio, we know that there will be clouds and rain. We know the time by the flight overhead of the big planes going north and south, and some of the pilots know us so well that on summer nights they blink their lights in greeting as they pass through the clear, still sky overhead.

In the barns and the fields Al and Simon know their cows— a hundred and twenty of them—by name, and they know their dispositions and what they like or do not like, from Jean, the bossy old Guernsey who must be started homeward first on her way from pasture before the others will go properly, to Inez, the Holstein, smart and temperamental, who once struck up a feud with Mummy, the feed-room cat, and was observed on two occasions shaking Mummy as a dog might shake her, when the unfortunate cat came within reach.

As Philip, who lived with us until he grew up and went away on his own, once said, "The trouble with Malabar is that it's always characters—characters never people . . . even down to the

ducks." That's true of most farm people and especially true of
farm people in hill country where over each rise in the land, just
beyond each patch of woods, there lies a new world. In the old
days before automobiles and telephones, "character" developed
in old age into eccentricity. Today the change is not so great, but
the independence, the strength of opinion and willingness to
fight for an opinion still remain. These are not regimented people
herding at night into subways to return to a cave somewhere
high up in a skyscraper, living as man was never meant to live.

For the young people a farm is a kind of Paradise. One never
hears the whine of the city child, "Mama, what shall I do now?"
On [297] a farm no day is ever long enough for the young person
to crowd into its meager twenty-four hours all there is to be done.
That, too, is true of the good farmer himself. No day is long
enough. There is fishing and swimming, explorations of the
woods and the caves, trapping, messing about the big tractors,
playing in the great mows, a hundred exciting things to do which
each day are new and each day adventurous.

But most of all there is the earth and the animals through
which one comes very close to eternity and to the secrets of the
universe. Out of Gus, the Mallard duck, who comes up from the
pond every evening to eat with the dogs, out of Stinker, the bull,
with his wise eyes and placid disposition, out of all the dogs
which run ahead leaping and barking and luring the small boys
farther and farther into the fields, a child learns much, and most
of all that warmth and love of Nature which is perhaps the greatest of all resources, not only because its variety and beauty is inexhaustible but because slowly it creates a sense of balance and
of values, of philosophy and even of wise resignation to man's
own significance which bring the great rewards of wisdom and
understanding and tolerance. It is not by senseless accident that
the vast majority of the great men and women of the nation and
those who have built it have come from farms or hamlets.

There is in all the world no finer figure than a sturdy farmer
standing, his feet well planted in the earth, looking over his rich
fields and his beautiful shiny cattle. He has a security and an
independence unknown to any other member of society, yet,
unlike the trapper or the hunter, he is very much a part of society, perhaps its most important member. The sharp eyes with

the crow's-feet circling them like small halos, the sunburned neck, the big strong hands, all tell their story of values and of living not only overlooked but unknown to far too many of those who live wholly in an industrial civilization where time clocks and machines rule man instead of man ruling them.

Nothing is more beautiful than the big farm kitchen. It has changed with the times. The refrigerator, the electric stove, the quick-freeze and the cold room have supplanted the cellar, the root storage and the great black old range with its tank of boiling water on the side. The woodpile is gone from outside the door and the horses no longer steam as they stand patiently while the farmer comes in for a cup of coffee and a cinnamon bun. We tell the time nowadays not by the whistle of the old steam locomotives but by the [298] passage overhead of the big flying flagship. But the good smell is still there in the kitchen and the farmer's wife is the same at heart, although in these times she is not bent with rheumatism at forty from carrying water and wood and bending over a washboard. At forty she is likely to be spry and young and busy with her clubs and neighborhood activities—as young-looking as her eighteen-year-old daughter who is a leader in the 4-H Club. And her husband does not rise at daylight and come in weary and bent long after dark. He keeps city hours, but during the day his work is half fun, because the drudgery has gone out of it. He is out of doors with the smell of fresh-turned earth rising to him from the furrow, the sight of a darting cock pheasant rising before his eyes in a kind of brilliant hymn to the morning. He, too, is young and sturdy at middle age and able to go places with his boys, to fish and hunt with them and attend their meetings.

A lot of things have changed on the farm of today, but the essence of the farm and the open country remains the same. The freedom is unchanged and the sense of security and independence and the good rich food and the beauty that lies for the seeing eye on every side and, above all, that satisfaction, as great as that of Leonardo or Shakespeare or any other creative artist, in having made something great and beautiful out of nothing. The farmer may leave his stamp upon the whole of the landscape seen from his window, and it can be as great and beautiful a creation as Michelangelo's David, for the farmer who takes over a desolate farm, ruined by some evil and ignorant predecessor, and turns it into a Paradise of beauty and abundance is one of the greatest of artists.

Of course, I am talking about the good farmer, the real farmer, and not that category of men who remain on the land because circumstance dropped them there and who go on, hating their land, hating their work and their animals because they have never discovered that they do not belong there, that they have no right to carry in trust the greatest of all gifts Nature can bring to man— a piece of good land, with the independence, the security, the excitement and even the splendor that go with it. The good farmer, working with Nature rather than fighting or trying to outwit her, may have what he wants of those treasures which are the only real ones and the ones by which man lives—his family, his power to create and construct the understanding of his relationship to the universe, and the deep, religious, humble sense of his own insignificance in God's creation.[299]

The good farmer of today can have all the good things that his father knew and many that his father never knew, for in the modern world he lives with all the comforts of a luxurious city house plus countless beauties and rewards forever unknown to the city dweller. More than any other member of our society— indeed, perhaps alone in our society—the farmer has learned how to use machinery to serve him rather than his serving machinery. That is a very great secret indeed and one which the other members of our society need desperately to learn.[300]

VIII
The New Centripety

*Joseph Hudnut*_____

THE INVISIBLE CITY

Joseph Hudnut, "The Invisible City," in *Architecture and the Spirit of Man* (Cambridge, Mass., Harvard University Press, 1949).*

Perhaps because I was born and brought up in the country I have always wanted to live near the heart of a great city. Even now I look forward to the day when I can live again in New York: in a little flat, say, at the corner of Broadway and Forty-second Street. I should like to be clothed again in the strength and space of that city; to taste again the diversity of its fashions and humors; to feel about me the encompassment and drift of its opinion. I am not alone in New York even when I am alone. The city furnishes and fortifies my mind.

I once owned a farm near Westport, Connecticut, and for twelve years I tried valiantly to simulate that compassion for rusticity which was and still is fashionable. I was not successful. I could not after the first careless rapture dissemble my boredom with a cottage which was as quaint as a daisy chain at a Vassar commencement and as full of Ye Spirit of Ye Olden Tyme as an eggnog at Christmas. It was all very well so long as I had the fun of adding things on; but when I had added on a loggia, a terrace, a garage, an outside stairway, a gazebo, and all the money I could borrow my week-ends became something to be got through with. Every recollection of my "little place in the country" is filled with a definite vexation and ennui. My memory flies from it like a bird from its cage to those familiar symbols of urbanism which each Monday morning greeted my return to New York: the houses gathering ever more closely around me [157] across the Bronx, the iron bridges over the Harlem River, the long tunnel expectant of the day's adventure, the sudden light-filled space of the Grand Central Station.

The literature of the world is filled with a poet's conspiracy against the city: with advertisements of the city's clamors and indecencies, with the illusion of the country's solace. Only God, we are reminded, can make a tree. As if He had no part in the making of poems and cities!

I am not of course speaking of holidays in the country or of traveling in the country. These are altogether different experiences from that of *living* in the country. Of course I take pleasure in meadows and woods, in mountains and in the gentle forms of New England villages, nor have I forgotten the taste of strawberries fresh from the vine. I am not speaking of recreation or of play, essential ingredients in every life, nor of reverie and the contemplation of sunsets, but of the notion that a rural environment is more congenial to human happiness than the environment of a city. I am thinking of that fantasy of feeling which projects a paramount virtue and health on the country way of life and especially I am thinking of that strange inconsistency of our minds which in spite of poetic sensibilities and discomforts innumerable holds us in the city. My friends in New York talk constantly of escape and yet do not escape. If they had to live there they wouldn't exchange the tip of the Woolworth Building for all that part of the continent which—doubtless through no fault of its own—lies westward of the Hudson River. There is a paradox here which ought to be resolved.

We say that we are imprisoned in cities by economic necessity. A casuistry, surely. There is nothing in the business of making a living, whether it be by way of manufacturing or merchandising or professional service, which absolutely demands a civic environment. Our enterprises grow to larger proportions amid huge concentrations of populations and yet taken as a whole [158] they breed no richer or more numerous rewards than they would if population and place of work were both scattered over the countryside. We could break up our cities without serious consequence to our economy.

Leonardo, in 1486, laid at the feet of Ludovico Sforza a practical plan for dispersing the city of Milan into ten satellite towns so that the people "should not be packed together like goats and pollute the air for one another." Four hundred years later Ebenezer Howard offered London the same program; and today the British Ministry of Town and Country Planning is again flirting at no small expense with that seductive phantom. If we pay little attention to these physicians of our society it is because we do not wish to do so.

The city's pleasures, then? We are held here by crowds and neon lights, by the excitement and comedy of streets and shop windows, by theaters, spectator sports and places of recreation, by the arts which flourish only amid brick and asphalt landscapes?

These are the distant magnets for country-bred youth but they do not explain those acres of our interminable cities in which such pleasures exist in the merest shreds. The pale colorations woven into the tedious fabrics of Queens and the Bronx would seem to afford a dull recompense for mountain vistas and the voices of forest streams; and even if the delights which lie along the spine of Manhattan be considered sufficient to anchor a few thousand there we ought not to overlook the millions of New Yorkers who taste these delights infrequently or not at all. In Chicago there are tens of thousands who have never ventured within the enrapturing atmosphere of the Loop.

We are held in the city neither by pleasure nor by economic necessity but by a hunger which transcends both practical and sensuous experience, a hunger seldom revealed by appearances, seldom acknowledged in our consciousness. We are held in the [159] city by our need of a collective life; by our need of be-

longing and sharing; by our need of that direction and frame
which our individual lives gain from a larger life lived together.

There are city habits and city thoughts, city moralities and
loyalties, city harmonies of valuations which surround us in cities
with an authority and system which, whatever may be the tur-
moil in which they exist, are yet friendly to the human spirit and
essential to its well-being. Beneath the visible city laid out in
patterns of streets and houses there lies an invisible city laid out
in patterns of idea and behavior which channels the citizen with
silent persistent pressures and, beneath the confusion, noise, and
struggle of the material and visible city, makes itself known and
reconciles us to all of these.

We have lived in that invisible city a very long time and are
patterned more comfortably than we suppose to its congenial
mold. It was in the invisible city that we grew over centuries into
what we are today, shaped less by forest, wind, and soil than by
the social relationships and activities which are city-engendered.
Our human nature was created, not as some imagine in treetops
and caves, but in that invisible city. It was there that we learned
the art of living together, developed the shield of values and relationships which protect us, least armored of animals, from the
hostile powers that array us, and it was that there we came to
know the destiny which on earth we must share together. In the
invisible city, frail crystallization of idea and habit of thought,
we learned, circumscribed by forest, river, and the near horizon,
to meet the recurrent crises of birth, adolescence, and death, of
flood and famine and the malice of our gods. There we learned
to organize ourselves with language, conference, magic, education, and law; to use tools, fire, animals, and seed; to possess
property and women; to trade and manufacture; and out of all
these to build that structure of meanings which reconciled our
new-discovered spirit not merely to the [160] nonhuman world
which surrounds us but to the growing complexities of our economies and the tyrannies of our swift technologies.

Under the mechanizations and the new freedoms with which
science has transformed the material and actual city, under steel,
electricity, and machine, under subway, hospital, and grand
hotel, under democracy, progressive education, and assembly-
line manufacture lie the firm strata of experience gathered across

the centuries in the invisible city. Mound above mound, a thousand Troys laid on Troy, these lift us above the arid plain of biological and economic existence. The roots of our minds reach deeply into these deposits and draw from them the law of our present vision and behavior. We are not always aware of that law so light is its accustomed authority, so nice is our conformity to its channelings; nor do we always understand, wrapped in the business of living, how these give steadfastness and direction to our lives.

Every creature on this earth finds happiness in that setting which gives scope to his peculiar energies. Tigers are happy in the jungle, birds in the shade-bestowing trees, and men in the free air of cities. Each living thing attained its present attributes by adjustments long continued between itself and the world which encircled it. Each has its home having been fashioned by his home. Creature and environment are parts of a whole. Tigers, birds, and men do not always know that they are happy; but take them out of their familiar elements and they soon know what it is to be unhappy.

Our poets are too ready to give the city to the devil. The city, I think, was the tool with which God made man. Perhaps it is the tool with which He is making man.

Almost from the beginnings of human history the invisible city has been the theme of the social art of architecture. The musician,[161] the dancer, the poet were the channels through which the experience and emotion of individuals were made known but the architect celebrated the intangible fabric of communal feeling discovered by him beneath street and wall, beneath family, ambition, and the market, beneath the tumult of politics and war —discovered by him and by him advertised in his many-voiced art.

There is a mode of that art having as its materials not buildings or gardens or public places merely, but the totalities of cities: a mode of architecture—sometimes anonymous, sometimes guided by genius—sometimes swift in process, sometimes operative over slow centuries—which sets forth in the language of form that civic consciousness without which cities are only biological conveniences; which seizes upon that consciousness and holds it before us in a thousand different interpretations, each universal in substance and yet specific to time and circumstance. The practitioner of that architecture is the collective soul, silent for a moment beneath our present turbulence of circumstance, but certain of renewal and regained authority. Our necessity paves a channel for that inevitable progress. Our hunger prepares the table which shall nourish it.

We are too apt nowadays to think of architecture as a minister of individual comfort and delight, and even when we remember that architecture may be an element in civic patterns it exists in our minds as decoration or ceremonial background. The design of cities has become a matter of traffic highways and housing projects—with here and there a splash of peristyle and ordered space to give dignity to a city hall. The idea of form in cities, of cities which exhibit in their aggregates of shelter, space, and tree an ideal and pattern of life, of cities which are works of art: this idea seems to be lost under the present urgencies of our mechanizations. In the great traditions of architecture this idea was not, as it is today, thus alien to our minds.[162]

Architecture did not impose itself upon the practical activities of a city, was not an intruder into social or economic life, was not inconsistent with politics, war or individual ambition, but marched with all of these holding before all the shining symbols which revealed the direction and unity of the general life.

An invisible Athens existed beneath the visible Athens and was the deep source of its splendor. The Athenians were well aware of their city as commercial utility and political instrument, but their imaginations were not, happily, limited to that awareness. Themistocles planned the city with a regard for profit and empire not less strict than was Burnham's solicitude for the railroads of Chicago. The roads to Athenian supremacy were the trade routes which led to Egypt and the Black Sea and the great harbor of the Piraeus was laid out with the intent to keep open these freedom-freighted avenues. The quays were wide, straight, and well protected, the warehouses and arsenals were ordered and convenient for maritime trade, the exchanges for corn, wool, metals, dyes, and slaves were designed in accordance with the rigid and functional science developed in the technological schools of Miletus. The plan of the Piraeus, so far as it has been revealed under the foundations of the modern city, seems to have followed a practical and systematic geometry not unlike that which Le Corbusier proposed for modern Paris: the traffic regulated, the quarters clearly bounded, the public works set apart from the homes of the people. The art of civic design—that art which Aristotle called a "sociological architecture"—was a useful art, appropriate and at home under the life-filled porticoes of the crowded agorae.

That art nevertheless was not limited by the technologies of enterprise. It was not the architecture of commerce—of the Piraeus whose arms embraced the sea-borne traffic of a hundred nations—nor the architecture of politics, nor yet the architecture of their homes, threaded with narrow and tortuous streets,[163] which best served the Athenian people, but the shining temples built out of loyalties and memories, out of great deeds accomplished together, out of gratitudes never to be forgotten in the collective heart. This was the city the Persians could not destroy, the invisible city, proud, exultant, and eternal, which the people had guarded behind the wooden walls of Salamis. Symbol and sentinel of that city the Acropolis stood above the clash of party and of class, a harmony crowning a harmony, the white crest of a wave which had gathered strength across centuries. The Acropolis was not a political document or a civic decoration or an abstraction of art—still less a "cultural center," pale refuge such as we build for our besieged civilization—but a spiritual reality which kindled the collective life and yet was intimate also to the life of every Athenian.

I am sure that the Romans, whose lives were lived under stately porticoes and amid the pomp of great temples found in that background an ever present dignity which must have followed them even into the poverty and confusions of the crowded, many-storied *insulae*. The wide forums and the glittering thermae did not arise merely from the vanity of emperors and the corruption of the people. These were the songs in which the Roman soul made itself known above the cries of the circus and the clash of civil swords. The Gothic cathedrals were, in part at least, prayers of thanksgiving for a joy discovered in the revival of cities, and the *piazze* into which Venice poured her compressed splendor are jubilant with that new enfranchisement. These are not each an ornament added to a city but summations of a city's spirit to which houses and streets, walls, canals, and the domes of public buildings are the harmonious counterparts. Florence, Padua, Cordoba; the Paris of Richelieu, the Philadelphia of Franklin: each of these might have been the work of a single architect so consistent is the ordinance and expression of their streets and structures. With what persistence have they held [164] their characters over the years in spite of political crisis and economic change! Because the men who lived in these cities lived also within the city's pattern of idea, from which no citizen could imagine himself apart, the pattern in which they clothed themselves became, even without their conscious consent, the mirror which revealed the city's anonymous heart. In that mirror the citizen recognized his own dignity and his faith. The architecture of the city—a term which included all of the city's structures and ordered space—confirmed that which men believed about themselves.

All things—even the suns—are subject to deformations. Trees are gnarled and twisted by the sea winds, green fields turn to dust under drought and sun, and peace-loving men become savages amid the frenzies of war. Through long progressions the million species of the earth reach each its characteristic form and yet none is invulnerable to accident. A sudden crisis may arrest any progress—a violent alteration in wind or sun, an invasion of new enemies, a storm too rough for accustomed measures of security—and distortion, blight, and adventitious growth may overcome the healthiest organism.

So it was with the city under the fierce impact of the Industrial Revolutions and of that explosive mercantilism which at the end of the eighteenth century scattered the European peoples over the earth. Cities, new and old, grew rapidly to unprecedented dimensions and as they grew shattered that humanity of texture and expression which had once been impressed upon them by collective thought and feeling long continued. No longer do our cities exhibit in their outward aspects that framework of social purpose, that cement of manners, conventions, and moralities, that *tradition* built by slow change and patient compromise which once gave character and beauty to the city's life.

The symbol and chief actor in this disintegration was the factory [165]—the factory and its accomplice, the railroad, together with the thousand other children of iron and steam. We did not guess when we admitted the factory to our cities that it would destroy their patterns; destroy them utterly and with that destruction provoke the questionings and discontents which color our present judgments of cities. Servile and seemingly innocent utilities, born of windmill and mountain stream, growing slowly in the green forests beside their white waterfalls, their many windows caressed by sunshine and fresh winds, there was little in the first factories that was prescient of Birmingham and Chicago. No one was aware of crisis. Across the countryside, silently, unnoticed, factory and city began their unequal duel.

Nevertheless it was inevitable that the two should meet on closer ground. People must work where they live: the factory must invade the city, or the city come to the factory. The railroad and the steam engine were prompt to respond to that necessity; these united city and factory; united them but not as the elements of an art are united in a pattern, not as new functions are united by slow development to a growing organism, but as aliens forced together by outside pressure, as a foreign body is thrust into living tissue. The factory came into the city not as architecture but as machine. Unlike the temple and the theater, the house and the market place, the factory was built, not out of love and the commerce of society but out of calculation and economic necessities. A consequence, not of feeling but of ingenuity, a device by which men—and children—lent themselves to machines and machines to men, the factory was little else than pulley and wheel grown to vast proportions.

We know how that growth, once the factory was firmly planted within the city, eclipsed in speed and consequence all other growth in the long history of mankind. Within a single century pulley and wheel gathered the city within their giant shadows and gave the city a new law. Pulley and wheel raised new values [166] for the city to live by; refashioned the city's manners, speech, and faith; recoined the city's time; remade in its own image the city's streets and squares. The people of the city must then arrange their lives in accordance with its uncongenial necessities; government must listen to its decrees; religion rewrite her mythologies to condone its tyrannies; and social custom, family life, recreation and the arts, the ambitions of men and their standards of right and wrong, must be made conformable to these mechanical rhythms, to these uniformities of process and product. The cathedral, once generator and guardian of cities, had cherished and consoled all who lived at its side. The palace, also a generator of cities, ennobled the citizens with an ordinance and art of living; the distant trading posts bound together with common enterprise and shared destiny those who gathered around them; and even the fortress inspired in those who must live beneath its walls a loyalty from which they drew a communal strength. The factory merely used the city. As if in response to some blind biological law the city transformed itself from home and commonwealth into storehouse and machine.

The giant lizards could not survive a sudden change of climate. It may be that man now confronts that peril also. Could that be one of the secret causes of the giant wars which now convulse the earth?

Please do not misunderstand me. I am not for imitations of Venice and Athens set down in Cleveland and San Francisco. Our cities are the homes of our great industries and they must take the way of industry. I am for mechanized cities and for every technological improvement in cities; nor would I hide these under cloaks of romance or academic decorums. Neither do I believe that we can restore the old and beautiful patterns of society by inviting our civic populations to enter shining new houses laid out for them by architects confident of their art [167] to transform the universe. Our architecture, and especially the architecture of our cities, will be created by our society to whose mood and necessities the architect is instrument. I am for no Utopia.

Nevertheless I have faith in the power of man to shape his environment in accordance with his inward needs and I know that that reshaping is most essential for human happiness. Beneath these wheels and pulleys, these endless turnings and meaningless propulsions, there still lies that invisible city in which we must live or perish. That city has desperate need of architecture: of an architecture peculiar to itself, unlike any other architecture, and yet as constant as any other in its affirmation of purpose and dignity.

Sometimes when I am in Rockefeller Center, where skyscrapers, music halls, gardens, and shops innumerable crowd into an islanded harmony I imagine that I feel the promise of that new renaissance of our art. A city rises about me; I am in a theater prepared for me as if by ancient usage and rehearsal. At such times I like to believe that architecture may indeed reassume its forgotten importance as outward frame and envelope of a communal life, being shaped once more by the commerce of a society that is civilized, polite, and urbane.

Civilized, polite, and urbane—each word rooted in a word that means *the city*.[168]

Robert Moses _____

THE SPREADING CITY

Robert Moses, "The Spreading City," in Working for the People: Promise and Performance in Public Service (New York, Harper and Brothers, 1956).*

The urban trend, whether we like it or not, is undeniable. The shift from country to town is steady. There is little wavering in the graph but, like all statistics, these require both definition and honest interpretation.

The country is, of course, the area marked in green on the maps, whether wide open or thinly populated. The town—that is another matter. The town is not only the city in the legal sense but the large village as well, whether incorporated or not, the township in some areas, the metropolis in others. In measuring the trend toward the more compact, populous places, we must remember that as people move into cities many in the same cities move into the outskirts, the suburbs and the satellite towns.

* Reprinted by permission of Robert Moses.

Besides those who move from place to place because of their work, an astonishing number of people have homes in town and in the country. They divide their time about equally between an apartment in town and a house, camp or shack of some kind elsewhere. We have millions of city people of all income brackets who spend every weekend in the country and others who have made a habit of regular visits to national and state parks.

The city man is a weekend salt-water fisherman by instinct. He requires something unpaved, unencumbered, and monotonous to keep him sane. Perhaps it is an admission against interest to say that there are many of us who simply cannot take the city the week around.[83] Our parkways, turnpikes, expressways, thruways and other roads, which are being multiplied and improved to keep pace with the output of cars and the demands of the traveling public, will increase enormously the pressure on our highway system and promote mutual attraction and gradual unification of the country and the town.

Meanwhile, the healthy, natural movement of young couples with growing families to houses and apartments at moderate prices in outlying areas of the city and in the suburbs has been accelerated. No compulsion, no artificial stimulus is needed to drive people out of town.

PREJUDICE AND POPULATION SHIFTS

Increasing leisure, longer paid vacations, larger pensions, earlier retirement, older people with the itch for travel and with unsatisfied curiosity about distant places break down more and more the artificial differences between the city man and the country man. The big question is whether the traveler seeks to broaden his horizons or to confirm his prejudices.

We should not pay too much attention to the dweller in the shadow of the "El" who would rather be a lamppost in Chicago than the whole Painted Desert. Or to the confirmed Gothamite who boasts that the city is the finest summer resort and that, as Mr. Dooley remarked: "Ivrything that's worth havin' goes to th' city; the counthry takes what's left." And by the same token, keep in mind that Thoreau spent only a relatively short time continuously in his crude shack at Walden Pond. There is no sense in assuming irreconcilable conflict between city and country people. We are not neatly divided between hayseeds and slickers. Acres have claims as well as concentrations of people, but there are no provable superior virtues attaching to the country or city when moral, spiritual, mental, or even health and hygienic factors are under consideration.

Cities were in many cases originally created for protection. This is about the only logic of urban growth which is no longer significant. All the other reasons for the establishment of growing cities are as influential today as they were when the pioneers founded them on the seaboard, the river, the valley, the hill, the rail center, the crossroads,[84] the focal point of a farming, mining, fishing, manufacturing or other center, or the source of plentiful labor.

Academic planners and those who cannot stand urban competition or tolerate a certain amount of noise, tension, hurry, and the anonymity of urban life, advocate decentralization of cities and dispersion of population. But their prejudices will not materially influence the logic of the situation. There are good reasons why most cities persist. Those which decline do so because they no longer serve a function in the larger economy of the nation.

SOME ADVANTAGES OF CONCENTRATION

It is not to be forgotten that civilization is an outgrowth and attribute of cities. Farms produce food; oceans support commerce; the suburbs are dormitories; the mines teem with energy and the forests with the solitude which promotes thought—but civilization flourishes only in concentrated urban communities. You need not live in a city, but you must be nearby or visit now and then if you expect to be recognized as a civilized man. A city need not be large but a village is not a city. To quote the lines of Vachel Lindsay:

> Let not your town be large, remembering
> That little Athens was the muses' home,

> That Oxford is the heart of London still,
> That Florence gave the Renaissance to Rome.
> —"ON THE BUILDING OF SPRINGFIELD" [1]

The American is restless and imitative. He likes contrast, change and assembly-line stuff. I believe it was Henry Mencken who described him sourly as an Elk in a Ford. Well, ours may not be a great civilization as measured by philosophers. It is no Cinque-Cento Italian Renassance when it comes to aristocracy of the arts, but it has its points. This is the one nation on earth in which the average man can also be the well-rounded man with two residences, one in town and the other in the country. You do not have to be a millionaire here to own a flivver and a country bungalow.

A proper reading of history shows that the permanence of cities is [85] more significant than their decay. War and the acts of God have from time to time outraged them, but those which were established at navigable waters, at important crossroads and centers, strategic places of one kind or another, persist.

A one-industry town may dry up with its only attraction, but this is the exception not the rule. For every Auburn which fades as its bold peasantry declines, there is a Birmingham which still flourishes. Ol' Man River—Mississippi, Danube or Columbia—keeps on rolling along and most of the cities he has spawned on his banks still flourish. A city cannot live on Tyrian purple, or the sale of graven images of Diana, or on depleted mines, honky-tonks or rundown aristocracy; but London, Stalingrad, Amsterdam rise from rubble because they were and continue to be the logical and traditional places for concentration and because they continue to have the men, the enterprise and the pride to keep up with or ahead of the times.

The trouble with the prophets of doom of cities is that they do not think like the people who live in them. Lewis Mumford, Frank Lloyd Wright and their followers who damn urbanization because they cannot stand the gaff of city life no doubt honestly believe that all city people hate their existence. They do not realize that Brooklynites adore Brooklyn, idolize the Dodgers

---

[1] From *General William Booth Enters Into Heaven;* copyright 1916 by The Macmillan Company. Reprinted by permission of the publisher.

because they symbolize it, and cheer themselves hoarse at the mention of its name. Can Mumford and the aesthetes, and Frank Lloyd Wright and the back-to-the-land boys be right and three million Brooklynites be wrong? The community may survive a long time because there are, as Webster said of his old alma mater, those who love it, and because there are also those who cannot get away.

A town, like a British remittance man in Canada, can be supported by distant relatives. Some of our old villages are helped by natives who have gone to big cities and made good. We have towns that, like Colonial Williamsburg, have become museums and monuments which stir memories but have no grip on ambitious boys and girls. There are, to be sure, not many such communities in our new country. Those that exist should keep up standards but should not try to compete with rushing, raucous, new places. It is better to live on charm than to be an imitation Babylon.[86]

Only the city can afford the arts in their broadest and most developed sense, because it takes population to keep art centers alive and flourishing. The same reasoning applies to great medical centers which require the most nearly complete clinical facilities, to management headquarters of banking and big business, and to many mercantile establishments which have to be close together.

The nearby country as well as the suburb is meaningless without the city. Los Angeles supports a veritable paradise of truck farmers and orchards almost at its borders, and New York is the big market for the potatoes, ducks and shellfish of Long Island. Proximity of city and country, warm shorefront and glacial heights, ranch and bungalow, is what makes California such a strong rival of the Atlantic and Gulf seaboards and the Middle West. Our entire economy is dependent on urban, suburban and rural integration.

Obviously, city life is not doomed, although some particular town may be static, advancing or going back. In studying any particular community, there is no quick, smooth categorical answer to the never-ending challenges of growth and change. Intelligent citizens should study the main forces at work, the pulls and pressures. Much depends on the traditions of the town, on its

The **Triborough Bridge area** of New York City. Robert Moses, who became head of the Triborough Bridge Authority in 1934, was instrumental in the completion of the bridge, its approaches, and the 144-acre park, a portion of which is shown in this photograph. The bridge links three areas of the city: Manhattan, the Bronx, and Queens.

special interests, on types of leadership and the strength of advocates of conservative improvement as against radical and revolutionary uprooting.

DIVERSITY IN METROPOLITAN AREAS

It is a great mistake to assume that the overbuilt and deliberately overcrowded midtown section of every big city is the city, and that nothing else in it counts. Parts of big towns are like suburbs and even country. The significant and often prevailing and controlling outskirts, peripheries and relatively quiet residential places where respectable people keep the noiseless tenor of their way—places which make no pretense of being "stems," Broadway crossroads, "hot spots," "loops" and what not, and with no special bids to visitors—are more characteristic of the city, more redolent of its quality and flavor than the places ballyhooed by barkers and touted by advertisers. The barkers always show off the city slums, the Harlems, Bowery, Basin streets, Chinatowns, Little Italy, the former ghettoes, and so on, and picture [87] them as a fixed, unchangeable, inevitable feature of city life. But it simply is not so.

In our cities the shallows murmur, but the deeps are dumb. There are more churchgoers than cabaret hounds, but they make less noise. The jazz joints, with their raucous snare drums and trumpets, are more obtrusive but much less important than the long-drawn aisles and fretted vaults where, as the poet said, the pealing anthem swells the note of praise.

The spreading suburbs also have their logic, not only as dormitories for commuters and garden spots for their wives and children, but also as places from which, by rail and road, the manifold attractions of the city can easily be reached without the distractions and handicaps of city life.

It is sad to see venal, weak or complacent local officials, indifferent to recent history, permitting the subdividers, real estate developers and their co-conspirators and victims to repeat the same tricks in the suburbs which made the slums of the cities a few generations ago—small lots, narrow streets, with parks, schools, and utilities of all kinds waiting for future assessments

on unsuspecting purchasers. Higher standards must come from
the average citizen. Water cannot rise above its own level.

The suburbs, too, often are leaderless. I worry more about the
suburbs than about the cities. In the cities we are at least aware
of and are trying to undo the errors of the past. In the suburbs
these felonies are being compounded and perpetuated.

SOME SUBURBAN PROBLEMS

I do not believe that the metropolis is obsolete. The city is still
the center of gravity of modern civilization. Parts of it of course
are antiquated, especially slums and rundown, depressed areas
which are the results of the past selfishness of capital, the weakness of government and the indifference of the citizenry. We
have at least been educated above this level to some understanding of the difficulties, costs and sacrifices which must be made to
remedy conditions which under better leadership would never
have occurred.

Our big cities must be rebuilt, not abandoned. While this is
being [88] done the suburbs will continue to grow amazingly, and
open country previously considered beyond commuting distance
will become suburban. But let us not fool ourselves about the
spreading city. There are just as many problems involved in
rapid, uncontrolled, suburban growth as in the rebuilding of
substandard midtown urban sections.

As we reflect on suburban growth we begin to recognize that
this is not an unmixed blessing. I am not at all sure that the problems of the suburbs are not more serious and less understood
than those of the city. I have never yet seen one of these big
plans for suburban "developments" start out with a proper diag-
nosis of future problems.

The Levittown community on Long Island is an example. Here
the builders took a number of farms, open land, and built some
17,000 houses to accomodate 75,000 people. When you live in the
heart of the city you have facilities which, while they may not be
just to your liking, do provide schools, streets, sewers, water,
electric and gas utilities and some established forms of transportation. When you go out in the open country, however, all these

problems gradually rear their ugly heads to plague you. I have seen them develop. You decide that putting in cesspools is safe to start with, but soon you are taking water out of the same ground to drink, no doubt at a different level, and then a water supply problem arises. Nobody pays much attention to drainage, and all of a sudden you have to do something about storm sewers.

Somebody is going to get the bills for that. Some one will be assessed. Bills also have got to be paid for sewage plants. Cesspools and well water for 75,000 people do not mix for any length of time. Transportation and schools must be provided. There is no use going through the roster of necessities. They descend upon the community as a whole after the developer, the fellow who has moved these people or industries to virgin territory has departed and closed his account books.

"RUS IN URBE"

Only a pretentious scribbler would glory in the boast that Augustus Caesar found Rome built of brick and left it built of marble. Our watchword should be that we found our city a wilderness of stone [89] and steel, crowded and inaccessible, and that we opened it to light and air, planted it with the green of parks and the laughter of playgrounds, and carved out wide spokes and rims for parkways and expressways to make the city and country one.

I dismiss as unworthy of serious consideration the gloomy prophets who label cities as obsolete because of the possibility of atomic bombing. If the hydrogen bombs actually fall, we shall all be finished. Meanwhile, apprehension and premature terror can paralyze us before anything really happens. These are just the objectives the Communists aim at in their cold, psychological warfare.

It is the ambition of every official responsible for the rebuilding and improvement of cities to increase the open spaces, reduce the coverage of land, salvage, restore and preserve natural resources; in fact, to approximate the old Roman idea of *rus in urbe*, the country in the city.

The city, rebuilt, modernized and humanized, will always be the great magnet which draws from the hinterland the eager, the young, the curious, the ambitious, the talented. These, from the dawn of history, have gravitated to big places where the incentives are most dramatic, where competition is strongest and rewards great. Ours is an emerging new people of many stocks and talents in a land of extraordinary variety. Country and city, we are knitted together.

Our suburbs will in time somehow attain bouquet, flavor, character and personality. The residents, mostly young couples with small children, will form friendships. Acquaintances will cross the parkways and highways which separate one development from another. Marriages will cement the Montagus and Capulets of these scattered communities. Thus eventually they will produce leaders with vision and pride and by some mysterious alchemy develop a sense of unity.[90]

Christopher Tunnard

THE LEAF AND THE STONE

Christopher Tunnard, "The Leaf and the Stone," in *The City of Man* (New York, Charles Scribner's Sons, 1953).*

There are primitive communities in many parts of the world today in which tree worship is still practiced. There are also to be found in highly civilized communities certain advanced groups—mainly architects, planners and their disciples—who worship all forms of greenery indiscriminately. So great is the devotion of these latter-day hamadryads to the forms of nature that they wish to be surrounded by them at all times and in all places

*Reprinted with the permission of Charles Scribner's Sons from *The City of Man*, pp. 235–239, 240, 243, 246, 247, 249, 250, 251–258, by Christopher Tunnard. (These extracts appeared first as part of an article titled "The Leaf and the Stone" in the *Magazine of Art*.)

—even in the heart of the city, where until recently nature was seldom seen. This new cult is trying to abolish the old and seemingly irreducible dualism between nature and man, the tame and the wild, the country and the city. In doing so, it denies many hitherto-cherished concepts of civic design, some of which must be mentioned here to put the new movement in perspective.[235]

There used to be a region called the country and a place called the town. Since Ruskin's day this distinction has become less clear: "At least fifty acres of beautiful country outside London," the sage of Denmark Hill once railed, "have been Demoralized by the increasing urge of the Upper Classes to live where they can get some gossip in their idleness and show each other their dresses." Since the mid-nineteenth century the situation has grown worse—more people want to live closer to nature *and* to the dress shops, to fresher air and wider spaces; it was not long, therefore, before a solution in city planning terms was forthcoming.

"There are in reality not only, as is so constantly assumed, two alternatives—town life and country life—but a third alternative, in which all the advantages of the most energetic and active town life, with all the beauty and delight of the country, may be secured in perfect combination. . . ." So wrote Ebenezer Howard, the inventor of the garden city, proposing the adoption of *"town-country,"* a not-altogether happy solution for the problems of contemporary living. Note the phrase "beauty and delight of the country,"—a typically town-bred way of referring to cultivated nature; one feels that the countryside would be unhappy partner in this forced marriage, under the subjection, in fact, of the town itself which still dominates the planner's thinking. Is there not a confusion here? In trying to improve what Henry James calls "the terrible town," not only Howard, but every other nineteenth century utopian planner was trying to change it into something else, not realizing that towns must be allowed their own diathesis in order to be effective as communities. As a result almost all the ideal towns proposed in the age of antipathy to urban "ugliness" lack any atmosphere or character which would ensure this popularity. Even the garden city, dissolved in green, lacks appeal to any but the dedicated, in much the same way as the meatless dinner [236] appeals only to the vegetarian; but it should not be imagined that Howard's idea was without influence. As several authorities have pointed out, his theory has been more effective in changing the character of the city itself than in creating its antithesis . . . town-country or the garden city proper.

˝ This is not to deny that the forms of nature have their legitimate part to play in man's own private place, the city; in the furnishing, the elevation, and especially in the plan. We need not subscribe to the extreme views of the Abbé Laugier, who in his *Essai sur l'Architecture* published in 1755 suggested that French cities be planned like forests to avoid "the excesses of regularity and symmetry;" nor will the problem again arise which confronted the courtiers of the Margrave of Baden-Durlach when, escaping from their too flattering attentions, he sought refuge in a wood. The city plan, being an art form, will never be an exact mirror of nature, in spite of the pseudo-biological approach of the devotees of "organic planning;" although it may with virtue acknowledge the presence of nature and heighten our enjoyment of man-made environment by contrast.

What is the evidence of history in the attempted resolution of this problem? A few general observations can be made here. First, it is clear that with only occasional exceptions there is a hard and fast line drawn between town and country until well on into the sixteenth century. This is not to say that town extensions, and even suburbs, did not exist—one had to travel outside the walls of Athens to visit the garden of Epicurus or Plato's academy, and by the Augustan age it was positively fashionable to live in the not too distant country—but the character of the city and of even the nearest cluster of Roman villas [was] vastly different, and no attempt was made to bring natural forms into the city pattern except in the privacy of the garden. Sometimes it happened that nature was already there and was [238] not destroyed when the city grew, but mostly the city was quite literally streets, buildings, fountains and squares—bare of natural ornamentation. . . .[239]

The seventeenth century brought nature into the city plan in a unique and unsurpassed fashion, but first let us look at the preceding century, which gave us the first modern cities and in which certainly we should expect to find evidences of the coming trend. The Italians of the Renaissance, who were pioneers in the discovery of modern landscape, arrived at the new attitude simply by reviving a late classical feeling for esthetically agreeable scenery and the change was neither drastic nor sudden. Wild nature was still kept in its place and even to men of the later Renaissance the idea of "town-country" was unthinkable. There was the world and the city—the latter certainly to be escaped from, when the weather was too hot or the plague threatened, but always the center of government, and of culture,—a separate place. . . .[240]

The Renaissance city in its more advanced forms remains the truest expression of the power of man to create an esthetically satisfying environment. It had, as we have seen, no need for nature within the gates. . . .

Green space as part of the organic structure of the city comes with the seventeenth century and the establishment of new forms based on changing social behavior. . . . The significant change comes with the building of Marie de Medici's Luxembourg Palace in 1620. These grounds have been open to the public for over three hundred years. . . .[243]

This . . . is the beginning of the marriage of nature with the urban complex, a union arranged by the French, as Sitte remarks, to suit their philosophy of human control in all things which Malebranche raised to its height in the seventeenth century. . . .[246]

Paris was never modeled on a garden, but it was the first school for the introduction of nature into cities, and the least idiosyncratic one. By the mid-eighteenth century, before London had many of its green squares, Paris had conquered the problem of the treatment of open space in cities. She had a manicured air and a fresh look, with her public and private pleasure grounds, open squares like the Place Vendôme and the Place de la Concorde, green avenues and Elysian fields. Everything was in its place, like smaller jewels in the Monarch's crown. And while large parts of the city had the appearance of a beautiful garden, the gardening became a part of the architecture, to produce a hitherto unequaled urban ensemble. . . .[247]

Misopolitan feeling becomes stronger throughout the nineteenth century as the city grows more horrible—the utopians, reformers like Buckingham, architects—all the planners of ideal cities represent a movement to approximate nature in their schemes. . . .[249]

The notion of the eventual abandonment of the city for a life in more "natural" surroundings has a strange persistence; it received an enormous impetus from the garden city movement after 1898. . . .[250]

Turning from prototype plans to those which may be more accurately termed contemporary, it appears at first glance that the picturesque-romantic school has triumphed over the advocates of controlled natural forms (neo-classic), who have not been heard from for twenty years. While utilitarian planning still holds its place, neo-romantic urbanism predominates among the intellectuals of the planning movement. What are the evidences?

1. The two most popular over-all forms are a modification of the curvilinear plan (which originated in the last years of the romantic period) and adaptations of the linear plan (of technological origin). The curvilinear plan was introduced into the United States by Alexander Jackson Davis and Andrew Jackson Downing and used later by Olmsted and Vaux. It has been modified by the cul-de-sac and adapted to modern traffic requirements (e.g. a more gently curving street pattern, less arbitrary forms). In this country, it has seen popular adaptations in the activities of subdividers (Levittown) and in the shape of completely new [251] towns (Norris and Oak Ridge, Tenn.). In England, it has reached official status, being employed by municipalities and housing authorities (Becontree, Wythenshawe). It is frequently used because curved streets are thought to be pleasanter than straight ones, a notion not devoid of sentimental implications, or because it can be easily adapted to irregular topography. The modified linear plan appears, with the foregoing, in the work of contemporary planners like Le Corbusier. It may take the form of urban units arranged along a communication spine, or of a series of superblocks, connected by traffic arteries or linear parks.

In both cases the detailed planning of residential areas is likely to derive from picturesque antecedents, although its rationalization will often be based on scientific argument. "Free" arrangements of buildings in green space have taken the place of the more strictly disciplined *zeilenbau* pattern and although [252] density and economic requirements often necessitate group[s] in the form of courts or squares, the most "advanced" school of planners prefers the staggered row and the isolated tower in picturesque balance.

2. The character of contemporary architecture now approaching full popularity is romantic-mannerist in feeling, with emphasis in the case of the International school on silhouette, and in that of the "Organic" school on horizontal line (identity with nature and the earth). Both schools rely heavily on landscaping or the proximity of natural surroundings to offset or complement their architecture. In the case of the "Organic" style, green forms are used in conjunction with the building to reach toward the uncultivated or to tie the building to the ground. In the case of the "International" style, they are introduced to provide scale and for purely esthetic pleasure in foliage and branch structure. This demand for the proximity of natural forms is philosophically based on the contemporary ideal of a harmony between nature and man, of "biological decency" toward the forms of nature; *not,* it should be noted, on the rival principle of absolute control of nature by man himself. This partnership of man and nature, the feeling of "oneness" has been largely spurred by the writings of Dewey, and to a lesser extent by Riegl and Minkowski, whose anti-compartmentalized worlds in which the sciences and the arts, technology and creativity are to be brought together have an extraordinary attraction to the architect trying to create an environment of universal appeal. His failure to appeal lies in the impossibility of providing a satisfactory form of urbanized nature which will fulfill all the outdoor social needs [253] of urban life, as city building based on picturesque principles alone must always fail. As long as the focal point of the city, the very core of its activity, is treated as an island of green, these intellectualized plans will remain unsatisfying.

It is on Le Corbusier's shoulders that the major responsibility rests for the wide-spread attempts to dissolve the city in an ocean of green. Beginning in the twenties with an awkward mechanical solution for the metropolis, he has moved through the period of the "radiant" city and has now arrived at a new conception: "We may try another: the installation of a 'green City' . . . all around it an immense countryside will be freed; fields, meadows, forests . . . NATURE CAN BE ENTERED IN THE LEASE! Nature lived before the town arose; the town chased her away, filling her place with stones, with bricks, and with asphalt." Describing the "green city" he remarks significantly: "The pact is signed with nature . . . Through the four seasons stand the trees, friends of men. Great blocks of dwellings run through the town. What does it matter? They are behind the screen of trees." In America, Ludwig Hilberseimer actually shows how the city can be made to disappear [254] in trees—"the city will be within the landscape and the landscape within the city."

To recapitulate: In the theory of city-building there have been periods in which 1. the city excluded nature except in the manicured form of gardens, which have never formed an integrated part of the overall plan 2. the forms of nature were used with the forms of architecture to create the plan, and 3. the forms of nature have been given a role approaching dominance in the plan. It has been suggested that the first two were creative and appropriate attitudes, but that the third is based on a misconception of the urban function in contemporary society. It remains then to indicate an alternative approach. Obviously, the Renaissance and Baroque attitudes have lost their relevance; the city has grown too large to draw a line past which nature cannot cross, and social needs have changed since the days of the Sun King.

But is there an approach which can be satisfying to contemporary social and esthetic needs?

First, let us be aware that any attitude toward nature is fundamentally a part of our whole conception of the city; not just a matter of providing recreation space and green lungs for an expanding urban population. We must accept the existence of a continuing dualism in the concept of environmental planning. The search for town-country can lead only to extreme solutions such as those already outlined. Perhaps the distinction between urban and rural surroundings should be heightened rather than decreased; but in any case a pragmatic approach should reveal the role which each should play. What is "country," in planning terms? A resource base, to be preserved, cultivated and constantly renewed in fertility. Its population will always be less, acre for acre, than that of the city, but access to the amenities of life will become increasingly important. And "town"? A processing and distributing center, requiring larger [255] concentrations of population; also, if we can agree with the Aristotelian concept and with modern urban sociologists, a cultural fountainhead. Whether or not the giant city, through decentralization, will become smaller and the countryside become interspersed with new centers as a result, as Lewis Mumford suggests, there is likely to be a continuing urban form and a continuing rural pattern, distinct in function and design. For the urban center, with which we are concerned here, this condition of things will mean a continuing search for solution to specific urban problems, based on the existence of urban concentration.

Green forms will be always necessary and an integrated part of the urban pattern. Their use should, however, be preceded by a better social investigation than the dis-urbanists have made. We have now achieved a scientific analysis of the *quantity* of open space necessary for recreational purposes. Standards of the National Recreation Association and the American Public Health Association are admirable in their thoroughness and have been broken down into various types of open space development with suggested general locations for each in the city plan. These recommended open spaces however do not usually take an excessive proportion of the total area of the community and there is sufficient reason that they should not do so, green space being expensive and usually difficult to maintain in urban surroundings. The introduction of green walls, green verges, extensive tree-lined boulevards and purely decorative green areas which are undesirable for recreational use is to be discouraged, as is the whole concept of greenery for its own sake. Trees used for shade, noise buffers and windbreaks are, on the other hand, highly desirable, and, when they are properly integrated with social use, extremely effective in civic design. The introduction of trees into the very heart of the city can be accomplished in this way; the trouble is that our neo-romantic [256] approach has envisaged something like the New England village common occupying the center of megalopolis. It should not be imagined that the scientific introduction of green forms will produce a city resembling Baroque Paris; on the contrary, this approach should result in the creation of new city patterns; the absolute control of natural forms in the modern city should be the only similarity noticeable between it and that first great period of nature in towns. The writer will yield to no one in his admiration for the adventitious tree or green space, seen unexpectedly as a foil to architectural works; certainly we should welcome the casual hand or the occasional picturesque note, and in this we should be following the Italian renaissance tradition. Here we come close to gardening, and the gardens of a city should be many and various—like paintings on the wall of a living-room, their form and content may differ widely.

The plea is thus for realistic urbanism, rather than neo-romantic dis-urbanism, and it is to be expected that a change in attitude on the part of urbanists would produce a very different type of plan from the ones now being advanced. Open space in cities not planned as amorphous green areas dotted with trees but given a form complementing and increasing enjoyment [257] of architecture—with grass and trees only where they are essential to the plan.

We should be thinking in terms of the spaces for pageantry and parades, for street markets, for games, for the place where the statue of the founder stands, to satisfy the needs of all members of the family—not in terms of parks alone. Natural forms will appear in some of these spaces, not by any means in all. It is a question of interpreting social needs in terms of open space design, of exploring beyond the stock limits of commercial, traffic and recreational areas to determine a better social basis of urban form. The promenade, the market square and the carousel were right for seventeenth century Paris: our complex activities and interests today surely require outlets more imaginative than a stretch of grass, trees and shrubberies can provide. With new outlets should appear new forms; the recent proposals in England for urban *precincts* have already suggested forms very different from the usual block, street and square. Certain classical principles of tree planting would also completely change the character of the modern parking lot.

A rejection of the neo-romantic attitude to urbanised nature would also have a salutary effect on architectural design. The architect would not be able to take refuge in the trees and would be faced once again with the challenge of spatial unity—the relationship of structures and space which demands that consideration of proportion and fine building, which is civic design. "Today the urbanist fills his open space with trees," comments the historian Pierre Lavedan, "but he would not think of filling an apartment with furniture in this way. Furnishing should never destroy the impression of unity—it should be subordinated to architecture, to the great advantage of both elements." This urban lesson still remains to be learned by those architects, landscape architects and civic designers whose love-affair with nature is based not on understanding but on impetuous desire.[258]

Henry Hope Reed, Jr._____

THE GOLDEN CITY

Henry Hope Reed, Jr., *The Golden City* (Garden City, N.Y., Doubleday, 1959).*

In spite of the triumphs of the American Renaissance the daemonic forces of abstract nihilism prevailed. The men who made the classical contribution had approached the Golden City, but somehow too many of them accepted it casually. Fond parents, with some misgivings, they handed their patrimony to their successors as Apollo gave the reins of the sun chariot to Phaëthon and fashion raged unbridled as nature uncontrolled. To them it could not seem possible that the classical would not endure, any more than the chariot of the sun would leave its course, and some of them who have seen it go down stand bewildered at the spectacle. It is hard to believe that the heirs of Alexander Johnston Cassatt and Samuel Rea at the helm of the Pennsylvania Railroad would place the visual canker of the new ticket booths in one of McKim's proudest efforts and yet such has come to pass. The chariot of fashion has long since abandoned the classical path of taste and now it brings destruction on every side.

We think of gutted Park Avenue or the new lamppost of the New York street, an open razor gashing the sky, or of the rude entrance to a new apartment house. Small towns have been as much the victims as large cities. A charming crossroads such as that of Rhinebeck on the Hudson is made waste by an ungainly gas station. The countryside has been spoiled for the eye. It is not only the approaches of our cities, such as at Denver, where the highways are lined with chaos and ugliness; it is out in the fields and the woods. Liber and gracious Ceres, fauns and dryad girls, and the great god Pan have fled before man's insensibility. We exploit our countryside as the angler who put aside his rod for explosives. Into the American landscape go explosives of the expanding community, and havoc rules.

As we blandly go about our business, we blame the urban and rural chaos on the automobile, the super-highway, the real estate subdivision, and speculation. A glance at our history would remind us that this has happened before, especially when the great railroad network threaded its way through the land, but with the American Renaissance the City Beautiful tamed the steam engine. The New York Central System covered its Manhattan tracks to create the magnificent terminal and Park Avenue; Chicago, on beholding Burnham's plan, brought order to its riverbanks and Michigan Avenue. Orderly communities arose on the outskirts of cities guided by the artist; some of them were given squares with uniform architectural treatment,[99] one of the best being that of Lake Forest by Howard Van Doren Shaw. But when the automobile and the super-highway were to appear on the scene in our time, the chariot of art was already in reckless hands, the lessons of the past were being derided, and we were not prepared for the future's growth and expansion.

The city had held the center of the stage in the American Renaissance, and to it the artists had given their best, from churches to civic centers. It was the inevitable consequence of the unity Chicago initiated in 1893. Nor was it an accident that in the countryside beauty was nourished, both by the landscape architect and the conservationist. The first real attempt to preserve our great natural resources in forest and scenery occurred in the 1900's under Theodore Roosevelt.

The classical image embraces all in its frame. It was this hated image, with the city at its center, that our false prophets and our Phaëthons have abused, and they succeeded in destroying it by the time the forces of material expansion were in the land. Yet they believe that they can answer the problem with suggestions of merging city and country, of breaking up the metropolis into fragments of small cities and subsistence homesteads, a world so jejune that it would condemn us forever to the setting of soap operas.

Some Secessionists accept the growing urban complex and

dying landscape as part of present existence. They praise the
rapidly changing scene for its invention and display of energy,
its dynamism, as something essentially American. There is as
much unreality in the acceptance of the urban sprawl for the city
of the future—Los Angeles is an oft-cited example—as in turning
to soap-opera solutions. It is not unlike the approach of so many
contemporary painters to life when they offer disorder to the beholder on the one hand or sketchiness on the other. To pass from
a gallery filled with abstract pictures and caricatures, the work
of men who have never dared to commit themselves, into one
filled with classical work is to know relief. Here is the substance
we are seeking, which we call *reality,* the reality of human existence. It is the world of men and women, all flesh, blood, and
spirit. It welcomes the Promethean spark and gives savor to the
daily ritual. The artist has dared to have an aim, he has peopled
his canvas with figures in action, he is telling a story and telling
it well.

The question of aim, what we are trying to do, where we are
going, is paramount, and we might as well begin there, at the
beginning. The aim of America is to build the great democratic
society to achieve the good life for all. In its visual form it is the
achievement of the classical image in a free world. For that reason Jefferson turned to "Roman taste, genius and magnificence."
Our exploits and our triumphs were to be commemorated in
classical terms, the conviction made permanent of the worth of
the American ideal. It was a bold stroke of L'Enfant to turn to
the most royal garden in Europe as model for the capital of a
republic; Versailles gave shape to Washington, which was to become the Golden City, the cynosure of the world. No less bold
was the adoption of the dome set on a drum as symbol of the
democratic state. We have seen how the federal government held
to the classical image, refusing to join in stylistic battles. In the
1880's the extraordinary drive to strengthen the image came when
the men from the Beaux Arts [100] saw what had to be done. Chicago's Michigan Avenue, New York's Grand Central complex, the
San Francisco Civic Center, and the Great Plaza in Washington
were the proudest rewards.

For all Jefferson's dislike of the city he was not afraid to build
one; instinctively he saw it at the center of his dream and his

reality. It was a city's taste that he offered his countrymen "to reconcile to them the respect of the world and procure them its praise," as he wrote to James Madison. This is the city which is the apotheosis of civilization, where the past, present, and future are joined, where every generation must bring some monument to know immortality. Here are to be found the treasures which moth and rust do not corrupt. Not just any city shape will do, only the classical can give a conscious pattern in the form of a fully articulated plan, the product of unity, which can be accepted in visual terms. Here the city does not reach out to destroy but insists on protecting the countryside, its sacred complement. Order, in plan, prospect, and content is of the essence; the axis, after all, is man's invention, a part of his struggle over the turnings and twistings of nature. . . .

We need the reality which recognizes the hierarchy in civic design, by giving greater importance to places where the public does or might congregate. For that reason government buildings take precedence as foci in the urban scene and offer that sense of identification which binds the community together. Forgotten, or bruised, as they often are today by Secessionist tampering, they invite dejection and indifference. In San Francisco the Civic Center has already been mauled by fumbling Modernists and there is even talk of carrying it further by adding an abstract courthouse. Enough damage has been done already without compounding it. As an alternative Stanford Stevenson, an interested amateur who resides in Berkeley, across the bay, offers a courthouse in the high classical manner for the present parking lot at the southeast corner of the plaza. His façade of high-arched bays is inspired by those of George W. Kelham's library nearby, while the detailing pays compliment to the work of Arthur Brown. Rusticated arched entrances, masked [101] keystones, gold lanterns, and statues are offered in profusion. Fulton Street, between the courthouse and the San Francisco Public Library, is seen as a court of honor with elevated promenades to conceal some ramps lately installed by Modernists. Stevenson suggests a triple row of clipped sycamores, a fountain, vases, and statues as embellishment.

We have seen that, in terms of public use, it has been an American contribution to make temples of their banks and pal-

aces of their railroad stations and department stores, such as
Marshall Field's in Chicago. Splendor once reserved for royal
residences and noble mansions was brought to the people and it
continually sought out new types of buildings for its province.
Only today have we given up this tradition. Our housing projects
are good examples of our failure. Here we have cities within a
city, in several instances communities of twenty-five thousand,
and yet the projects have no shape, turn their backs on the communities about them, and have no place in the urban hierarchy.
To show the classical answer, John Barrington Bayley has designed a housing project for the western end of 125th Street in
the center of Harlem. The main thoroughfare of one of the city's
more famous quarters needs a setting of distinction, one which
will pay compliment to the Hudson River nearby as well as to
the city. He has set his buildings on formal lines around a central
point, the focus in this instance being an equestrian statue of
General Grant. Monumental façades are joined by arches and
take the form of exedras to convey a sense of grandeur, embracing
the streets and inviting the people to enter instead of forming
walls to exclude them. Furthermore he has designed it to accommodate families on more than one income level. His is a truly
democratic solution in the Roman spirit, where people of different
means can live and meet instead of the public-housing ghetto
or the residential subdivisions based [102] . . . on income level.
In housing projects it would permit shops, drugstores, bars, news-
stands and other amenities. Such flexibility and freedom, so
much a part of the classical, are simply not part of the current
vocabulary.

There are many chinks in the hierarchy of the urban scene.
The squares, plazas, circles, and parks are too rare; one can go
for blocks without finding a statue or a simple monument and in
most cities triumphal arches, rostral columns, and just plain columns are wanting. Strangest of all in a nation which loves music,
the dance, the theater, and opera is the glaring absence of places
to shelter the performing arts. For every million of population
there should be a grand opera house, for every half million a
ballet or light-opera theater, for every quarter million a municipal repertory theater with a permanent company. The few that
have been built follow the example of the Shed at Lenox and the

few that have been inherited are becoming fewer, what with the opera house in Boston being torn down to make way for a parking lot. Above all, our national capital has no grand opera house or great theaters. It is incredible that they do not exist in a city which shares the power to rule the destinies of the world. . . .[105]

Victor Gruen————————————————————

IN DEFENSE OF THE CITY

Victor Gruen, "In Defense of the City," *Progressive Architecture*, XL (July, 1959).*

We have been dissatisfied with the functioning and the environmental qualities of our cities for a long time. Traffic congestion, slums, and blight did not manifest themselves yesterday or today. They have been with us for many years, but until recently we believed that we could escape to new frontiers and start there a better urban life. First the Midwest, then the West, and then the open countryside surrounding each of our crowded cities were the targets of urban refugees. Only now are we beginning to realize that not only are we running short of open spaces but also that the hopes which we had that things would be better in new areas have proved vain. The new cities of the Midwest and West are beset by traffic congestion, by slums, by ugliness, by inefficiency, and by economic deterioration to the same degree as the older ones along the Eastern seaboard. In some cases, we have even managed to add to the old list new evils, like the smog in Los Angeles.

Moving out to the suburbs did not bring us the advantages of contact with nature, as we had once hoped. We have carried with us all the disadvantages of the city, at the same time losing most of the advantages of urban life.

Now we are starting to realize that there are no places left to escape to, no new urban frontiers to be opened, no easy way out. We now feel the necessity for analyzing what is wrong with our [116] cities and what can be done to make the urban pattern more workable and more livable.

It is high time that we do so. A new generation is growing up, a generation which has never known what the pleasures and advantages of true urban life can be. Our demands, our expectations with regard to city life are on the downgrade. The only inkling which our younger generation has of the fact that a city can be more than a place to work in is derived from their journeys to European cities and older settlements, most of them in other parts of the world, such as the ones here pictured. Thus if we do not act decisively in our generation, the danger exists that the awareness of the advantages of urban culture and urban life might disappear, and with it the expressions of urban culture which have been the basis of most human progress from antiquity to the present. . . .

Space shortage is aggravated by the fact that not only has the human population of the United States grown from 20 millions to 170 millions in one hundred years, but also an additional population group with an insatiable hunger for space has invaded our nation. This new group is the automobile population, which has grown from zero in 1850 to about 60 million "hoods" at the present time. In addition, we are now engaged in activities which are characteristic of conspicuous space consumption in urban areas, activities which were unknown a hundred years ago: airfields for jet planes, horizontally spreading industrial plants, and a network of highways, expressways, freeways, and toll roads which with their ramps and cloverleaves take a heavy bite out of space inventory.

The great majority of our cities were laid out and built when the supply of space seemed inexhaustible, at [a] time when the automobile, the airplane, and the conditions of mass production and mass consumption were unknown.

Most of the problems of our urban areas stem from the fact that we have failed to take cognizance of the revolutionary [117] changes which have taken place in the last fifty years. We have continued to squander space and land aimlessly and wastefully, scattering urban development over the countryside until the metropolitan areas of one city flow into those of others. By this failure, we have created disorderly and anarchistic conditions. We have made our cities unlivable and unworkable, until they have become economically impractical and have ceased to give human enjoyment. To a significant degree, we have lost the advantages of urbanism and those qualities of a mode of life which are termed "urbane." . . .

A city is obviously a comparatively large human settlement, but size alone is not decisive. We have in this country townships with a large population (for example, the township of Hempstead, Long Island, has 750,000 inhabitants) which could not be termed cities. On the other hand, in our own past and in other countries there have been communities of a few thousand souls with truly urban characteristics, such as the city of Athens in Greek antiquity. There are cities of 50,000 in Europe which successfully support an opera, legitimate theaters, libraries, and museums, and which have distinctive flavors in their characteristic architecture, art, public life, and cooking. The city of Venice, Italy, with a small permanent population, is visited by hundreds of thousands yearly who want to enjoy its urban culture. On the other hand, there are cities with populations of a million or more which signify to their inhabitants only places in which one can eat, work, or sleep—and be annoyed with the necessity of bucking traffic on the way to work and on the way home. In contrast to cities with true urban character, these concentrations do not receive or expect expressions of loyalty or attachment from their citizens. They are not in a position to offer enjoyment or pleasure, and they therefore have a hard time collecting taxes even for the most necessary expenditures. . . .[118]

There is scarcely a city in the United States where measures have not been taken—or are not planned—to alleviate the situation. But in the great majority of cases, these steps have a stop-gap character. They take the form of traffic regulations, signaling devices, one-way street systems, "scramble" crossings, and other general measures which have the aim of facilitating automobile traffic in the most congested city areas. The construction of municipal and private parking garages, highways, parkways, new tunnels and bridges, all undertaken in the hope that new life blood could be pumped into downtown areas by providing better facilities for automobile traffic, have only resulted in increased congestion and in a loosening of the urban fabric until many of our city centers resemble tremendous parking lots rendered inefficient by the remaining islands of structures. Even ambitious new developments like the Golden Triangle in Pittsburgh, though they substitute new and large modern office buildings for the former slums, often result in an anti-urban pattern in which buildings are placed far apart from each other, hindering human communication, and in which the wide spaces between the buildings are filled with moving and stored vehicles.

What is needed to cure the deep-seated disease of our urban areas is much more than stop-gap measures. We need a basic planning philosophy which can serve as a foundation for long-range planning efforts. . . .

There are two cities in the United States which have retained a large quantity of urban spirit and character though they also have been severely damaged by the general development. They are New York and San Francisco. It is significant that they have one important characteristic in common: both of these cities are confined, in their downtown areas, by natural boundaries. Both are peninsulas surrounded by bodies of water. On the other hand, those cities where physical barriers such as bodies of water or mountains do not exist, are the ones which have spread in all directions and which have lost the advantages of urban life to the greatest degree.

Many older cities have kept their urban cores intact through the fact that they were originally surrounded by walls and fortifications. Paris and Vienna derived their urban character, which still remains, from the fact that their centers were originally forced into a compact pattern by city walls which were razed only in the late 19th or early 20th Century. It is perhaps significant that a settlement which grew outside city fortifications is called in German *Vorstadt*, which means "before city," or a settlement which one reaches and experiences in anticipation of the city. This is in contrast to our English word *suburb* which signifies a lower category of *urbs*, with the connotation of *substandard*.

The advantages of a compact and cohesive city pattern, though it might have been originally enforced by the desire to protect oneself from animals or humans or by the existence of a physical boundary, are obvious. Some fortified cities remain fortified even today against urban sprawl. (It is significant in this connection that the city of Manila in the Philippine Islands refers to its downtown area as *intro muros,* or "inside the city walls.") . . .[119]

The main threads of today's urban pattern are streets, roads, highways. In the fabric of the spreading urban scene, they usually appear in gridiron formation. Their function is a two-fold one. They serve, first, as lineations along which all structures designed for human activities are arranged—from maternity hospital to mortuary, from cathedral to hot-dog stand, from mansions to Skid Row saloons. The second function they are expected to fulfill is to serve as tracks for a bewildering number of rubber-wheeled vehicles.

The tragedy is that these two uses are utterly incompatible; one use defeats the other. Buildings serving human activities located on the banks of rushing traffic streams are undesirable and unlivable. Traffic carriers bordered by structures which constantly receive and emit people and vehicles must necessarily be overcongested. We seem to understand that ranch houses located on both sides of an airport landing strip are not idyllic. Some time ago we concluded that railroad trains do not belong on Main Street. But we stick stubbornly to the notion that we must have automobile traffic rushing by our front porch, though it is denser and less disciplined than scheduled airplane or railroad traffic.

In the freeway system we have found the natural habitat for the mechanical being. The entrance ramps are marked with signs: "FORBIDDEN TO PEDESTRIANS." The human being on foot can rightly demand *his* own natural habitat—an area of restfulness and quiet, unmolested by mechanical noises and technological smells, with an opportunity to walk and a chance to look around, observe, and think without being pushed, maimed or killed by any of the machines which we have invented. It would only be fulfilling the laws of elementary justice to mark entrances to such reserves with signs: "FORBIDDEN TO AUTOMOBILES."

Basically, the aim of a new planning philosophy must be to sort out and make order—to separate flesh from machines, vehicles from people, and various types of vehicles from each other. To attain this aim, we must abandon the gridlike arrangement characteristic of today's urban pattern. It will have to be replaced by a *cellular or cluster arrangement,* similar in structure to the organisms which nature has created and within which it has arranged everything from molecules and cells to the planetary system. Urban cells will be of different sizes; in some cases they may serve a single purpose (residential, perhaps) and in others a multiplicity of purposes. Cells will be separated from each other; the larger they are, the wider the separation. The urban cells will be arranged in clusters. A number of them might be arranged around a working and business, cultural and social nucleus. A number of such community clusters, separated from each other by open land, might be grouped in a larger constellation around a more potent activity cell; and a large number of such constellations might ring a powerful solar body, the downtown core of a metropolitan area. The open land between cells, clusters of cells, and constellations of cells within the galaxy of a metropolitan area will serve agricultural purposes, and could become orchards, recreational areas, sports facilities, lakes and ponds. Within them will also move all means of transportation, radially as well as in concentric fashion. The concrete ribbons of freeways and highways, the rails of rapid transit transportation and railroads, separate lanes for express bus service, all will touch in an encircling fashion the various elements of the urban organism—but they will never cut through it. In some cases, they might move underground or overhead, but the human activity areas themselves will remain reserved for the use of human beings on their two feet. They will be pedestrian islands, and walking will be the main activity. Only in the busiest and most concentrated areas will the walkers be aided by small, slow-moving electric buses of the exhibition type, or, where connection between two areas is involved, by moving sidewalks or similar devices.

Traffic areas within human activity centers, which now often occupy up to 50 per cent of the total ground area, will have to remain open only for emergency vehicles. Thus additional space for new structures and for the creation of a more compact, more interesting and more exciting environment will be created.

The size of each nucleus or cell would be governed by "limits of walkability." These limits are dependent on time, distance, and desirability. Time and distance are constant factors; desirability is measured largely by the amount of pleasure derived from walking. Obviously, this amount is near zero in the desert or in a tremendous parking lot and of considerable size in an environment which provides superior comfort and ever-renewing impulses for sight, sound, scent and touch. . . .

The planning philosophy outlined has nowhere yet been translated into reality, but elements of this emerging urban pattern have become apparent during the last decade. In some cases we have to go to the suburbs to find them. In others, they are still only on paper. But in some instances they are close to true implementation.[130]

Examples of cluster-type formations within suburban areas are to be found in the field of regional shopping centers. Though located mostly in outlying suburban areas, they are of utmost importance to our considerations.

The best of the shopping centers represent successful planning experiments, proving that the cell-like organization works.

In their fullest interpretation they include the principles established earlier: a cluster-type arrangement of structures serving retail, cultural, and recreational purposes around attractive, landscaped pedestrian areas; car-storage areas and terminals for public transportation directly adjoining the building cluster; multiple-lane ring roads surrounding the car-storage area. They separate service traffic effectively from private automobile traffic and bus traffic by routing service roads underground and installing all loading facilities in the basements of the buildings. The largest examples of the regional shopping center are equal in size to the downtown areas of good-sized towns. Northland, in Detroit, for example, with 1,100,000 square feet of rentable space, with its theater, auditorium, community center, exhibit areas, and many restaurants, has become the crystallization point of a large area. It is visited by 70,000 persons a day, some utilizing transportation by a number of bus lines and others using its nearly 10,000 parking spaces.

Photo Warren Reynolds of Infinity, Inc., courtesy, Victor Gruen Associates

Nature controlled in the modern American city; the city altered to take nature into public account. The locale: interior of the main court of the **Southdale Shopping Center** in Edina, a suburb of Minneapolis, Minnesota. The objects suspended from the ceiling at the far left form a metal sculpture. The bench at the lower left is curved slightly to fit the human form. Inside the tall screened cage are singing birds. One manifestation, to date, of the synthesist tradition in the United States.

In the Southdale area in Edina, near Minneapolis, a number of cluster arrangements are planned and partly executed.[132] One is the Southdale Shopping Center, with its covered and air-conditioned pedestrian area. Another is a regional health center, with a medical building already constructed, which will ultimately include hospitals, nurses' quarters, and pharmaceutical laboratories all grouped around a large parklike pedestrian area. Other cell-type developments in the Southdale area are a large residential development and an office-building and amusement-center core. . . .[133]

The success of regional shopping centers has led to downtown "mall" schemes.

Many merchants now believe that the pedestrian mall concept could be transferred to the center of the city by eliminating automobile traffic from at least sections of one street. The "Shopper's Paradise" in Springfield, Oregon, was an experiment to establish such a mall for a short time and thus to persuade citizens and authorities that it would be desirable. Albany, Oregon, is a similar case. Both experiments found mixed reactions; the fact that they were not totally successful indicates that the creation of a new downtown environment cannot be effected only by a subtraction—the elimination of automobile traffic. It must be part of an integrated planning effort which will create improvement of [150] public transportation, better perimeter accessibility for private automobiles, the establishment of terminal facilities in appropriate locations, and the enlivening of roads formerly devoted to automobile traffic by new features and events. Plans developed by Raymond and May Associates for the village of Mount Kisco, New York, and the city of Glen Cove point the way in the right direction. These are activities indicating the emerging pattern short of total downtown replanning. . . .[151]

Planning accomplishes in the physical sense what legislation does in the moral realm. None of us could enjoy freedom and liberty if laws did not protect us from their abuses. Translating this into the planning vernacular, it is obvious that nobody can enjoy our urban areas, our countryside, and our landscape if we do not protect ourselves against their abuse. If highways are planned with intelligence and from a long-range point of view based on a sound planning philosophy of the kind expressed in these pages, they will cease being destroyers of community life and can become the shapers of urban organisms. Traffic, which has become a nuisance, can be made efficient. Driving the private automobile, now a burden, can again become enjoyable. The view from our windows, which is now directed toward disorder, ugliness, and smog, can become a delight. Our cities, which too often now are anonymous, dull, ugly, and dirty places, can stimulate civic pride and become an important part of our lives.[162]

Guides to Study

ANALYSIS OF THE READINGS AND ILLUSTRATIONS

I. The Major Plans

The questions below pertain to these community designs:

L'Enfant, Plan of Washington, D.C. (1791)
Howard, The Garden City (1898)
Burnham and Bennett, Plan of Chicago (1909)
Le Corbusier, City of Three Million Inhabitants (1922) and The Voisin Plan (1924)
Wright, Broadacre City (1935)

1. What assumptions underlie each of these plans regarding (*a*) the worth to society of business (trade, commerce) relative to that of other activities, such as agriculture? (*b*) the comparative value of art and science (or technology)? (*c*) the extent to which the citizen's sensory or aesthetic reactions to his urban surroundings should be taken into account? (*d*) the quality of human life in existing cities? in an ideal city?

2. What two or three elements does each man consider *primarily* important in his proposed design?

3. Which of the designers allows a place in his scheme for individual creative work, such as sculpturing, composing music, or devising mathematical theories? Which one includes the human need of privacy or solitude in his plan?

4. What role does the machine play in these designs?

5. Which planner has the most imagination? Which is the most rational?

II. All of the Readings

The following questions are intended as guides to your analysis of the readings and as topics for essays. For a *short* essay on a question embracing many authors, you will probably find it advisable to write on no more than three or four.

1. Compare the attitudes of the following writers toward Europe: Crèvecoeur, L'Enfant, Jefferson, Turner, Downing, and Reed. For which of these writers is his attitude toward Europe a determining factor in his ideas about community life in America?

2. Compare the opinions of these writers regarding private property: Thoreau, George, Bellamy, Kropotkin, Wright, and Brownell. In each case, does the writer's opinion on private property seem to be a cause or a result of his views on other aspects of social life?

3. Compare the attitudes of Jefferson, Emerson, Kropotkin, Geddes, Mumford, Brownell, and Bromfield toward science (excluding technology). Relate these attitudes to the individual author's conception of a desirable community life.

4. Compare the attitudes of these writers toward technology: Jefferson, Thoreau, Bellamy, Kropotkin, Stein, Mumford, the Goodmans, Le Corbusier, Borsodi, the Southerners, Bromfield, Moses, and Gruen. Explain how their attitudes on this subject affect their main arguments concerning the city or the country.

5. According to Crèvecoeur, Emerson, Turner, Bellamy, Ruskin, Olmsted, Perry, Sitte, and Brownell, what role does environment play in the conditioning of human behavior? (Look for tacit as well as stated premises.) Do those men who most emphasize the effect of environment on man also exhibit the strongest interest in community planning?

6. Which of the following authors value a certain common quality of human life rather than variety or individuality in human life: Thoreau, Bellamy, Perry, the Goodmans, Le Corbusier, the Southerners, Wright, Brownell, Hudnut, Tunnard, and Gruen? Do their views on this subect enter significantly into their central arguments concerning community life?

7. What attitude toward centralized political, economic, or social authority do Crèvecoeur, Emerson, Thoreau, Bellamy, Mumford, the Goodmans, Le Corbusier, Borsodi, the Southerners, Wright, and Bromfield express or imply? Is there an inverse relationship between the man's attitude on this matter and his interest in personal freedom?

8. How concerned do Emerson, George, Burnham and Bennett, Perry, Stein, Brownell, and Gruen appear to be, respectively, about the lowest social or economic classes in the nation? How would you explain their degree of concern, in each instance?

9. Which of the following seems revolutionary in idea or intent: Thoreau, George, Bellamy, Ruskin, Kropotkin, Mumford, Le Corbusier, the Southerners, Wright, Moses, or Gruen? Which conservative? Which reformist? What are your criteria for your judgments?

10. Arrange these names in order of their apparent degree of familiarity with the actual work of farming: Crèvecoeur, Jefferson, Emerson, Thoreau, Kropotkin, Borsodi, the Southerners, Wright, Brownell, Bromfield. Surveying this list, would you say that the writer's degree of farming experience was an apt test of the worth of his ideas?

11. George, Turner, Bellamy, Burnham and Bennett, Geddes, Mac-Kaye, Mumford, Le Corbusier, the Southerners, Bromfield, Hudnut, Moses, Reed, and Gruen all take it for granted that human action is prompted by economics or aesthetics or some equivalent force. Some of them see more than one such power moving men and therefore history. Identify the force for each. With which writers do you most agree? Why?

12. Which of these men tends to think inductively: L'Enfant, George, Kropotkin, Mumford, Le Corbusier, the Southerners, Wright, Tunnard, Reed? Which deductively? Does there appear to be any connection between this logical-psychological characteristic of the various men and the degree to which each is either dogmatic or open-minded?

13. How would you rank the following as to the relative acuteness of their visual or aesthetic responses to the world about them: Thoreau, Bellamy, Ruskin, Howard, Downing, MacKaye, the Goodmans, Sitte, Le Corbusier, Bromfield, Hudnut, Moses, and Reed? Does their sensitivity in this respect have any bearing on the type of community they prefer?

14. Is the "magnet" analogy equally a cliché for Burnham (-Bennett) and Howard? Or does it come alive for one of them?

15. What do Jefferson, Emerson, Kropotkin, Geddes, Mumford, Brownell, Hudnut, and Moses say or imply about book-knowledge? With which of these opinions do you most agree? Why?

16. Compare the declamations of Downing and the Goodmans on the ailanthus tree. What do their differences of opinion indicate, if anything, about more fundamental disagreements on the function of nature in the city?

17. Ruskin, Downing, Olmsted, Sitte, and Reed base certain of their architectural or other pronouncements on taste (that is, on personal predilections for particular kinds of beauty, excellence, and the like). Do their tastes agree in essentials?

18. Which of these authors have a basically simple idea of "society" and which a complex one: Thoreau, Geddes, Perry, Mumford, the Goodmans, Le Corbusier, Brownell, Hudnut, Moses? Which one seems to you closest to the truth?

19. Is the viewpoint of Howard and Stein on the building of new towns inconsistent with Geddes' evolutionism?

20. What similarities are there in Sitte's and Geddes' arguments? How do these points of agreement set both men off from Burnham and Bennett? From Le Corbusier?

21. Do you find important parallels in the Borsodi and Thoreau experiments, or were the two ventures undertaken for fundamentally different purposes?

22. What are the crucial disagreements of Lytle and Bromfield regarding the proper mode of farming? Could both men be labeled "agrarians"?

23. What, precisely, does Sitte mean by "natural"? How many meanings of the words "nature" or "natural" can you discover among the selections in this book?

24. Which of the writers view the city from within, transparently as it were? Which of them view it from without, opaquely?

25. Are all of the writers represented in this book ambivalent toward the city, or only some of them?

III. The Illustrations

1. If we take the illustrations of the Azilum site and of Walden Pond as representing the kinds of nature admired respectively by Crèvecoeur and Thoreau, what differences do you find in their points of view?

2. Compare the modern aerial view of Washington, D.C., with the L'Enfant design. Does the city differ radically in any particulars from the design? What technological innovations unforeseen in L'Enfant's era appear to have modified the carrying out of his design?

   Then compare the two views of Central Park. Is the Park today substantially the same as it was in the mid-nineteenth century? Has technological change altered its character?

Examine Diagrams 2 and 3 from the Howard selection as possible designs on which Greenbelt, Maryland was based. Judging by
the photograph of Greenbelt, would you say these designs were
followed closely or not?

3. What personal or social significance do bodies of water have,
respectively, for Thoreau, Olmsted and Vaux, and Robert Moses?
Answer this question by placing each of the three pertinent illustrations in the context of the selection it accompanies. Do your conclusions about the three authors lead you to broader conclusions on
their fundamental beliefs concerning man, nature, or community
life? If so, what are they?

IDEAS FOR ESSAYS

I. The Major Plans

Write a well-constructed and interesting comparative analysis of
the five major plans along one of these lines:

1) geometry as a means of differentiating the designs;
2) the five planners' differing attitudes toward tradition;
3) Thoreau's probable critique of each of the plans.

II. All of the Readings

See the note on this section under "Analysis of the Readings and
Illustrations" (above, page 394).

III. The Illustrations

Using the appropriate readings to supplement but not to replace
the illustrations, write on one of these topics:

1) differences in the conception of cultivated nature as revealed
in the illustrations of Central Park, the Appalachian Trail,
Radburn, Greenbelt, the 1922 Le Corbusier "City," Malabar
Farm, the Triborough Bridge area, and the interior of the
Southdale Shopping Center;
2) the significance of the presence or absence of human beings
in a selected number of the illustrations;
3) the role of the machine (technology) in the actualities of
(a) Bonanza farming, (b) the Greenbelt community, (c) the
relationship of the city of Buffalo to the adjacent areas,
(d) Malabar Farm, and (e) the Southdale Shopping Center.

FURTHER INQUIRY

Excerpts usually involve some distortion of meaning or emphasis
in the original text. Most of the books and articles from which the
selections in this anthology are taken should therefore be read
in their entirety.

Not all of them, however, are worth reading whole. One does
not need to plow all of Downing's rural essays to learn his point
of view; and while it can be argued that one should read all of
the seven Ruskin volumes represented here in order to further
his education, the average reader may consider that a rather un-
selective use of his time.

And so to move discriminatingly into the related areas of
American urban and agrarian thought, the student may wish to
begin with *Walden, Looking Backward,* and *Communitas.* The
three books are available in inexpensive paperbound editions.
Moreover, each one is of modest length; each offers a strong and
individual argument; each is in its own way well written; and
each opens up a wide range of ideas and experience.

Thereafter, any of the works listed below will make more
sense. If necessary, to be sure, one may plunge into them directly
for research purposes.

CARR, Edward H., *The Soviet Impact on the Western World.* New
York, Macmillan, 1947.

CONKIN, Paul K., *Tomorrow a New World: The New Deal Community Program.* Ithaca, N.Y., Cornell University Press, 1959.

EGBERT, Donald Drew, and PERSONS, Stow, *Socialism and American
Life,* 2 vols. Princeton, Princeton University Press, 1952.

FORD, Henry, and CROWTHER, Samuel, *Today and Tomorrow.* Garden
City, Doubleday, Page, 1926.

Fortune Editors, *The Exploding Metropolis.* Garden City, Anchor
Books, 1958.

The Future Metropolis: Winter 1961 issue of *Daedalus: Journal of
the American Academy of Arts and Sciences.*

[GEDDES, Patrick] *Patrick Geddes in India,* ed. by Jaqueline Tyrwhitt.
London, Lund Humphries, 1947.

GRISWOLD, A. Whitney, *Farming and Democracy*. New York, Harcourt, Brace, 1948.

GRUEN, Victor, and SMITH, Larry, *Shopping Towns USA*. New York, Reinhold, 1960.

JACOBS, JANE, *The Death and Life of Great American Cities*. New York, Random House, 1961.

KIERAN, John, *A Natural History of New York City*. Boston, Houghton Mifflin, 1959.

KOUWENHOVEN, John A., *The Columbia Historical Portrait of New York: An Essay in Graphic History*. Garden City, Doubleday, 1953.

LETHABY, William R., *Form in Civilization: Collected Papers on Art and Labour*. London, Oxford University Press, 1922.

LYNCH, Kevin, *The Image of the City*. Cambridge, Mass., Technology Press, 1960.

MUMFORD, Lewis, *City Development*. New York, Harcourt, Brace, 1945.

———, *The City in History*. New York, Harcourt, Brace, and World, 1961.

———, *The Culture of Cities*. New York, Harcourt, Brace, 1938.

———, *From the Ground Up*. New York, Harvest Books, 1956.

SMITH, Henry Nash, *Virgin Land: The American West as Symbol and Myth*. Cambridge, Mass., Harvard University Press, 1950.

TUNNARD, Christopher, and REED, Henry Hope, Jr., *American Skyline*. New York, Mentor Books, 1956.